Time Out

Sydney Guide

Penguin Books

PENGUIN BOOKS

Published by the Penguin Group
Penguin Books Ltd., 27 Wrights Lane, London, W8 5TZ, England
Penguin Books USA Inc., 375 Hudson Street, New York, New York 10014, USA
Penguin Books Australia Ltd., Ringwood, Victoria, Australia
Penguin Books Canada Ltd., 10 Alcorn Avenue, Toronto, Ontario, Canada M4V 3B2
Penguin Books (NZ) Ltd., 183–190 Wairau Road, Auckland 10, New Zealand

Penguin Books Ltd., Registered offices: Harmondsworth, Middlesex, England

First published 1997
10 9 8 7 6 5 4 3 2 1

Copyright © Time Out Group Ltd., 1997
All rights reserved

Colour reprographics by Precise Litho, 34–35 Great Sutton Street, London EC1
Mono reprographics, printed and bound by William Clowes Ltd, Beccles, Suffolk NR34 9QE

Edited and designed by

Time Out Magazine Limited
Universal House
251 Tottenham Court Road
London W1P OAB
Tel: 0171 813 3000
Fax: 0171 813 6001
Email: net@timeout.co.uk
http://www.timeout.co.uk

Editorial

Managing Editor Peter Fiennes
Editor Caroline Taverne
Consultant Editors Jon Casimir, Helen Greenwood
Copy Editor Kei Kikuchi
Researcher Eva Lewicki
Indexer Jacqueline Brind

Design

Art Director Warren Beeby
Art Editor John Oakey
Designers Paul Tansley, Mandy Martin
Design Assistants Carrie Lambe, Marcus Ludewig
Picture Editor Catherine Hardcastle
Picture Researcher Michaela Freeman

Advertising

Group Advertisement Director Lesley Gill
Sales Director Mark Phillips
Advertisement Sales (Sydney) Samuel Childes Pty Ltd

Administration

Publisher Tony Elliott
Managing Director Mike Hardwick
Financial Director Kevin Ellis
Marketing Director Gillian Auld
Production Manager Mark Lamond

Features in this guide were written and researched by:

Introduction Jon Casimir, Helen Greenwood. **Essential Information** Caroline Taverne. **Getting Around**
Caroline Taverne. **Accommodation** Eva Lewicki. **Sydney by Season** Julie Delvecchio. **Sightseeing** Eva
Lewicki (*The Far Side* James Cockington). **The Great Outdoors** Malcolm Knox. **Architecture** Bill
McMahon. **History** John Birmingham. **Sydney by Area** Helen Greenwood, John Newton (Central Sydney);
Brook Turner (Eastern Suburbs); Shelli-Anne Couch (Inner West); Monique Farmer (Newtown & the South);
Daniel Lewis (Parramatta & the West); Andrew Conway (North Shore, Northern Beaches). **Restaurants**
John Newton (*Winewise* Helen Greenwood). **Cafés & Bars** Ruth Ritchie. **Shopping & Services** Sam Griffin.
Museums & Galleries Anne Loxley. **Literary Sydney** Matt Condon. **Media** Jon Casimir. **Nightlife** Sean
Nicholls. **Film** Peter Galvin. **Music: Classical & Opera** Miriam Cosic. **Music: Rock, Folk & Jazz** Jon
Casimir, John Clare (Jazz). **Sport & Fitness** Malcolm Knox (*Odds on Favourites* Jon Casimir). **Theatre &
Dance** Angela Bennie. **Business** Andrew Conway. **Babies & Children** Hilary McDowell. **Queer Sydney**
Stephen Dunne. **Students & Backpackers** Julie Delvecchio. **Women's Sydney** Eva Lewicki. **Trips Out of
Town** Daniel Scott. **Survival** Caroline Taverne.

The Editors would like to thank the following: Deborah Brill; Hugh Galloway; Emil Goh; Ianthé & Darvan
Sinnetamby.

Maps by Mapworld, 71 Blandy Road, Henley-on-Thames, Oxon, RG9 1QB

Photography by Jon Perugia except for ppiii, 11, 28, 35, 37, 41, 44, 46, 50(r), 51, 52, 69, 75, 203, 215,
226, 227 Arnhel de Serra; pp59, 64, 65 Hulton Getty; p61 Image Library/State Library of NSW; p70(b)
Allsport; pp194, 226(b) John Fairfax Picture Library; pp241, 244, 246, 248, 251, 253, 255, 259 Daniel
Scott. The photographs on pp15(t), 164, 173, 202, 212, 213, 237, 243 were supplied by the featured
establishments.

Contents

Essential Information

The vital logistics of staying in Sydney.

For more information on surviving in Sydney, from embassy addresses or late-opening chemists, to finding work, *see chapter* **Survival**. For a list of abbreviations used in this guide, *see page vi* **About the Guide**.

Visas

All travellers except Australian passport holders must have a visa to enter Australia. New Zealanders – who are granted a special category visa – can obtain this on arrival, but everyone else needs to apply in advance. Visas can be obtained through selected travel agents (they can be issued electronically in the US and Singapore), by post (allow a minimum of three weeks) or in person from Australia House in London, the Australian Embassy in Dublin, or the Australian Consulate in Manchester. Be prepared to queue if you want to arrange your visa in person.

Types of Visa

There are three different types of tourist visa. The first is free and allows a stay of up to three months with multiple entries over a 12-month period. If you want to stay for more than three months, you'll have to pay a fee of £18. There's also a fee of £18 if you want a three-month visa with the option of multiple entries beyond a 12-month period. Those travelling on business have the option of a one-month single entry visa (free), or a three-month multiple entry visa (£18). Visas can be extended in Australia through offices of the Department of Immigration and Ethnic Affairs, but this is expensive (between $100 and $140). If you have close relatives in Australia (parent,

spouse, child or sibling) you can apply for a close family visa, which has fewer restrictions than the other types. You don't need a photograph when applying for a visa, but you do need a valid passport with at least six months to go on it. You might also be asked for proof of a return ticket.

If you are going to be in Australia for more than three months, you might be asked to provide evidence that you have sufficient means to support yourself during your stay, probably in the form of a bank or building society statement. Be prepared to prove that you have at least £3,000 for a stay of six months. *See chapter* **Survival** for details on working holiday visas.

Australian Visa Information Service
(0891 600 333). **Open** 24-hour recorded information.

Australian High Commission
Visitor Visa Section, Australia House, Strand, London WC2B 4LA (0171 379 4334). **Open** 9.30am-3.30pm Mon-Fri.

Australian Consulate
Client Services Section, Chatsworth House, Lever Street, Manchester M1 2QL (0161 228 1344). **Open** 8.30am-1.30pm Mon-Fri.

Australian Embassy
Fitzwilton House, Wilton Terrace, Dublin 2, Ireland (353 1 676 1517). **Open** 10am-12.30pm; 2-3.30pm Mon-Thur; 9am-noon Fri.

Immigration & Customs

Before landing on Australian soil, you will be given an immigration form to fill out, as well as Customs and Agriculture Declaration forms. The immigration process can take a while, as the rule of thumb is if in doubt, declare everything. Australian plant and animal quarantine rules are particularly rigorous. All goods of animal or plant origin must be declared, and you can't import any fresh fruit or vegetables. There are quarantine bins at the airport before you pass through immigration, so you can ditch the remains of your in-flight picnic.

Duty Free
The duty free allowance for anyone over the age of 18 is one litre of alcohol and 250 cigarettes, plus goods to the value of $400.

Emergencies

In an emergency, for police, fire brigade or ambulance, **dial 000**.

Departure Tax

All overseas visitors over the age of 12 must pay a departure tax of $27 on leaving Australia. This is sometimes incorporated into the price of a return airline ticket, but otherwise has to be paid in Australian currency at the airport when you leave. If you plan on taking out cash to the value of $5,000 in Australian and/or any foreign currency, you must fill in a Customs report.

Health & Insurance

Apart from the occasional notorious exception, there are few extreme health hazards in Australia. The Australian Medicare system has a reciprocal agreement with Finland, Italy, Malta, the Netherlands, New Zealand, Sweden and the UK, which entitles residents of these countries to necessary medical and hospital treatment. This agreement does not cover all eventualities (for example, ambulance fees or dental costs), and only applies to public hospitals and casualty departments. If you have travel insurance, check the small print to see whether it requires you to register with Medicare before making a claim; if it doesn't, or if you don't have insurance, you can claim a Medicare rebate by taking your passport and visa, together with the medical bill, along to any Medicare centre. For more information and details on how to apply for a Medicare card, phone or write to the information service below. *See also* chapter **Survival** for a list of medical services.

Medicare Information Service

GPO Box 9822, Sydney 2001 (13 2011). **Open** 8.30am-4.30pm Mon-Fri.

Money

In 1966 Australia went decimal and relinquished pounds, shillings and pence for the Australian dollar ($) and cent (¢). Paper money – actually brightly coloured polymer with clear plastic forgery-proof holograms – comes in $100, $50, $20, $10 and $5 denominations. Coins come in bronze-coloured $2 and $1 pieces, and silver 50¢, 20¢, 10¢, and 5¢ pieces. The 2¢ and 1¢ coins were recently phased out, so you might find prices in shops rounded up or down to the nearest 5¢ on your total bill. At the time of writing, the tourist exchange rate was A$1.85 to £1.

Plastic

Credit cards – particularly Mastercard, Visa and American Express, but also Diners Club and the Australian/New Zealand Bankcard – are widely accepted and invaluable for leaving a deposit if you want to hire a bike or a car, or for booking a hotel over the phone. You can also use credit cards to get cash from any bank (take some form of photo ID) and many cashpoint machines (ATMs).

Lost or Stolen Credit Cards & Travellers' Cheques

American Express credit cards (9886 0666), travellers' cheques (9886 0689); **Diners Club International** (1800 331 199); **Visa** (1800 801 256).

Banks

The central branches of the major high-street banks are listed below, all of which have foreign exchange facilities and outlets throughout the city. Trading hours are 9.30am-4pm Mon-Thur, 9.30am-5pm Fri. Major city branches often open longer, as do outlets in suburban shopping centres. Of the banks listed below, Westpac doesn't charge a transaction fee if you're cashing travellers' cheques. The others charge between $5 and $8.

ANZ

Corner of Bathurst and Castlereagh Streets, Sydney (9267 2055). CityRail Town Hall.

Commonwealth Bank

48 Martin Place, Sydney (9378 2000). CityRail Martin Place.

National Australia Bank

300 Elizabeth Street, Sydney (9215 6789). CityRail Central.

Westpac

60 Martin Place, Sydney (9226 3366). CityRail Martin Place.

Bureaux de Change

Foreign currency and travellers' cheques can be cashed at any of the banks listed above. Thomas Cook also has a foreign exchange branch in the international terminal at the airport, which is open seven days a week, 5.30am-10pm (9317 2100).

American Express

92 Pitt Street, Sydney (9239 0666). CityRail Martin Place. **Open** 8.30am-5.30pm Mon-Fri; 9am-noon (travel), 9am-3pm (foreign exchange) Sat.
Offers foreign exchange facilities as well as money orders, poste restante and more.

Thomas Cook

Shop 64, Queen Victoria Building, 22 George Street, Sydney (9264 1133). CityRail Town Hall. **Open** 8.30am-6pm Mon-Wed, Fri; 8.30am-9pm Thur; 9am-6pm Sat; 11am-5pm Sun.
Foreign exchange facilities only. Phone for details of other branches in the city.

Post

Post to Europe can take between four and ten days. According to Australia Post, about 90 per cent of letters within the metropolitan area arrive the next business day. Postcards to the UK and Europe cost $1, and 95¢ to the USA. Letters cost $1.20 and $1.05 respectively, and all international aerogrammes cost 70¢. Most post office branches open from 9am to 5pm, Mon-Fri. Any suburban branch will receive post for you, otherwise have it sent poste restante to the General Post Office. Stamps can also be bought at some newsagents and general stores.

General Post Office

159-171 Pitt Street, Martin Place, Sydney (9230 7834). CityRail Martin Place or Wynyard. **Open** 8.15am-5.30pm Mon-Fri; 8.30am-noon Sat.

This is the main post office for poste restante (take some form of photo ID with you when collecting mail), as well as providing the usual Australia Post fax service, express delivery, parcel post and stamps. *See also chapter* **Sightseeing**.

Telephones

Before the end of 1997, all Australian telephone numbers will have increased to eight digits, from their current six or seven. At the time of writing, all Sydney numbers had already changed; NSW and ACT codes will change by August 1997. For a note on these, *see chapter* **Trips Out of Town**. You can also phone the Numbering Information Helpline for more information between 8am and midnight daily (1800 888 888).

The telephone system is run by Telstra (called Telecom Australia before recent deregulation), with Optus, its only rival, offering a competitive pricing system for long-distance calls (as yet only from private phones). There are plenty of public phones dotted around the city, as well as in bars and cafés, at post offices and at the Telstra Payphone Centre (*see below*). Most accept coins ($1, 50¢, 20¢, 10¢) and phonecards. Some also accept the major credit cards (AmEx, DC, MC, V).

The country code for Australia is 61; the area code for Sydney (and NSW from August 1997) is 02.

International (IDD) Calls

To make an international call from Australia, dial 0011 + country code + area code (minus the 0) + phone number.

Canada	1
New Zealand	64
UK	44
USA	1

The easiest way to make reverse-charge (collect) or charge card international calls is by dialling the relevant country's OTC Country Direct number, which will put you in touch with that country's operator. Or simply dial International Bookings (0101), who will make the call for you.

Canada	0014 881 150
New Zealand	0014 881 640
UK (BT)	0014 881 440
USA Direct (AT&T)	0014 881 011

To find out other OTC Country Direct numbers, dial 0103.

Useful Numbers

International directory assistance	0103
National directory assistance	0175
Sydney directory assistance	013
Wake-up calls	0173
Faults & service helpline	1100
Sydney weather	1196
News	1199

Rates

Local calls (within a 25km radius) cost a flat rate of 40¢ from public phones and 25¢ from private ones, although some payphones (usually those in bars and hotels) have a 60¢ minimum. Rates for international calls start at 99¢ a minute (6pm-9am Mon-Fri and all weekend), and $1.28 a minute at peak time (9am-6pm Mon-Fri). There's a 12¢ connection charge. If you want to know the cost of the international call you have just made, dial 0012 before 0011, and the cost will be telephoned back to you (for a small fee) at the end of your call.

Phonecards

Telstra phonecards can be bought from newsagents, chemists, kiosks and tourist information centres. They come in $20, $10 and $5 units.

Faxlink

If you want to send an international fax, dial 0015 instead of 0011.

Useful Information (at a price)

A recorded message will tell you how much you are about to be charged on these numbers, which contain information on anything from the racing results to a teenage tarot line. A complete list can be found on the back of the Yellow Pages.

Local Time	0055 12149
International Time/Weather	0055 26152
National/International News	0055 12351
Sports News/Results	0055 50159
What's On in Sydney	0055 11464
Weather by Fax	1902 266 536

Telstra Payphone Centre

130 Pitt Street, Sydney (9233 1177). CityRail Martin Place. **Open** 9am-6pm Mon-Fri; 10am-4pm Sat.
There are banks of telephones in booths where you can make endless calls in comfort. Phones accept coins, phonecards (which you can buy at the counter) and credit cards.

Tourist Information

For a list of Sydney-related websites, *see chapter* **Media**.

Bondi Visitors Information Centre

Bondi Beachside Inn, corner of Campbell Parade and Roscoe Street, Bondi Beach (9130 5311). Bus 380, 382, L82. **Open** 9am-5pm Mon-Fri.

Darling Harbour Visitors Centre

Palm Grove, between Cockle Bay and Tumbalong Park, Darling Harbour (9286 0111). Bus 456/ferry Darling Harbour. **Open** 9am-5.30pm daily.

Countrylink NSW Travel Centre

11-31 York Street, corner of Margaret Street, Sydney (9224 2742/13 2077). CityRail Wynyard. **Open** 9am-5pm Mon-Fri; 9am-1pm Sat.
Branches: phone 13 2232 for the location of your nearest.

Historic Houses Trust

Lyndhurst, 61 Darghan Street, Glebe (9692 8366). Bus 431, 432, 433. **Open** (telephone enquiries only) 9am-5pm Mon-Fri.

Manly Visitors Information Bureau

South Steyne, Manly (9977 1088). Ferry Manly. **Open** 10am-4pm daily.

NSW National Parks & Wildlife Service

Cadman's Cottage, 110 George Street, The Rocks (9247 8861). CityRail/ferry Circular Quay. **Open** 10am-3pm Mon; 9am-4.30pm Tue-Fri; 11am-4pm Sat, Sun.

Parramatta Visitors Centre

Corner of Church and Market Streets, Parramatta (9630 3703). CityRail/ferry Parramatta. **Open** 10am-4pm Mon-Fri; 9am-1pm Sat; 10.30am-3pm Sun.

The Rocks Visitors Centre

106 George Street, The Rocks (9255 1788). CityRail/ferry Circular Quay. **Open** 9am-5pm daily.

Sydney Info

Level 3, Town Hall House, 456 Kent Street, Sydney (9265 9007). CityRail Town Hall. **Open** telephone enquiries only 8am-7pm Mon-Fri; 9am-12.30pm Sat. Information on the city provided by the State Library.

Sydney Visitors Information Kiosk

Martin Place, Sydney (9235 2424). CityRail Martin Place. **Open** 9am-5pm Mon-Fri.

Disabled Access

The Australian Council for the Rehabilitation of the Disabled (ACROD) publishes a book called *Accessing Sydney*, which costs $15 if you collect it in person or $18 by post, and is available from their NSW office listed below. It lists all the places, building and services that are wheelchair accessible in Sydney. The State Library operates a very helpful information line, which is a good starting point for disabled visitors to Sydney. People with Disabilities (NSW) Inc is a lobbying organisation dedicated to enhancing and protecting the rights of the disabled. It provides community information and runs the Disability Complaints Service (9319 6549). Other useful publications include *Access for All*, which is free and published by the National Parks and Wildlife Service (*see above* **Tourist Information**).

The National Information Communications Awareness Network (NICAN) is a Canberra-based federal government organisation. It provides information on recreation, tourism, sports and the arts for people with disabilities throughout Australia.

ACROD

NSW Division, 55 Charles Street, Ryde (9809 4488). Bus 458, 461, 500, 511, 512. **Open** 9am-5pm Mon-Fri.

NICAN

PO Box 407, Curtin, ACT 2605 (1800 806 769).

People with Disabilities (NSW) Inc

Ground Floor, 52 Pitt Street, Redfern (9319 6622). **Open** 9am-5pm Mon-Fri.

State Library of NSW

Disability Information (9230 1622). **Open** 9am-5pm Mon-Fri.

Opening Times

In many areas, shops stay open late into the night and also open on Sundays (particularly along Oxford Street and in Kings Cross), while every neighbourhood has its late-night convenience store. Otherwise, opening hours vary between 8.30am and 9am to 5pm or 5.30pm. Thursday is late-night opening (usually until 9.30pm). Some shops close at noon on Saturdays.

Safety

Sydney is a fairly safe city, although car theft and burglary are on the increase. However, the rules that apply to any large city apply here: use common sense about flashing your money or valuables around and avoid lonely or poorly lit streets. Watch out for pickpockets in crowded places, particularly in areas such as Kings Cross, the red-light district with a well-earned reputation for no end of nefarious activities. In an emergency, dial 000. *See chapter* **Survival** for the number of the Crime Stopper helpline and the location of your nearest police station.

Alcohol

The legal age for buying/consuming alcohol is 18.

Smoking

Smoking is banned on public transport and in many office buildings and public places, as well as in most cinemas and theatres. Pubs and bars, however, rarely restrict smoking, though under popular pressure many restaurants now have no-smoking areas.

Time

New South Wales operates on Eastern Standard Time (GMT+10). Between October and March, Daylight Savings Time comes into operation and the clocks go back one hour. There are three different time zones within Australia – the others are Western Standard Time (GMT+8) and Central Standard Time (GMT+9.5). Confusingly, Queensland doesn't recognise Daylight Savings Time like the rest of the eastern states, so if you're catching a flight to the Great Barrier Reef between the end of October and the end of March, double check local time.

Tipping

On the whole, tipping isn't the financially debilitating process it is in the US. It is appreciated in restaurants and cafés, where 10 per cent is the norm. In taxis, just round the fare up to the nearest dollar (Sydney is possibly the only city in the world where a taxi driver will offer to round the fare down so as not to bother with change).

Electricity

The Australian domestic electricity supply is 230-250V, 50Hz AC. UK appliances work with an adaptor; US 110V appliances also need a transformer.

Weights & Measures

Australia has been metric for more than 20 years; distances and measurements in this guide are given in both metric and imperial.

Getting Around

*Sydney's efficient transport system offers the added pleasure of
messing about on the water.*

There's no doubt about it: Sydney sprawls. With 112 kilometres (180 miles) of shoreline and a greater metropolitan area that stretches from Ku-Ring-Gai Chase National Park in the north to the Royal National Park in the south and the Blue Mountains in the west, there's a lot of it to get around. The central area, however, is relatively compact, and not only well served by public transport, but small enough to explore on foot. Getting between suburbs can be harder (and slower), especially those which aren't served by the train system. As we went to press, a light rail network was under construction between Central Station and Pyrmont, and there were plans afoot to extend the tramways into the centre of the city, from Central Station to Circular Quay. The first 'Light Rail Vehicles' are due to trundle into operation in mid-1997.

MAPS

For detailed maps of central Sydney and of selected suburbs, *see pages 275-290.* If you're staying in Sydney for any length of time, it is worth investing in a copy of Gregory's Street Directory, which comes in various forms – including a handy paperback compact edition ($15.95) – and can be found in most bookshops and newsagents. Street names, and often house numbers, are not at all clearly marked in Sydney: look for street names at traffic light-level or, occasionally, carved into the curb. Free street maps are available from the Countrylink NSW Travel Centre or the Martin Place information kiosk (*see chapter* **Essential Information**).

Public Transport

Sydney's public transport system is made up of trains, buses and ferries. The combined system is efficiently run, and not too expensive if you invest in a travel pass (*see page 8*), but it works best at transporting commuters in and out of the city centre. Getting across town and travelling between suburbs can sometimes be a laborious process, which goes a long way towards explaining why Sydneysiders are so attached to their cars. For a

The CityRail network connects the central city with Sydney's sprawling 'burbs.

map of State Transit ferry and train routes, and a bus map of the central area *see pages 289-290*.

Public Transport Infoline
(13 1500). **Open** 6am-10pm daily.
State Transit is responsible for operating CityRail trains, Sydney Buses and Sydney Ferries. For information on these services, including timetable and route details, phone the above number.

Lost Property
To track down your mislaid belongings, phone 9245 5777 (buses/ferries) or 9379 3000 (CityRail).

Travel Passes

There are several sorts of travel pass covering the State Transit system, and they are worth buying if you intend to use public transport to any extent. You can buy them at CityRail stations, most newsagents on bus routes, ticket vending machines at Circular Quay or Manly Wharf, and from State Transit sales outlets. The options run to any number of bus-only, bus/ferry permutations. The weekly Red, Green, Yellow, Pink, Brown and Purple 'TravelPasses' allow different combinations of travel on buses, ferries or CityRail within the State Transit travel zones. Prices start at $20 for the Red TravelPass. If you use your TravelPass after 3pm on the first day, it will be valid for that day plus seven further full days. If you make your first journey before 3pm, the pass is only valid for six full days.

Other TravelPass options include the following: **BusTripper** (travel on buses for one day); **DayPass** (unlimited travel on buses and ferries for one day); **DayRover** (travel within Zone 7 on all buses, ferries and CityRail trains for one day); **TravelTen** (each ticket is valid for ten bus journeys and can be used any time within a year of purchase).

TravelPasses are not valid on the Sydney Explorer, Bondi & Bay Explorer or Airport Express buses. Nor can they be used on Jetcats before 7pm (when the last ferry leaves).

Children under the age of four travel free on State Transit; under-16s travel half-price, as do students and pensioners with the appropriate ID.

Bus

Buses are slow but fairly frequent, and offer a better way of seeing the city than by CityRail, which operates underground within the centre. They are the only option for getting to areas such

To & from the airport

Kingsford Smith Airport is in Mascot near Botany Bay, roughly 11 kilometres (seven miles) south-east of the city centre. The domestic and international terminals are connected by an express bus which runs every 20 minutes ($2.50 adults, $1.50 children). For a list of airline phone numbers, *see chapter* **Survival**.

Airline Information Sydney Airport
Flight information (0055 51844). **Open** 24 hours daily.
Daily recorded information on national and international arrivals and departures. Calls are charged at a rate of 75¢ a minute. Have your flight number to hand if you don't want to listen to a long list of airlines.

By Public Transport

The **Airport Express**, run by State Transit, operates roughly every ten minutes between 5am and 11pm daily. Stops include Central Station, the Town Hall, the Queen Victoria Building, Wynyard, Circular Quay and The Rocks, as well as Oxford Street, Kings Cross, Potts Point and Elizabeth Bay. Route 300 goes as far as The Rocks, and route 350 travels via Kings Cross to Elizabeth Bay. A single fare costs $5 (adults) or $3 (under-16s); a return is $8 (adults) or $4 (under-16s). The journey to The Rocks takes roughly 35 minutes. For more information phone the **Public Transport Infoline** (*see above*).

By Airport Shuttle

Kingsford Smith Transport (9667 0663) runs a bus service to and from the airport. The fare is $6 single, $10 return, and it stops at selected hotels in the centre of town. You must book a seat at least three hours in advance for the return journey to the airport.

By Taxi

A journey from the airport to Circular Quay takes 20-25 minutes, depending on the traffic and the time of day, and costs around $20. There's a taxi rank outside the international arrivals building. For a list of taxi companies, *see page 10*.

By Car

Avis, Budget, Hertz and Thrifty all have car rental desks at Kingsford Smith Airport. For their telephone numbers, and information on getting around Sydney by car *see page 10*.

as Bondi Beach, Coogee or the northern beaches, which aren't served by train. The minimum adult fare is $1.20. Pay the driver or validate your travel pass in the green machine at the door. Bus route numbers beginning with an 'X' are express services, which operate between the outer suburbs and major centres on the way into the city. Stops are marked 'Express'. Limited-stop or 'L' services operate on some of the longer routes to provide faster trips to and from the city. For private bus tours of the city, as well as details of the Sydney Explorer and Bondi & Bay Explorer buses, *see chapter* **Sightseeing**.

BUS TERMINALS

There are main bus terminals at Wynyard (York Street), Spring/Gresham Streets, Millers Point (Argyle Street), Opera House (Forecourt), Circular Quay, Queen Victoria Building (York Street) and Railway Square.

State Transit Bus Information Kiosk

Corner of Loftus and Alfred Streets, Circular Quay (9219 1680). **Open** 8am-8pm Mon-Fri; 8am-6pm Sat, Sun. **Branches**: Carrington Street, Wynyard (13 1500); Queen Victoria Building (9264 5482).

Ferry

Travelling by ferry is one of the great joys of Sydney, where fingers of water protrude into the heart of the city. Taking the ferry from Manly to Circular Quay or from Circular Quay to Woolwich Point is one of the best (and cheapest) sightseeing trips around. There are 27 vessels in the State Transit fleet, ranging from nippy Jetcats to more stately boats that ply the water between the north and south shores. All 33 ferry wharves are served from Circular Quay ferry terminal, where Sydney Ferries operates out of Wharfs 2-5.

Departure times and fares vary, but getting a Ferry Ten TravelPass is probably the most economical option if you plan to use the ferries much. You can pick up timetables for individual routes from the information centre listed below, or phone the Public Transport Infoline.

Sydney Ferries Information Centre

Opposite Wharf 4, Circular Quay (9207 3170). Ferry, bus or CityRail to Circular Quay. **Open** 7.30am-6.30pm Mon-Sat; 8.30am-5.30pm Sun.

Hegarty's Ferries

(Information 9206 1167).
This is a private company which operates between Wharf 6 of Circular Quay and the north shore, and caters for rush-hour commuters.

Train

Fast and fairly frequent double-decker CityRail trains connect the city centre with the outer suburbs. It's worth taking the train to the north shore for the pleasure of travelling across the Harbour Bridge with time enough to inspect the views. For a map of the CityRail network, *see page 290*. Beyond the metropolitan area, CountryLink trains serve the extensive NSW railway network from Central Station. *See chapter* **Trips Out of Town** for more details.

Travelling at Night

Around midnight, the privatised Nightride bus service comes into operation and runs through the night: the Public Transport Infoline will provide times and routes of these buses. All have radio links to taxi operators, so you can arrange for a taxi to meet you at your destination. CityRail trains run from roughly 5am to midnight within the centre of town; there are special 'Night Safe' areas where you can wait for trains, and after 8pm only two carriages – next to the guard's compartment – are open to passengers. Ferries tend to run from 6am to midnight (times vary with each route). There's a late-night taxi rank (6.30pm-7.30am) on the corner of Pitt and Goulburn Streets.

Disabled Travellers

CityRail is in the process of introducing a network of Easy Access stations in major suburban centres which have interchange facilities with other transport services. Planned features include lifts or ramps and help points with hearing loops. Most ferries are wheelchair accessible, and help is available if you need it. Phone the Public Transport Infoline for more information. For more details about disabled access in Sydney and NSW *see chapter* **Essential Information**.

Wheelchair Accessible Taxis (9332 0200)

Taxis

Taxis are fairly easy to flag down in the street (unless it's raining) and they are cheap. There are taxi ranks at major points throughout the city (for example, at Circular Quay, Central and Wynyard Stations, in Elizabeth Street at Chifley Square, in Market Street by the State Theatre and in

Elizabeth Bay on Macleay Street). The standard fare is $1 booking fee, $3 flagfall and $1 per km. Major taxi companies include the following:

Legion Cabs (9289 9000)
Premier Taxis (9897 4000)
RSL Cabs (9699 0144)
Taxis Combined Services (9332 8888)

If you're not happy with the service, let the **Taxi Complaint Hotline** (9549 3722) know. If you've left something behind in a cab, phone **Taxi Lost Property** on 9361 8252.

Water Taxis

These are great fun, but expensive. The bill usually depends on the time of day and the number of passengers, but the fare for two from Circular Quay to Watsons Bay, for example, comes to around $40.

Harbour Shuttles (9810 5010)
Harbour Taxi Boats (9555 1155)
Taxis Afloat (9955 3222)

Driving

Driving in Sydney can be the traffic-congested, pollution-promoting experience it is in any other large city and, as any Sydneysider will tell you, parking is a pain. However, if you are planning to explore the coast, the mountains or the less accessible reaches of the National Parks, it is worth hiring a car.

The state Roads and Traffic Authority (RTA) publishes a leaflet called *Driving Safely in New South Wales*, which details local regulations and helpful hints on dealing with kangaroos on the road (avoid them whenever possible). Overseas visitors can drive on their domestic licence for a limited time, though an international one is better (available from the AA, RAC and other international motoring organisations). You must have your licence with you when driving; there are on-the-spot fines if you don't. The fine for not wearing a seat-belt is $100, and all children under the age of 12 must travel in an approved child restraint.

Vehicles drive on the left throughout Australia. In NSW, the speed limit is 60kph (38 mph) in areas with street lights; the maximum is 110kph (70 mph); and there are speed cameras in city and rural locations to make sure you observe them. Speed regulations vary from state to state, so keep an eye out for changes in speed limits if you are crossing a state line. The legal blood alcohol limit is 0.05; if you are under 25 and in your first three years of driving, the limit is 0.02, which means no alcohol. You can be stopped and breathalysed at any time, and the penalties for being over the limit are severe.

Petrol stations are fairly plentiful, particularly on main roads, and most accept all the major credit cards. At the time of writing, petrol cost from 70¢ to 80¢ per litre.

The toll for the Harbour Bridge and tunnel is $2 for southbound cars. For a list of central city carparks *see chapter* **Survival**.

Car Rental

The major car rental companies listed below are the ones that also have outlets at the airport. They all offer various discounted deals and their rates vary almost hourly, so what we've quoted is merely an indication of their prices. Hundreds more companies are listed in the Yellow Pages, although those offering special deals should be approached with caution: always read the small print first before you commit yourself to renting a car. You

The monorail

The controversial 'monster rail' is an expensive way of getting around, especially as it doesn't go anywhere. The raised three-and-a-half-kilometre track loops Darling Harbour and functions as a sightseeing trip for tourists, who are treated to views over the harbour and some of Sydney's biggest building sites, plus occasional eye-contact with startled office workers, as the trains swish past their windows. There are seven stops. Travelling anti-clockwise, they are: Darling Park (for Sydney Aquarium); Harbourside (for the National Maritime Museum); Convention (for the Convention Centre and Motor Museum); Haymarket (for the Powerhouse Museum, Chinatown and the Entertainment Centre); World Square (for the George Street cinemas); Park Plaza (for the Town Hall and Queen Victoria Building); and City Centre (serving Sydney Tower and the Queen Victoria Building among others). Trains run roughly every five minutes. And it's worth remembering not to stand under the rail when it's raining, or you will be showered with water as the next train passes overhead.

TNT Harbourlink Monorail

Open *18 Apr-25 Sept* 7am-9pm Mon-Wed; 7am-midnight Thur-Sat; 8am-9pm Sun; *26 Sept-17 Apr* 7am-midnight Mon-Sat; 8am-9pm Sun. **Tickets** $2.50 adults; $1.20 under-16s; free under-5s. **Daypass** (9am-7pm) $6.

have to be 21 or over to rent a car – some companies insist on a minimum age of 25.

Avis
214 William Street, Kings Cross (9357 2000). CityRail Kings Cross. **Open** 7.30am-6pm Mon-Thur, Sat, Sun; 7.30am-7pm Fri. **Rates** from $53 a day, unlimited km. **Credit** AmEx, BC, DC, JCB, MC, $TC, V. **Branches**: Central Reservations (9353 9000); Sydney Airport (9667 0667).

Budget
Corner of William and Crown Streets, Kings Cross (9339 8888). CityRail Kings Cross. **Open** 7.30am-7pm Mon-Fri; 7.30am-6pm Sat, Sun. **Rates** from $49 a day, unlimited km. **Credit** AmEx, BC, DC, JCB, MC, $TC, V. **Branches**: Central Reservations (13 2727); Sydney Airport (9669 2121).

Hertz
65 William Street, Kings Cross (9360 6621). CityRail Kings Cross. **Rates** from $49 a day, unlimited km. **Open** 7.30am-6pm Mon-Fri; 7.30am-5pm Sat, Sun. **Credit** AmEx, BC, DC, JCB, MC, $TC, V. **Branches**: Central Reservations (13 3039); Sydney Airport (9669 2444).

Thrifty
75 William Street, Kings Cross (9380 5399). CityRail Kings Cross. **Rates** from $49 a day, unlimited km. **Open** 7.30am-6pm daily. **Credit** AmEx, BC, DC, JCB, MC, $TC, V. **Branches**: National Reservations Centre (1800 652 008); Sydney Airport (9669 6677).

Second-hand Cars

There is a market in Kings Cross where travellers can buy (and in some cases sell back) second-hand cars. Before embarking on this, get hold of a copy of the National Roads & Motorists Association's (NRMA) free booklet, *The Worry Free Guide to Buying a Car*, which is a mine of useful information.

NRMA Insurance Ltd
151 Clarence Street (9292 9230/24-hour information 13 2132). CityRail Wynyard. **Open** 8am-5pm Mon-Fri; 9am-noon Sat.
The NSW motoring organisation has reciprocal agreements with other international organisations, including the AA, which entitle members to such services as free towing and breakdown assistance. The centre on Clarence Street also provides travel advice, maps and brochures on topics like buying a car, off-road driving and general car maintenance.

Kings Cross Car Market
Kings Cross Carpark, Level 2, Ward Avenue, Kings Cross (9358 5000)/24-hour information 1 902 263 180). CityRail Kings Cross. **Open** 9am-6.30pm daily. **No credit cards**.
Only 'genuine travellers' are allowed to sell their cars here – not local residents or dealers. There are members of staff on hand to offer helpful advice to both buyers and sellers. There is also a leaflet containing advice on what to look for before making a purchase.

Cycling

If you can stand the hills, the six-lane highways that carve up the city and the drivers who think signalling is for sissies, cycling can be a good way of getting around the city. Even better are the cycle tracks in parks such as Centennial Park. For more information *see chapter* **The Great Outdoors**.

Walking

Walking is sometimes the most practical way of getting around, and it is certainly the most scenic way of exploring. There are dozens of harbour and ocean walks, from the Manly Scenic Walk to one that goes from Circular Quay to the Art Gallery of NSW, via the Opera House and Mrs Macquarie's Chair. For more details *see chapters* **Sightseeing**, **The Great Outdoors** *and* **Sydney by Area**.

For the fastest route to Manly, take the nippy Jetcat. See page 9.

Accommodation

Want a room with a view? Prefer backpacker bohemia and self-catering simplicity? Or perhaps you hanker after some Old World colonial charm? It's all here.

First, the bad news. Sydney hotels are struggling to keep pace with the city's burgeoning tourist and corporate trade. Arrivals of overseas visitors increased by 12.1 per cent in 1995; the number of nights spent by international backpackers leapt by 28 per cent. So, despite the steady increase in accommodation availability (at the last count, 236 hotels, motels and guesthouses were offering some 66,199 beds in the city) many places are continuously running at over 90 per cent capacity.

The busiest periods are between November and May. Between mid-December and late January – a time which coincides not only with the festive season but also the summer school holidays and the annual Sydney Festival – is busiest of all. The Gay & Lesbian Mardi Gras in February and the Easter festivities in March and April are also popular periods. So if you're planning to visit Sydney during these months, book ahead.

Now for the good news. You don't have to be wealthy to stay in Sydney. Between $70 and $100 will get you a very acceptable double room, in the heart of the metropolis if you so desire it. If you are backpacking, there are some excellent new hostels to be found, many of which are equally geared to suitcase-carriers. Universities also have cheap rooms available during the holidays just when there's a dearth of them elsewhere (December to mid-February). And if money's no object, there are currently 13 five-star hotels in the city.

A word about the term 'hotel'. In Australia, this also refers to a pub, which may not necessarily have accommodation. The ones that do have rooms vary enormously in standard, ranging from the seedy to the superlative. The good ones, some of which are listed below, offer great value for money and are usually well situated. However, pubs can be noisy places to stay, especially if the bar has live music. To ensure peace and quiet, ask for a room at the top.

*Take a dip beneath the stars at the **Observatory Hotel**. See page 15.*

*The **Sebel of Sydney**. See page 17.*

USEFUL ORGANISATIONS

A real asset to travellers is the newly formed, government-funded Countrylink New South Wales Travel Centre. It stocks up-to-date guides to all the accommodation available in the city, including serviced apartments, hostels and camp-sites. It will also negotiate deals with a wide range of city hotels, getting up to 50 per cent chopped off the usual rates. Contact the centre for a current list (for the address *see chapter* **Essential Information**). You can book the hotel of your choice directly through the centre with a credit card.

If you are a member of a motoring organisation such as the AA or RAC, you can pick up the af-filiated NRMA's 'Holiday Guides for Members' booklets which contain information and discounts ranging from 10 to 40 per cent on selected hotels. *See chapter* **Essential Information** *for listings.*

Unless otherwise stated, the rates quoted below are for a double room, mercifully with no hidden extras or taxes to pay. It's always worth asking for stand-by prices, weekly rates or 'specials'; you may well get them, even in the peak season. No hotelier likes an empty room.

1800 telephone numbers can be dialled free of charge within Australia.

Top Dollar

Inter-Continental

117 Macquarie Street, Sydney, NSW 2000 (9320 0200/1800 221 828/fax 9240 1240). CityRail/ferry Circular Quay. **Rooms** *497.* **Rates** *$360-$675.* **Credit** AmEx, BC, JCB, MC, V.
The turn-of-the-century Treasury Building has been restored and transformed into a 31-floor, five star hotel that oozes her-itage credentials and old world charm. It overlooks the Harbour, Botanic Gardens and the Opera House and includes all the luxuries you'd expect at this level: indoor pool, fully equipped gym and panoramic views of the city, as well as several restaurants and bars. The handsome skylit palm

court area, with its vaulted sandstone arcades, is the place to sip tea or something stronger.
Hotel services *Air-conditioning. Babysitting. Bars. Beauty salon. Business services. Carpark. Conference facilities. Currency exchange. Disabled: access. Fax. Gym. Laundry service. Limousine service. Multi-lingual staff. Non-smoking floors. Restaurants. Swimming pool.* **Room services** *Hair-drier. Minibar. Room service (24-hour). Safe. Tea/coffee-making facilities. Telephone. TV (in-house movies).*

Observatory Hotel

89-113 Kent Street, Millers Point, Sydney, NSW 2000 (9256 2222/fax 9256 2233). CityRail/ferry Circular Quay. **Rooms** *80, plus 20 executive suites.* **Rates** *$425-$1,500.* **Credit** AmEx, BC, DC, MC, TC, V.
Looking at the early-Colonial elegance of the Observatory Hotel, it's difficult to believe that the place was built just four years ago. But little things give the game away. Like the com-plimentary flotation tank session to help combat jetlag. And the fully equipped basement gym furnished with personal trainers and satellite TV. And a 20-metre indoor heated pool, with the Southern Hemisphere constellations depicted in fibre-optic lights on the ceiling. And a Jacuzzi. Go up to your room, and in that polished mahogany armoire you will find a personal fax machine, a CD player, a VCR and TV with 24-hour CNN. Plus four telephones and modem facilities on two separate lines. Security-minded? Request a room on floors two or three, accessible only by security keys which activate the lift. Reassured? Then soak in your over-sized marble bath and nibble at those complimentary strawberries, or relax on your four-poster bed and call up 24-hour room service. The management wants you to feel that the place is a home from home. And you do, you do.
Hotel services *Air-conditioning. Babysitting. Bar. Beauty salon. Business services. Carpark. Fax. Conference facilities. Currency exchange. Disabled: access; specially adapted rooms. Fax. Gym (incl flotation tank, sauna, swimming pool).*

*Unbeatable location: the **Park Hyatt**, page 17.*

*Hairdresser. Laundry service. Limousine service.
Multilingual staff. Non-smoking rooms. Restaurants. Ticket
agency.* **Room services** *Hair-drier. Minibar. Radio/CD
player. Refrigerator. Room service (24-hour). Safe.
Tea/coffee-making facilities. Telephone. TV (satellite). VCR.*

Park Hyatt

*7 Hickson Road, The Rocks, Sydney, NSW 2000 (9241
1234/fax 9256 1555). CityRail/ferry Circular Quay.*
Rooms 122, plus 36 suites. **Rates** *rooms* $480-$620;
studio $700-$750; *suites* $850-$3,500. **Credit** AmEx, BC,
DC, JCB, MC, TC, V.
Feeling tired after that long, long flight? Relax. Your personal 24-hour butler understands. He'll usher you up to your
suite, unpack your luggage, shine your shoes and fix you
that Scotch. After all, you are staying at the most exclusive
hotel in Sydney. How much? If you have to ask, you can't
afford it. So, what are you paying for? Three things: location,
location and location. Look below and you can see the
Bounty. And smack in front of you is the Opera House. Want
a closer look? Use your strategically placed personal telescope. Now go into your dressing room, change into your
cossie, and relax in the rooftop Jacuzzi. Look up. That's
Sydney Harbour Bridge. Feeling better now? You're in good
company. Bruce Willis, Demi Moore, Robin Williams and a
host of other celebs quite like it too.
Hotel services *Air-conditioning. Babysitting. Bar.
Beauty salon. Business services. Butler service. Carpark.
Fax. Conference facilities. Currency exchange. Disabled:
access; specially adapted rooms. Fax. Gym. Hairdresser.
Interpreting services. Laundry service. Limousine service.
Multilingual staff. Non-smoking rooms. Restaurants. Roof
terrace. Sauna. Swimming pool. Ticket agency.* **Room
services** *Hair-drier. Minibar. Refrigerator. Radio. Room
service (24-hour). Safe. Tea/coffee-making facilities.
Telephone. TV. VCR.*

The Regent, Sydney

*199 George Street, Sydney, NSW 2000 (9238 0000/fax
9251 2851/email regentsyd1.@att.net.au). CityRail/ferry
Circular Quay.* **Rooms** 596. **Rates** $250-$2,000. **Credit**
AmEx, BC, DC, JCB, MC, TC, V.
Like the Sebel (*see below*), this is one of the city's original
five-star hotels – and nobody does it better. The Regent is
famous for its sleek personal service, an executive chef
whose dining room is the envy of other establishments, and
a buzzy sense of Sydney careering towards 2000. The hotel
is spectacularly placed on the harbour, and the wonderfully
large lobby has great views.
Hotel services *Air-conditioning. Babysitting. Bars.
Beauty salon. Business services. Carpark. Conference
facilities. Currency exchange. Disabled: access. Fax. Health
club. Interpreting service. Limousine service. Multi-lingual
staff. Non-smoking rooms. Restaurants. Swimming pool.
Ticket agency.* **Room services** *Butler service. Daily
newspaper. Fax. Room service (24-hour). Radio.
Telephone. TV.*

Ritz-Carlton Sydney

*93 Macquarie Street, Sydney, NSW 2000 (9252
4600/fax 9252 4286). CityRail/ferry Circular Quay.*
Rooms 93, plus 13 suites. **Rates** *rooms* $279-$369; *suites*
$400-$1,200. **Credit** AmEx, BC, DC, JCB, MC, TC, V.
A two-minute stroll from the Opera House and opposite the
Royal Botanic Gardens. Like its larger sister hotel in Double
Bay (9362 4455/fax 9362 4744), it was built only this decade,
yet bears all the trademarks of the Ritz-Carlton chain: oil
paintings, antique furniture, Persian rugs, chandeliers, crack-
ling log fires. It was here that the Rolling Stones requested
– and got – interconnecting doors specially added to link
their rooms. Also popular with business people, the hotel's
luxuries include a heated rooftop pool. There are even
Corporate Woman Rooms which couples or single women
can book at no extra charge. As well as an extra door lock,

Small and chic – L'Otel. See page 20.

these gender-sensitive boudoirs offer such feminine must-
haves as fresh flowers, low-cal beverages, full-length mirror
and a velvet bag containing stockings, hairbrush and mois-
turisers. The more expensive rooms include use of the club
lounge, which serves complimentary food and drink all day.
Hotel services *Air-conditioning. Babysitting. Bar.
Business services. Carpark. Conference facilities. Currency
exchange. Disabled: access. Fax. Gym. Laundry service.
Limousine service. Multilingual staff. Non-smoking rooms.
Restaurants. Roof terrace. Sauna. Swimming pool. Ticket
agency.* **Room services** *Hair-drier. Minibar. Radio.
Refrigerator. Room service (24-hour). Tea/coffee-making
facilities. Telephone. TV (satellite).*

Sebel of Sydney

*23 Elizabeth Bay Road, Elizabeth Bay, NSW 2011 (9358
3244/fax 9357 1926). Bus 327.* **Rooms** 143, plus 22
suites. **Rates** *rooms* $205-$295; *junior suites* $450; *major
suites* $700. **Credit** AmEx, BC, DC, JCB, MC, TC, V.
The Sebel's age – just 34 years – qualifies it as the oldest five-
star establishment in Sydney. Add to that its position overlooking Rushcutters Bay and legendary service, and you get
a hotel that has long been a favourite with entertainers. From
Bob Hope to Barry Manilow, Tina Turner to Tom Selleck, the
cocktail bar has seen them all come and go – and has signed
photos on its dark panelled walls to prove it. The six major
suites are named after former regulars. The Sir Robert
Helpman suite, described as 'ideal for honeymooners', incorporates a spa and a wall depicting a Mediterranean coastline.
It seems, however, that David Bowie is no longer in favour
at the Sebel: his suite has been converted into a gym.
Hotel services *Air-conditioning. Babysitting. Bar.
Business services. Carpark. Conference facilities. Currency
exchange. Disabled: access; specially adapted rooms. Fax.
Gym. Laundry service. Limousine service. Multilingual staff.
Non-smoking floors. Restaurants. Roof terrace. Sauna.*

For the popular **Potts Point House**, *see p23.*

Swimming pool. Ticket agency. **Room services** Hair-drier. Minibar. Radio. Refrigerator. Room service (24-hour) Tea/coffee-making facilities. Telephone. TV (satellite).

Sheraton on the Park

161 Elizabeth Street, Sydney, NSW 2000 (9286 6000/fax 9286 6686). CityRail St James. **Rooms** 559. **Rates** *rooms* from $340; *suites* from $790. **Credit** AmEx, BC, DC, MC, $TC, V.
Instead of the usual harbour views, this handsome branch of the world-wide chain looks out over the lush foliage of Hyde Park. The sweeping staircases and marble pillars of the grand lobby lead up to suitably luxurious rooms with black marble and granite bathrooms and various deluxe amenities including three telephones, in-house movies and CD players.
Hotel services *Air-conditioning. Babysitting. Bars. Business services. Carpark. Conference facilities. Currency exchange. Disabled: access. Fax. Health club & gym. Laundry service. Limousine service. Multilingual staff. Non-smoking floors. Restaurants Swimming pool. Ticket agency.* **Room services** *Hair-drier. Minibar. Radio. Refrigerator. Room service (24-hour). Safe. Tea/coffee-making facilities. Telephone. TV (in-house movies).*

Moderate to Expensive

Cranbrook International

601 New South Head Road, Rose Bay, NSW 2029 (9327 7770/fax 9327 8361). Ferry Rose Bay/325 bus. **Rooms** 46 (all en suite). **Rates** *single* $65; *double/twin* $90-$125; *family suite* $125-$145; *penthouse* $220. **Credit** AmEx, BC, DC, MC, TC, V.
Pretty Rose Bay, just 20 minutes from Circular Quay by bus or ferry, is a playground for tourists and Sydneysiders,

offering sailing, windsurfing, scuba-diving, golf, water-skiing and tennis. Seaplanes also fly from here (*see chapter* **Sightseeing** for more details). Cranbrook, the only hotel in the area, offers both 'standard' and 'deluxe' rooms in two separate wings, the best with views directly over the bay. The penthouse suite is opulently furnished with chesterfields, a dining table seating six, a kitchen and a Jacuzzi.
Hotel services *Air-conditioning. Babysitting. Bar. Carpark. Conference facilities. Currency exchange. Disabled: access. Fax. Laundry service. Limousine service. Multilingual staff. Non-smoking rooms. Restaurant. Swimming pool. Ticket agency.* **Room services** *Hair-drier. Minibar. Radio. Refrigerator. Room service (7am-9pm). Tea/coffee-making facilities. Telephone. TV.*

Gazebo Hotel

2 Elizabeth Bay Road, Elizabeth Bay, NSW 2011 (9358 1999/1800 221 495/fax 9356 2951). CityRail Kings Cross. **Rooms** 384 (all en suite), plus 11 suites. **Rates** *rooms* $190-$210; *suites* $270-$420. **Credit** AmEx, BC, DC, JCB, MC, TC, V.
Close enough to take advantage of all its eateries, live music pubs, shops and nightlife, but distanced slightly from the bustle of Kings Cross, the Gazebo is a four-star Australian-owned and operated hotel. Most rooms have great views of the harbour, the city skyline or the eastern suburbs from their balconies. The best outlook of all is provided by the **Windows Over Sydney** rooftop restaurant and bar on the seventeenth floor.
Hotel services *Air-conditioning. Babysitting. Bar. Business services. Carpark. Conference facilities. Currency exchange. Disabled: access; specially adapted room. Fax. Laundry service. Limousine service. Multilingual staff. Non-smoking floors. Restaurants. Roof terrace. Sauna. Swimming pool. Ticket agency.* **Room services** *Hair-drier. Minibar. Radio. Refrigerator Room service (24-hour). Tea/coffee-making facilities. Telephone. VCR (on request).*

Manly Pacific Parkroyal

55 North Steyne, Manly, NSW 2095 (9977 7666/fax 9977 7822). Ferry Manly. **Rooms** 169 (all en suite). **Rates** $165-$250. **Credit** AmEx, BC, DC, JCB, MC, TC, V.
Right on the famous surf beach, and just 12 minutes by Jetcat from Circular Quay, this stunningly located, though blandly designed, modern hotel is in the business of providing ocean views every which way you look. And if you don't fancy sand in your swimwear, go for a dip in the rooftop pool.
Hotel services *Air-conditioning. Babysitting. Bar. Business services. Carpark. Conference facilities. Currency exchange. Disabled: access. Fax. Gym. Interpreting services. Laundry service. Limousine service. Multilingual staff. Non-smoking floor. Restaurants. Roof terrace. Swimming pool. Ticket agency.* **Room services** *Hair-drier. Ironing facilities. Minibar. Radio. Refrigerator. Room service (24-hour). Tea/coffee-making facilities. Telephone. TV (in-house movies). VCR.*

Novotel

100 Murray Street, Pyrmont, NSW 2009 (9934 0000/1800 642 244/fax 9934 0099). Monorail Convention Square/443 bus. **Rooms** 527 (all en suite). **Rates** $225-$490. **Credit** AmEx, BC, JCB, MC, TC, V.
The Novotel is built for those who like their amenities abundant and equate big with best. With over 500 rooms – most have terrific city and harbour views – and more than 800 staff, this is a Darling Harbour landmark. Surrounded by a multitude of tourist attractions the hotel also has an undercover walkway to Sydney Convention & Exhibition Centre and Festival Marketplace, while the city centre and Chinatown are a few minutes' taxi or bus ride away. Extras include a fully equipped business centre and an outdoor heated pool.
Hotel services *Air-conditioning. Babysitting. Bar. Beauty salon. Business centre. Carpark. Conference facilities. Currency exchange. Disabled: access; toilets;*

specially adapted rooms. Fax. Gym. Laundry service. Limousine service. Multilingual staff. Non-smoking rooms. Restaurants. Sauna. Swimming pool. Tennis court. Ticket agency. **Room services** Hair-drier. Minibar. Radio. Refrigerator. Room service (24-hour). Tea/coffee-making facilities. Telephone. TV (satellite). VCR.

Wynyard Vista Hotel

7-9 York Street, Sydney, NSW 2000 (9290 1840/1800 652 090/fax 9290 1870). CityRail Wynyard. **Rooms** 211 (all en suite). **Rates** single $120; double $140. **Credit** AmEx, BC, DC, JCB, MC, TC, V.

This large, newly established hotel is keen to build up its clientele and for that reason offers excellent rates through the Countrylink NSW Travel Centre. Centrally located next to Wynyard Station, with all major attractions nearby, rooms are comfortable and there is an imaginative buffet restaurant on the ground floor, operated by Sri Lankan chefs. Visit the Japanese garden roof terrace for superlative city views. **Hotel services** Air-conditioning. Babysitting. Bar. Business services. Carpark. Conference facilities. Currency exchange. Fax. Garden. Laundry service. Limousine service. Multilingual staff. Non-smoking floor. Restaurant. Safety deposit boxes. Ticket agency. **Room services** Hair-drier. Minibar. Radio. Refrigerator. Room service (24-hour). Telephone. TV (in-house movies).

Small & Chic

L'Otel

114 Darlinghurst Road, Darlinghurst, NSW 2010 (9360 6868/fax 9331 4536). CityRail Kings Cross. **Rooms** 14 (all en suite). **Rates** $80-$150. **Credit** AmEx, BC, DC, MC, $TC, V.

A small, stylish hotel with bare-brick rooms individually decorated in French provincial and 1950s retro style, and furnished with opulent queen-size beds. Trompe-l'œil effects, imaginatively painted furniture, huge fireplaces and masses of modern art add to the interest. More practically, each room has its own kitchenette. On the ground floor there is an exhibition of work by contemporary artists and a trendy café offering a mouthwatering choice at breakfast. **Hotel services** Air-conditioning. Bar. Carpark. Fax. Laundry service. Limousine service. Multilingual staff. Restaurant. Safe. **Room services** Hair-drier. Refrigerator. Minibar. Room service (7.30am-11.30pm). Telephone. TV. VCR.

Pasadena on Pittwater

1858 Pittwater Road, Church Point, NSW 2105 (9979 6633/fax 9979 6147). Ferry Manly then 155 bus. **Rooms** 14 (all en suite). **Rates** $100-$120. **Credit** AmEx, BC, DC, MC, TC, V.

With spectacular views over the water to Ku-Ring-Gai Chase National Park and Scotland Island, Church Point is an ideal place to unwind for a few nights, and well worth the one-hour ferry and bus journey from the centre of town. The secluded Pasadena offers airy cane-furnished rooms and an elegant waterfront restaurant. Alternatively, guests can dine at the hotel's Italian café next door. Boats can be rented from $30 an hour. If you're feeling flush, fly over by seaplane from Rose Bay or Cronulla ($225 for up to 4 passengers), an experience in itself on a windy day. **Hotel services** Air-conditioning. Bottle shop. Carpark. Conference facilities. Fax. Garden. Laundry service. Limousine service. Multilingual staff. Safe. Seaplane service. **Room services** Hair-drier. Radio. Refrigerator. Room service (limited). Telephone. TV.

Ravesi's

Corner of Campbell Parade and Hall Street, Bondi Beach, NSW 2026 (9365 4422/fax 9365 1482). Buses 380, 382. **Rooms** 11 en suite, plus 5 split-level suites. **Rates**

rooms $95-$180; suites $155-$250. **Credit** AmEx, BC, DC, MC, $TC, V.

A charming small hotel above the Bondi bistro of the same name. Cane furnishings, queen-size beds and marble bathrooms are standard. And, if your budget runs to it, there are rooms with unsurpassed views over the famous beach itself. Enjoy the same views by taking a lazy breakfast or lunch on the verandah. **Hotel services** Air-conditioning. Bar. Babysitting. Carpark. Conference facilities. Disabled: access; specially adapted rooms. Fax. Laundry service. Limousine service. Restaurant. **Room services** Hair-drier. Radio. Refrigerator. Room service (7.30am-10pm). Tea/coffee-making facilities. Telephone. TV.

Regents Court Hotel

18 Springfield Avenue, Potts Point, NSW 2011 (9358 1533/fax 9358 1833). CityRail Kings Cross. **Rooms** 29. **Rates** $170-$185. **Credit** AmEx, BC, DC, MC, V.

Dark, slick and moderne, this chic boutique hotel is favoured by young actors and filmbiz types. Based in a recently restored 1920s building in a leafy cul-de-sac near Kings Cross, the hotel has 29 spacious suites, many furnished with 1920s and 1930s design classics by the likes of Corbusier, Eames and Newson. All suites have kitchens, stocked with fresh coffee, tea and home-made cakes and biscuits. The staff are particularly keen and helpful. Check out the rooftop terrace, a popular venue for celebrity interviews. **Hotel services** Air-conditioning. Babysitting. Business services. Carpark. Fax. Laundry service. Non-smoking rooms. Roof terrace. **Room services** Hair-drier. Ironing board. Kitchen. Telephone (2 lines). TV. VCR.

The Russell

143A George Street, The Rocks, Sydney, NSW 2000 (9241 3543/fax 9252 1652). CityRail/ferry Circular Quay. **Rooms** 29 (18 en suite). **Rates** single $95-$220; double $105-$230. **Credit** AmEx, BC, DC, MC, $TC, V.

Frequently accoladed and very popular, The Russell strives to maintain 'the charm and elegance of a bygone era'. It prides itself on hospitality and elegant rooms individually furnished with period pieces. High ceilings, marble fireplaces, Victorian bedsteads, heavy drapes and fresh flowers abound. On the first floor there's a comfortable lounge/bar with a balcony offering views over Circular Quay. Breakfast can be eaten on the sunny roof terrace or in the rather swish Boulders Restaurant below. **Hotel services** Bar. Carpark. Fax. Laundry service. Limousine service. Multilingual staff. Restaurant. Roof terrace. **Room services** Hair-drier. Radio. Telephone. TV.

Sullivans Hotel

21 Oxford Street, Paddington, NSW 2021 (9361 0211/9360 3735/email sydney@sullivans.com.au). Bus 378, 380, 382. **Rooms** 66 (all en suite). **Rates** $105. **Credit** AmEx, BC, DC, MC, TC, V.

Friendly family-run hotel in the heart of cosmopolitan Paddo, with its cinemas, shops and cafés. Many of the recently refurbished rooms overlook the landscaped courtyard, complete with swimming pool. Free guest bicycles are available for those wishing to work off the complimentary evening chocolates with a pedal through nearby Centennial or Moore Parks. **Hotel services** Air-conditioning. Babysitting. Business services. Carpark. Currency exchange. Fax. Laundry service. Limousine service. Multilingual staff. Restaurant. Safety deposit boxes. Swimming pool. **Room services** Hair-drier. Radio. Refrigerator. Tea/coffee-making facilities. Telephone. TV.

Victoria Court Hotel

122 Victoria Street, Potts Point, NSW 2011 (9357 3200/1800 630 505/fax 9357 7606/email vicsyd@ozemail.com.au) CityRail Kings Cross. **Rooms** 23 (all en suite). **Rates** single/double $60-$180 (incl breakfast). **Credit** AmEx, BC, DC, MC, $TC, V.

Bed & breakfast

All over Sydney there are households offering that famous Aussie hospitality. The Bed & Breakfast Booking Service will arrange accommodation with experienced and welcoming hosts; some will even take you on bushwalks or tours of the region.

Bed & Breakfast Booking Service
PO Box 298, Edgecliff, NSW 2027 (9314 7203/fax 9314 6823). **Rates** *from single $40; double $70.*

Periwinkle Guest House
18-19 East Esplanade, Manly, NSW 2095 (9977 4668/ fax 9977 6308). Ferry Manly. **Rooms** 17 (10 en suite). **Rates** *single $70-$80; double $85-$95; triple $100-$115; family room $115-$135 (incl breakfast).* **Credit** BC, MC, V.
The visitors' book at this Federation-style guesthouse says it all. Almost everyone has written: 'Lovely as usual' or 'Great to be back!' Tucked in a quiet corner of Manly Cove, the Periwinkle is a friendly place based in two Victorian houses linked by wrought-iron lacework verandahs, which form a verdant inner courtyard with seating and a barbecue. The best rooms overlook the harbour, and are furnished with period furniture and deep Victorian baths.
Hotel services *Carpark. Fax. Function room. Washing-machine/drier. No smoking.* **Room services** *Hair-drier. Refrigerator. TV.*

Riverview B&B
16 Wallace Street, Greenwich Point, NSW 2065 (9906 7550/mobile 019 912 192/fax 9906 7617). Ferry Greenwich Point. **Rooms** 3 (none en suite). **Rates** *single $60; double/twin $85.* **No credit cards.**
This rambling Federation-style house was once Peter Finch's boyhood home. It is now run as a comfortable B&B, with fluffy bathrobes, fresh flowers and tantalising home cooking. It's superbly located near Greenwich Point, which is a short ferry ride from Circular Quay. The friendly hosts (and their corgis) will accompany guests on local bushwalks or take them on drives to harbour look-outs at no extra cost. Work off the hearty breakfast (bagels, smoked salmon, crêpes with fresh ricotta) at the local tennis courts or nearby harbourside pool.
Hotel services *Garden. Laundry service. Multilingual staff. No smoking.* **Room services** *Hair-drier. Radio.*

Tricketts Luxury B&B
270 Glebe Point Road, Glebe, NSW 2037 (9552 1141/ fax 9692 9462). Bus 431. **Rooms** 7 (all en suite).

Rates (incl breakfast) *single $95; double $120.* **No credit cards.**
Highly recommended for a relaxing stay is this tastefully restored Victorian mansion. The former ballroom (*above*), now a drawing room, is furnished with period furniture, pool table, piano and Persian rugs on polished parquet flooring. Bedrooms have underfloor heating and are furnished with queen-size beds, cane chairs, Welsh slate tables and Victorian dressers; the Honeymoon Room throws in a miners settle. There is not a TV to be found anywhere, greatly encouraging conversation between guests.
Hotel services *Barbecue. Carpark. Fax. Garden. No smoking. Pool table.* **Room services** *Hair-drier. Radio.*

Recommended for a romantic stay is this historic boutique hotel. A tinkling fountain in the courtyard conservatory greets visitors, while the best rooms have marble fireplaces, huge mirrors, glitzy chandeliers, four-poster beds and wrought-iron balconies. Breakfast is taken in the conservatory, which adjoins a comfortable lounge. The staff are very hospitable and there are good deals available through the Countrylink NSW Travel Centre.
Hotel services *Air-conditioning. Business services. Carpark. Fax. Laundry service. Limousine service. Multilingual staff. Non-smoking rooms.* **Room services** *Hair-drier. Radio. Refrigerator. Tea/coffee-making facilities. Telephone. TV.*

Pub Hotels

Coogee Bay Hotel
Corner of Coogee Bay Road and Arden Street, Coogee, NSW 2034 (9665 0000/fax 9664 2103). Bus 373. **Rooms** 35 (all en suite), plus 52 suites. **Rates** *single $68; double $70-$120; suites $120-$140.* **Credit** AmEx, BC, DC, MC, $TC, V.
An award-winning corner hotel with stylish ocean-view suites; other rooms have beach views. Downstairs you can eat in the pretty brasserie or char-grill your own steak and eat alfresco in the courtyard. The hotel is also a popular live-music venue for local and international bands.

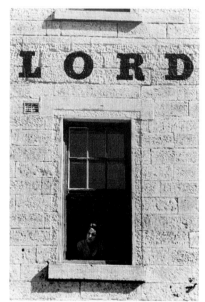

*They're admirable views at the **Lord Nelson**.*

Hotel services *Air-conditioning. Bars. Carpark. Conference facilities. Courtyard. Fax. Laundry service. Limousine service. Multilingual staff. Pool tables. TAB.* **Room services** *Hair-drier. Minibar. Radio. Refrigerator. Telephone. TV (satellite).*

Grand Hotel

30 Hunter Street, Sydney, NSW 2000 (9232 3755/fax 9232 1073). CityRail Wynyard. **Rooms** 19 (none en suite). **Rates** *from single* $60; *double/twin* $80; *family room* $100. **Credit** AmEx, BC, DC, MC, $TC, V.

One of the oldest surviving pubs in the CBD, sitting on the historic Tank Stream, the first settlers' precious water supply. Now offering rather stronger liquid refreshments, the Grand also has some of the nicest pub accommodation around. Downstairs there is a pleasant pool room and busy bar; request a quiet top-floor room.

Hotel services *Bars. Fax. Pool room.* **Room services** *Radio. Refrigerator. Tea/coffee-making facilities. TV.*

Hotel Bondi

178 Campbell Parade, Bondi Beach, NSW 2026 (9130 3271/fax 9130 7974). Bus 380, 382. **Rooms** 46 (30 en suite). **Rates** *single* $35-$50; *double* $65-$120. **Credit** AmEx, BC, DC, MC, $TC, V.

This huge, heritage-listed, family-owned hotel is a Bondi landmark. Locals come here to eat fish and chips, catch the sport on satellite TV, shoot pool or just relax in the bar overlooking the sweep of Bondi Beach. There are karaoke nights and weekend discos. Upstairs are newly renovated soundproofed rooms, including some impressive ocean-view self-contained suites (sleeping 4) with sleek kitchens. All guests get to use the terrific beach-view balcony.

Hotel services *Air-conditioning. Bars. Bottle shop. Carpark. Fax. Laundry service. Pool hall. Restaurant. Washing-machines/driers.* **Room services** *Radio. Refrigerator. Tea/coffee-making facilities. Telephone. TV.*

Lord Nelson Brewery Hotel

19 Kent Street, The Rocks, NSW 2000 (9251 4044/fax 9251 1532). CityRail/ferry Circular Quay. **Rooms** 5 (none en suite). **Rates** (incl breakfast) *single/double* $60-$80; *triple* $100. **Credit** AmEx, BC, DC, MC, $TC, V.

An 1841 sandstone hotel in a prime position overlooking Observatory Hill. It claims to be the oldest pub in the city, and has Victorian-style guest rooms complete with the original bare sandstone walls to keep the rooms cool. On the first floor is a pretty brasserie with views towards the Harbour Bridge. The atmospheric bar downstairs – its walls lined with framed naval charts detailing the Battle of Trafalgar – brews its own beer. Book ahead.

Hotel services *Bar. Fax. Restaurant.* **Room services** *Telephone. TV.*

Mercantile Hotel

25 George Street, The Rocks, NSW 2000 (9247 4306/ 9247 3570/fax 9247 7047). CityRail/ferry Circular Quay. **Rooms** 15 (4 en suite). **Rates** (incl breakfast) *single* $65; *double/twin* $85; *suite/triple* $100-$120. **Credit** AmEx, BC, DC, MC, TC, V.

One of the city's oldest hotels surprisingly offers the most luxurious accommodation you'll find for the price. The striking listed building has large, quiet, rag-rolled suites unlisted in most guide books. They come with marble fireplaces, carved mahogany beds and corner Jacuzzis. Double rooms have huge period bathrooms. At weekends the canopied Rocks market takes place in the street below. The lively bar, known as 'the Irish pub', is the only place to be on St Patrick's Day; it has live Irish and bush music every weekend.

Hotel services *Air-conditioning. Bar. Fax. Laundry service. Live music. Pool tables. Restaurant. Roof terrace.* **Room services** *Hair-drier. Radio. TV (cable).*

O'Malley's Hotel

228 William Street, Kings Cross, NSW 2011 (9357 2211/fax 9357 2656). CityRail Kings Cross. **Rooms** 15 (10 en suite). **Rates** (incl breakfast) *single* $55-$70; *twin/double* $60-$75. **Credit** AmEx, BC, MC, $TC, V.

Rates are reasonable at this listed, restored hotel. The rooms are spacious and comfortably furnished in mid-Victorian country style with added touches like turned-down beds and phones in the bathrooms. Downstairs is the liveliest Irish bar in the Cross, with jazz, soul, rock or traditional Irish bands playing nightly. The top floor rooms are quiet if you need that early night. Booking in advance is a good idea, particularly at Easter during Mardi Gras and around September's Rugby League Grand Final.

Hotel services *Air-conditioning. Bar. Business services. Carpark. Casino. Fax. Laundry service. Live music. Limousine service. Multilingual staff.* **Room services** *Hair-drier. Radio. Refrigerator. Room service (7.30am-10pm). Safe. Telephone. TV.*

Palisade Hotel

35-37 Bettington Street, Millers Point, NSW 2000 (9247 2272/fax 9247 2040). CityRail/ferry Circular Quay. **Rooms** 10 (none en suite). **Rates** *from* $80. **Credit** AmEx, BC, JCB, MC, $TC, V.

Peacefully situated on the cusp of The Rocks, the 1916 Palisade Hotel offers pleasantly furnished rooms, some with large balconies overlooking the harbour. Downstairs is a quiet bar with a log fire and there's an excellent, informal restaurant on the first floor.

Hotel services *Bar. Roof garden. Restaurant.*

Budget

Alishan International Guesthouse

100 Glebe Point Road, Glebe, NSW 2037 (9566 4048/fax 9525 4686). Bus 431, 433, 434. **Rooms** 19 (14 en suite).

Rates *single* $20 (dorm), $70 (en suite); *double* $85.
Credit BC, MC, TC, V.
A Victorian mansion renovated Japanese style, and equally popular with suitcase-carriers and backpackers. The airy dining room/lounge has a cool black stone floor and sleek black furnishings, with a new, well-equipped kitchen attached. The simple rooms, some with balconies, have pine beds with futon mattresses. There are good-sized family rooms and four-bed dorms overlooking the courtyard, which has both a barbecue and Jacuzzi.
Hotel services *Barbecue. Carpark. Disabled: access; specially adapted room. Fax. Garden. Jacuzzi. Kitchen. Laundry service. No smoking. Safe. Washing-machine/drier.* **Room services** *Hair-drier. Refrigerator. Tea/coffee-making facilities. TV.*

Australian Sunrise Lodge

485 King Street, Newtown, NSW 2042 (9550 4999/ fax 9550 4457). Bus 422. **Rooms** 20 (14 en suite).
Rates *single/double* $45-$65; *family room* $85.
Credit AmEx, BC, DC, JCB, MC, $TC, V.
Located in King Street – famous for its cheap restaurants, New Age shops and artisan outlets – this is a small and quiet family-run lodge. With parquet flooring throughout, guest rooms (many with balconies overlooking a courtyard) are well equipped, down to a microwave and toaster. There is also a small communal kitchen and lounge. The family room sleeps six, making it cost-effective for sharers.
Hotel services *Carpark. Disabled: access. Fax. Kitchen. Lounge. No smoking. Payphone.* **Room services** *Hair-drier. Microwave. Radio. Refrigerator. Tea/coffee-making facilities. Toaster. TV. VCR (on request).*

Billabong Gardens

5-11 Egan Street, Newtown, NSW 2042 (9550 3236/ fax 9550 4352). Bus 422, 423, 426, 428. **Rooms** 140 (70 en suite). **Rates** *dorm* $16-$18; *double/twin* $35-$65.
Credit TC.
This new, luxury hostel easily justifies its five-star rating. It's well located on a quiet road beside Newtown's lively King Street. It offers both private rooms with bathrooms and dormitories; children are also well catered for. Natural materials and indigenous plants have been used throughout the light and airy building, which centres around a courtyard with a solar-heated pool, spa and barbecue. Terracotta floors lead off to exposed-brick, pine-furnished rooms, which are cleaned daily. There is a comfortable TV lounge and an excellent kitchen. Security is good and there is 24-hour access.
Hotel services *Barbecue. Carpark. Fax. Garden. Kitchen. Pool table. Non-smoking rooms. Safe. Spa. Swimming pool. TV (satellite). Washing-machine/drier.* **Room services** *Refrigerator. Tea/coffee-making facilities (private rooms only). TV.*

Elevera Private Hotel

2 Manns Avenue, Neutral Bay, NSW 2089 (9929 7441). Ferry Neutral Bay (Hayes Street). **Rooms** 40 (none en suite). **Rates** *single* $110 weekly. **No credit cards**.
Set in a leafy garden, this north shore boarding house provides secure budget accommodation for women only. The TV lounge is furnished with comfy armchairs, mahogany furniture and a piano. Bedrooms are small but well furnished with dressers and wardrobes; rooms on the top two floors are nice and bright. Old-fashioned but well kept kitchens are provided on each floor. Sunny shared balconies are generously dotted around and there is a pretty roof terrace.
Hotel services *Carpark. Garden. Kitchens. TV lounge. Washing-machine/drier.*

Potts Point House

154 Victoria Street, Potts Point, NSW 2011 (9368 0733/ mobile 0418 200 966/fax 9261 2208). CityRail Kings Cross. **Rooms** 9 (none en suite). **Rates** *dorm* $20; *double* $40; *triple* $60. **Credit** AmEx, BC, DC, MC, TC, V.

Guests rave about this charming, cheap, newly renovated Victorian boarding house. A stripped-pine and stained-glass hallway leads off to spacious Ikea-furnished rooms, some with wrought-iron balconies. Adjoining the small courtyard is a pleasant well equipped kitchen/lounge. The three bathrooms and all bedrooms are serviced daily. The affable landlord is happy to accommodate both overnight stays and weekly boarders, including room-sharers. Book ahead.
Hotel services *Fax. Garden. Kitchen. Payphone.* **Room services** *TV.*

Y on the Park Hotel

5-11 Wentworth Avenue, Sydney, NSW 2010 (9264 2451/fax 9285 6288). CityRail Museum. **Rooms** 250 (17 en suite). **Rates** *dorm* $24; *single* $52-$70; *double/twin* $70-$95; *triple* $85-$100. **Credit** BC, MC, $TC, V.
This excellent, large and newly refurbished hotel offers central and secure budget accommodation for everyone from single professionals and young families in private en suite rooms to backpackers in dorms. Rooms have large mirrored wardrobes, safes and desks. There's a friendly atmosphere and plenty of shared areas to relax in. Various classes are available (for example, yoga) and, although there are no cooking facilities, the ground-floor cafeteria is open daily. The hostel is at the top of traffic-congested Oxford Street, but quieter rooms overlooking the central courtyard can be requested. Although you don't have to be a member to stay, the usual YMCA/YWCA rules apply: there's a curfew between 3am and 5am; no guests are allowed in rooms after 10.30pm; no smoking or alcohol is allowed on the premises.
Hotel services *Air-conditioning. Babysitting. Business services. Classes. Conference facilities. Disabled: access; toilets. Fax. Garden. Interpreting services. Laundry service. Multilingual staff. No smoking. Restaurant. Safety deposit boxes. Tea/coffee-making facilities. TV lounges.* **Room services** *Hair-drier. Radio (on request).*

Self-catering

All Season New Hampshire Apartments

2 Springfield Avenue, Potts Point, NSW 2011 (9356 3222/fax 9357 2296). CityRail Kings Cross. **Apartments** 45. **Rates** *1-bed* $120-$160; *2-bed* $165-$221. **Credit** AmEx, BC, DC, MC, TC, V.
An upbeat clientele gives both a buzz to the friendly staff and a charge to the atmosphere here. The luxury apartments – furnished in modern country style – are favoured by musicians, many of whom have their signed 8x10s in the hallway. All apartments have balconies, some with spectacular views of the Harbour Bridge, the Opera House and Fort Denison. Oddly, the noisiest songsters here are not the entertainers but the sulphur-crested cockatoos who turn up for breakfast. As they also tend to rip up the artificial turf, Parks and Wildlife advised sprinkling pepper over the entire roof as a deterrent. 'The only result,' the manager told the *Sydney Morning Herald*, 'was a request for salt as well. If you stand still, they'll start eating your shoes.'
Hotel services *Air-conditioning. Bar. Business services. Carpark. Disabled: access; specially adapted rooms. Fax. Interpreting services. Laundry service. Limousine service. Multilingual staff. Non-smoking rooms. Restaurant. Roof terrace. Swimming pool. Ticket agency.* **Room services** *Hair-drier. Kitchen. Radio. Refrigerator. Room service (breakfast & dinner). Telephone. TV (in-house movies). VCR.*

Bondi Beachside Inn

152 Campbell Parade, Bondi Beach, NSW 2026 (9130 5311/fax 9365 2646). Bus 380, 382. **Rooms** 70 (all en suite), plus 2-bed apartment. **Rates** *rooms* $62-$91; *2-bed apartment* $118-$138. **Credit** AmEx, BC, DC, MC, $TC, V.
This family-friendly, modern beachfront seven-floor inn is great value: $81 buys you an airy double with plenty of

clothes-hanging space, dining facilities, a kitchenette (cooker optional) and an ocean-view balcony. The excellent two-bed apartment sleeps up to six. Booking ahead is essential in the high season. Free security carparking.

Hotel services *Air-conditioning. Babysitting. Carpark. Fax. Multilingual staff.* **Room services** *Kitchen. Tea/coffee-making facilities. Radio. Refrigerator. Telephone. TV.*

Bondi Serviced Apartments

164-166 Bondi Road, Bondi, NSW 2026 (9363 5529/ mobile 015 407 621). Bus 380, 382. **Apartments** 10. **Rates** $285-$410 weekly. **Credit** BC, TC.
These pleasant and efficiently-run apartments – 15 minutes' walk from the beach – can sleep up to four people but are better suited to one or two. The minimum stay is one week, and the rates decrease according to season and length of stay. Get an apartment at the back, away from busy Bondi Road, if possible. Good value.

Apartment services *Carpark. Laundry service.* **Room services** *Balcony. Clothes line. Hair-drier (on request). Ironing facilities. Kitchen. Radio. Telephone (on request). TV.*

Coogee Sands Motor Inn

161 Dolphin Street, Coogee, NSW 2034 (9665 8588/ 1800 819 403/fax 9664 1406). Bus 373; free airport pick-up. **Rooms** 50 (all en suite). **Rates** $75-$120. **Credit** AmEx, BC, DC, MC, $TC, V.
Located just 10 minutes from Sydney Cricket Ground, the Royal Agricultural Society Showgrounds and Randwick Racecourse, and 15 minutes from the airport and the CBD, this is a gay-friendly inn, also popular with interstate couples and families. The beachfront en suite rooms, which have kitchenettes and baths as well as showers, are airy and reasonably priced. The ocean-view roof terrace sports a pool, barbecue and dining facilities. Rates include airport transfers and three weeks' free security parking for guests away visiting other parts of the country. There are also special deals available through the Countrylink NSW Travel Centre.

Hotel services *Air-conditioning. Babysitting. Bar. Barbecue. Carpark. Cooking facilities. Conference facilities. Disabled: access; specially adapted room; toilets. Fax. Laundry service. Limousine service. Multilingual staff. Restaurant. Roof terrace. Safe. Swimming pool.* **Room services** *Hair-drier. Radio. Refrigerator. Room service (6.30-8.30am, 6-10pm). Telephone. TV.*

Cremorne Point Manor

6 Cremorne Road, Cremorne Point, NSW 2090 (9953 7899/fax 9904 1265). Ferry Cremorne Point. **Rooms** 31 (23 en suite). **Rates** *single* $35-$65; *twin/double* $79; *triple* $95. **Credit** AmEx, BC, MC, TC, V.
The exclusive harbourside suburb of Cremorne Point offers bush, birdlife and bracing coastal walks; it's the place most Sydneysiders would choose to live if only their bank managers practised philanthropy. With regular ferries running until midnight into Circular Quay, it's also a great spot to stay. The Federation-style Manor, just five minutes' walk from the wharf, offers good and affordable accommodation with harbour views. There are pleasant rooms, practical Ikea-style kitchens, a leafy courtyard and several other outdoor areas to sit, eat and enjoy the views. Staff are helpful and single rates are particularly low. Book through the Countrylink NSW Travel Centre for a 10 per cent discount.

Hotel services *Fax. Kitchen. Washing-machine/drier.* **Room services** *Hair-drier. Radio. Refrigerator. Tea/coffee-making facilities. TV.*

Currawong Beach Cottages

PO Box 4, Palm Beach, NSW 2108 (9974 4141/fax 9974 1328). Bus 190 to Palm Beach Wharf then ferry to Currawong Beach. **Rates** *4 nights* $150-$250; *weekly* $300-$400. **No credit cards.**

Escape the rat race cheaply by renting one of these nine council-owned, basic beach huts, accessible only by ferry. There is a safe, sheltered swimming beach ideal for children, tennis courts, a practice golf course and bushwalking trails through Ku-Ring-Gai Chase National Park. Each cottage sleeps five, and you must supply your own linen and groceries. The huts are extremely popular, so booking well in advance is essential and must be by phone or in writing.

Communal services *Tennis courts. Golf driving range. Telephone.* **Hut services** *Kitchen.*

Kings Cross Holiday Apartments

169 William Street, Kings Cross, NSW 2011 (9361 0637/fax 9331 1366). CityRail Kings Cross. **Rates** *nightly* $80-$100; *weekly* $500-$600. **Credit** AmEx, BC, DC, JCB, MC, $TC, V.
Ideal for working backpackers or groups simply wanting cheap accommodation, these apartments comfortably sleep four each, rivalling hostel prices. Rollaways can be supplied for extra guests and security parking is free. The block is on a busy street above a car-rental outlet; request a top-floor apartment and you'll not only get a quiet night but also a harbour view.

Hotel services *Carpark. Fax.* **Room services** *Kitchen. Radio. Refrigerator. Tea/coffee-making facilities. TV. Washing-machine/drier.*

Youth Hostels

Contact the YHA (422 Kent Street, Sydney, NSW 2001; 9261 1111/fax 9261 1969) for a free information pack giving membership details and a list of Australian youth hostels. *See also* **Alishan International Guesthouse, Billabong Gardens** and **Y on the Park Hotel** *under* Budget.

Backpackers Beachside

28 Raglan Street, Manly, NSW 2095 (9977 3411/ fax 9977 4379). Ferry Manly. **Rooms** 23 (1 en suite). **Rates** *dorm* $15; *double* $40. **Credit** (for bills over $100) BC, MC, $TC, V.
It's not difficult to see why guests seem happy at this attractive and secure brick hostel, 100 metres from the beach and five minutes' walk from Manly Wharf. Carrying the NRMA four-rucksack award, the place is spotless, with shared areas cleaned daily and rooms (doubles and three-bed dorms) twice weekly. Guests may eat either in the large, well-equipped kitchen or on the outside deck. The place is good for work contacts, there is an efficient mailing and message service, and regular day trips are arranged. Beach paraphernalia, such as boogie boards and volleyballs, may be borrowed free.

Hotel services *Fax. Garden terrace. Payphone. No smoking. Safe. TV (satellite). Washing-machine/drier.*

Coogee Beach Backpackers

94 Beach Street, Coogee, NSW 2034 (9315 8000/after 5pm 9665 7735/fax 9664 1258). Bus 372, 373/24-hour courtesy bus. **Beds** 100. **Rates** *dorm* $16-$18; *twin* $35. **Credit** $TC.
A friendly hostel providing free 24-hour pick-ups from anywhere in the city. The majority of guests are working backpackers and receive assistance through the hostel's employment agency contacts. Help is also given with sorting out bank accounts and tax file numbers. Accommodation is split between three houses, each with ocean views from shared balconies. The common areas are cleaned twice daily, the rooms weekly, and linen and blankets can be provided. Unusually, guests can receive calls at any time, as the phones are manned 24 hours a day. Regular coach trips and weekly beach barbecues are arranged and there is no curfew.

Hotel services *Barbecues. Carpark. Courtesy bus. Fax. Kitchens. Payphone. TV. VCR. Washing-machines/driers.*

Eva's Backpackers
*6 Orwell Street, Kings Cross, NSW 2011 (9358 2185/
fax 9358 3259). CityRail Kings Cross.* **Beds** 96. **Rates**
dorm $17-$20; *double* $36-$40. **Credit** BC, MC, TC, V.
One of the friendliest and cleanest hostels in the Cross,
located on a quiet road close to all amenities, nightclubs and
pubs. There are bright rooms, 24-hour reception and great
city views from the rooftop garden. It's very popular (particularly with Germans), so book well in advance.
Hotel services *Barbecue. Fax. Kitchen. Multilingual
staff. Non-smoking rooms. Payphone. Roof terrace. TV
lounge. VCR. Washing-machines/driers.*

Lamrock Hostel
*7 Lamrock Avenue, Bondi Beach, NSW 2026 (9365
0221/fax 9365 3404). Bus 380, 382.* **Rooms** 8 dorms
(4 en suite); 2 rooms (1 en suite). **Beds** 60. **Rates** *dorm*
$15; *twin* $50. **Credit** AmEx, MC. TC, V.
The only purpose-built hostel left in Bondi. Carrying the
NRMA three-rucksack award, it's located just 100 metres
from the beach. There are private twin suites in addition to
the four-bed dorms, half of which have their own bathrooms.
The hostel also rents out flats. The Lamrock is geared to
working backpackers and can supply good job contacts;
alternatively, you can hire surfboards and boogie boards.
Reception is manned 24 hours a day and there's no curfew.
Hotel services *Barbecue. Carpark. Disabled: access.
Fax. Kitchen. Multilingual staff. Payphones. Terrace. TV.*
Room services *Refrigerator.*

Wattle House
*44 Hereford Street, Glebe, NSW 2037 (9552 4997).
Bus 431, 433, 434.* **Rooms** 9 (none en suite). **Rates**
dorm $18; *double* $22. **No credit cards.**
This restored Victorian terraced house caters for working
backpackers and is located on a quiet road close to Glebe's
arthouse cinema and pavement cafés. Unusually, for a hostel, all rooms have fireplaces, mirrors, bedside lamps, linen
and quilts ('doonas'). The garden contains not only the ubiquitous barbecue but also a 'reading room', complete with
books and a drinks machine.
Hotel services *Barbecue. Garden. Kitchen. Multilingual
staff. No smoking. TV.*

Camping, Caravan & Cabin Parks

The Greater Metropolitan Area of Sydney is pep-
pered with campsites and caravan parks. Most
also offer cheap, fully equipped cabins and/or
villas, right in the heart of the bush or on the beach.
Additional attractions include hiking, horseriding,
windsurfing or scuba-diving, and most parks have
a shop and swimming pool. For a complete list,
contact the Countrylink NSW Travel Centre (*see
chapter* **Essential Information**). Also of use
is the NRMA's excellent *Camping & Caravan
Directory*. The National Parks and Wildlife Service
publishes a comprehensive booklet on NSW national parks (*see chapter* **The Great Outdoors**).
You may camp, caravan or rent a cabin at all the
places listed below unless otherwise stipulated.

The Basin
*PO Box 134, Forestville, NSW 2087 (9451 8124/fax
9451 7390). Bus 190 to Palm Beach Wharf then ferry to
The Basin. By car: Military Road; Spit Road; Burnt
Bridge Creek Deviation; Condamine Street; Pittwater
Road; Barrenjoey Road to Palm Beach Wharf carpark;
then ferry to The Basin.* **No credit cards.**

This scenic campsite on the western foreshores of Pittwater
(Ku-Ring-Gai Chase National Park), is a Sydneysider favourite. There are walking tracks on the West Head peninsula and wonderful views over the bay. No caravans or cabins.

East's Lane Cove River Van Village
*Plassey Road, Macquarie Park, NSW 2113 (9805 0500/
fax 9805 1676). CityRail Chatswood then 500 or 551
bus. By car: Epping Road then Delhi Road.* **Credit** BC,
MC, TC, V.
Near a nature reserve in national parkland, with great bushwalks and birdlife. There's a pool, a shop and cabins to rent
from $50 a night.

Grand Pines Tourist Park
*289 The Grand Parade, Sans Souci, NSW 2219 (9529
7329/fax 9583 1550). Bus 301, 302 to Ramsgate Plaza
then 100-metre walk. By car: Princes Highway; Rocky Point
Road; Ramsgate Road; then Alfred Street.* **Credit** $TC.
A caravan park on scenic Botany Bay (entrance 112 Alfred
Street, Ramsgate) with a 24-hour supermarket and cabins to
rent from $50 for two persons per night. No camping.

Lakeside Caravan Park
*Lake Park Road, Narrabeen, NSW 2101 (9913 7845/
fax 9970 6385). Bus 190 to Pittwater Road. By car:
Pittwater Road then turn right after Narrabeen Bridge.*
Credit BC, MC, $TC, V.
This four-star lakeside spot above Narrabeen Beach has 20
seven-berth cabins and 20 five-berth villas (from $64 a night).

La Mancha Cara-Park
*901 Pacific Highway, Berowra, NSW 2081 (9456 1766/
fax 9456 2067). CityRail Hornsby then bus to Berowra.
By car: Pacific Highway.* **Credit** BC, MC, V.
Four-star facilities in a Spanish-style waterfront setting, with
access to thousands of acres of national park. Amenities
include a guest lounge, games room, mini-market, pool,
squash courts, sauna, spa and playground. There's excellent
fishing and boating on Berowra Waters. The park is 35km
(22 miles) from the centre of Sydney and close to public transport. Cabins cost from $59 a night.

Silver Beach Tourist Park
*288 Prince Charles Parade, Kurnell, NSW 2231 (9668
8215/fax 9668 9061). CityRail Cronulla then bus to
Kurnell. By car: take Princes Highway (Route 1); Rocky
Point Road; Taren Point Road; then Captain Cook Drive.*
Credit BC, MC, V.
Silver Beach is on a quiet, unspoilt stretch of seafront near
Captain Cook's landing spot in Botany Bay. Attractions
include horseriding, tennis, water-skiing, windsurfing, sail-
ing, scuba-diving and fishing. Cabins cost from $50 a night.

University Accommodation

During the holidays, many university colleges open
their doors to casual visitors at low rates. The dates
of semester breaks vary, but are usually late November to late February; during Easter; and in
June/July. Most universities also have a short break
around the end of September and early October.
Colleges often let visitors use university sports
facilities for a nominal charge and most also allow
use of in-house facilities such as kitchens and TV
lounges. Linen is supplied but you should bring
your own towels. Phone **University of New
South Wales** (9385 1000/fax 9313 6346) or
University of Sydney (9351 3312/fax 9552 7055)
for more information.

Sydney
by Season

Sydney's yearly roster of festivals, street parties, beach bashes and cultural events.

In the summer, Sydney is the city of the great southerly change. Around 5pm it hits – a strong billowing wind, almost from nowhere, after a warm balmy day. Picnickers can be seen hurriedly packing up their gear and scurrying in from the rain. Overall, though, Sydney has an enviably moderate climate, with warm to hot summers, cool to cold winters and reliable rainfall all year round.

Spring brings blossoming flowers and clear blue days, with temperatures barely warm enough to shed the woollies but clement enough to enjoy a spell in the sunlight. Just the season, in fact, to lie around in one of Sydney's splendid parks – Hyde Park or the Royal Botanic Gardens being the perfect location for such springtime (in)activity.

In summer, most people live in shorts and T-shirts. November and December are the months which bring with them the most sunshine: the sun bakes the city for around eight hours a day, and temperatures can reach into the thirties.

Temperatures

Don't forget that Australia is in the southern hemisphere, so the seasons are the opposite to those north of the equator. The figures listed below give the maximum average daily temperature in Sydney.

January	26°C
February	25°C
March	25°C
April	22°C
May	19°C
June	17°C
July	16°C
August	17°C
September	20°C
October	22°C
November	24°C
December	25°C

In autumn, the city is swept by strong, swirling winds, while winter mornings and nights mean low temperatures which can dip down to 6°. Winter daily maximums hover between 15° and 18°, and occasional snow falls in the Blue Mountains.

Spring

Aurora New World Festival
Darling Harbour (9286 0100/fax 9281 1052). CityRail Town Hall/ferry Darling Harbour. **Date** 2 weeks in September or October.
There's a strong Olympic focus to Aurora. The festival highlights changing lifestyles leading up to the new millennium, drawing on the music, food, art and crafts of the countries represented in the Olympic rings – Oceania, Europe, Asia, Africa and America.

Carnivale
Information from 164 Liverpool Road, Ashfield, NSW 2131 (9716 2878/fax 9716 2990). **Date** 3 weeks in September.
Multi-cultural festival of music and dance, held at various venues all over Sydney and NSW.

Sydney Spring Festival of New Music
Information (9224 2742/13 2077). **Date** September.
Run by Australian pianist Roger Woodward, this intensive, month-long festival of contemporary music presents the best local musicians and two or three visiting ensembles, and has featured such luminaries as Horatiu Radalescu and Arvo Paart in the past.

Festival of Culture
Sydney Opera House, Bennelong Point (9250 7111). CityRail/ferry Circular Quay. **Date** one weekend in September or October.
This festival is one of Australia's largest multicultural events. It brings together some the best performers, from within Sydney and abroad, in a bustling weekend of entertainment, food and crafts.

Glebe Street Fair
Glebe Point Road, Glebe (9692 0051). Bus 431, 433. **Date** 10am-7pm penultimate Sunday in November.
As Sydney's largest street carnival, the Glebe Street Fair marks the end of springtime festivities. Every year some 150,000 people venture to the inner city suburb of Glebe to visit the 300 different market stalls which line the streets. On offer is fine art, craft and clothing, together with food from all over the world. The fair also incorporates multimedia installations, skateboard competitions and giant street decorations.

Manly Jazz Festival

Information (9977 1088). **Date** Labor Day weekend in October.

Take the ferry over to Manly and head for the Corso to hear dozens of bands playing everything from contemporary to trad, fusion and bop.

Summer

The Australian Ballet

Information from Australian Ballet, Level 15, 115 Pitt Street, Sydney NSW 2000 (9223 9522). **Date** November/December and March/April.

This Melbourne-based company prides itself on bringing the best of the traditional classics (such as *Swan Lake*) to Sydney, while scouting for new Australian works. The ballets are performed at the **Sydney Opera House**, and tickets start at $31, though concessions are available. *See also chapter* **Theatre & Dance**.

Christmas on Bondi Beach

Date 25 December.

Thousands of travellers from around the world gather on the beach each year for an impromptu party. Unless a cross between Dante's Inferno and a toga party is your scene, it's best avoided.

Sydney to Hobart Yacht Race

Information from CYCA, New Beach Road, Darling Point 2027. **Date** race starts 1pm 26 December, from Sydney Harbour.

Hundreds of keen and competitive yachtsmen, and as many supporters, turn out on Boxing Day for the start of the notoriously gruelling race to Hobart in Tasmania. The spectacular sight of hundreds of sails filling the harbour, as the racers make their way between the North and South Heads and out into the Tasman Sea, is unmissable. Book a seat on a ferry well in advance, or secure your place on the foreshore.

The Sydney Festival

Information (9265 0444). **Date** runs throughout January.

A festival of massive proportions, which takes place at various venues throughout the city and features a broad collection of performance in dance, theatre and installation art. Musical highlights include **Midsummer Jazz**, **Symphony in the Park** and **Opera in the Park**, all of which present glorious music in an outdoor setting.

The Light Fantastic Summer Festival

Darling Harbour (9286 0100/fax 9281 1052). CityRail Town Hall/ferry Darling Harbour. **Date** December and January, for roughly a month.

An annual show of glitzy entertainment with waterski displays, inflatable mazes and twilight concerts. The festival's highlight is the firework display, which takes place every weekend during the summer months.

Chinese New Year

Date January or February.

Head to Chinatown for the traditional New Year's festivities, complete with firecrackers.

Sydney Writers Festival

State Library of NSW, Macquarie Street, Sydney (9230 1499). CityRail Martin Place. **Date** one week in January.

International and Australian writers converge on the city as part of the Sydney Festival, for an annual dose of readings, workshops and conferences. Great writers and innovative programming. The event may move to September or October in 1998.

Australia Day

Information from the Australia Day Council, PO Box N548, Grosvenor Place, Sydney 2000 (9247 2130/fax 9241 4405). **Date** 26 January.

Festivities take place all over the city in the annual celebration of European settlement in Australia. Arrive early to secure a good spot on the foreshore of the harbour, but note that parking is a near impossibility. The main Australia Day concert usually takes place in The Domain, and features a range of Australian artists and musicians. There are excellent firework displays at Darling Harbour.

Sydney Fringe Festival
Information from the Bondi Pavilion, Queen Elizabeth Drive, Bondi Beach (9365 0112). **Date** January-February, for 17 days.
This festival of comedy, film and dance combines the best of Sydney's fringe arts. Performances take place in venues around the city, including free shows (4-6pm daily) on Bondi Beach.

Gay & Lesbian Mardi Gras
Information from 21-23 Erskinville Road, Newtown 2042 (9557 4332/fax 95166 4446). **Date** throughout February. *Parade* 1 March 1997; 28 February 1998. **Route** from Elizabeth Street (Town Hall Station) to Royal Agricultural Showground, Moore Park.
It has been said that is isn't what you do at the Sydney Gay & Lesbian Mardi Gras, it's how you do it. In true Mardi Gras style, the scene is flamboyant and lively, with music

Sunny side up

The dangers of the Australian sun cannot be overemphasised. The sun can, and does, kill (Australia has one of the highest rates of skin cancer in the world). And since research suggests that the weather will be getting hotter and sunnier over the next few years, and that Australia is particularly vulnerable to the holes in the ozone layer over the southern hemisphere, it is wise to follow the government's awareness-raising advice and **Slip, Slop, Slap**. Slip on a shirt, slop on some sunscreen and slap on a hat.

These precautions covers the basics of taking care in the sun. Good quality sunglasses are a good investment, too – they eliminate almost 100 per cent of direct, reflected or scattered ultra-violet rays and protect the sensitive area around the eyes. The wraparound variety provide the best protection against eye damage.

The most dangerous time to expose your skin to the sun is between 11am and 3pm, when most of the day's ultra-violet rays occurs. During this time, skin begins to burn within 15 minutes of exposure. Don't stay in the sun for more than a couple of hours. Though fair-skinned people are at greater risk of developing skin cancer, those of all skin types should be aware of the dangers.

REMEMBER
* Use a sunscreen with a SPF of 15 or more. It should be water resistant and be applied 20 minutes before going out in the sun.
* Wear a hat.
* Wear a long-sleeved shirt.
* Wear wraparound sunglasses.
* Stay in the shade whenever possible.
* Try to avoid exposure between 10am and 2pm (11am and 3pm during daylight saving, between October and March).

booming from Oxford Street, the epicentre of gay and lesbian culture. If you want to watch the parade, get there early and bring a milk crate to stand on, because eager viewers spill into the hundreds of thousands. It's not uncommon for people to resort to standing on shop awnings, or hiring nearby hotel rooms for birdseye viewing of the hundreds of floats. The parade itself starts at 8pm, and culminates in an all-out party for the gay and lesbian community at the Hordern Pavilion (10pm-8am). This costs about $60 a ticket (*see chapter* **Queer Sydney**).

Norton Street Festival

Norton Street, between Marion and William Streets, Leichhardt (9692 0051). Bus 440, 445, 470. **Date** 10am-7pm, the Sunday two weeks before Easter.
The Norton Street Festival celebrates the contribution the Italian community has made in shaping Australia's cultural landscape. Norton Street, in inner city Leichhardt, remains the hub of Italian commercial and social activity as well as being the setting for Sydney's original café society. The festival brings together a feast of great food, wine, art, theatre and music, with everything from traditional puppetry and experimental street theatre to DJs spinning dance discs.

St Patrick's Day

Information (9211 3410). **Date** 17 March.
The one day on which Australians will happily swap their Victoria Bitter for a glass of Guinness. Sydney's Irish pubs overflow onto the streets, and the climax of this all-day and night party is a 250,000-strong street parade through the city.

Royal Easter Show

Sydney Showground, Moore Park, Driver Avenue, Paddington (9331 9111). Bus 339, 355, 378, 380, 382. **Date** 21 March-5 April 1997; 3 April-18 April 1998.
A chance to meet the bush without having to travel far from the centre of town, and an opportunity for rural Australia to showcase its finest produce. The Royal Easter Show brings cows, horses, chickens, candy floss (called fairy floss), expensive rides, showbags and much, much more to Sydney. Since the site has been earmarked for Rupert's Fox studios development, the Show will move to Homebush Bay in 1988 (phone for details).

Hoopla! Circus and Street Theatre Festival

Darling Harbour (9286 0100/fax 9281 1052). CityRail Town Hall/ferry Darling Harbour. **Date** March-April, for two weeks.
For two weeks, Darling Harbour is transformed into a giant three ring circus. Street theatre, jugglers, acrobats and puppeteers fill the public areas in a colourful and lively spectacular.

The **City to Surf Run***: it's supposed to be fun.*

kinds. An array of tour operators and travel agents set up booths where qualified staff will answer queries on costs and accommodation, and hand out brochures.

City to Surf Run

Information from Countrylink NSW (9224 2742/13 2077). **Date** August.
The community fun run starts in the central city at the Town Hall and finishes – 14km later – at Bondi Beach. Upwards of 30,000 runners, some world class but mostly amateur joggers, usually participate.

Sydney Marathon

Information from Countrylink NSW (9224 2742/13 2077). **Date** August
A 42km course, run by athletes from all over the world, some trying to beat the 2 hour 14 minute record.

Winter

Bandemonium Winter Music Festival

Darling Harbour (9286 0100/fax 9281 1052). CityRail Town Hall/ferry Darling Harbour. **Date** 2 weeks in June-July.
Jazz, world music and hits from Broadway musicals make up this festival. It's the highlight event of the Sydney Shires In Winter promotion, co-ordinated by Countrylink NSW (9224 2742/13 2077).

Holiday and Travel Show

Sydney Convention and Exhibition Centre, Darling Harbour (9282 5000/9360 3500). CityRail Town Hall/ferry Darling Harbour/monorail Convention. **Date** three days in June.
Here's where to find out anything and everything you need to know about travel within Australia and beyond. It's a once-a-year chance to get no-pressure advice on trips of all

Public holidays

New Year's Day	1 January
Australia Day	26 January
Good Friday	March/April
Easter Monday	April
Anzac Day	25 April
Queen's Birthday	2nd Monday in June
Bank Holiday	Early August
Labor Day	1st Monday in October
Christmas Day	25 December
Boxing Day	26 December

Sightseeing

Water, water, everywhere, and countless vantage points. No wonder Sydneysiders think theirs is the most beautiful city in the world.

Sydney is blessed with one of the world's most glorious settings, placed as it is between the rolling surf of the Pacific Ocean and the primeval Blue Mountains several dozen kilometres inland. The city is a big one, with around 600 suburbs and localities plus 70 beaches to its name. But don't be deterred; most sights are within walking distance of the shining natural harbour at its centre. Other attractions can be reached by cheap and scenic ferry rides from Circular Quay – without question the best way to travel in Sydney – or found on the Red Bus Explorer route (*see page 41* **Trips & Tours**). For an off-the-beaten-track tour of the suburbs, *see chapter* **Sydney by Area**.

Harbourside

Circular Quay
CityRail/ferry Circular Quay.
There is something thrilling about the bustle of Circular Quay. Commuters and day-trippers board and disembark from a constant stream of ferries, JetCats and water taxis, while tourists and teenagers idle in the 24-hour cafés drinking cappuccino, listening to buskers and admiring the harbour views. Fast food kiosks sell pastries, fish and chips, and the best kebabs outside of Greece. There are information stands proffering an abundance of free literature and, handily, most sightseeing tours, by bus as well as boat, leave from here. The State Transit ferries run services to all reaches of the harbour, and a large variety of private cruises is also available. The harbour is particularly lovely at night, when the Opera House and Fort Denison are lit up like birthday cakes. The best viewpoint is by Sydney Cove Passenger Terminal on the high concourse.

Darling Harbour
(Darling Harbour Info Line 1902 260 568/Tumbalong Park 9286 0100). CityRail Town Hall then 10-minute walk/Monorail Darling Park or Harbourside/ferry Darling Harbour. **Open** *Harbourside Marketplace* 10am-9pm Mon-Sat; 10am-7pm Sun; *Tumbalong Park* 24 hours daily.
Like many cities trying to maximise their tourist income, Sydney has followed the tried and tested path of creating an open space surrounded by tourist-oriented shops and restaurants. What other cities don't have, of course, is the rather wonderful view of the harbour waters along one side and the towering Sydney skyline on the other. Inside the shopping complex, the ground floor is devoted almost exclusively to a huge food hall where you can buy every major food group known to man. An adjoining games area contains the usual array of video shoot-'em-ups and virtual car races, and for some reason it's peopled with fluffy toys that can be shot as well. The 200 shops that inhabit the **Harbourside Festival Marketplace** range from purveyors of ubiquitous tourist tack to some of the more upmarket fashion chains. The obligatory opal shop has loose gemstones scattered ankle-deep on the floor where you can select your own. Near the

Harbourside complex is **Tumbalong Park**, an undulating and turfed children's area. Surrounded by water cascades, streams and fountains, the park contains some creative climbing and sliding structures. Other Darling Harbour attractions include the new giant **IMAX** cinema (*see chapter* **Film**), **Sydney Aquarium** (*see p31*), the **Chinese Garden** (*see p35*), the new **Sydney Casino** (*see chapter* **Nightlife**), the **Australian National Maritime Museum** and **Powerhouse Museum** (*see chapter* **Museums & Galleries**) and the much-maligned Monorail (*see chapter* **Getting Around**).

Fort Denison
Pinchgut Island. Ferry (phone 9555 9844 for details). **Tours** noon, 2pm daily. **Tickets** (incl ferry & tour) $8.50 adults; $6 concessions. **Credit** BC, DC, JCB, MC, TC, V.
As your boat draws near, you might be surprised to see Fort Denison – the nation's small but proud monument built, absurdly, to protect her from the might of threatening warships – adorned with feather dusters. These, the guide explains, ward off the pesky seagulls. Oddly, the birds all gather instead in front of the One O'Clock gun, which is fired daily. Had an alternative proposal gone through, you would be gazing upon something entirely different: a full-size replica of the Statue of Liberty. Pinchgut Island originally served as a prison. Its first resident, Thomas Hill, was marooned here for a week in 1788 as punishment for taking biscuits. Over the following eight years, convicts were regularly dumped here alone – the authorities found the sharks to be vigilant wardens. By the mid-nineteenth century, however, the potential threat of the Empire's distant enemies had inspired the addition of the fort, along with the distinctive Martello tower. Today, Fort Denison offers visitors a cannon museum, a working tide gauge and a bell tower offering unparalleled views of the harbour. Romantic wedding receptions are catered for, but day-trippers must bring their own sandwiches. There are plans underway to change the smelly barracks into a cafeteria; it remains to be seen whether a more commercial Pinchgut will retain its indefinable charm.

The Rocks
The Rocks Visitors Centre, 106 George Street, The Rocks (9255 1788). CityRail/ferry Circular Quay. **Open** 9am-5pm daily.
In January 1788, after an eight-month voyage from Plymouth, UK, the First Fleet stumbled ashore at Sydney Cove. Their brief was to 'build where you can, and build cheap'. The Rocks, named after the rough terrain, grew and survived for almost two centuries as a working-class area, until the 1960s when it was almost demolished to create an Australian Manhattan. Civic protest saved the day and the 'birthplace of the nation' was finally restored for posterity in 1970. Now under the wing of the Sydney Cove Authority, The Rocks nevertheless has to pay its own way, and many historic buildings have been turned over to commercial use. The nineteenth-century **Campbells Storehouses** ingeniously contain restaurants on the harbour's edge. **Cadman's Cottage**, probably the nation's oldest house, turns a brisk trade in souvenirs. For more up-market shopping, the revamped **Argyle Centre** (Argyle Street) houses local and international fashion outlets. You can still buy a

Don't miss

Bondi Beach p35
Ferry ride to Woolwich p39
Hyde Park Barracks p32
Queen Victoria Building p33
Manly Scenic Walk p41
Royal Botanic Gardens p41
Sydney Harbour Bridge p31
Sydney Opera House p32
View from The Gap p39, p42
Waratah Park p43

beer at a hotel, including the splendid **Mercantile** at the tip of George Street; **Garrison Church**, beyond Observatory Hill, continues to be used by the Australian Army. **Susannah Place**, a row of brick terraces on Gloucester Street, displays original wares in its windows. The Victorian **Observatory** (*see p34*) is also still in use. However, the **General Hospital** is now just a row of shops, the 'Ragged School' is long gone, the gaslights are replica, and the Sewer Lane stench has been replaced by the more agreeable smell of sizzling steaks. The Rocks Visitors Centre, which shows free films and conducts tours, is a good starting-point.

Sydney Aquarium
Aquarium Pier, Darling Harbour (9262 2300). CityRail Town Hall/monorail Darling Park/ferry Aquarium. **Open** 9.30am-9pm daily; *seal sanctuary* 9.30am-sunset daily. **Tickets** $14.90 adults; $7-$11 concessions; $34.90 family ticket. **Credit** AmEx, BC, DC, JCB, MC, TC, V.
A blue starfish the size of a cocker spaniel is plastered to the side of its tank; a creature shimmers past wearing a black negligée; monstrous eel-like faces leer out of pipes; a lobster that would comfortably feed a party of eight swaggers about the bottom of the pool… This is the entrancing Great Barrier Reef section, just one of 50 tanks collectively holding around 5,000 sea creatures, in habitats ranging from tropical to Antarctic, at the 'world's most spectacular aquarium'. Also on view are inert estuarine crocodiles, a seal sanctuary and two huge floating oceanariums, one holding Sydney Harbour species and the other, entitled the Open Ocean, containing a vast shark collection. Viewed from transparent underwater tunnels, the sharks glide past, some of them frankly due for a good floss. Bodyguarding the sharks are the menacing rays, wide and flat enough to use as teatrays.

Sydney Harbour Bridge
Entrance to pylon via stairs on Cumberland Street, The Rocks, or from near Milsons Point CityRail on the north shore. (Information 9218 6888). **Open** 10am-5pm daily. **Admission** $2 adults; $1 concessions. **No credit cards**.
Long before the Opera House was built, Sydney had 'the Coathanger' as its symbol. Though now an elderly structure, it was for a long time the world's largest single-span bridge, and has 200,000 vehicles crossing its 503-metre (1,651-ft) length daily. Sydneysiders had dreamt of a bridge to link the north and south harbour shores for a century before construction finally began in 1923, by which time the ferries were struggling with 40 million passengers a year. Tutankhamun's tomb had just been discovered, and the bridge reflects this historic event in the styling of its Egyptian pylons. A total of 1,400 workers toiled on the 134-metre (440-ft) high bridge for eight years, without safety rails; 16 lost their lives. The opening ceremony in 1932, broadcast around the world, was interrupted by a lone horseman – disaffected Irishman Francis de Groot – who galloped forward and slashed the ribbon with his sword, declaring the bridge open in the name of 'the decent citizens of New South Wales'. After the police had removed him (he was later fined £5), the ribbon was hurriedly tied back together and the ceremony continued. The bridge was internationally

For the zoo with a view, see page 32.

declared to be 'one of the seven wonders of the modern world'. You can currently climb 200 steps up to the Pylon Lookout for excellent harbour views. Guided tours are now given of the entire span. All 'arch walkers' must take a mandatory breath test before the tour and wear waterproof suits firmly connected by harnesses to the hand rail. The climb goes to the very top of the 50-storey high structure. Appropriately, a former bridge-painter was invited to take the first of these tours: Paul 'Crocodile Dundee' Hogan.

Sydney Opera House

Bennelong Point, Circular Quay (box office 9250 7777/ information 9250 7111/fax 9251 3943). CityRail/ ferry Circular Quay or 438 bus. **Open** *box office 9am-8.30pm Mon-Sat; 2 hours before show Sun; tours 9am-4pm daily.* **Credit** AmEx, BC, DC, MC, V.

Set in a heavenly harbour, its cream wings reminiscent of the sails of the First Fleet, the Sydney Opera House is now the city's most famous icon. Yet it took 14 troubled years at a cost of $102 million to build – $95m more than anticipated. In true Aussie style, the shortfall was met by lotteries. The cultural cathedral has never been seen by its creator, Danish architect Joern Utzon, who departed halfway through the project, never to return. A lot of head-scratching took place before the eventual opening night in 1973 when, just to set the seal on the bizarre series of events, an impromptu onstage appearance was made by two small possums.

In its four main auditoria the opera house holds an impressive 3,000 opera, concert, theatre, film and dance performances a year. There are also free lunchtime organ recitals in the Concert Hall which, at 25m (82ft) high and with seating for 2,690, is the jewel in the crown. Previous artistes range from kd lang to the Pope, but the accolade of 'first performer' rightfully belongs to Paul Robeson who, in 1960, at the invitation of the militant builders union, sang 'Old Man River' at the construction site. *See also chapters* **Music: Classical & Opera** *and* **Theatre & Dance**.

Taronga Zoo

Bradleys Head Road, Mosman (9969 2777). Ferry Taronga Zoo, Athol Wharf/247 bus. **Open** *9am-5pm daily.* **Admission** $14.95 adults; $8.90-$7.50 concessions. **Credit** AmEx, BC, DC, JCB, MC, TC, V.

The 'zoo with a view' no longer permits koala-cuddling, although you can have your photo taken beside one of the sleepy critters. You may also pat the more intrepid wallabies and kangaroos in the Australian Walkabout area. At the new Serpentaria, you can smile at a croc, pose with a python or just keep your distance. Other attractions include the Seal Theatre, whose star performer is a cute specimen weighing in at 750kg (wait until she grows up); and the brilliant new parrot aviary. April 1997 saw the opening of the African Tropical Forest for gorillas. There are terrific harbour views to be had everywhere, including from a cable car. It's a huge zoo and tricky to find your way around (someone will probably come across the new McDonald's Orang-utan Rainforest soon) so allow at least three hours for a visit. There are several eateries. Alternatively, you can picnic or use one of the on-site barbecues (but bring your own chops).

Historic Houses & Buildings

Elizabeth Bay House

7 Onslow Avenue, Elizabeth Bay (9356 3022). Bus 311. **Open** *10am-4.30pm Tue-Sun.* **Admission** $5 adults; $3 concessions; $12 family ticket. **No credit cards**.

Designed by John Verge and completed in 1838, this handsome Greek Revival villa was Sydney's most prestigious house until the construction of Government House (*see below*). Alexander Macleay, the first owner, was Colonial Secretary of New South Wales at the time, but after falling into financial difficulties he was forced to move out in 1845. Some of the furniture subsequently ended up in Government House.

Dominating the house is the elliptical stairhall saloon which contains the finest staircase in Australian colonial architecture. The other rooms, no less imposing, are furnished as they would have been in 1845. Originally set in a 54-acre garden, long gone to property developers, the house still commands splendid views over Elizabeth Bay and the harbour.

Elizabeth Farm

70 Alice Street, Rosehill (9635 9488). CityRail Rosehill Racecourse. **Open** *10am-5pm daily.* **Admission** $5 adults; $3 concessions; $12 family ticket. **No credit cards**.

Elizabeth Farm is notable for two things. Firstly, it became the birthplace of the Australian wool industry when John Macarthur imported merino sheep for breeding at the site; the exhibitions and slide show inside provide a more detailed history. Secondly, the main building, with its deep, shady verandahs and stone-flagged floors, became the prototype for the Australian homestead. The original 191-ha (250-acre) property now comprises only the main building, restored to its 1830s condition with a matching, recreated Victorian garden behind. Parts of the original 1793 construction remain and the interior has been simply furnished in period style.

General Post Office

159-171 Pitt Street, Martin Place, Sydney (9230 7834). CityRail Martin Place or Wynyard. **Open** *8.15am-5.30pm Mon-Fri; 8.30am-noon Sat.*

This recently restored High Victorian building, with its lavish sculpture and handsome clock tower, took 28 years to build. Completed in time for the 1888 gala centennial, it boasted the city's first electric lifts and the latest telegraphic equipment. The large clock had to be removed during World War II for fear Japanese bombers might zero in on the landmark.

Government House

Royal Botanic Gardens, Sydney (9931 5222/9931 5200). CityRail/ferry Circular Quay. **Open** *house 10am-3pm Fri-Sun; garden 10am-4pm daily.* **Admission** free.

Designed by William IV's architect Edward Blore in 1834, the plans for Government House had to be modified to take account of local conditions, such as the Australian sun being in the north rather than the south. However, the original gothic revival concept remained and today's visitors can still enjoy the crenellated battlements and grossly detailed interiors. Past governors have dabbled in decorations and extensions with rather weird and unsettling results. However, the State Rooms – including dining room, drawing rooms and ballroom – have been marvellously restored to an appropriate level of opulence, and are now the best example of Victorian pomp and grandeur in the country.

Hyde Park Barracks

Queens Square, Macquarie Street, Sydney (9223 8922). CityRail Martin Place or St James. **Open** *10am-5pm daily.* **Admission** $5 adults; $3 concessions; $12 family ticket. **Credit** AmEx, BC, DC, MC, V.

The Hyde Park Barracks were originally built by Francis Greenway in 1817 to house 600 male convicts. Subsequently used as the Immigration Women's Depot and Asylum as well as law courts and government offices, the building eventually metamorphosed into a museum. The top level now houses the recreated convict barracks, though thankfully the element of squalor is missing. Rough hammocks hang side by side in the long rooms, while recorded snippets of conversation surround you. A computer database allows you to follow the official records of any convict you choose from initial conviction via much flogging to eventual rehabilitation, in some cases. The women's section on level two is no less thought-provoking. These (mostly Irish) women were escaping an awful existence to start what must have been an equally burdensome new life in a harsh colony. There is the usual talk of ghosts here, of course, but records show that no male convict ever died on the premises. If you want to check for yourself, an overnight stay in a hammock can be arranged, but for some reason there is a long waiting list. *Disabled: access; toilets.*

Justice and Police Museum

Corner of Albert and Phillip Streets, Sydney (9252 1144). CityRail/ferry Circular Quay. **Open** *Feb-Dec* 10am-5pm Sun; *Jan* 10am-5pm Mon-Thur, Sun. **Admission** $5 adults; $3 concessions; $12 family ticket. **No credit cards**.
The nation's fascination with its bushrangers is highly evident in this museum. Inside there is a good display of plaster-cast heads of prisoners as well as mug shots, assorted deadly weapons and newspaper reports of the more sensational crimes. Also on view is a police charge room and remand cells, which look as though the officers have just nipped out for a smoko. A restored Magistrates' Court is used to hone budding lawyers' courtroom technique.

Luna Park

Olympic Drive, Milsons Point (9922 6644). CityRail/ferry Milsons Point. Closed to the public.
The huge clown face that grins out from beneath the Harbour Bridge on the north shore, fronts a 1930s amusement park, complete with old-fashioned Ferris wheel, shooting gallery, dodgems and miniature rides for children. Closed in the mid-1980s, redeveloped and re-opened in the early 1990s, it was closed again in February 1996. The park currently awaits reprieve or further redevelopment, whichever comes first. It occupies what is probably the most valuable 12$\frac{1}{2}$ ha (31 acres) of land in Australia, so there's a clue.

Parliament House

Macquarie Street, Sydney (9230 2111). CityRail Martin Place. **Open** 9.30am-4pm Mon-Fri. **Admission** free.
Nowhere else in the world can you simply walk in off the street straight into the lobby of the local elective chambers. The staff at Parliament House will show you the perfectly preserved nineteenth-century debating chambers of the Legislative Assembly (Lower House) and Legislative Council (Upper House) on request, although you get better value from joining one of the tour groups that constantly traipse through. Sydney's Parliament is largely modelled on its mother House in London; there's a Speaker and Black Rod, and even the colour scheme follows the British tradition of green for one chamber and red for the other. Between the two is the Jubilee Room, once the main library, but now a committee room. Parliamentary papers are kept along the upper part of the high walls, while the lower reaches contain a chronological exhibition of the building's restoration and redevelopment.

Queen Victoria Building

455 George Street, Sydney (information 9264 1955; tours 9264 9209). CityRail Town Hall. **Open** 9am-6pm Mon-Wed, Fri, Sat; 9am-9pm Thur; 11am-5pm Sun.
The Queen Victoria Building, designed to resemble a Byzantine palace, occupies an entire block on George Street, and once dominated the Sydney skyline with its dramatic domed roof. Built in 1898 to celebrate Queen Victoria's golden jubilee, the QVB originally housed street markets, and later gamely survived long periods of neglect. Demolition threats were finally quashed in the 1980s when a healthy $75 million budget restored the QVB to its original grandeur. It's now home to 200 outlets, including boutiques, jewellers, cafés and restaurants. There are plenty of designer labels to be found here, along with Australiana gift shops stocking more didgeridoos than a tourist can shake a store card at. Of particular note are the magnificent coloured-leadlight wheel windows, the original floor tiles, the cast-iron circular staircase and the original lift. Although it's unpromoted, try to get a peek at the magnificent peaches-and-cream ballroom on the third floor – a full three storeys high replete with palms, pillars and a grand piano. On the hour, shoppers

The **State Library of NSW**.

gather on Gallery Two to watch the Royal Automata Clock display a moving royal pageant. The execution of Charles I goes down a storm.

State Library of NSW

Macquarie Street, Sydney (9230 1414). CityRail Martin Place. **Open** 9am-9pm Mon-Fri; 11am-5pm Sat, Sun. **Tours** *General Reference Library* 2.30pm Tue-Thur; *Mitchell Wing* 11am Tue, Thur. **Admission** free.
The State Library is essentially two libraries in one: the modern General Reference Library allows you access to over two million books, CD-ROMs and other media stored over five floors below ground; while the older Mitchell Wing holds the world's greatest collection of Australiana. This includes the original journals of James Cook and the log book of Captain Bligh. There are guided tours of both libraries, which explain their workings and give some historical background. Two very popular sections of the GRL are the Legal Information Service and the Family History Service, while the Mitchell Wing has its grandiose and skylighted reading room.

State Theatre

49 Market Street, Sydney (9373 6645/tours 9231 4629). CityRail Town Hall or Wynyard. **Open** box office 9am-5.30pm Mon-Sat (until 8pm on performance nights). **Credit** AmEx, BC, DC, MC, V.
Opened in 1929 – the last of the great picture palaces – this breathtaking 2,000-seater theatre was faithfully refurbished back in 1980. Entering through the Gothic Hall, you pass through magnificent Renaissance bronze doors into the Grand Assembly, and on through to the Butterfly Room, the Pioneer Room and the Pompadour Room. The splendid interior includes The Beauties of the Dress Circle, with its 18 chandeliers. Now one of the city's main venues for live entertainment, the theatre also hosts the annual Sydney Film Festival. *See also chapters* **Film** *and* **Theatre & Dance**.

Sydney Hospital

8 Macquarie Street, Sydney (9382 7111). CityRail Martin Place. **Open** 8am-8pm daily. **Admission** free.
Originally known as the Rum Hospital because its construction was financed by government-controlled rum sales, Sydney Hospital is the city's only early institutional building still performing its original function. If you want to know what the Rum Hospital looked like, cast your eyes to Parliament House (*see p33*) and the Sydney Mint Museum (*see below*) on either side of the current grand Victorian building which thoughtlessly replaced the centre of an eye-catching trio. Inside, the original marble floors, magnificent windows and colour scheme have been carefully restored. The lobby contains a list of those who donated to its construction and the respective amounts – Dame Nellie Melba kicked in £100, as much as some of the business giants of the day. There are free guided tours on the first Wednesday of every month, otherwise groups can apply to the press office to arrange their own tour. Without a guide, visitors are restricted to a short wander through the lobby and courtyard.

Sydney Mint Museum

Queen's Square, Sydney (9217 0313). CityRail Martin Place or St James. **Open** 10am-5pm daily. **Admission** $5 adults; $2 concessions; $12 family ticket. **No credit cards**.
One of Australia's oldest public buildings and originally a wing of the 'Rum Hospital'. The building became the nation's first Mint in 1853 and is now a museum which spreads over a series of small rooms and into the coining factory across the courtyard. 'The Power of Gold' room is probably the best place to learn the importance of the goldrush to Australia's prosperity. There is also an exhibition of coins and medals, plus a coining machine with which you can press your own souvenir token.

Sydney Observatory

Observatory Hill, The Rocks (9217 0485). CityRail/ferry Circular Quay. **Open** *museum* 2-5pm Mon-Fri; 10am-5pm Sat, Sun; *night programmes* phone for details. **Admission** *museum* free; *night programmes* (booking essential) $6 adults; $3 concessions. **No credit cards**.
Constructed in 1858, the modestly built Sydney Observatory has gained international recognition for its 80-year contribution to the International Astrographic Catalogue, the first complete atlas of the sky. Now that the Observatory is a hands-on museum of astronomy, its charming Victorian building is incongruously equipped with the latest hardware. With the aid of a new 40-cm (16-in) diameter telescope (and size matters here) daytime visitors can view Venus or a binary star system 4.34 million light years away. There are also various interactive machines that tick you off loudly if you give wrong answers. Night visitors might see any planet out as far as Neptune. Observatory Hill also has wonderful night views of twinkling lights in the harbour below, making it one of the most romantic spots in town.

Sydney Town Hall

483 George Street, Sydney (9265 9189/concert details 9265 9007). CityRail Town Hall. **Open** 8am-6pm Mon-Fri. **Admission** free.
Built on a graveyard and completed in 1889, Sydney Town Hall is a towering High Victorian building topped by a clock tower with a two-ton bell. A multimillion-dollar restoration has since made it a popular setting for wedding receptions as well as an established venue for concerts and conferences. The Vestibule, with its highly coloured domed ceiling hung with a huge, glittering crystal chandelier, features some of the earliest examples of Australian-made stained glass and is stunning. Behind it, the Centennial Hall, with an entire wall dominated by the magnificent 8,500-pipe organ, was used for important concerts before the advent of the Opera House. With a holding capacity of 2,500, it was once the largest of its kind in the world and is now treasured as one of the two

grandest surviving nineteenth-century halls in Australia (the other being the Great Hall of Sydney University). It's worth catching one of the regular free organ concerts.

Vaucluse House

Wentworth Road, Vaucluse (9388 7922). Bus 325. **Open** 10am-4.30pm Tue-Sun. **Admission** $5 adults; $3 concessions; $12 family ticket. **No credit cards**.
Vaucluse House was built long before film stars moved into the area. It is, in fact, the oldest 'house museum' in Australia, nestling prettily in a moated nineteenth-century estate surrounded by 10 ha (25 acres) of prime land, with its own sheltered beach on Vaucluse Bay. From 1827 to 1862 it was the opulent home of William Charles Wentworth, explorer, politician, barrister, businessman, newspaper magnate and one of the most influential Australian-born colonists. The house originally stood in 209 ha (515 acres) and needed 26 servants to tend the master's children, who just kept coming. Then there were his vineyards, orchards and beloved racehorses. The Historic Houses Trust has endeavoured to keep the place much as it was: a wood fire burns in the generously sized grate in the kitchen and hefty copper pans line the walls. A tin bath, taken on European travels, still displays its Victoria Station, London, sticker. The drawing room has the full sumptuous works, including a door that hides a secret – ask a guide to open it.

Victoria Barracks

Oxford Street, Paddington (9339 3000). Bus 378, 380, 382. **Open** *tour* 10.30am-noon Thur; *museum* 9.30am-2.30pm Thur, Sun. **Admission** free.
Built by convicts and officially opened in 1850, this barracks complex seems much too pretty to be wasted on soldiering. The simple Victorian colonnaded buildings border a large, grassy drill square on two sides. Armed guards appear in front of certain doors, dressed in period uniforms dating back to the earliest colonial days. The museum is interesting enough for those who enjoy uniforms, guns and medals, and the staff everywhere seem to be on permanent smiley PR duty. The museum also harbours a Redcoat ghost, Charlie, who hanged himself while incarcerated for shooting his sergeant. His spectre appears frequently enough to cause some soldiers to refuse guard duty in that area at night. Every Tuesday at 10am there is a formal change of the guard with marching band.

Churches & Cathedrals

Great Synagogue

166 Castlereagh Street, Sydney (9267 2477). CityRail Town Hall. **Open** *services* 5.30pm Fri; 8.45am Sat; *tours* noon Tue, Thur. **Admission** free.
Somewhat dwarfed by the office blocks that surround it, the Great Synagogue (consecrated in 1878) is a lavish confection of French gothic with large amounts of Byzantine thrown in. The superb wheel window at the front repeats the design of the wrought-iron gates outside while inside, the cast-iron columns holding up the balcony where the women sit are capped with intricate plaster designs. The ceiling, deep blue with gold-leaf stars, depicts the Creation. Unusually, for a synagogue, the central Bimah, where the rabbis and cantors read from the Torah, has been moved to the back to accommodate a greater congregation. Tours include a short sound-and-light show on the history of the Great Synagogue and the Jewish community in Australia. There is also a small museum in the basement.

St Andrew's Cathedral

Sydney Square, corner of George and Bathurst Streets, Sydney (9265 1661). CityRail Town Hall. **Open** 8am-5.30pm Mon-Fri; 9am-4pm Sat; 8am-8.30pm Sun; *services* 8.30am, 10.30am, 6.30pm Sun; *tours* 11am, 1.45pm Mon-Fri; 11.45am Sun. **Admission** free.

A massive, late gothic edifice started with astonishing confidence by Governor Macquarie (who named it after the Scottish saint) when Sydney was the size of a small village, St Andrew's Cathedral was finally consecrated in 1868. Interesting touches link the cathedral to the motherland: the side chapel's marble floor came from St Paul's and much of the stonework from Westminster Abbey in London. Military commemorations honour the landings at Gallipoli and the prison camp at Changi in Singapore. There is a full weekly programme of services with and without choir.

St James' Church
173 King Street, Sydney (9232 3022). CityRail St James or Martin Place. **Open** 9am-5pm daily; *services* 8am, 9am, 11am Sun. **Admission** free.
The oldest Sydney church began life on Francis Greenway's drawing board as a courthouse. However, a review of expenditure resulted in a swift change-of-use decision and the building was converted into a church before its completion. The intended holding cells were neatly transformed into a crypt. The altar is flanked by two sets of organ pipes and topped by a copper half-dome, while the side windows are beautiful memorials to past parishioners. A small chapel off to the right holds several services during the day.

St Mary's Cathedral
Corner of College and Cathedral Streets, Sydney (9232 3788). CityRail St James. **Open** 6.30am-6.30pm daily; *services* sung mass 10.30am Sun; *tours* noon Sun. **Admission** free.
At 100m (328ft) long with a 30 metre-high (98 ft) nave, St Mary's Cathedral dwarfs many of the European models from which it took inspiration. This substantial gothic masterpiece, complete with flying buttresses, opened in 1882,

Bondi Beach

There are plenty of other beaches close to the city that provide Sydneysiders with their regular dose of R&R. But the most famous of all is the spectacular golden sweep of Bondi Beach – spiritual home of the faithful Bondi Icebergs and regular haunt of Sydney surfers. Its fame can't be said to rest only on aesthetic grounds – there are cleaner beaches all along the coastline, and ones with fewer souvenir shops and less traffic. Where Bondi scores is on location: it's the city's closest beach, easily accessible by bus (L80, L82, 380, 382). And therein lies its downfall, for Bondi has long been victim of its own success. Polystyrene cups pepper the sand at peak hours, graffiti abounds and no one has seen fit to give the poor old pavilion a lick of paint. But this doesn't deter from its raffish charms and Bondi has enjoyed a revival of late. Countless groovy cafés and restaurants have opened, as well as decent places to stay. A string of surf shops caters for every wave-riding need and on Sundays, the alternative market draws big crowds. After all, Bondi Beach is, and probably always will be, a national institution. (For Tamarama, Bronte, Clovelly and Coogee Beaches, among others *see chapter* **The Great Outdoors**.)

Take control, rent Budget

Experience the freedom to do what you want, when you want. Rent your own set of wheels from Budget. Whether you're after the versatility of a 4WD, the comfort of a campervan or the convenience of a sedan, Budget has exactly what you need. All at competitive prices, with the option of one way rentals.

For bookings call your travel agent or Budget on:

Australia	13 28 48
New Zealand	0800 652 227
United States	1800 527 0700
Canada	1800 268 8900
United Kingdom	0800 181 181
France	0510 0001
Italy	6 229 356 20
Germany	89 66 695 128
Switzerland	1 813 5797
Netherlands	23 567 1222

Budget.

All The Difference In The World.

ResponseAbility BUD08/04

replacing an earlier structure that burnt down. The crypt floor alone is worth inspection: several hundred square metres of marble mosaic form a fantastic sequence depicting the six days of creation, held together with enamelled Celtic scrollwork; it's like standing on a vast medieval manuscript. The best time to visit is during the 10.30am Sunday morning mass, when you get the full works, with choirboys, incense and organ music.

Parks & Gardens

Centennial Park

Between Oxford Street and Alison Road (9339 6699). Bus 200, 314-6, 321, 327, 329, 330, 355, 359, 360, 361, 400. **Open** *Mar, April, Sept* 6am-6pm, *May-Aug* 6.30am-5.30pm, *Oct-Feb* 6am-8pm, daily. **Admission** free.
Glorious Centennial Park is the perfect place to see Australians in their natural habitat. Go on a sunny Sunday afternoon and you feel as though you have stumbled upon a terrific street party. The bush, open spaces, cycle tracks and park walks attract ramblers, rollerbladers, horse-riders, kite-fliers, chess players, cyclists, baseball players, picnickers and dog lovers in droves. Such is the immensity of the place it still feels quite uncrowded, although the café is always busy. Head for the lakes to watch chubby eels and aggressive fish compete with irritable white swans for thrown bread (the smart money's on the seagulls). For more on rollerblading and cycling *see chapter* **The Great Outdoors**. *See also chapter* **Cafés & Bars**.

Chinese Garden

Darling Harbour (9281 6863). CityRail Town Hall/ monorail Haymarket. **Open** 9.30am-sunset daily. **Admission** $3 adults; $1.50 concessions. **No credit cards.**
Unless you're prepared to arm wrestle for your share of tranquil spots, avoid this place at the weekend when it's full of grimly determined tourists. Designed by the Guangdong Landscape Bureau in China to celebrate the bicentenary of 1988, the Garden of Friendship gives up a fresh vista around

every corner. Here you'll find waterfalls, weeping willows, water lillies, wandering galleries and wooden bridges. For an extra five bucks, you or any accompanying short persons can dress up in traditional Chinese garb and pose orientally by the pagoda. Afterwards, go up to the teahouse balcony and order a cup of shui hsien tea. Then enjoy the best view of all: the entire park reflected in the Lake of Brightness, stuffed full of chubby koi.

The Domain

Adjacent to Royal Botanic Gardens. CityRail Martin Place or St James. **Open** 24 hours daily. **Admission** free.
Home to Sunday soap-box orators, The Domain park has long been the place for civic protest. Huge crowds gathered here in 1917 to protest against World War I conscription, and in 1931 over 100,000 demonstrated against the Governor's dismissal of Premier Jack Lang. The Domain is also where to find the Art Gallery of New South Wales (*see chapter* **Museums & Galleries**) and memorials to poets Robert Burns and Henry Lawson. The park itself is rather dull and Mrs Macquarie's Road, although it offers good views over the naval docks and Woolloomooloo Bay, is spoilt by heavy traffic. But it's all worth it for the final sensational view: Mrs Macquarie's Chair overlooking the harbour (*see p39* **Views & Vistas**).

Hyde Park

Between Elizabeth and College Streets, Sydney. CityRail Museum/St James. **Open** 24 hours daily. **Admission** free.
Hyde Park, named after its London counterpart, used to have a rowdy reputation; it was more of a venue for private sports meetings, sideshows, wrestling and boxing matches than a park. Until the late 1820s, it also served as Sydney's racecourse. Now it's a tranquil green space and fitting home to elegant Australian memorials, including the famous 1934 art deco Anzac Memorial, commemorating those who served in World War I, and the graceful Archibald Fountain, commemorating the Australian-French Alliance of 1914-18. The main avenue of fig trees to the north is especially striking. During the Sydney Festival in January the park erupts with free entertainment (*see chapter* **Sydney by Season**).

Plant yourself in a quiet corner of the **Royal Botanic Gardens**. *See page 41.*

Sydney

Views & vistas

The visitor is spoilt for choice when it comes to viewpoints in Sydney; there's practically one at the top of every street. In the city centre, there are rooftop bars at the **ANA**, **Inter-Continental** and **Gazebo Hotels**, and the toilets at **Forty One** restaurant have to be the most scenic around (*see chapters* **Restaurants** *and* **Cafés & Bars**). On the south side of the harbour try the **Sydney Opera House** steps for a bracing close-up of the waters and on the other side of Farm Cove, **Mrs Macquarie's Chair** offers a glorious panorama, starting with the Opera House on the left, the Harbour Bridge, Kirribilli House across the harbour, Pinchgut Island ahead and the dockyards of Woolloomooloo on the right, with plenty of yachts in between.

At the end of the Old South Head Road lies **The Gap** with its weathered and grotesquely shaped rocks. Walk on to the very tip of the peninsula, to **South Head**, and you can gaze out over the ocean or look back into Sydney Harbour. Down to the left lies Watsons Bay with its restaurants, parks and winding streets. Across to the north is, of course, **North Head**, the other half of Sydney Harbour's portal; this can be reached from Manly and offers similar views but without the crush of tourists.

The north shore has its own array of viewing spots including **Milsons Point** directly under the Harbour Bridge, the plush suburb that includes **Cremorne Point** and **Bradleys Head** with its picnic areas on the road past Taronga Zoo. **Woolwich Point** at the tip of Hunters Hill (even the ferry ride is scenic) is popular on New Year's Eve when fireworks light up the harbour sky.

Moving up the coast, there are uplifting views from **Queenscliff** (go to the end of Queenscliff Road), **McKillop Park** at South Curl Curl (with another view around the corner at the Carrington Street car park overlooking the pool and surfers). **Newport** offers tranquil views over Pittwater (the Newport Arms is a good convivial viewing place), as does **Bayview Park** off Pittwater Road.

Sydney Tower

Centrepoint, corner of Market and Pitt Streets, Sydney (9233 3844). CityRail St James or Town Hall/monorail City Centre. **Open** 9.30am-9.30pm Mon-Fri, Sun; 9.30am-11.30pm Sat. **Admission** $9 adults; $4-$7 concessions; $20 family ticket. **Credit** $TC.
A must-see for anybody once in their life, Sydney's tallest building (*below* 305m, 1,000ft) offers a 360-degree view that ranges from the street immediately below to Terrigal Beach 100km (62 miles) away to the north. Use of the high-powered binoculars for landmark-spotting is free, but pick a clear day or you'll be wasting your time. Alternatively, a night-time viewing will provide its own spectacular light show. There is a café/bar a few steps below the main viewing deck which offers equally riveting views and its prices are mercifully free of the rip-off-the-tourist mentality. There are also two swankier revolving restaurants on other levels with prices to match.

VETRO

Restaurant Wine Bar
Plaza Level, Grosvenor Place
225 George Street
Sydney NSW 2000
Ph: (02) 9247 8787

Monday & Tuesday   7.00am - 6.00pm
Wednesday - Friday 7.00am - late

Nielsen Park

Graycliffe Avenue, Vaucluse. Bus 325. **Open** 5am-10pm daily. **Admission** free.

With its generous number of shady trees, Nielsen Park is the coolest outdoor place in the city. But the big drawcard is the beach offering panoramic views over Port Jackson. Protected by a shark-proof enclosure in summer, the beach shrinks to a narrow strip at high tide, but there are plenty of steps to lie about on. Nicely poised between beach and flora is the unexpectedly pretty Nielsen Park Kiosk (*see chapter* **Cafés & Bars**). Dogs and ball games are banned, making the park a predominantly adult (topless sunbathing is permitted) and fairly peaceful spot.

Royal Botanic Gardens

Mrs Macquarie's Road (9231 8125). **Open** *park* 6.30am-sunset daily; *Sydney Tropical Centre* 10am-4pm daily. **Admission** *park* free; *Sydney Tropical Centre* $5 adults; $2 concessions; $12 family ticket. **Credit** BC, MC, $TC, V.

Encompassing Farm Cove are the 74 broad green acres of the Royal Botanic Gardens, which include the site of Australia's first vegetable patch. You can still see the spot where, two centuries ago, Governor Arthur Phillip first planted his big yams. Sydneysiders play footie here or picnic, while ibises (sporting beaks that could tear off an arm along with a proffered egg sandwich), stride about with an air of greed mixed with terror. Most tourists initially head straight for the Sydney Tropical Centre, fronted by a stunning black-glass pyramid; heavily concreted innards, however, betray its early 1970s origins, detracting from the intended impression that you are in the middle of a tropical rainforest. Instead, take advantage of the free guided walks conducted every morning at 10.30am, beginning outside the visitors centre. Alternatively, take the 'trackless train' which stops at all areas of interest, neatly ending up at the Opera House.

For boat tours, see page 44.

On Foot

The Rocks Walking Tours

106 George Street, The Rocks (9247 6678). CityRail/ ferry Circular Quay. **Tickets** $10 adults; $6.50 children.

Highly recommended anecdotal tour of the most historic part of Sydney where the itinerary can be modified according to customers' preferences. It starts from The Rocks Visitor Centre.

Walkabout with Sydney Ferries

Free leaflet from Ferry Information Office, opposite Wharf 4, Circular Quay (13 1500).

Thirteen terrific walks around Sydney and the suburbs (including the Manly Scenic Walk) put together by Sydney Ferries. Pick up a free leaflet and take your pick.

By Air

Balloon Adventures of Australia

16 Lyte Place, Prospect (9622 5267). **Tickets** $100-$175.

Hot air balloon flights over the Camden Valley where John Macarthur started Australia off in the wool business. View the Blue Mountains to the west and the Sydney skyline to the east, then devour a champagne breakfast on landing.

Red Baron Scenic Flights

PO Box 76, Georges Hall, NSW 2198 (9791 0643). **Tickets** $110-$450.

Traditional open-cockpit biplane flight over Sydney. For greater thrills, try an Aerobatic Thrill Seeker flight.

South Pacific Seaplanes

PO Box 490, Cronulla, NSW 2230 (9544 0077). **Tickets** $35-$425.

Return flights to more than 20 restaurants and hotels near the water, plus beach picnic flights where you get to choose the beach and scenic flights.

Sydney Heli-Scenic

Wharf 6, Circular Quay or Information Booth, Harbourside, Darling Harbour (9247 5151/93173402). **Tickets** $140-$220.

Helicopter tour that flits above Sydney Harbour and out over Bondi Beach. Night flights are also available.

By Motorbike

Eastcoast Tours

Wharf 6, Circular Quay or Information Booth, Harbourside, Darling Harbour (9247 5151/9544 2400). **Tickets** $65-$325.

The way to see Sydney with the smells and sounds close up – the wind in your face and the throbbing engine of a Harley Davidson between your legs, while you clutch the waist of a manly Australian. All bike gear provided.

Easy Rider Motorbike Tours

The Rocks Market, George Street, The Rocks (9247 2477). **Tickets** $25-$650.

Also featuring the classic Harley Davidson, but this company offers shorter rides around the city centre for the faint-hearted.

By Bus

Here are a few highlights from the many bus tours on offer in the city. The best value pack as far as local tours go is the Sydney Pass, product of the combined efforts of the municipal bus, rail and

The far side

Bondi is boring. The Opera House sucks. If you want to get the true flavour of Australia, these are the places you should visit.

Mistral Point

Off Marine Parade, Maroubra. Bus 395, 396.

At Mistral Point, just north of Maroubra Beach, there is a cliff with almost mystical significance. In 1974, during the making of the cult psycho-biker movie *Stone*, stuntman Peter Armstrong rode a motorcycle off this 50 metrehigh cliff into the ocean. He lived, although the bike never ran the same again. The jump qualified for the *Guinness Book of Records* and is one reason for the movie's continued success in video stores (a skinny-dip sequence involving a current TV lifestyle hostess is another). Kawasaki-riding movie freaks are frequently seen making a pilgrimage to the site of Australia's most spectacular film location.

The Gap

Watsons Bay. Bus 234, 325.

The Gap (*below*) is Sydney's best known terminal exit zone – popular with bankrupt businessmen, jilted lovers and, lately, part-time models. While there are no signs indicating 'suicides, this way', every taxi driver knows where the place is and will gladly drop you off, provided you pay the fare in advance. When ghoulmeister Alfred Hitchcock visited Australia in 1960, The Gap was top of his list of tourist locations. Be warned: during busy periods there may be a short delay. Please form an orderly queue. No pushing.

181 Birriga Road

Bellevue Hill. Bus 387.

While Hitchcock merely looked, English comedian Tony Hancock acted. In June 1968 – fighting alcoholism and trying to resurrect his career – Hancock was staying in a bungalow flat at the rear of 181 Birriga Road when he ended the pain with copious amounts of vodka and barbiturates. His suicide note read, in part: 'Things seemed to go wrong too many times.' While there is no plaque or shrine in honour of the sad funny man, some say that on moonlit nights you can see a ghostly figure in a Homburg hat arguing with Sid James. Please note this is a private residence.

Tool Shed

See chapter **Queer Sydney** *for listings.*

This emporium, in the heart of Sydney's so-called pink triangle, is not a hardware shop except in the sexual sense. Displayed here are many of the industrial implements used to prove man's inhumanity to man, of a consenting adult nature, of course. Those from a sheltered background may be shocked by the wide variety of fist-shaped objects available. Do not ask for a demonstration.

Drag Bag

2 Brisbane Street, Surry Hills (9261 3333).
CityRail Museum.

Just a dildo's toss away from Oxford Street is a retail outlet called Drag Bag, on the top floor of the Beyond Woman Factory. A mini-department store for potential Priscillas and fellow queens of the desert, the shop is also popular with larger-than-life real women seeking those hard-to-find size 14 stilettos.

Bourbon and Beefsteak Bar

24 Darlinghurst Road, Kings Cross (9358 1144).
CityRail Kings Cross.

Situated in the heart of Kings Cross, sleaze capital of Sydney, is the famous 24-hour Bourbon and Beefsteak bar and restaurant. Always packed with drunken sales reps and giggling secretaries, the front bar at 4am on a Saturday can resemble a scene from Dante's *Inferno*. The place was allegedly set up to make visiting American crime lords feel at home, and the decor is reminiscent of a Mafia garage sale. Still, it's the only place in Australia where you can order Steak Sinatra, a dish celebrating the visit of Ol' Blue Eyes back in the 1970s.

Horsley Park Gun Shop

1848 Horsley Drive, Horsley Park (9620 1235).

Way out west in a suburb called Horsley Park lies Australia's – and the Southern Hemisphere's – largest gun shop. Even more impressive is the array of taxidermied heads mounted on the wall, including species that perhaps even David Attenborough doesn't know about. Too late, Davo, they're already dead.

Viking Tavern

Now Milperra Palms, 189 Beaconsfield Road, Milperra (9771 2722). CityRail Ravesby then 20-minute walk.

On Father's Day in 1984, the car park of the Viking Tavern in the western suburb of Milperra was the scene of Australia's best known biker war. The skirmish between members of the Comancheros and the Bandidos resulted in seven being shot and 21 injured. While arguments over

amphetamine distribution are commonplace in Sydney pubs, even those involved agree that this one got a little out of hand. As a country with so few historic battle zones, perhaps this is the nearest thing to Hastings or Waterloo that Australia can offer visitors.

Pacific Sheepskin Products

14 Rennie Street, Wetherill Park (9756 1922).
Pacific Sheepskin Products is the major distributor of Australia's main contribution to world fashion: the ugg boot. Looking like a pair of furry wellies, uggs give the wearer an appealing yeti-like appearance. The ugg was a proudly Australian icon until the brand was sold last year to an American corporation, which explains why such major celebrities as Pamela Lee Anderson, Bruce Springsteen and Willie Nelson have been spotted looking ridiculous in a pair. Wade O'Brien, boss of Pacific Sheepskin, boasts that it was his father who came up with the concept of the comfy sheepskin boot. But even Wade is unsure which genius thought up the word 'ugg'. Though

once you've seen a pair, it's unthinkable that they could be called anything else.

Palm Beach

Bus 190, 193.
Fans of Aussie soaps have to travel to Melbourne if they want to visit the popular Ramsay Street shrine where *Neighbours* is filmed. The best Sydney can offer soapa-holics is Palm Beach and neighbouring Whale Beach, a millionaire-only zone 30km (19 miles) north of the city. This is where most of the outside scenes in *Home and Away* are filmed. You can swim in the same rock pool as your fave sun-bronzed hunk or spunk. Just remember, Australians are notoriously blasé about stars, treating them with the same lack of attention they reserve for members of their immediate family. You should do the same.

Sydney Cricket Ground

See chapter **Sport & Fitness** *for listings.*
Sydney Cricket Ground has been the site of many of England's most humiliating Test match defeats. A tour of the ground is a must for any sports lover and an even more of a must for fans of legendary Australian broadcaster Richie Benaud. A feature of the Sportspace tour (9380 0383) is an automaton of the man in the cream jacket, which is so un-lifelike that meeting the real man could prove a disappointment. Robotic Richie is much more exciting.

Westpac Museum

6 Playfair Street, The Rocks (9251 1419).
CityRail/ferry Circular Quay.
Apart from inspecting cyber-Richie, our tip for the most boring thing to do in Sydney is to visit the Westpac Museum. Westpac is a bank, and unless you have a per-verse fascination with Australia's fiscal history you will be bored rigid by this exhibition. Still, admission is free and, OK, the dioramas of pioneering banking methods may be mildly entertaining. But probably not.

Norman Lindsay's Home & Gallery

See chapter **Trips Out of Town** *for listings.*
Set in the mountains about 80km (50 miles) west of the centre of town is the family home of artist Norman Lindsay, Australia's raunchiest painter and sculptor, who died in 1969. This was the location for *Sirens*, the movie that featured Elle Macpherson's breasts, and some actors. But judging by his paintings and sculptures, Lindsay pre-ferred his women big: more Dawn French than 'The Body'. There is more naked flesh on display here than on an *Electric Blue Wobbling Whoppers* video, which makes it ironic that most of the visitors appear to be little old ladies enjoying tea and scones.

Waratah Park

Namba Road, Duffys Forest (9450 2377). By car: Pacific Highway to Pymble then Route 3.
Fans of Oz's best known television import after Kylie Minogue will be rushing to Waratah Park to interact with Skippy. The TV series was filmed here, but the original kangaroo has been replaced by distant and dumber relatives. These substitutes don't drive cars or make emer-gency phone calls. The dusty office of ranger Matt Hammond (as featured on TV's *Eurotrash*) remains, but sadly Ed Deveraux no longer works here.

ferry services. Three, five and seven-day passes give you unlimited access to the Red Sydney Explorer, the Blue Bondi & Bay Explorer, the Airport Express and all ferry cruises.

Australian Pacific Tours

102 George Street, The Rocks (13 1304). **Tickets** $35-$66.
Three city and suburbs trips are available, which take in Sydney sights, beach life and super furry animals.

Blue Bondi & Bay Explorer

Information (13 1500).
Concentrates on the eastern side of town, stopping at Kings Cross and Rose Bay Convent before hitting the beaches of Bondi, Bronte, Clovelly and Coogee. A short run northwards takes in Watsons Bay and The Gap Park. It departs every 30 minutes from Circular Quay, but you can board anywhere you see the 20 blue signs. A day ticket costs $20 from the driver.

Clipper Gray Line Tours

Shop 1, Lower Level, Overseas Shipping Terminal,
Circular Quay (9319 4666/9241 3993).
Tickets $32-$369.
Clipper offers Sydney sights combined with a wildlife park sortie where you can cuddle a 'roo. Alternative trips cover the northern beaches too.

Murrays Australia

Shop 3, Overseas Shipping Terminal, Circular Quay
(9252 3590). **Tickets** $32-$82.
Choose from Australian bush creatures, surfing beaches, historic buildings, killer sharks or cosmopolitan centres.

Red Sydney Explorer

Information (13 1500).
Unlimited travel in air-conditioned comfort around the highlights of Sydney. It covers Sydney Cove, the Opera House, Royal Botanic Gardens, Mrs Macquarie's Chair, Art Gallery of NSW, Kings Cross, Chinatown, Powerhouse Museum, Sydney Casino, Darling Harbour, Harbour Bridge, Queen Victoria Building, The Rocks and more. Jump on and off as you please. A day ticket costs $20 from the driver.

By Boat

There are over 25 different Sydney Harbour cruises on offer every day and the best way to choose one is to get *The Complete Guide to Harbour Cruises* from the Quayside Booking Centre at Wharf 6, Circular Quay or the Information Booth, Harbourside, Darling Harbour.

Bounty

Wharf 6, Circular Quay (9247 5151). **Tickets** from £43.
A replica of the vessel lost by Captain Bligh in the famous mutiny sets off twice daily, and you can help set sail or just sip your wine and watch.

Captain Cook Cruises

Wharf 6, Circular Quay (9206 1122). **Tickets** from $16.
One of the biggest cruise operators with a large choice of vessels, daytime and night-time cruises, various meal combinations and commentaries in nine languages.

River Cat to Parramatta

Wharf 6, Circular Quay (13 1500). **Tickets** $4.60.
Fast and comfortable run inland that takes passengers past unspoilt bays, untouristy suburbs and the site of the 2000 Olympics to Parramatta, birthplace of the Australian wool industry and the commercial centre of western Sydney.

Sydney by Sail

Wharf 6, Circular Quay (9247 5151). **Tickets** from $39.
More intimate exposure to the harbour waters. Sit back and absorb the sights or learn to sail in the world's best setting.

The Harbour City: for the best vantage points, see page 39.

The Great Outdoors

You don't have to go far to get away from it all: there are parks, islands, bushwalks and an embarrassment of beaches, all within the city limits.

Sydney is very much an outdoor city. Most of its major events take place in the open air. An extraordinary number of restaurants, cafés and pubs have alfresco areas for patrons to congregate on hot summer nights – and summer now seems to take up about eight months of the year. But most of the city's sense of identity is based on sky, sand and water. Sydney people think of themselves as outgoing, outdoors types, permanently ready to head off for a picnic or a spot of water-skiing. Sharing the Sun Equals Health attitude of Californians, Sydneysiders believe themselves to be fit, tanned, laid-back people – all as a result of climate and geography. This, of course, is and isn't the truth.

Sydney's beaches and national parks are its pride and joy. In much the same way that Australians will tell you how attached they are to the outback, even though they've never been there, a Sydneysider who never ventures beyond remote-control range of his television will still insist that the city's natural beauty is why they love living there. A shamefully small number of locals actually use the beaches and national parks, especially during the week. The residents take an amazing amount for granted – which makes it all the better for visitors to appreciate the peace and beauty of these living treasures.

Forget the fact that the great outdoors – bushwalks, beaches, cycle paths or the expanse of Sydney Harbour – is full of nasty little critters that bite to kill. A city of four million humans provides safety in sufficient numbers to have driven most of the beasties out to quieter climes. So you can swim, hike, surf or sail with relative peace of mind.

Parklife

You needn't go far to get away from it all. The Sydney metropolitan area has ten national parks, administered by the NSW National Parks & Wildlife Service (NPWS). These areas are dedicated permanently 'for public enjoyment, education and inspiration', according to the NPWS

charter. And they are protected from all development apart from that which is needed for their management. They are chosen for their outstanding ecology, geology, rare flora and fauna, scenic grandeur, wilderness and historical interest. In Australia, this means in particular places of early Aboriginal settlement.

Starting in the north, **Ku-Ring-Gai Chase** is one of Sydney's wealthiest municipalities. The national park winds among the affluent suburbs of St Ives and Turramurra to the south and up to Broken Bay in the north. Every visitor to Sydney should take in the West Head lookout, which gives views over the mouth of the Hawkesbury River and the northern beaches. Ku-Ring-Gai's walking tracks lead to significant examples of Aboriginal rock art. Guided walks and canoe and boat tours can also be arranged.

Marramarra, near Wisemans Ferry to the north-west, is only accessible to serious bushwalkers. But it's also the only national park with no restrictions on camping.

Further west lies **Cattai**, a popular picnic spot in the north, situated on the Hawkesbury River in one of the first areas of Sydney settled by Europeans. An 1820 sandstock-brick cottage is preserved in the park, as is a small farm named 'Friendship', after the first boat that sailed up the river to this point.

Tucked below Ku-Ring-Gai is the much smaller **Garigal**, linking Sydney's north shore suburbs with the northern beaches. The western side of the park hugs Middle Harbour Creek, which leads into Sydney Harbour. A walking track by the creek offers historical interest (Arthur Phillip, first Governor of New South Wales, explored here) and some rare native ash and stringybark trees. The track has four picnic areas.

Lane Cove National Park picks up where Garigal leaves off, meandering along the banks of Lane Cove River through the suburbs of Killara, Chatswood and Ryde. It is one of the most popular recreation areas in the Sydney region, hosting hundreds of barbecues, impromptu cricket and football games. It is filled with cyclists, canoeists and a paddlewheel boat at the weekends and on school holidays. There are 41 picnic areas and a caravan/camping park. Unfortunately, swimming is prohibited because of the pollution.

At the heart of the metropolis is what many consider to be the city's finest achievement: **Sydney Harbour National Park** – the preservation of 388 hectares (959 acres) of the country's prime waterfront real estate. It is broken up into seven chunks along the northern and southern rims of the harbour, and includes three harbour islands (*see page 53* **Island Flings**). The views from North Head (near Manly), up the harbour's gullet to the city, are mesmerising. Nielsen Park in Vaucluse, on the south side, has a shark-netted beach and extensive picnic grounds. The walk from The Spit Bridge in Middle Harbour to Manly, along the foreshore, is the city's most popular bushwalk.

Heading south brings you to **Botany Bay National Park**, split over both sides of the historic bay's mouth. Significant sites here include Captain Cook's Landing Place and La Perouse. The southern part has several kilometres of bushwalks, while the northern section (La Perouse) has a museum commemorating the earliest white settlement.

Inland, amid the riverside suburbs of Picnic Point, Revesby Heights, Padstow Heights, Alfords Point and Illawong in Sydney's south-west, you'll find the **Georges River National Park**. This small (324-hectare/800-acre) national park has some bushwalks, but is used more for picnicking, fishing and water-skiing.

Sydney's biggest national park (15,000 hectares/37,000 acres) marks off the metropolitan area's southern boundary. The **Royal National Park** attracts thousands of visitors a week, who come for the views over the southern coastline, the variety of walking tracks, the excellent swimming at ocean beaches and freshwater holes, and the picturesque camping sites. Canoes and rowing boats can be hired from the boatshed at Audley, the park's nerve centre. The park was badly damaged in the 1994 bushfires, but has regenerated with remarkable speed.

Barbie cues

Australians are prideful about their barbecues. They claim this is because they invented them. Wrong: *homo erectus* was throwing steaks on the barbie long before he moved to Australia. In fact, Australian men are particularly protective about the barbecue because this offers them a once-a-year chance to show they have some use in the art of food preparation.

In an age where every male bastion seems to be falling, the barbecue remains sacrosanct. Sexual

Just on the other side of the Princes Highway is **Heathcote National Park**. This almost untouched area is popular among seasoned bushwalkers and birdwatchers. It has no road access and camping permits are issued by the NPWS.

General Information

The NPWS produces an excellent free colour booklet, *National Parks in New South Wales*, which lists facilities available at each place. The national parks listed below charge an admission fee of $7.50 per car and $3 per adult, and concessions are also available. The exceptions are Cattai, which charges $1 per adult, and Sydney Harbour, which is free. Unless otherwise indicated, none of the parks accept credit cards. All provide disabled access and toilets. For a map showing their location *see page 278*.

NSW National Parks & Wildlife Service

Cadman's Cottage, 110 George Street, The Rocks (9247 8861/9555 9844). CityRail/ferry Circular Quay. **Open** 10am-3pm Mon; 9am-4.30pm Tue-Fri; 11am-4pm Sat, Sun. **Branch** 33 Bridge Street, Hurstville, NSW 2220 (9585 6444).

National Parks

Cattai

Wisemans Ferry Road, Cattai (4572 8404). **Open** sunrise-sunset daily. **Credit** (for bills over $10) BC, MC, V. **Getting there** *No public transport. By car* Pacific Highway to Hornsby; Galston Road; Pitt Town Road; then Cattai Road.

Botany Bay

Captain Cook Drive, Kurnell (9668 9111). **Open** 7am-7.30pm daily. **Getting there** *By public transport* CityRail Cronulla then 67 bus. *By car* Princes Highway; Rocky Point Road; Taren Point Road; then Captain Cook Drive.

Garigal

Davidson Picnic Area, Roseville Bridge, off Warringah Road, Forestville (9451 3479). **Open** *park* sunrise-sunset daily; *picnic area* sunrise-3.30pm Mon-Fri; sunrise-sunset Sat, Sun. **Getting there** *By public transport* 169, 172, 173 bus. *By car* Eastern Way then Warringah Road.

Georges River

Henry Lawson Drive, Revesby Heights (9772 2159/9542 0648). **Open** 7am-sunset daily. **Getting there** *By public transport* CityRail Revesby then 5-minutes by taxi. *By car* Hume Highway to Villawood; then south on Henry Lawson Drive.

---

segregation at an Australian barbecue is as strict as at a teenage social dance. The men congregate around the appliance itself. The proprietor/chef identifies himself with his tongs (the only cooking implement he knows how to wield) and his apron. The apron will often bear the imprint of a naked woman, a pair of plastic breasts or a suitably witty line, such as 'KISS MY COOK'.

Barbecue etiquette is simple but mandatory. The chef must never be without a drink. For this purpose, he is surrounded by a cadre of fellow males, ostensibly there to admire his cooking and offer advice on when his meat is ready to turn. In fact, they are watching his drink, to make sure it never runs dry. The women do the real work of making salads, setting tables, serving crisps and other pre-barbie nibbles. Nevertheless, it is a cardinal sin to praise anything other than the meat. An approving remark about the potato salad or the coleslaw is likely to be taken as an insult to the chef's manhood.

Over time, Australians have become more eclectic about what they will give the barbecue treatment. The orthodoxy used to be sausages, steak and lamb chops. Onions and rissoles made their débuts in the 1970s; variously flavoured sausages in the 1980s. Now, seafood is especially popular – mostly baby octopus, prawns and whole fish – as are brochettes of meat, capsicum (pepper) and

onion. Australians will call these 'shish kebabs', but don't believe them. There are enough good Middle Eastern restaurants in Sydney to find out what a real shish kebab tastes like. Tomato ketchup has been complemented by a growing interest in barbecue marinades, and the Asian influences on Australian cooking have been such that barbecues can now involve noodles and tofu. Barbecued chicken is a speciality, as is – for the better-equipped – a pig on a rotisserie.

The barbecue is such an institution of Australian life that most public parks have them. Often you have to bring your own fuel, but some parks provide it. Use is a matter of first come first served, so competition can be intense, particularly on summer public holidays. In some parks, you can arrive at 10.30am yet not get your meat on the hotplate until 2pm.

So when you visit someone at home, don't worry about the little furnace in the backyard. It's not a pet crematorium, just the barbie. The smell of meat cooking over a flame, wafting across a park or backyard, is one of the essential Aussie experiences. If you're lucky enough to be invited to a barbecue, bring your meat, bring some beer, and prepare to stand in the background. Don't interfere. When your meat arrives back on your plate, burnt and dry, don't criticise: Australian barbecue chefs can't stand the sight of blood.

Sydney Scenic Flight

See **ALL** the sights of the most beautiful city in the world, from above. This is not a joyflight, but a scenic discovery tour of Sydney.

A grand tour exploring Sydney City, Opera House, Harbour Bridge, Darling Harbour, Southern Beaches, Northern Beaches, Sydney's best real estate, and every other sight worth seeing and photographing.

Tour details:
- Multi-lingual ground staff
- Hotel-Heliport transfers
- Complimentary refreshments
- Tour operates 09:00 to 17:00
- Flight time: 25 minutes (approximately)
- Minimum booking - 2 passengers

Phone: (02) 9317 3402
Fax: (02) 9667 3142

Heathcote
Heathcote Road, Heathcote (9542 0648). **Open** sunrise-sunset daily. **Getting there** *By public transport* CityRail Heathcote or Waterfall then entry to park via walking tracks. *By car* Princes Highway.

Ku-Ring-Gai Chase
Ku-Ring-Gai Chase Road, Mount Colah (NPWS office 9457 9322/The Wildlife Shop 9457 9310/Kalkari Visitor Centre 9457 9853). **Open** sunrise-sunset daily. **Getting there** *By public transport* CityRail Berowra, Cowan, Hawkesbury River, Mount Colah or Mount Ku-Ring-Gai then taxi/190 bus to Palm Beach then ferry over Pittwater. *By car* Pacific Highway.

Lane Cove
Lady Game Drive, Chatswood (9412 1811). **Open** 9am-sunset daily. **Getting there** *By public transport* CityRail Chatswood/550, 551 bus. *By car* Pacific Highway to Chatswood; Fullers Road; Millwood Avenue; entrance at Fullers Bridge.

Marramarra
Between Old Northern Road, Berowra Creek and Hawkesbury River (9457 9322). **Open** 24 hours daily. **Getting there** *No public transport. By car* Pacific Highway to Hornsby; Galston Road to Galston; Middle Dural Road; then Old Northern Road.

Royal National Park
Farnell Avenue, District of Royal National Park, Audley (9542 0666). **Open** 9am-sunset daily. **Getting there** *By public transport* CityRail Engadine, Heathcote, Loftus, Otford or Waterfall then entry to park via walking tracks. *By car* Princes Highway.

Sydney Harbour National Park
(9337 5355). For locations see page 281. **Open** sunrise-sunset daily. **Admission** free.

High-flyers

There is no better way to see Sydney than from a bird's-eye view – approaching the airport on your inbound flight should whet the appetite. There are many helicopter and light-plane operations based at Kingsford Smith and Bankstown Airports, while hot-air balloons that rise from the city's out-skirts fly over Sydney and the surrounding regions. For **Balloon Adventures of Australia, Red Baron Scenic Flights** *and* **Sydney Heli-Scenic** *see chapter* **Sightseeing**.

Hang-gliding & Paragliding
Beginners can experience the thrill of soaring under a hang-glider or parachute with **Air Support** (9450 2674), for $110 per half-hour in a tandem arrangement with a licensed flier. Flights go over the northern beaches, although there are also operations south of Sydney, around the Royal National Park. Nine- or ten-day courses to become a qualified hang-glider or paraglider cost $965 and $950 respectively. Course price includes textbooks, gear and third-party insurance. The hang-gliding takes place mainly over the northern beaches, the paragliding on southern escarpments between Kurnell and Wollongong.

Parachuting & Skydiving
Tandem flights for beginners are available at the **Sydney Skydiving Centre** (9791 9155) – you jump from 3,700 metres with an instructor who does all the work ($230 Mon-Fri, $295 weekends). The jumps are over Picton, in Sydney's south-west. You can pay to have your jump videoed by another skydiver who comes down at the same time (an extra $70 Mon-Fri, $85 weekends). The more adventurous might opt for freefall courses, which cost $340 (Mon-Fri) for the two-nighter or $370 for an all-day course (Sat). You jump from 3,050 metres, with two instructors holding on to you who let go when it's time for you to pull the cord. The company has a website at http://www.wp.com/sydney_skydivers

Paraflying
This unusual activity is like aerial water-skiing: you are attached to a parachute pulled along by a speeding boat. The season lasts from October to May, and **Sydney Harbour Paraflying** (9977 6781/ 9977 5296) is based at Manly Wharf. A flight, which lasts about seven minutes, costs $39 for an adult or $29 for a child. You can elect to stay dry or get wet.

Seafarers

Nearly every cove and inlet of Sydney Harbour has its own marina – it's one of Sydney's most distinctive features. These marinas offer all types of sailing boat and cruiser hire. Alternatively, get some canoe-how and pootle about on the water under your own paddle-power.

Canoeing
The **NSW Canoe Association** (9660 4597) will give you a guide to the many places where you can go for recreational canoeing in Sydney. National parks with rivers, such as Lane Cove and the Royal, have boatsheds from which you can hire canoes at low rates.

Sailing
The **Charter Boat Information Service** (9552 1827) allows you to navigate your way through the jungle of charter boat advertisements. It provides information on sailing, fishing and houseboats, as well as dinner cruises and party boat hire.

If you want to learn to sail, the **Pacific Sailing School** (9326 2399) is one of the many schools in Sydney Harbour, Middle Harbour and the Port Hacking area. Situated at the **Cruising Yacht Club** (9363 9731) on Rushcutters Bay, the Pacific Sailing School offers courses in crewing and sailing on boats from seven to 20 metres in length (23-66 feet). The courses (of five three-hour lessons) cost $395 each, and its cheaper if you take more than one course.

Windsurfing
Windsurfing, or sailboarding, is a fad that never went away in Sydney. One of Sydney's great attractions is that it offers flat-water opportunities on Pittwater, the Narrabeen Lakes, Sydney Harbour, Botany Bay and Port Hacking, or surf challenges at various beaches – the most popular being Palm and Long Reef.

The **Balmoral Sailing School** (9960 5344) is the best of Sydney's sailboarding schools and its

Once more unto the beach

Beaches in Sydney and their inhabitants are like European countries. They all have cultures and geographies of their own, they all hate each other, and they all think they're the best. A visitor to Sydney must bear in mind that to stand on Bondi Beach and praise Manly is an invitation to assault. There are more differences between one beach and its neighbour than there are between the beaches and the inland suburbs.

The first cultural division is between beaches north and south of Sydney Harbour. (For prime beaches within the harbour, such as **Balmoral**, **Lady Jane** in Watsons Bay and **Shark Beach** in Vaucluse, *see chapter* **Sydney by Area**. For a map of the harbour and its islands and beaches, *see page 281*.) In northerners' eyes, the southern beaches are polluted, overcrowded, overdeveloped and full of 'ethnics'. To southerners, the northern beaches are deadly boring, too far away from the city and full of snobs.

Bondi is the first of the southern beaches (*see also page 35*). Sydney's most famous, it used to be best known for its 'blind mullets' (the floating faecal matter that washed in from a nearby sewage outlet) and the busloads of elderly Japanese tourists who paced the beach in their suits and shoes. Nowadays, the beach is relatively clean and the locals have returned (though the tourists are still there, of course). Tilted to the south, Bondi is an excellent surfing and swimming beach. Highly residential, Bondi's culture is a blend of yuppies, unemployed actors and Jewish immigrants from Eastern Europe. South of Bondi are **Tamarama** (also known as 'Glamarama'), **Bronte**, **Clovelly** and **Coogee**. The last two are flat-water beaches, favoured by families, and considerably quieter than Bondi. Further down is **Maroubra**, a wide and windswept stretch of sand notorious for the territorial aggression of its local surfers.

The surf and swimming strip is broken by Botany Bay, to the south of which are **Wanda** and **Cronulla** Beaches. Due to their isolation and predominantly Anglo-Australian culture, these beaches have more in common with the northern beaches than with the Bondi-Maroubra zone.

The first surfing beach north of Sydney Harbour is **Manly**, known as 'God's Own Country'. Situated on a narrow spit between the harbour and the ocean, Manly is the most commercially developed beach in the north. It has a lot of hotels and backpacker hostels, and when the swell

is running from the east it has the best surf in Sydney. Like Bondi, Manly has improved its pollution record considerably since the 1980s. North of Manly are **Freshwater**, **Curl Curl**, **Dee Why**, **Long Reef**, **Collaroy**, **Narrabeen** and **Warriewood**. Each has its own personality and surfing conditions. Generally speaking, these are the white working-class beaches, with parochial local populations and a distrust of outsiders. Long Reef and North Narrabeen have arguably Sydney's best breaks for the committed surfer.

The beaches of the extreme north become wealthier and more exclusive the further you get from the city. **Mona Vale**, **Bungan** and **Newport** are unpretentious; **Bilgola** is secluded and picturesque; **Avalon** has a village atmosphere and Sydney's northernmost backpackers' hostel; while **Whale** and **Palm Beaches** are where the rest of Sydney comes on special days when they want to look at multimillion-dollar houses (*see also page 100*).

Some of Sydney's beaches are topless (but not all), and a few are nudist: going starkers is legal at Reef Beach near Manly, Obelisk Beach at Mosman, Lady Jane Beach at Watsons Bay and Werrong Beach in the Royal National Park.

BEACHES WHERE YOU ARE MOST LIKELY TO...

See another tourist **Bondi** and **Manly**
Spot a famous actor or director **Whale**
Be in the nude **Lady Jane**
Feel ugly **Tamarama**
Get run over by a Rolls Royce **Palm**
Get run over by a surfboard **Maroubra**
Have the surf of your life **North Narrabeen**
Drown **South Narrabeen**
Have a picnic **Bronte**
Be alone **Bungan**

prices reflect this; $145 gets you two 2½-hour lessons on successive days, with wetsuits and shower included. If you do the course, you get a board for $25 for three hours on the following weekend to practise. Situated at Balmoral Beach (flat-water), the school will call you to arrange the best times for wind conditions and tides – and won't charge if it's raining or otherwise inclement.

Fully rigged windsurfers are inexpensive to hire. **Long Reef Sailboards & Surf** (9971 1212/ 9599 2814) charges $49 a day for conventional boards and $55 a day for wave-jumpers. It also has an office at Brighton-le-Sands (Botany Bay), where boards can be hired for $20 an hour.

Surfing

Every beach of significance in Sydney has a surf lifesaving club. Most of these hire out surfboards and bodyboards for less than $10 an hour. From there, you just have to know your level. For learning to surf Palm Beach's 'Kiddies' Corner' (at the south end) is perfect. The waves are invariably small and smooth, as the name suggests. Every beach's surf has its own characteristics and, of course, conditions vary from day to day. But it is safe to say that Bondi has a good consistent break, Manly has plenty of room, Dee Why is receptive to easterly swells, Cronulla is isolated but competitive, and Maroubra is big and windy. For the top-line surfer, the greatest rewards will be found at North Narrabeen, Newport's north-end peak, Long Reef, Queenscliff (the north end of Manly),

and Wanda. Garie Beach in the Royal National Park is also well known, if distant. The **NSW Surfriders Association** (9970 7066) is always ready to offer advice. *See also page 50* **Once More Unto The Beach**.

Swimming

There are cordoned-off areas (indicated by flags) patrolled by surf lifesavers for beach swimmers. Major beaches like Bondi and Manly keep boardriders out of large sections of the beach. If you transgress, a man with a megaphone will warn you off and impound your board on failure to comply. Bodysurfing is best at Bondi, Whale, Freshwater and Bronte. If you like ocean swimming but hate waves, the best beaches are Coogee and Clovelly in the south, and Shelly in the north.

Deep-sea Fishing

Sydney is not as well known for offshore fishing as Queensland, but at certain times of the year – notably the autumn and spring migratory seasons – seriously big sporting fish, including marlin, can be caught.

The people at **Charter Boat 'Mystery Bay'** (9969 6482) claim to know all the best spots off Sydney for snapper, kingfish, flathead and ocean perch. The 17-metre (57 foot) boat leaves Mosman Bay at 6am on weekends, and cruises anywhere from one to ten kilometres outside Sydney Heads, north or south, depending on the conditions.

If you don't fancy your chances at the helm, step aboard one of the many sailing tours.

Island flings

Port Jackson, as Sydney Harbour is properly called, is sprinkled with islands. One of them, **Fort Denison** on Pinchgut Island (*see chapter* **Sightseeing**), is a historic site. Three are part of Sydney Harbour National Park (*see page 49*). However, you should note that visitor numbers for the islands listed below are limited, and they are accessible only by private boat, chartered ferry or water taxi. For a map showing their location *see page 281*.

The largest and most popular harbour island is **Shark**. It has picnic shelters, toilets and running water. As the NPWS is busily promoting its harbour islands, booking in advance is mandatory. No more than 500 people are allowed on the island at any one time.

Lying just off Darling Point, with the swanky suburbs of Rushcutters Bay and Double Bay either side, **Clarke Island** is another popular picnic spot. You can't go on the island with more than 15 people in your group, and permits are required.

Rodd Island, situated west of the Harbour Bridge in Iron Cove (between Rozelle and Drummoyne), has toilets, running water and picnic shelters. Visitors must book with the NPWS and again, numbers are strictly limited – a maximum of 100 people at any one time.

All three islands are open daily all year round, from 9am to 6pm in winter, and until 8pm in the summer. Adults pay $3, under-5s go free. For more details or to book transport to the islands visit or phone the NPWS office at Cadman's Cottage (*see page 47*). Alternatively, arrange your trip through a private ferry company such as Banks Marine, for which advance booking is essential.

Banks Marine

(9555 1222). **Fares** *ferry* $10 return; *water taxi* $25 each way for first person ($5 per additional passenger). **Times** *from Rose Bay Wharf* 10am, 11am, noon Sat, Sun; *from islands* 3pm, 4pm, 5pm Sat, Sun. **Credit** BC.

Forget the surf at Bondi; try rollerblading.

It returns at around 2.30pm. The boat takes a minimum of 18 people, maximum 23. For $50 you get bait, tackle and a licence to tell tall stories. A returnable $250 group deposit applies.

Scuba-diving

The difference between snorkelling and scuba-diving is that to snorkel, you need equipment but no licence; for scuba-diving, you must present a licence to be able to buy or hire equipment. Luckily, Sydney has masses of diving schools. Manly is especially well served, with its sheltered Fairy Bower area the ideal place to learn. The **Manly Dive Centre** (9977 4355) has four-day beginner courses for $325, including a free boat dive (normally $60). This leads to the first grade of certification. Advanced courses are available for $250.

Dive centres are not just limited to the coastal suburbs – swing a cat in Sydney, in any suburb, and you will find a dive shop. The best diving areas are Fairy Bower in Manly, Coogee, Bondi, Gordons Bay (where there is a protected marine wildlife park) and Whale Beach. Sydney is also three hours south of one of Australia's most spectacular diving spots, Fly Point at Port Stephens (*see chapter* **Trips Out of Town**). If you don't have time to go to the Great Barrier Reef, Fly Point is the next best thing.

Cycling

With its undulating terrain and unrestrained drivers, Sydney is a rough place for cyclists. Local councils have been slow to provide cycle tracks. Accordingly,

the wearing of helmets is compulsory. Nevertheless, cycling's various branches are all increasing in popularity. Central Sydney's most suitable and enjoyable place for recreational riding is Centennial Park, which is threaded with roads and tracks for bikes. **Centennial Park Cycles** at 50 Clovelly Road (9398 5027/9398 8138) hires out mountain bikes for $8 the first hour ($4 for each additional hour), and standard bikes for $6 the first hour ($4 each additional hour). If you're thinking of buying your own two-wheeled wonder, try the **Clarence Street Cyclery** (*see chapter* **Shopping & Services**).

The **Australian Cycling Federation** (9281 8688) can provide information on clubs, racing and mountain bike-riding locations, and appropriate prices for hire and purchase. **BMX NSW** (4739 4008) gives information on bicycle motocross facilities. **Bicycle NSW** (9283 5200) publishes a useful book called *Cycling Around Sydney* ($10), with details of recommended cycle routes and paths, as well other booklets aimed at improving the safety and pleasure of getting around town on two wheels. For sports store and cycle shop listings *see* chapter **Shopping & Services**.

Rollerblading (Inline Skating)

There are certain areas in Sydney where you can't walk down the street without getting bowled over by a stream of rollerbladers. The promenades of Manly and Bondi Beaches are especially popular, and Bondi has two half-pipes for inliners and skateboarders. After lobbying their local councils for many years, rollerbladers and skateboarders have had ramps and other facilities built in parks throughout Sydney's suburbs.

Centennial Park, with its flat roads and moderate traffic, is a haven for inline skaters. **Centennial Park Cycles** (*see above*) hires out blades for $15 the first hour ($5 per additional hour). Skates can also be hired from surf shops at the beaches. Inline skating does not yet require a helmet to be worn by law.

Roller-skating

It didn't quite die. Sydney has about half a dozen remaining roller-skating rinks, all of which are open to inline skaters too. **Skate Plus** (9524 0611) in Caringbah (south of Botany Bay) is open on Friday evenings, Saturdays and Sundays, plus weekdays during school holidays. Prices range from $6 to $7.50 for a 2-2½-hour session. Roller-skate hire is $1, inline skate hire $2.

Horseriding

Centennial Park is the only area in central Sydney for horseriding. **Centennial Park Horse Hire & Riding School** (9361 4513) offers individual one-hour lessons for $45, group lessons for $35 per person, and rides around the park's five-kilometre circuit for $25. Showers are provided, and booking is essential. On Sydney's outskirts, there are several paddocks and trail rides for all standards of riders. The most notable areas are Kurnell in the south, Campbelltown in the south-west, Belrose and Terry Hills in the north, and Box Hill and Kurrajong in the west. The **Sydney Equestrian Centre** (9360 7882) can provide more information.

Motorcycling

Motorcycling in Sydney is no longer limited strictly to the licensed. In recent years, a few operations have sprung up to take Harley Davidson tours around the beaches, city or surrounding countryside. *See chapter* **Sightseeing** for more information.

Fishing

Fishing is one of Sydney's biggest participation sports. Go to any beach, headland, riverbank or bridge on a summer afternoon and you will find crowds of families and lone anglers waiting for a bite. The NSW branch of the **Game Fishing Association of Australia** (9521 6444) can provide some information on catch regulations, but the best up-to-date sources for where to fish are the weekend newspapers and tackle shops. Among Sydney's most popular fishing spots are Bare Island at La Perouse, Bungan Head, Manly Beach and Coogee Beach.

Rock-climbing & Abseiling

Abseiling, rock-climbing and canyoning are possible in the environs of Sydney, with lessons and tours for beginners available as well as hire shops for the experienced. Novices can get information from **Outward Bound Australia** (9261 2200), **Wild Perspectives** (9869 0300) and the **Australian School of Mountaineering** (*see page 250*).

Experienced climbers should try asking for locations at an indoor climbing centre or at the **Paddy Pallin** equipment shop (*see chapter* **Shopping & Services**). Indoor centres include the **Edge Adventure Sports** in Castle Hill, Parramatta (9899 8228) and **Rocknaseum** in Caringbah (9524 3944). **Mountain Designs** (9267 3822) is central Sydney's only indoor climbing wall. An eight-hour beginner course here costs $200, with all gear included.

Caving

An underground activity in more ways than one, caving in Sydney can take you into subterranean zones such as sewers and disused power tunnels, through which passage is not 100 per cent approved by law. There are totally legal caves to be explored outside Sydney, however, in the Blue Mountains. For information try the **Sydney Speleological Society** in Burwood (9660 8102).

Waiting for a bite in Lavender Bay, near Milsons Point.

Architecture

Highlights of the city's urban decoration, from convict creations to bold blocks making fashion statements.

Traces of Sydney's earliest inhabitants are limited to rock carvings and middens (piles of the remains of generations of sustained shellfish eating). The nearest the city has to a contemporary building that reflects Aboriginal culture is the **Museum of Sydney** (*see chapter* **Museums & Galleries**) which contains a sculpture listing the names of all the tribes of the Sydney Basin.

Therefore Sydney's earliest buildings are relatively recent, and date back to its days as a penal colony. Governor Phillip brought little more than a collection of tents and a prefabricated two-storey house for himself, when he led the First Fleet into Sydney Cove in 1788. The city's oldest house dates from nearly 30 years later. The tiny, stone **Cadman's Cottage** (110 George Street, The Rocks), was built in 1816 to house the Governor's boat crew and is now the headquarters of the National Parks and Wildlife Service, hemmed in by the towering skyscrapers of the CBD. Walking uphill from Cadman's Cottage you'll find other buildings dating from a similar period: the bond stores, also on George Street, have now mostly been converted into shops and offices.

Nearby, you can see evidence of the toil of the early convict labour-force in the **Argyle Cut**, a road cut through the sandstone cliffs to provide access to the ridge of Miller's Point. If you go through the cut, you'll come to a row of neatly terraced white houses built in the style of Georgian England.

CONVICT CREATIONS

The architect **Francis Greenway** was deported to Botany Bay for forgery, but found a patron in the governor of the colony, the enlightened Lachlan Macquarie. After his appointment as Civil Architect, Greenway built some 40 public structures – in both Georgian and Gothic styles, reflecting the fashions of the period – a few of which survive today.

Georgian buildings by Greenway include the fine **Hyde Park Barracks** and what is today the **Mint Museum**, both located on Macquarie Street. He was also responsible for the graceful **St James' Church** nearby, which originally had arrows stamped over its copper roof to prevent the sheeting from being stolen (*see chapter* **Sightseeing** for details of all three). Greenway also built the **Macquarie Lighthouse** at South Head – originally in timber, and it was later copied in stone.

Among Greenway's surviving Gothic buildings is the grandiose **Conservatorium of Music**, much altered since its original conception as the stables for Government House.

For examples of early settlers' houses and mansions, take a look at **Vaucluse House** (*see page 34*) or the collection of houses preserved in Parramatta and now open to the public: parts of the original 1793 construction of **Elizabeth Farm** still survive, now surrounded by suburban blight (*see page 32*), and **Experiment Farm Cottage** (9 Ruse Street; 9635 5655) is a fine example of an early nineteenth-century homestead. Also in Parramatta is **Old Government House** (*see page 93*), originally a country retreat for the colony's early rulers.

NAVAL ARCHITECTURE

For its first 150 years Sydney was a maritime city: its economic and material subsistence came from the sea. Many of the buildings surrounding the harbour were built to support and protect this trade. **Fort Denison** (*see page 30*) is a remarkable sandstone fortress built to defend the harbour from the threat of invasion. Also defensive, though not military, and with an equally good setting, is the **Quarantine Station** at North Head just south of Manly, a collection of nineteenth-century buildings built to house suspected carriers of infectious diseases. Both are now run by the National Parks Authority and are open to the public.

A NEW ARISTOCRACY

The colony's growing prosperity in the nineteenth century began to be reflected in the quality of its housing. Mansions were erected by the city's leading families. Among those that have been restored and are open to the public are **Elizabeth Bay House** (*see page 32*), a local example of the Greek Revival style designed by John Verge in 1832, and completed in 1838. Also by Verge is the nearby **Tusculum Villa** on Manning Street in Potts Point, the foyer of which is sometimes open to the public.

SYDNEY YELLOWBLOCK

The distinctive feature of Sydney architecture is its sandstone. This is the same soft stone that makes up the sea cliffs that run from Coogee to North Head and which became the favourite material of public buildings within the colony.

Denton Corker Marshall's sky-scraping **Governor Phillip Tower**. *See page 58.*

Large government buildings such as the **Lands Department Building** on the corner of Loftus and Bridge Street, and the **General Post Office** on Martin Place (*see page 32*) were constructed from sandstone. The sandstone is made up of sedimentary deposits of river sand laid down in strata and compressed to form rock. The yellow colour comes from iron traces washed through the stone. When exposed to the atmosphere, the iron oxidises to give the distinctive yellow colour. If you look at some of these buildings, you can see the sedimentary layers on many of the blocks. The very best sandstone, with an even texture and colour, came from quarries in Pyrmont and Miller's Point.

FEDERATION HOUSES

Towards the end of the nineteenth century, Australian Colonists had begun to feel more confident in their identity as Australians. In the ten years before Federation finally took place in 1901, a new style of architecture reflecting this began to emerge, known as the Federation style.

New suburbs such as **Daceyville**, in the southeast, were built in a 'parks and gardens' manner. The style was characterised by single storey bungalows with timber detailing on wide verandahs, in some cases reminiscent of the architecture of colonial India. Decoration within the houses is based on native Australian flora and fauna.

BETWEEN THE WARS

Sydney has its share of art deco architecture, the best examples being in Kings Cross. Take a walk down **Macleay Street** to see large apartment blocks such as the **Macleay Regis** or **Birtley Towers** at Birtley Place. The latter – designed by Emil Soderstern in 1934 – looks something like a set from *Batman*.

The southern end of **Bondi Beach** still has several relics of the Spanish Mission style. One of the best of these was designed by E. Sarkey in 1928, and is on Sir Thomas Mitchell Road, which leads off Campbell Parade. The flats here have a long tapering courtyard set off by palm trees. Another great building in this style is the **Roxy Cinema** (69 George Street, Parramatta; 9633 5257), designed by Herbert and Wilson in 1930.

Another of the great delights of Sydney is its array of seaside architecture, particularly the old baths. Best of these is **Wylie's Baths** at Coogee Beach (*see page 84*), which was recently restored by the firm of Allen Jack & Cottier.

WALTER BURLEY GRIFFIN

A must for any keen architectural traveller is a visit to **Castlecrag**, on the north shore overlooking Middle Harbour. This was the suburb developed by American-born architect Walter Burley Griffin and his partner Marion Mahoney. They met in the offices of Frank Lloyd Wright in Chicago, and came to live in Sydney for the period between the two world wars, having won the international competition to design the national capital of **Canberra** in 1912 (*see page 253*). Both Marion and Walter were ardent theosophists, and the suburb of Castlecrag was laid out according to its strict guidelines.

POST WAR

International modernism didn't fully hit the shores of Australia until after 1945. Its most prominent advocate was Harry Seidler, who arrived in Australia after graduating from the Harvard Graduate School of Walter Gropius. In 1950 he designed a house for his mother, Rose, which won New South Wale's premier architecture award, the Sulman Prize. **Rose Seidler House** is now a museum, and open to the public (*see page 161*). Seidler was also responsible for the **MLC Centre** (*see page 135*); and if you want to see International Modernism at the kooky end of the spectrum, visit Seidler's **Capita Building**, to see how he contorted the structure to make a mockery of local building regulations and create a building with gardens 20 floors in the air (and almost nothing at ground level).

Sydney Opera House (*see page 32*), designed by Danish architect Joern Utzon, remains the best-loved building in Sydney. Although never completed to Utzon's detail (the State Government gave him the boot), the white ceramic-covered 'sails' were his, and remain a wonder. With its place opposite the Sydney Harbour Bridge and beside Circular Quay, the Opera House completes a fabulous urban tableau.

Also worth inspecting are the **State Government Offices** on Macquarie Street (at the corner of Bent Street). Designed by Ken Woolley, this is a 1960s building complete with Miesian-style bronze cladding.

Greenway's **Macquarie Lighthouse**. *Page 56.*

CONTEMPORARY ARCHITECTURE

Sydney's contemporary architecture is dominated by schlock office developments, adaptive re-use projects, and round Olympic piles built on what is rumoured to be toxic land. Much of the best work, however, is small-scale, and there is also a flourishing culture of interior design.

Easily accessible, and well worth the visit, is Pier Four at Walsh Bay. It houses the **Sydney Theatre Company** (*see page 214*) and has a restaurant at the furthest end. The project, by Vivian Fraser, won the Sulman Prize and is an excellent example of building re-use, in this case of an old timber wharf.

The **Queen Victoria Building** (*see page 33*), was a fruit market in the 1890s, but was adapted in the 1980s into a shopping centre; even if you aren't interested in the merchandise on offer, the original building has been handsomely restored.

To see a 1960s building put to re-use, visit **Overseas Passenger Terminal** at Circular Quay. Here, an existing passenger terminal – originally one third larger – has actually been reduced in size to create a new harbourside plaza, and to allow the incorporation of function centres and restaurants.

The best of the upmarket architecture in the city is found in the work of Denton Corker Marshall, in their **Governor Phillip** and **Governor Macquarie Towers**, which occupy a block side-by-side on the corner of Phillip and Bridge Streets, the latter of which houses the Museum of Sydney, on the site of the first Government House (*see page 159*). This is bold architecture making a fashion statement. While the interior spaces at street level aren't great (despite some fabulous details), the exterior areas – particularly their relationship to the nineteenth-century buildings on either side – are a knockout.

You'll have to head for the hip side of town to see the latest in urban decorations. Walk along Oxford Street, starting at College Street at the tip of Hyde Park. You'll pass through the heart of queer Sydney, with a great range of camp window dressing and some mixed retail designs. Eventually you come to the intersection of South Dowling Street, where the chic **Grand Pacific Blue Room** (*see page 111*) has made re-use of the Greek Community Centre, and the brand new **Verona** complex (*see page 188*) has been designed by the firm of Tonkin Zulaikha. It's the very epitome of 'lifestyle' architecture, where you can buy some clothes, see a film, get a massage, and eat.

If you keep going up Oxford Street, you'll reach the heartland of swinging interior design in the shape of **La Mensa** (*see page 113*). It was designed, by Luigi Rosselli, along the lines of a Mediterranean cafeteria: order a plate of ModMed delicacies and check out the fashion shops; you'll want a break after all that architectural gazing.

History

Key Events

65,000 BC
Aborigines move down from the northern areas of the continent. A tribal group known as the Dharug occupy the bushland around what is now Sydney Harbour.

29 April 1770
James Cook and Joseph Banks sail the Endeavour into Botany Bay, originally naming it Stingray Bay. Cook calls the eastern coast New South Wales.

26 January 1788
After a false start at Botany Bay, the First Fleet arrives at Sydney Cove under the command of Governor Arthur Phillip. Of 1,030 people who disembark, 548 are male convicts, 188 female. Based around the freshwater Tank Stream, the settlement is named Sydney Cove, after British Secretary of State Viscount Sydney.

1789
A smallpox epidemic annihilates the local Aborigines.

March 1804
Several hundred convicts rebel and capture the small agricultural outpost of Castle Hill on 4 March, as a prelude to an unsuccessful plan to capture all of Sydney. The rebellion is put down over the next week and the ringleaders hanged.

26 January 1808
Soldiers of the New South Wales Corps, known as the Rum Corps for their controlling interest in the lucrative colonial grog trade, overthrow Governor William Bligh (of Bounty fame). This bloodless *coup d'état* is known as the Rum Rebellion.

1810-21
Governor Lachlan Macquarie modernises and civilises the city. With convict architect Francis Greenway, he is responsible for many of the fine colonial buildings which still line Macquarie Street and parts of the centre of town.

1813
WC Wentworth, George Blaxland and William Lawson become the first Europeans to cross the Blue Mountains, gaining access to the fertile western plains beyond.

1820
The city covers roughly one square mile.

22 May 1840
The transportation of convicts to New South Wales is outlawed by the British Government.

20 July 1842
The city of Sydney is officially incorporated; the first councillors are elected in November.

1850
Sydney University is founded.

1851
The first gold-rush commences after big discoveries near Bathurst in New South Wales. The city grows at a fantastic rate as fortune-seekers pour into the colony from around the world. Sydney's population rises from 54,000 to 96,000 by 1861.

1855
A railway linking Sydney to Parramatta is completed.

1858
Men are granted the vote in New South Wales.

November 1878
Seamen strike over the use of Chinese labour on coastal shipping, crippling waterfront operations in Sydney and setting in train a movement which would eventually lead to the White Australia Policy. Fevered popular support for the unionists turns ugly as arson attacks and violent assaults on the local Chinese community increase.

January-August 1900
Bubonic plague breaks out in Sydney, centred on the squalid slum area of The Rocks. Most of the original suburb is demolished as panic sweeps through the city. Nearly 100 people die.

1 January 1901
Federation: the antipodean colonies unite to form the independent Commonwealth of Australia. Sydney dominates the state of New South Wales. Holding a third

of the State's population (nearly half a million), it is nine times larger than its nearest rival, Newcastle. This dominance increases over the next 100 years.

2 November 1902

WH Gocher scandalises the city by bathing during daylight hours at Manly Beach and is arrested but not prosecuted. Four years later, laws banning daylight beach bathing are scrapped. Also in 1902, women are granted the vote.

1908

Canberra is chosen as the site of the federal capital.

1914-1918

Some 60,000 of the 330,000 Australian troops sent overseas to fight in France, the Middle East and at Gallipoli, perish.

1922-1930

The Empire Settlement Scheme moves hundreds of thousands of working-class families from the industrial towns of Great Britain to the shores of Sydney. It is curtailed by the Great Depression and a growing realisation that the UK cannot keep exporting her population.

19 June 1931

'Bloody Friday'. A crowd of thousands watch armed police and poor tenants fight a vicious battle over an eviction notice on a house in Newtown. Such evictions and clashes are common during the Depression.

19 March 1932

The Sydney Harbour Bridge is opened but the ceremony is marred by Francis de Groot, of the far right New Guard, who charges up to the ribbon on his horse and slashes through it with a sabre in the name of God, Queen and weird proto-fascist politics.

31 May 1942

Three Japanese submarines steal into Sydney Harbour and torpedo a ferry housing Allied naval officers, killing 19 of them.

1947

The great post-war immigration boom begins as millions of British and continental European migrants are assisted in moving to Australia. Most eventually settle in Sydney or Melbourne.

c1948-1974

The Sydney Push, a loose collection of libertarian boozers and mad fornicators based around a number of inner-city pubs and the University of Sydney spawns Clive James, Germaine Greer and Robert Hughes, among others.

1960-1964

Aborigines are granted the vote and included in census figures for the first time.

1965-1972

Australia sends troops to fight in Vietnam; American GIs on leave take advantage of Kings Cross nightlife for their R&R; the peace movement picks up pace in Sydney. In 1972 the Australian Labor Party gains power for the first time in over 20 years. Under Prime Minister Gough Whitlam, troops are withdrawn from Vietnam.

November 1971

Builders' unions place work bans, known as green bans on development projects in the historic Rocks area adjacent to Circular Quay, and in Victoria Street, heralding the birth of the urban conservation movement.

20 October 1973

Sydney Opera House officially opens.

11 November 1975

Governor General Sir John Kerr, the British monarch's representative in Australia, sacks the country's Labor Government. The conservative Opposition had gained a one vote advantage in the Senate and were refusing to pass the Government's money bills. Serious movement towards an Australian republic can be traced to this day.

April 1978

The first of hundreds of thousands of Vietnamese refugees begin to enter the country. The first arrivals are illegal, stealing into Darwin on fishing boats.

24 June 1978

The first Gay & Lesbian Mardi Gras march ends in violence after police attack 1,000 marchers. By the 1990s Mardi Gras has become the largest community-based street parade in the world, watched by over half a million spectators and a handful of religious nutters, praying for rain.

1985-1986

A gang war for control of Sydney's huge prostitution, gambling and drug rackets rages across the city. Criminals gun each other down in the street. A rough, tangled series of alliances form around long-time crime bosses Lenni Macpherson and Neddy Smith. Over the next few years a web of business connections between Sydney's underworld and the police force is exposed. By 1996, with a Royal Commission tearing the police force apart, it is estimated by the city's leading newspapers that up to 80% of plain-clothes detectives are corrupt.

1988

Bicentennial celebrations draw one million people to Sydney Harbour for Australia Day. The festivities around the rest of the country sort of fade away amid Aboriginal protests and accusations that Sydney has hijacked the anniversary.

March 1989

A growing wave of public outrage at pollution on Sydney's beaches culminates at the end of the month in a rock concert on Bondi Beach to protest against the dumping of sewage in the ocean. A quarter of a million people attend, forcing the state government to address their concerns with a new deep-ocean sewage outfall.

1992

Sydney Harbour Tunnel opens.

24 September 1993

Hundreds of thousands of Sydnesiders stay up way past their bedtime to hear Juan Antonio Samaranch give the 2000 Olympics to 'Sid-er-nee'. A giant party at Circular Quay attended by over 100,000 revellers rocks on until dawn. The celebration can be heard miles away.

January 1994

On 'Black Friday' the city is ringed by fire, as bushfires blaze out of control for weeks. Thousands of homes are evacuated and 250 are destroyed. Four residents in outlying suburbs who are unable to escape the wall of flame – which moves at 70kmph (43mph) – die in their homes and backyard pools.

1996

A conservative Coalition government wins power under Prime Minister John Howard, ousting the Labor Party led by staunch republican Paul Keating.

History

The good, the bad and the ugly moments of Sydney's turbulent past, from harsh penal colony to bright light of the Pacific Age.

Aborigines

Captain Cook's final journal entry on the Aborigines he encountered displayed the navigator's charming, if naïve, belief in the myth of the noble savage. 'From what I have said of the natives of New Holland they may appear to some to be the most wretched people on Earth,' he wrote. 'But in reality they are far more happier than we Europeans.' Cook thought the Aborigines a blessed and happy race because they knew nothing of the petty material and political obsessions of white men. While fellow travellers such as naturalist Joseph Banks were bemused and even at times disturbed at the natives' lack of interest in the proffered baubles and trinkets, Cook thought them 'happy in not knowing the use of them'. He thought of Australian life, with its fine climate in which earth and sea furnished all necessities as being a 'Tranquillity which is not disturbed by the Inequality of Condition.'

Unfortunately Cook's full journal, including his observations on the Aborigines, was not published until nearly 100 years had passed. When it was finally printed in 1893, attitudes to Australia's original inhabitants had hardened into something much more violent, best evinced by the journal's editor, Captain WJL Wharton, who added his own obnoxious and completely inaccurate footnote to Cook's observations.

'The native Australians may be happy in their condition,' grumbled Wharton, 'but they are without doubt among the lowest of mankind. Confirmed cannibals, they lose no opportunity of gratifying their love of human flesh. Mothers will kill and eat their own children.' The Whartons of the time were convinced that it was the manifest, Darwinian destiny of the white man to exterminate the inferior or races, whether indirectly through the effects of introduced diseases, or directly through massacre and the policy of 'dispersal' (an early Australian version of a later twentieth-century euphemism, ethnic cleansing). The Aborigines of 1770 probably guessed at what was to come. When Cook put ashore at Botany Bay, a couple of nervous warriors confronted the landing party and tried to threaten them with spears. 'All they seem'd to want for us was to be gone,' he wrote.

Instead, within a few years of the First Fleet's arrival 18 years later, many of Sydney's Aborigines were gone, killed or driven away by the smallpox epidemic of 1789. They had no knowledge of the disease, of how to treat or contain it, and of course they had no immunity to it. The incubation period of up to two weeks, during which time the host appeared healthy while actually being highly infectious, combined with tribal rituals which encouraged the transmission of the virus to devastating effect. Painful eruptions and scabbing of the feet meant that those who survived the ravages of the illness were unable to hunt or gather food.

By the time Jacques Arago visited the settlement in 1819, as part of a French scientific expedition, the condition of the Aborigines had been thoroughly reduced and debauched. The self-interested benevolence of the first Governor, Arthur Phillip, who knew the colony's early survival was dependent on the indulgence of the locals, had been supplanted in the ruling establishment by a cruel and nearly witless contempt. (According to Robert Hughes in *The Fatal Shore*, the convicts had always regarded the blacks with scorn, having nobody but them to look down on.) Riding out to the estate of a wealthy local merchant, Arago was horrified to come upon the businessman's three daughters gathered on the front lawn to laugh and twitter at the spectacle of some drunken natives bashing each other to death. Arago writes that they were the finest and most well bred of young ladies who, like their parents, thought nothing of plying the tribesmen with enough rum to encourage a fatally violent display of armed combat for the enjoyment of their guest.

It is not surprising that, given this sort of treatment, the Aborigines effectively disappeared from most of the recorded history of Sydney. They were officially expected to die out and were not even counted in the national census or accorded the rights of Australian citizenship until the 1960s. Only 300 or so survived in remnant bands 50 years after the arrival of the First Fleet. Only the most ghostly and fleeting references to them exist in public records after the 1850s. After that time, with their traditional lifestyle completely annihilated in the Sydney region, many of the Dharug people either moved west into camps on the Cumberland Plain, or along the Hawkesbury River in the settlement's hinterland. Others, the

The first inhabitants of Sydney now account for only 0.6% of her population.

children of racially mixed marriages, were swallowed up by the dominant white population, living and working among them with little or no ties to their original tribal groups.

Ironically, as the dispossession of Sydney's native population proceeded apace, a similar phenomenon in the bush was driving increasing numbers of outback Aborigines into the city. Intense mining and agricultural developments led to the dispersal of communities and even the forced break-up of families, as white government workers separated black children from their parents. Many of the Aborigines uprooted in this period moved into the less heavily supervised city areas. Small but identifiable black enclaves existed in the waterfront working-class suburb of Balmain, and many of these people were prominent in left-wing opposition to forced evictions from the area during the Depression years. Extensive family and tribal ties drew others to the inner city, particularly the old suburb of Redfern near the sprawling Central Railway Station, with its cheap housing and ready availability of factory work. World War II accelerated this process as labour shortages increased the demand for black factory workers. By the mid-1960s, nearly 12,000 Aborigines had made Redfern their home. Another significant settlement grew up at La Perouse on the shores of Botany Bay.

Redfern was the new frontier for urban blacks, many of whom were radicalised in the Land Rights movement and counter-cultural struggles of the late 1960s and early 1970s. The suburb housed Australia's first Aboriginal medical and legal services. It acted as a focal point and magnet, drawing ever more patronage from both governments and black people. In 1973, a reforming national government signed over ownership of a large parcel of land containing 58 condemned houses to the local community. An Aboriginal Housing Commission was established to renovate the properties and rent them out for the benefit of locals.

Unfortunately, these high ideals have since soured. Much of Redfern, like most of inner-city Sydney, has been gentrified by yuppies. The Aboriginal experiment has contracted to a few mean streets of blasted rubble and abandoned rotting tenements. Nearly 100 Aboriginal families still live in the properties donated in 1973, but they form one of Australia's few true ghettos. Once again, the white majority has encircled Sydney's black population and is waiting for them to disappear or be 'dispersed'.

Even middle-class blacks, those few who exist, seem to find Redfern something of an embarrassment. The most recent scheme to move on the families and redevelop the area came from within the Aboriginal Housing Commission itself. It was defeated, or more likely deferred, by strong resident action. The chances are slim of Olympic visitors and the international media being able to witness the ugliness of the destruction wrought on Sydney's original inhabitants. When they arrive in 2000 they will probably be greeted by an antipodean showcase of an 'authentic' redeveloped Aboriginal suburb.

'All they seem'd to want for us was to be gone'.

Immigrants

The dire results of white settlement for the Aborigines of Sydney stand in stark contrast to the rewards reaped by those settlers themselves within a few decades of their arrival. Even now, 200 years later, waves of migrants seeking better lives periodically descend on the city from the world's more benighted corners. The first white settlers, of course, had as little say and probably even less enthusiasm for their arrival than the Aborigines they eventually displaced.

Sydney was nothing more than a fearful, terribly isolated, open-air prison for the first 30 years of its existence, established to relieve the pressure on England's prisons, which had become dangerously overcrowded when the War of Independence brought transportation to America to a halt. The prospect of transportation to the colony was meant to strike terror into the hearts of England's criminals. However, while the laws of eighteenth-century England were unbelievably harsh, it would be a mistake to fall for the myth of the convicts as a lot of lovable agrarian rogues and Irish freedom fighters who happened to run foul of a savage ruling class. Most historians now accept that while the convicts were drawn almost entirely from the lower tiers of society, most were also habitual felons.

The vast majority of indictments handed down on the First Fleeters were for stealing, burglary and robbery with violence. None was convicted of poaching or political offences. Not one of the 188 female prisoners was transported for prostitution, although they were widely regarded as such and

some were referred to in their papers as being an 'unfortunate girl' or a 'woman of the town'.

Conditions were harsh at Sydney Cove. Thousands of lashings with the cat-o'-nine-tails – a vicious whip with nine knotted leather strips – were doled out for the most minor of offences and it was not long before the Governor had executed a few of his charges who proved themselves unable to abide by his fierce code of discipline, a central tenet of which was to let the Aborigines go about their business unmolested.

The spectre of starvation constantly hovered over the outpost. None of the settlers were agricultural specialists and the thin soils and sparse water supply did not lend themselves to European farming methods, something which Australian farmers have taken a long time to understand. In March 1790, Judge Advocate David Collins wrote: '… the whole settlement appeared as if famine had already thinned it of half its numbers. The little society that was in the place was broken up, and every man seemed left to brood in solitary silence over the dreary prospect before him.' Watkin Tench, another of Governor Phillip's officers, called these 'days of despair' when 'the hearts of men sunk'. Disease came riding in at the shoulder of famine to torment the colony between 1791 and 1792. The death rate easily matched London's during the worst days of the Great Plague. If such an illness took hold of the city today, it would depopulate it by hundreds of thousands of people.

Starving, hopeless and racked with illness, the convicts were set to the heavy task of timber-felling and saw-milling, brick and tile-making, building, farming and labouring. They were overseen by other convicts and consequently productivity was low; the overseers having had little experience at either supervision or the work they were supposed to be controlling. Those who didn't work in the heavy labour gangs were attached as servants to the colonial officers. The women mostly carried out domestic duties, especially laundry and needlework. Also contrary to popular myth, the convicts did not wear the grey, arrowed garb of legend. Most were clothed in the standard dress of the day. In very rare cases they were required to wear a stitched letter 'R', signifying to all that they were a Rogue.

The British government soon found transportation to be horrendously expensive and sought to have the infant colony subsidise the cost. Convicts became a substitute for the coolies and slaves of other colonies. They were used for increasingly economic goals, particularly as the colony's pastoral base developed. They were still, like all slave societies, an inefficient workforce and the colony soon moved from being a dumping ground for England's criminal population to being a dumping ground for her excess, under-employed working classes. Free immigrants, most often bonded to colonial employers, their passages subsidised by the sale of land, began to arrive from the 1830s. By 1840, just before transportation to NSW ended, the convict proportion of Sydney's population had declined to 30 per cent. By 1847 it was only 3.2 per cent, and fell away to nothing with the discovery of gold and the subsequent rush of migrants from around the globe in the 1850s.

Harsh as the lives of the exiles were, many came to see Australia as their only chance for a decent existence. Life for the urban poor in London at the time was short, nasty and brutish. The vast wealth of an untended continent and a hundred-year labour shortage meant that anybody willing to work had much better opportunities in Sydney and her outlying districts. This was especially so of the Irish, who made up such a large percentage of those transported. Contemporary reports paint a grim portrait of their plight at the turn of the nineteenth century. A Royal Commission of the time found that '… in good seasons the standard of living was desperately low; their food was so scanty they stinted themselves to one spare meal in the day; their houses were wretched hovels, with the whole family sleeping on straw or on the bare ground, sometimes without even a blanket to cover them. In lean years death stalked in the wake of this poverty, peasants lay dead in ditches with their mouths all coloured green by eating nettles, docks and all things they could rend up above ground.'

Many of the convicts – when they had served out their sentences – were given land to till, simply because the authorities had nobody else on hand for the job. There was no place in the infant society for the luxury of discrimination. In this way many of those who arrived as the wretched of the earth, finished their days as respectable merchants and business people. Jacques Arago had already noted this by 1819 when he wrote of convict reformation: 'The wrongdoer is employed in useful undertakings which repay him first in land, then in reputation, and finally in preferment. The thief, forswearing his evil ways, often obtains a magistracy and becomes here the very scourge of thieves… It is as if the air of this country, although breathed by savage tribes, purifies hearts and quickens in them every noble feeling.'

Noble feelings did not extend to everyone, however. Not to the Aborigines and definitely not to the 'Asiatic races', which the young colony came to fear would overrun the entire continent given half a chance. The Chinese, who formed the largest non-European group, were the source of most concern. In 1878 a national waterfront strike, which originated in Sydney over the issue of Chinese seamen, led to riots and attacks on the city's Chinese population. It also helped draw together some of the political strands which would

'Populate or perish'. Migration to Australia, 1953.

Botany Bay, windswept site of James Cook's original landing.

be woven into the White Australia Policy of the next century. The restrictive immigration laws that gave life to this policy were the first Acts passed by the new Australian Parliament in 1901.

By 1947 the population of Australia was 99.4 per cent European, and mostly Anglo-Saxon. Those continental Europeans who did make it through the tough filter of the country's race laws were mostly of Nordic stock. All of this changed within a few years after World War II. Australia had felt itself mortally threatened by Japan during that conflict and the post-war government adopted a new policy colloquially known as 'populate or perish'. They actively sought out millions of European migrants to fill their empty continent. It was hoped that British people might make up the bulk of this population surge, but the UK had been drained by two world wars and nearly two centuries of exporting its youth to the Empire. Southern Europeans, mostly Italians and Greeks, provided the numbers. In the main they settled in the booming industrial centres of Sydney and Melbourne; so many of them, in fact, that these two Australian cities became two of the largest 'Greek' cities in the world.

The New Australians, as they were known, settled into cheap, crowded tenements and terrace houses in the inner city where they could find plentiful unskilled work in nearby factories. Unlike their American counterparts, however, the migrants did not become ghettoised. Like the poor British convicts and migrants before them, they found a young society with nearly boundless opportunities for advancement. Rather than permanently clustering in Little Italys or Little Athens, they moved quickly into the middle classes and out to the suburbs, often to be replaced in their cheap houses by the next wave of migrants, and in the late 1960s, by increasing numbers of young, Anglo professionals returning to the city centre.

The latter were drawn partly by cheap real estate and partly by the new chic of living in an ethnic neighbourhood. Eventually, of course, these 'yuppies' drove out the migrant workers who are today concentrated in Sydney's far western suburbs. The inner city, however, has not reverted to the sleepy, English monoculture of the pre-war years. Millions of migrants from over 100 different cultures have transformed Sydney into one of the most cosmopolitan cities on earth. Only New York and Tel Aviv can rival her ethnic diversity.

The most recent wave of arrivals, Vietnamese and other south-east Asians, who have come in their thousands since the end of the Indochina wars, have repeated the story of their predecessors. In fact, they have settled into Sydney even more quickly and easily than their European forbears, transforming it yet again, as their own ancient civilisation has mingled and reacted with the strange hybrid culture of the Harbour City. In suburbs like Cabramatta you can walk the main shopping strip and think yourself transported to a market square in Thailand or Vietnam. At the same time the city's boardrooms, universities and political power centres have embraced the Asian migrants they fought so long to exclude from the entire country.

Sydney by numbers

Population	**3.8 million**
Area of Greater Sydney	**2,407 sq km (4,790sq miles)**
Sydney suburbs and localities	**600 (approx)**
Average daily hours of sunshine	**6.7**
Days without sunshine per year	**23**
Annual average rainfall	**122 cm (48 in)**
Average summer temperature	**22ºC (72ºF)**
Average winter temperature	**13ºC (55ºF)**
Proportion of households where a language other than English is spoken	**23%**
Proportion of population who speak Chinese	**10%**
Proportion of population who speak Italian	**10%**
Proportion of the population who are Aborigine	**0.6%**
Estimated gay population	**400,000**
Number of overseas visitors in 1996	**2,590,000**
Sydney's share of top 20 Oz tourist attractions	**12 (incl 9 out of the top 10)**
National parks in Greater Sydney	**10**
Known prehistoric rock painting sites	**5,500**
Area occupied by Sydney Harbour (Port Jackson)	**55 sq km (21 sq miles)**
Length of Harbour foreshore	**240 km (150 miles)**
Corpses pulled from Sydney Harbour each year	**15 (average)**
Number of beaches	**70**
Swimmers rescued by lifesavers (1994-95)	**11,455**
Number of hotels, motels and guesthouses	**236**
Most common crime: theft	**2,227 per 100,000**
Least common crime: murder	**2 per 100,000**
Proportion of NSW government revenue from gambling taxes	**13%**
Number of poker machines in NSW	**74,000**
Proportion of Sydneysiders who regularly smoke marijuana	**6-7%**

Suburb of sleaze: today's Kings Cross.

The Green Bans

If you approach the red-light district of Kings Cross from the city centre, the landmark which strikes you first is a huge fortress-like wall of ugly, early-1970s apartment blocks. It dominates a third of the high ridge line on which sits a strange mix of brothels, clubs, hotels and stratospherically priced residential buildings. Former prime ministers' Victorian terraces share the streets with rent boys, tourist traps and a police station reputed to be the most corrupt in all Christendom. Victoria Street, which contains the massive and hideous apartment blocks, is paradoxically one of the most beautiful thoroughfares in the city, a tree-lined avenue of meticulously restored colonial terraces amiably roughing it with restaurants, cafés (upmarket and otherwise) and a scattering of cheap backpacker hostels.

The apartment blocks are hidden from the street by a line of restored period buildings. This was not the developer's original intent and the battle to save Victoria Street was a long, bloody, sometimes murderous affair, which pitted the government and big money interests against a makeshift alliance of local residents, tough building unions and a strange cabal of anarchists, libertarians, street philosophers and mad drinkers.

The old inner city of pubs, small offices and rough tenements was devoured by rapacious development during the 1960s. The conservative state government entered into an arrangement with the developers, which guaranteed huge profits, generous campaign donations, knighthoods all round and the systematic destruction of great swathes of low-cost housing. Although much of the inner city had fallen into poverty and disrepair, the architecture itself often dated back to the convict era.

The reaction against this rampant exploitation began in 1971 in the wealthier suburbs, surprisingly, where a coalition of middle-class matrons got together to protect a small swathe of pristine forest known as Kelly's Bush. Having exhausted all legitimate routes of protest, they prevailed on the unionists of the Builders Labourers Federation to place a black ban on the site. The BLF was a progressive union with streetsmart officials. They knew that their members were the ones being displaced by unfettered development and thus took a major role in trying to ameliorate its effects. They banned work on Kelly's Bush and, in a flash of PR brilliance, called it a green ban rather than a black ban. Residents in other parts of Sydney began to turn to the union to save their own areas from demolition.

Green ban activity reached a height in Victoria Street. A developer, Frank Theeman, was attempting to demolish the whole street, which was at that time a working-class neighbourhood. The residents were resisting, costing Theeman millions of dollars in interest payments. He hired bouncers to stand over the locals and used his contacts with the state government and corrupt police to ensure that not only were the thugs allowed to operate unmolested, they were often supported by both plain-clothed and uniformed police. Residents were bashed with crowbars, kicked and beaten, and their buildings were vandalised and subject to arson attacks, one of which killed a young woman.

The residents were supported in their struggle by a group of libertarian activists known as the Sydney Push, and then by the hard men of the BLF. The Push had been a Sydney feature for two decades. It established the city's counter-culture in the early 1950s and was a breeding ground for many of the country's foremost intellectuals. Among others, the Push launched Germaine Greer, Clive James and Robert Hughes into the world. Push activists helped organise residents and co-ordinate actions with the BLF. When many of the locals were forced out by the violence, members of the Push squatted in the abandoned buildings and patrolled the street with unionists at night, guarding against attacks. They so delayed Theeman's plans that when construction finally went ahead, it was in a much reduced form which had to take account of changed community attitudes towards development. In this way, Sydney was able to retain a good deal of its early colonial architecture. Ironically, the buildings' original inhabitants never reaped the benefits, being pushed into the outer 'burbs far more effectively by the credit lines and mortgages of the newly wealthy young urban professionals than by Frank Theeman's thugs.

Party Town

Every Christmas Day thousands of young travellers from around the world gather on the famous crescent of Bondi Beach. They form into clans, often gathering around their national flags for ease of identification. Then they begin to drink. By nightfall, the beach is a cross between Dante's *Inferno* and a toga party – a monstrous, bestial scene of debauchery. It is considered an absolute must on any traveller's Down Under itinerary, along with the world-famously riotous Gay & Lesbian Mardi Gras.

Sydney has a hard-earned reputation as a party town, beginning with the legend of the founding orgy, mythologised by Robert Hughes in *The Fatal Shore*. This bacchanalian episode is supposed to have taken place when the women of the First Fleet finally disembarked and 'made merry' with the male prisoners, rutting like pigs in the red Sydney mud while a fierce storm raged overhead. Unfortunately, no first-hand accounts survive. Arthur Bowes Smyth, the surgeon on the Lady Penrhyn whose journals record the event, stayed aboard and didn't actually see anything.

Fun was pretty thin on the ground during Sydney's days as a prison camp. What little leisure time existed was often spent bushwalking or bathing in the harbour. The only known outdoor game was the mysterious 'cross sticks', a noisy, popular and probably violent game, the rules of which have been lost in time. There was a rough brand of cruel humour. Tree-fellers thought it a great laugh to point the handles of their axes at Aborigines who, thinking they were about to be shot, would scamper away in fear. Newly arrived immigrants were another favoured target. Locals found it easy to convince them that the merest insect or snake nip was a deadly bite, for which the cure was a hot iron placed on the wound. The *Government Gazette* had to publish a warning for newcomers about believing the word of the 'artful designing knaves' who encouraged them to walk to China. Just over the hills it was, they said.

The emergence of a prosperous middle-class went hand in hand with the growth of a stultifying Victorian morality. When Russian naval officer Pavel Mukhanov visited the colony in 1863, he and his fellow officers were invited to a society dance. The Russians professed themselves entranced to be attended in the wastes of the far Pacific by such delightful female company, but it was not to be for long. After a cup of tea and two waltzes the guests all hurried off home.

The city remained an outpost of censorious virtue until the Americans appeared in World War II to teach everyone how to have a good time. They left, having laid the groundwork for the waves of migrants who followed to loosen the last of Sydney's corset strings in the 1950s and 1960s. From an uptight, completely Anglo-Saxon enclave in 1939, Sydney became – in the span of a single generation – one of the most cosmopolitan and laid-back cities in the world.

The Olympic Games, which will precede celebrations for the centenary of Australian federation at the turn of the millennium, are expected to

The city lives up to its reputation as a party town during the annual Mardi Gras celebrations.

Only New York and Tel Aviv can rival Sydney's ethnic diversity.

confirm Sydney as one of the bright and shining lights of the Pacific Age. Many of the major facilities have already been completed, on time and under budget. Controversy does surround the city's claim to be staging the first truly 'green' Olympics, however, with many of the environmentally sensitive aspects of the massive project having been cancelled or downgraded. It is also doubtful whether Sydney's already strained transport system will be able to handle the traffic generated by the estimated million extra visitors. Nevertheless, no one is in any doubt that the games and the subsequent millennium celebrations will be the biggest party the city has ever seen.

Revellers stay up way past their bedtime to celebrate winning the 2000 Olympics.

Sydney by Area

Central Sydney

The preserved heritage of the spruced-up Rocks and the slick high-rise of the CBD are worlds away from the late-night sleaze of Kings Cross and the café society of neighbouring Darlinghurst.

Sydney may look like one big city, but don't let it fool you. It's as villagey as New York or Paris. Locals refer to the eastern suburbs or the inner west as if they were separate entities – which they are.

Architecturally, topographically and socially, the northern beaches, for instance, are a world away from the west or, as Sydney newsreaders quaintly refer to it, 'our west'. They even have different micro-climates: summer in breezy Maroubra is very different to stifling Mount Druitt. The tribes of Sydney are readily recognisable once you can tell the crucial difference between the upper north shore and the lower north shore – would life be complete without it? The following area-by-area guide should help you.

Many of the places that are mentioned in this chapter appear elsewhere in the guide. *See chapters* **Sightseeing**, **Restaurants**, **Café & Bars** *and* **Shopping & Services** in particular. For maps of the city, the harbour and local transport, *see pages 278-290.*

The CBD

The Central Business District, known universally as the CBD, looms above Circular Quay; a crenellated wall of high-rise gradually becoming more low-rise in the south, until it reaches Chinatown and the late Victorian, if somewhat crumbling, splendour of Central Station. Directly across Sydney Harbour is its younger rival, the business district of North Sydney.

The CBD is actually a cluster of several precincts, many of which have more to do with history or shopping than corporate culture. The regal monikers of Sydney's asphalt and concrete alleys reflect the obsession of early Australia with its beloved England: in street names like George, Kent, Clarence and Pitt.

In the past few years, this area, which used to shut down at night and offer little in the way of entertainment, has become livelier. Old office blocks are being renovated and transformed into residential dwellings. Restaurants and clubs are moving

Windows on a world of shopping at the **Queen Victoria Building**. *See page 76.*

back from the inner city into the CBD. By the time the Olympics hit town in 2000, it should be buzzing.

Though the centre is relatively compact, it can be quite a foot-slog traipsing around the city if you want to shop, play tourist and really breathe in the atmosphere. So take advantage of the endless buses that roar up and down George, Castlereagh and Elizabeth Streets, the CityRail trains and even the dreaded Disney-like monorail, which runs across to Darling Harbour.

The Rocks & Circular Quay

The historic area of The Rocks is one of the major sightseeing attractions in Sydney. Period buildings, tourist shops, restaurants, pubs, ferries and harbourside vistas guarantee that. As a result, locals have shunned The Rocks for the past ten years, writing it off as a place filled with noisy boozers, tacky souvenirs and commercialised history, all neatly packaged for busloads of Japanese tour groups. For many, the glamorous renovated **Overseas Passenger Terminal**, the upmarket **Rockpool** restaurant and the majestic **Museum of Contemporary Art** have been the only saving graces.

Things are changing, though. In the past couple of years, some of Sydney's best restaurateurs (**Sailor's Thai Canteen**, **bel mondo** and the **Palisade**) have moved in, and the **Argyle Centre** (12-18 Argyle Street; 9247 7782) has gone upmarket, now stocking local and overseas fashion brand names.

Off the main drag, towards Walsh Bay and under the thundering Bradfield Highway that feeds the **Harbour Bridge**, you can find a quieter and gentler experience, with tiny cottages, working wharfs and a couple of pubs vying for the honour of Sydney's oldest: the **Lord Nelson** on Kent Street and the **Hero of Waterloo** on Lower Fort Street.

On the eastern side of Circular Quay is Bennelong Point and Sydney's icon, the **Opera House**. The buildings between the quay and the Opera House are being converted into residential apartments and were the scene in 1996 of an unforgettable instance of Sydney's obsession with real estate. People queued overnight to be first in and pay between $500,000 and $3 million for one of the 129 units. Scuffles broke out and by 1.30pm the next day, only 23 apartments were left. Within 24 hours, some of them had gone up for resale – with a hefty price hike.

Macquarie Street

Tree-lined Macquarie Street is the closest thing the CBD has to a boulevard. It fairly drips with old money and resonates with history: here you will find the **State Library of NSW**, **Sydney Mint Museum**, **Parliament House** and **Sydney Hospital** on one side and handsome apartment blocks on the other. This genteel part of town is where the medicos, the well-heeled and the squat-ocracy (Sydney's attempt at aristocracy) have their suites. **The Domain** (laid out in 1810) and the

Cross that Bridge when you come to it, under the thundering Bradfield Highway.

*Darling Harbour's **Chinese Garden** (see page 77) and lip-smackin' **Chinatown**.*

Royal Botanic Gardens (created in 1856) form a green and pleasant rump to the city, leading down to the water at Farm Cove.

At Macquarie Street's southern end, **Hyde Park** offers a breather from the city's concrete wind tunnels. In summer, office workers and boutique assistants flop down on the grass, while ibises pick their long-legged way around the supine bodies. Hyde Park is a fine sight at night, too, with fairy lights in the trees and the glowing eyes of possums scampering up trunks and foraging among the plants.

The **City Bowling Club** (4 College Street; 9361 6474), by St Mary's Cathedral, has one of the prettiest locations in the city. But then, so do many of the bowling clubs in Sydney – no one can work out how bowlers manage to score such prestige spots.

Martin Place

Martin Place is where crowds gathered to celebrate the end of two World Wars and where the grand **General Post Office** marks the centre of Sydney. Lunchtime concerts, fountains and lots of seating make this an outdoor mecca for office workers, though at the weekend you are more likely to be knocked over by skateboarders.

The sandstone banks and office buildings that went up during the economic boom of wool and wheat jostle with modern monstrosities and the odd elegant skyscraper, such as Chifley Square. Sydney's core of commerce is bordered by Circular Quay, King, York and Phillip Streets. Suits and secretaries, cycle couriers and company cars do the capitalist crawl from the foyers of luxury five-star hotels to the legal district around Phillip Street, where you might catch sight of a be-wigged barrister, robes flapping, scurrying across the street. The people who look like touts at the entrances of office buildings are just having a cigarette: most workplaces are non-smoking these days. You might think yourself in any major city, if it weren't for the stunning glimpses of the Harbour Bridge – and the friendly rather than frenzied bustle.

Centrepoint

Heading south, past Chifley Square, you march into the heart of consumer Sydney. The main shopping district of the CBD – roughly bounded by Hunter, Elizabeth, George and Park Streets – takes as its epicentre Sydney's two department stores, **Grace Bros** (436 George Street) and **David Jones** (corner of Elizabeth and Market Streets). Nearby are the stately **Queen Victoria Building** and **Sydney Town Hall**. Pitt Street Mall has lots of buskers and never enough seats. At Christmas, a quartet of hopeful youngsters plays fine Vivaldi on the corner of George and Market Streets. **Sydney Tower** stands tallest at Centrepoint between Pitt Street Mall and Castlereagh Street. Watch out for the hourly mechanical clock displays in the mall.

Town Hall

The nondescript area between the Town Hall and Chinatown is dominated by the multiplex cinemas on George Street that process hordes of office workers and suburbanites in town to catch a movie and inhale some popcorn. **Planet Hollywood** (600 George Street; 9267 7827) recently set up shop opposite, with attendant hoopla and an orgy of stars whose last good films were in the 1980s. The tone in the area can be raucous, with Doc Martens, ferals and cool dudes coming to see a gig at Sydney's best venue, the **Metro**, or watch a film at the arthouse **Dendy**. Look a little harder and you'll find comic shops, record stores, discount houses and eateries in the area. And at 'Little Spain', the section of Liverpool Street between George and Sussex, you can find excellent tapas.

Chinatown & Haymarket

You can't miss the Asian influence in Sydney. It has been estimated that if the current rate of immigration continues, one Sydneysider in five will be all or part Asian by the year 2000.

The Chinese have been a presence in Sydney since the First Fleet landed in 1788: two of the ships' cooks were said to be Chinese. By 1891, the

Chinese population had reached 14,000, which dwindled to 4,000 as the White Australia Policy peaked in the 1950s. These days the Chinese community in NSW is 200,000 strong and most of them live in the state capital.

Vietnamese, including many of Chinese descent, arrived by the boatload in the late 1970s and started to boost the oriental numbers. China's 1989 Tiananmen Square disgrace was, in a perverse way, Australia's gain. Dissident students sought asylum in the antipodean haven, adding their northern culture to the predominantly Cantonese one.

The years leading up to China's takeover of Hong Kong have brought Hong Kong Chinese and their dollars to Sydney, buying up real estate and starting new businesses; there are four Chinese daily newspapers.

When you hit Chinatown, the vitality and energy of the Chinese community is obvious. Not that Sino-Sydneysiders live in a ghetto: there are established communities in Strathfield, Willoughby and Ashfield as well. But Chinatown is at the hub of it all. Once confined to Dixon Street, a somewhat tacky mall created in the early 1980s, Chinatown is expanding and changing at a phenomenal rate. It extends over Hay Street, down Thomas and Ultimo Streets, and across George Street.

Around the gates of Chinatown in Dixon Street, soil, sand and rock from Guangdong Province has

been buried. For the Chinese, it symbolises that Australia is their home and they can be buried there. Sussex Street has taken over from Dixon Street as the main strip. This brightly lit section, from Goulburn Street to Hay Street (where Paddy's Market returned a few years ago to the site of Sydney's original produce market) is filled with bustling activity from early morning to late at night. Grannies do their grocery shopping; plump businessmen wander around with mobile phones; families dress up for weekend lunch. Restaurants, shops, supermarkets and Chinese-language cinemas – and some well hidden gambling places – are all here. This is one of the few places in Sydney where you can get a meal and a drink at 2am.

In daylight hours, chic shops sell Agnès B and Katharine Hamnett watches, Versace and Romeo Gigli perfumes, Jean Paul Gaultier bags, and a range of bewilderingly hip gear that could only be worn by trendy, svelte Chinese girls with porcelain skin.

Daniel Chen, who left Shanghai when the Japanese marched in, and came to Australia with $5 in his pocket, is said to be the second richest Chinese Australian (property developer Bernard Chan is worth $100 million). He owns the **Burlington Centre Supermarket** on Thomas Street which stocks 12,000 assorted items, from varying grades of rice to pak choy, fresh abalone, pork lung and dried fish. Turnover is $10 million a year, contributing to Chen's business fortune of $65 million.

The days of wall-to-wall sweet and sour pork and chow mein are far behind. Tiny diners serve Peking-style dumplings, while others specialise in hand-made noodles, barbecued duck or seafood. Grand Hong Kong-style dining rooms with over-the-top chandeliers are always packed with Chinese and Anglos choosing delicacies from yum cha trolleys.

Down at the Hay Street end of Dixon Street is one of the best tea shops in Sydney, in the **Live Crafts Centre** (84 Dixon Street; 9281 2828), selling fine green teas from Taiwan and mainland China; don't be side-tracked by the bewildering array of trinkets and aquariums.

Darling Harbour, Pyrmont & Ultimo

The reclaimed waterfront of Darling Harbour boasts some fabulous modern architecture, courtesy of Phillip Cox, and a huge retail complex, courtesy of global greed. Thousands of people spend their time strolling by the water and wandering through the ersatz marketplace. So many attractions are down here – **Sydney Casino**, the **Australian National Maritime Museum**, the **IMAX Cinema**, **Sydney Aquarium**, the **Chinese Garden** and **Sydney Entertainment Centre** – that it's easy to overlook the most basic one: the view from the Pyrmont side of Darling Harbour of the western cityscape is one of the best in Sydney. And it's free.

Harbour hub at **Circular Quay**. *See page 75.*

Reached by the Pyrmont Bridge, which is now closed to traffic, Pyrmont used to be an industrial warehouse area for the docks. The handsome **Goldsbrough Mort** building is still there. The headland, which was once a combination of working-class cottages, refineries, quarries and engineering works, is rapidly turning into apartment buildings and office blocks as the city spreads ever westwards.

The biggest draw, though, is **Sydney Fish Markets**, one of the best in the world, perhaps second only to Tokyo's Tsukiji. From the auction rooms here, premium-grade tuna goes to Japan and ordinary retail punters can buy off-the-boat-fresh seafood from a dozen or more outlets. These fish shops are owned by a fraternity that is essentially Greek or Italian, but they all seem to have smiling Vietnamese girls behind their huge ice-loaded counters. Browse among the enticing mounds of salmon, snapper, John Dory and yabbies; or feel torn between hunger and sympathy, peering into lobster-crammed tanks. You can shop for fruit, veg and deli items here, or just pick up half a dozen Sydney rock oysters and find a sunny wharfside seat to picnic at.

Ultimo – south of Pyrmont and west of Chinatown – has evolved into a strange meeting place of media, academia and museum life. It used to be notorious for having some of Sydney's most squalid housing, and was later site of the municipal markets. Now Ultimo is home to the sprawling **University of Technology**, built up from the old Technical High School in Harris Street; the headquarters of the **Australian Broadcasting Corporation**; and the masterfully converted **Powerhouse Museum**.

East Sydney

Stand with your back to Hyde Park at Whitlam Square facing down Oxford Street to Taylor Square (neither of which are really squares, merely crossroads) and you're on the edge of the CBD and the inner city: a kind of a Burroughsian interzone, neither one thing nor the other, just the down and dirty entrance to that boulevard of broken stilettos, Oxford Street. All inner Sydney's tribes – Pierced, Pinkheads (tragic dye jobs), Proto-hippies and DINKs – seem to scurry through the interzone: it's no place for a saunter.

They're on their way to or from the mainly Victorian terraces crammed together on either side of this main drag which leads to the inner-city suburbs of East Sydney, Surry Hills, Darlinghurst and Kings Cross. But this first fragment of Oxford Street is also a curious kind of fashion centre, boasting a varied string of outlets: the celebrated **Cash Palace** (42 Oxford Street), bespoke designers of flash frocks, theatrical costumes and costume jewellery for everyone from debutantes to drag queens; the extravagant art deco shopfront of **Zink & Sons Tailors** (56 Oxford Street), proffering splendid suitings for the (few remaining) gentlemen of the eastern suburbs; **Nelson Leong**, one of the country's cleverest chicouturiers (72 Oxford Street); **Pandarra Country & Western**

Kings Cross – *hell on earth or pervert's paradise? See page 80.*

(96 Oxford Street) selling everything for the urban boot-scooter; and on the corner of Oxford and Crown Streets, **Gowing Brothers**, a branch of Sydney's Aussiest retail department store.

If a little tatty and windswept by day, the inter-zone by night thumps and pumps with music and light from a fistful of clubs catering to all possible gender fusions, whose simpler hungers are assuaged by any number of fast fooderies, none worthy of being singled out – although one pub should be: the **Burdekin Hotel** at 2 Oxford Street is the pick of the watering holes on this stretch.

Surry Hills & Redfern

Crown Street is the first major thororoughfare to cross Oxford Street and runs south to the ever so slightly tumbledown terraces of Surry Hills which, while long overshadowed by smarter Pad-dington to the east, is coming out of the shadows with some clever development of its own. The first couple of blocks above Oxford Street, once home to rag trade factories (most have now moved down the hill towards Central Station), have their own peculiar buzz: a quick turnover of tiny de-signer frock retailers, hole-in-the-wall cafés and hairdressers caters to the Pierced, the Pinkheads and the occasional stretch-riding slumming celeb – is that Naomi sliding out of a limo and into **Third Millenium** (328 Crown Street)? Folk round here tend to come out to play later in the day, especially on a Saturday.

There's movement further down Crown, where **The Dolphin** has been smartly spruced up (412 Crown Street; 9331 4800), as has the Clock Hotel (468 Crown Street; 9331 6364). Café honcho Bill Granger has moved in with **bills 2** (355 Crown Street) and more restaurants, cafés and retailers are sure to follow. Curiosities worth noting include the south-west American restaurants, **Coyote's** (294 Crown Street; 9361 4935) and **Yipiyiyo** (290 Crown Street; 9332 3114), sitting cheek by jowl, and the tranquil and fragrant Thai curio shop **Mrs Red & Sons** at number 427 (9310 4860).

Just around the corner you'll find one of the inner city's best kept secrets, the tiny **Passion de Fruit Cafe** (633 Bourke Street; 9690 1894), a haven for many of Sydney's professional food mavens. And we can't leave this patch without pointing out its worst kept secret, **Touch of Class** (377 Riley Street), the city's most lavish bordello.

Will the new display of chic in Surry Hills dis-place the area's current much-pierced and rain-bow-headed occupants? It's more than likely that they'll be gentrified out of their low-rent terraces; previously funky Paddington to the east – where some terraces change hands for upwards of $1 mil-lion – is now too chichi for words.

Surry Hills peters out west at Central Station (just beyond the rag trade centre on and around

Woolloomooloo, *Sydney's oldest suburb (p81).*

Foveaux Street) and south at Cleveland Street, the border with **Redfern**. This formerly down-at-heel area is right in the middle of intensive reinvention. Property developers are coming up with fashion-able titles such as Moore Park East for their sprawl-ing town house and apartment projects, as pockets of Redfern hurtle upmarket at a furious rate. Meanwhile, the traditional population of the area, the working-class labourers, recent immigrants and Aborigines, are finding themselves increas-ingly priced out, or squeezed into smaller precincts.

Darlinghurst

The next stop along Oxford Street is Taylor Square and Gilligan's Island, a much decorated and desecrated pedestrian haven and inner-city landmark whose constantly changing public sculpture, rapidly dying palm trees and popula-tion of brown-paper-bag-swiggers are a source of baffling amusement to locals. **Taylor Square**, like a scruffy Piccadilly Circus, is one of those places where if you hang out long enough, you'll see the whole of the inner city pass by – from crims making guest appearances at the courts over the road to chic gallery owners from Paddo and Woollahra scoffing pasta or tandoori in one of the wall-to-wall cafés and trats on the strip between Flinders and South Dowling Streets.

The romantically-named **Rushcutters Bay**. *See page 81.*

Landmarks worth noting just off Taylor Square include **Kinsela's** (383 Bourke Street), originally a funeral parlour, then a restaurant and theatre, now a useful bar and live music venue; the **Athenaikon Continental Cake Shop** (409 Bourke Street; 9360 4878) for the best baklava and olive bread in town; and **The Bagel House** (7 Flinders Street; 9360 7892) for coffee and bagels every which way. A little way along Darlinghurst Road, at the corner of Burton Street, is the **Jewish Museum**.

On the north side of Oxford Street, Darlinghurst Road begins its downhill run to the Cross. Now you enter Cockroach territory, Sydneyspeak for the predominant black-turtle-necked tribe in Darlinghurst and East Sydney. Take the time to wander through the old **Darlinghurst Gaol** – now East Sydney Institute of Technology, site of one of the city's best art schools (Forbes Street; 9339 8666) – a magnificent collection of sandstone buildings dating from the 1820s. Drop in at the library (in the old chapel) and they'll give you a handout on the gaol's history. A little imagination will take you back to the days when some 79 people were hanged here, including Edmund Farrell who attempted to murder the Prince of Wales (Queen Victoria's son) in the 1880s. The gaol was built on this site because it was a conspicuous hill, and would remind all that Sydney was a penal colony.

Back then, instead of negotiating the hustling hordes and screeching traffic of Darlinghurst Road, you'd have reached the Cross by scrambling through scrub and sand drifts, past farms and sandstone quarries, before finally clambering down wooden ladders to Woolloomooloo Bay. Along the Darlinghurst ridge, where the Kingsgate Hotel stands at the top of William Street, is where the city's important windmills were erected. Walk past on a blustery August day, and you'll see why.

Kings Cross

Kings Cross (the cross is formed by Darlinghust Road intersecting Victoria Street) is Soho's little sister, with a thick scab of fairly standard sleaze (Porky's Nitespot, The Love Machine, The Kinky Adult Shop *ad nauseam*) concentrated along The Strip, that stretch of Darlinghurst Road between William Street and the **El Alamein Fountain**. This area has long been the vice quarter of Sydney – Darlinghurst has been variously known as Razorhurst, Gunhurst and Dopehurst – and that reputation has stuck, right through to recent revelations of rampant police corruption.

Today's Cross, a long way from the hobohemia of the 1920s and 1930s, is a fading glittery hangover from the R&R (Rest & Recreation) days of the Vietnam War, when hordes of US soldiers descended with fistfuls of dollars and a desire to party the horrors of that dirty war out of their consciousness. Their appetites tended towards the carnal, and today's dreary parade of seedy strip clubs and massage parlours – frequented mostly by suburbanites and out-of-towners – is evidence of the way they got their kicks. It's ripe for another big change.

One of the first signs you see on entering the Cross, on the Hotel Capital (111 Darlinghurst Road), is a suggestive one: SAUNA, it leers. But honest, it really is just that. This traditional Korean bathhouse (called the **Relaxation Centre**) – with gender-segregated bathing, skin scrubs, body massages, wet and dry saunas and a dining area with great Korean soups – may be the only straight sauna joint on the Cross.

The Strip offers a curious mixture of swivel-necked tourists clutching their airline bags against pickpockets; the flotsam and jetsam of city lowlife who hang around the tourist traps, working their various scams; and the ordinary folk from various social levels who've always lived in the Cross – still unique in Sydney for hosting a combination of residential and commercial life which is much more common in the great European cities.

Once on The Strip, we suggest you resist the blandishments of touts as well as those of more direct purveyors of the pleasures of the flesh, stopping only to check the menu in the window of the **Astoria Restaurant** (7 Darlinghurst Road; 9358 6327) for a glimpse of how Sydneysiders used to eat. Steamed leg of chicken with mornay sauce is still $5 and wine trifle with ice cream $1.40 on the plates that time forgot. You might also fancy a cool drink at the **Bourbon & Beefsteak Bar**, another – far more successful – legacy of R&R days, and *Spectator* columnist Jeffrey Bernard's favourite Sydney hangout. By night the B&B attracts a curious mix of gawking tourists and workers in the local industries. At breakfast time it offers some of the best hash browns outside LA.

Potts Point & Woolloomooloo

By contrast, Macleay Street, with its columns of cool plane trees, is made for slow strolling and offers genuine architectural and culinary pleasures. Tall, impregnable apartment buildings like the neo-gothic **Franconia** (123 Macleay Street) offer a glimpse of the grandeur of the old Cross. Orwell Street, running west off Macleay, houses one of Sydney's finest art deco buildings, the old Minerva movie and live performance theatre, now called the **Metro** and, fittingly, home to Kennedy Miller Productions who brought the world *Mad Max* and *Babe*. Across the road at 39 Orwell Street is **The Crocodile Factory**, purveyor of Sydney's tackiest souvenirs: everything from kangaroo-scrotum purses to crocodile-paw backscratchers.

In this quarter you'll find some of Sydney's finest eateries (**Morans, Paramount, Cicada**, the **Pig & Olive**) along with a good selection of coffee shops for watching the world go by. And the world that goes by here is a far cry from the desperate world of The Strip – you could be on another planet, populated by chic Sydneysiders and hordes of sleek Japanese tourists pouring into and out of the **Landmark Hotel** (81 Macleay Street; 9368 3000).

Macleay Street runs into Wylde which runs out of puff at the **Garden Island Naval Base** on Woolloomooloo Bay, where you are greeted by the surreal sight of the Royal Australian Navy's fleet moored by the side of the road. Skirting the bay round to the **Royal Botanic Gardens** takes you past the **Art Gallery of New South Wales**.

The northern end of Victoria Street, parallel to Macleay, retains a handful of the grand Victorian terraces that once made it one of Sydney's most elegant streets. Sydney's lucky to have even these – at one stage, they were to be mostly demolished for high-rise developments. Victoria Street backs on to a cliff that drops down to Sydney's oldest suburb, Woolloomooloo, which stands partly on land filled with scuttled square riggers, and is now very well redesigned as a housing estate using many of the original buildings. You can walk down from Victoria Street via Horderns or Butlers Stairs. Alternatively, gaze down from the restaurant **Mezzaluna**, which offers a spectacular view over Woolloomooloo Bay to the city skyline.

Elizabeth Bay & Rushcutters Bay

Elizabeth Bay begins beyond **Fitzroy Gardens** at the southern end of Macleay Street. Here, instead of backpackers and rubberneckers, there are uncrowded streets lined with an attractive collection of apartments, dating from the 1930s to the present day, tumbling down to the harbour. Worth seeking out are **Elizabeth Bay House** and **Boomerang** (corner of Ithaca Road and Billyard Avenue), a 1930s Alhambresque fantasy which has been home to some of Sydney's highest fliers – and fastest fallers. On the edge of Elizabeth Bay is one of those neglected little parks that dot the harbourside like oases.

The next inlet east is the romantically named Rushcutters Bay, so called for the convicts who really did cut rushes here: two of them were the first Europeans to be killed by the local Aboriginal tribe, in May of 1778. Now there is a large and tranquil park lined by huge Moreton Bay figs. The bay is home to the **Cruising Yacht Club** (New Beach Road), whose marinas bristling with masts launch into a frenzy of activity every January when the club is the starting point for the bluewater classic Sydney to Hobart Yacht Race.

If you feel in need of a great cup of coffee, head back towards Oxford Street. On the southern end of Victoria Street is Caffeine Alley, where the Cockroaches take their favourite (legal) drug. From early morning to late afternoon (it's curiously quiet at night), resting writers, actors and film-makers, property developers and architects, psychiatrists and high-ranking public servants sip lattes and network in the cafés of their choice. If you're skinny and savvy enough, take yours at **Parmalat**, next door to the more famous **Bar Coluzzi**.

Eastern Suburbs

Gay chic, park life, fab shops and baywatching – in the east, life's a beach and then you buy.

For its habitués, Sydney *is* the eastern suburbs. Those who start out in the east tend to shift around within the area for the rest of their lives, and can't imagine why anyone would voluntarily live anywhere else.

But there is some method in their madness. Lifestyle is an article of faith in the east, and within the boundaries of middle-class affluence, it is a very diverse area. Pockets of serious wealth like Vaucluse and Bellevue Hill coexist with trendier Paddington ('Paddo') and the raffish charms of Bondi. Gay meets straight, parks abound despite the population density, and you are never more than a few minutes from a decent cup of coffee, a cool drink or some sort of waterside view.

Darlinghurst to Paddington

Taylor Square is the heart of gay Sydney. The epicentre of what is referred to, usually affectionately, as 'the ghetto', it marks the last leg of the annual Gay & Lesbian Mardi Gras and the edge of Darlinghurst (*see also page 79*). Going

east from Taylor Square, Oxford Street gets a little straighter, but no less fashionable, block-by-block to Centennial Park (buses 378, 380 and 382 go along the street). Bookstores, cinemas and clothes shops line the way with numerous cafés, pubs and wine bars, each filled with a slightly different crowd.

The Albury, which sits on the corner of Barcom Avenue, is a local landmark with two decades under its belt as a celebrated gay venue. Still the first home of Sydney drag, the place is like an outtake from *The Adventures of Priscilla Queen of the Desert* most nights.

Across the road is one of Sydney's original arthouse cinemas, the **Academy Twin**, and its newest competition, the stylish **Verona**, which combines cinema-going with a fashionable café and bar, shops and yoga studio. **Berkelouw Books** next door, **Ariel** across the road and **The Book Shop** back towards Taylor Square, provide plenty of good book-browsing opportunities.

Victoria Barracks, further along Oxford Street, predates most of Paddington and is more

*Every Saturday, **Paddington Market** is piled high with crafty goods. See page 83.*

than a little at odds with the area's current cosmopolitan atmosphere. Constructed with convict labour in the 1840s, and designed by Lieutenant Colonel George Barney, the complex was built to house soldiers and their officers.

From the Barracks to Centennial Park, Paddington is a relentlessly trendy mix of antique and homeware shops, boutiques, cafés, bars and pubs. The crowded **Paddington Market**, on the corner of Oxford and Newcombe Streets, is the highlight of the area every Saturday. Here you'll find a hotchpotch of local crafts, good cheap clothing (a number of Sydney designers started out here), fortune-tellers, masseurs and just about every other money-spinning wheeze you can think of.

Now one of Sydney's chicest suburbs, Paddo was regarded in previous decades as bohemian at best, and at worst a slum. Most of its celebrated terraces were built in the 1870s and 1880s, and are now the gentrified homes of upper-echelon yuppies. Head down Heeley Street (it runs north, off Oxford Street) to **Five Ways**, and you'll find a tiny hub of activity which epitomises the area – the surrounding leafy streets dotted with shops, pubs and galleries, and the Victorian houses with fancy wrought-iron balconies. Liverpool Street and Glenmore Road both have rows of the famous terraces, with Aussie motifs like fish ferns and waratahs worked into their cast-iron balconies.

Centennial Park & Moore Park

Where Oxford Street heads off towards Bondi Junction, you hit **Centennial Park**. The most popular breathing space and picnic spot in the eastern suburbs, this park is a 195-ha (482-acre) oasis of fields, artificial lakes, bridle paths and cycle tracks. Reaching all the way down to Randwick Racecourse and across to Queens Park, it was created in the 1880s on the site of the Lachlan Swamps as part of the state celebrations marking the centenary of the landing of the First Fleet.

The Royal Agricultural Society Showground, on the west side of Centennial Park (Cook Road), used to be the site of the annual **Sydney Royal Easter Show** in April, but is to be redeveloped by Fox Studios into a film studio and entertainment complex. Next to the showground, and approached from Moore Park Road, the huge white doughnuts that form **Sydney Football Stadium** and **Sydney Cricket Ground** light up the skyline for miles around at night.

Woollahra to Bondi Junction

Leading off Oxford Street, opposite the main Centennial Park gates, Queen Street is the closest thing in Sydney to an old-fashioned English high street outside the lower north shore. This 'village' of expensive antique shops, galleries and boutiques marks

Making a splash at **Wylie's Baths**. *Page 84.*

the beginning of the salubrious suburb of Woollahra. A walk from the end of Queen Street via Greycairn Place and Attunga Street to **Cooper Park** – which runs east into Bellevue Hill – is a pleasure in the jacaranda season (late November-December) when the area is awash with the vivid purple blossoms. From the eastern end of Cooper Park cross Victoria Road to find the small gem, **Bellevue Park**, which has knockout views down to the harbour.

The eastern suburbs, from Woollahra to Double Bay, Bellevue Hill, Bondi Junction and Bondi, are home to Sydney's Jewish community. On Friday evenings and Saturday mornings, the streets are alive with the faithful walking to and from the various synagogues dotted throughout the area, including the liberal **Temple Emanuel** (7 Ocean Street, Woollahra) and the **Central Synagogue** (15 Bon Accord Avenue, Bondi Junction).

Darling Point & Double Bay

Bordered by small but perfect Rushcutters Bay Park to the west and Edgecliff to the south, Darling Point is another of Sydney's most exclusive suburbs, commanding spectacular harbour views – the best of which can be sampled free from **McKell Park** at the tail end of Darling Point Road. Further up the street is **St Mark's** (53 Darling Point Road), a beautiful early Edmund Blacket church first consecrated in 1864 and still *de rigueur* for society weddings, including Elton John's ill-fated nuptials.

The next suburb east is Double Bay, Sydney's luxury shopping precinct also known as 'Double Pay'. Migration after World War II turned 'The Bay' into a sophisticated European village of restaurants, cafés, delicatessens and ritzy boutiques. Once an oasis in a city where coffee came in cans, escalating rental rates have gradually turned Double Bay into Sydney's answer to Rodeo Drive. Even if you don't pack a wad of sky's-the-limit plastic, it remains a good place to browse and grab a coffee. Highlights include **Lesley McKay's** stylish bookshop at 346 New South Head Road, the **Village Double Bay Twin Cinemas** opposite, antique and clothes shops, and the pleasant, harbourside **Steyne Park**.

Point Piper to Watsons Bay

These picturesque waterside suburbs are a blend of serious new and ageing money, with a beautiful foreshore that is open to everyone and easily enjoyed on the cheap. By ferry from Circular Quay, you can take in Darling Point, Double Bay, Rose Bay and Watsons Bay from the water, though the boat only stops at the Quay, Rose Bay and Watsons Bay, and routes change at the weekend.

From Double Bay, small harbour beaches dot the shorefront up to Point Piper, including **Redleaf Pool** and **Seven Shillings Beach**. Point Piper is all high-walled mansions, but you can enjoy the panoramic views that cost millions from tiny **Duff Reserve**: reached by very steep steps to the harbour near the end of Wolseley Road, it's a good picnic spot if you manage to beat the crowds there.

All that recommends Rose Bay are the seaplanes that stop at Lyne Park (for scenic flights *see chapter* **Sightseeing**) and **Woollahra Golf Course** (O'Sullivan Road; 9327 1943) which, unlike the very toffy **Royal Sydney Golf Course** next door, is open to the general golf-playing public.

The streets from Rose Bay to **Vaucluse** feature yet more millionaires' mansions, but do not despair, because the hidden jewels of the Hermitage Foreshore Reserve and **Sydney Harbour National Park**, which run around the peninsula, come as compensation. On the west side, a walking track starts at Bayview Hill Road, below the imposing stone edifice of **Rose Bay Convent**, and offers fab views of the Harbour Bridge as well as picnic spots aplenty and glimpses of the lifestyles of the rich and vulgar.

The walk emerges at restful **Nielsen Park** off Vaucluse Road, where there is an enclosed bay (**Shark Beach**) that is particularly beautiful on a summer evening, as well as a popular restaurant (*see chapter* **Restaurants**). Further along, on Wentworth Road, the estate that became **Vaucluse House** was bought by the explorer and politician William Charles Wentworth in 1827. Next to Vaucluse Road, **Parsley Bay** is a lesser-known but no less beautiful picnic and swimming spot.

Watsons Bay was Australia's first fishing village, according to legend. Now largely the province of the Doyles seafood chain, it has stunning views back across the harbour to the city and retains vestiges of its old charm, including some original weather-board houses and terraces. These are best seen by walking around from Watsons Bay Central Wharf to the First Fleet landing spot at Green Point, and on to Camp Cove, Lady Bay, South Head and the Hornby Lighthouse. The naval chapel in the military reserve on the opposite side of the peninsular looks straight out across the Tasman Sea and is open to the public on weekends.

The bite in the sheer cliffs that give **The Gap** its name has long been a favoured Sydney suicide spot. The Gap Park is the start of a spectacular cliff walk that runs south back into Vaucluse. Along the way, hidden high above the approach to Watsons Bay at the fork of the Old South Head Road, is another fine Edmund Blacket church, **St Peter's** (2 New South Head Road), which houses Australia's oldest pipe organ, an instrument dating from 1796, and once lent to the exiled Napoleon.

Bondi to Coogee

Bondi Junction is the major bus and rail link in the eastern suburbs, and its biggest shopping mall. Beyond it, **Bondi Beach** is the closest thing most Sydneysiders have to a sacred site. In recent years the faded 1920s charm of the suburb has been resurrected into a post-Paddo, post-Darlo trendiness. The rash of good cafés lining the main thoroughfare of Campbell Parade are usually packed at the weekend. Among them, the **Sports Bar(d)** and **Sean's Panaroma** are almost as much Bondi these days as the famous beach itself. Summer nights bring in punters by the carload, particularly around Christmas and on New Year's Eve, when Bondi is best given a wide berth.

Heading south from **Bondi Baths** on Notts Avenue (home of the famous all-weather Bondi Icebergs), there is a stunning walk along the cliffs to **Tamarama** and **Bronte Beach**, and on to Waverley Cemetery. Past the cemetery, the coastal walk continues on to Clovelly and then to **Coogee Beach**, historic Wylie's Baths and the deservedly popular Women's Pool. Bronte, Clovelly and Coogee have enjoyed a similar renaissance to that of Bondi (though to a lesser degree), resulting in a proliferation of cafés and restaurants, and corresponding escalation in property prices. Not surprisingly, the Bondi-Coogee walk is a popular one, particularly at weekends, so go during the week if you can.

Randwick & Kensington

Randwick has long been synonymous with the **racecourse** on Alison Road that borders Centennial Park. The **University of NSW** campus lies south of it, while the National Institute of Dramatic Art across the road (215 Anzac Parade; 9697 7600) is the Alma Mater of such stars as Judy Davis and Mel Gibson, and offers cheap tickets to student productions. Anzac Parade is one long highway, but it does have some highlights, including one of Sydney's most eccentric eateries, the **Grotta Capri Seafood Restaurant** (99 Anzac Parade; 9662 7111), where the food is fine and the decor wild (there's a huge cement grotto with fairy lights and glass rock pools set into the floor).

Beach to its own: Vaucluse's tranquil Shark Bay (above) and surfswept Bondi (below).

Inner West

Thespians like it in Birchgrove, therapists head for wholesome Glebe, while Leichhardt is Sydney's Little Italy.

Balmain, Birchgrove & Rozelle

Snuggled in the inner west's harbour, a six-minute ferry ride from Circular Quay (Wharf 5 to Thames Street, Darling Street or Elliott Street) or a 20-minute bus jaunt from the city centre, Balmain melds the traditional working class, the bourgeois renovator and discreetly, well-heeled residents.

Screen star Judy Davis and playwright David Williamson are among the thespians who live in exclusive Birchgrove – the tiny, tranquil suburb that skirts Snails Bay – with its own neat, white picket-fenced oval (location for Russell Crowe's movie *The Sum of Us*, and where cricketing legend Donald Bradman once played). The oval was originally a giant mud flat in the late 1880s, which the residents filled in over a period of ten years to create today's quaint recreational site. Prime estate here is the narrow and vehicle-riddled **Louisa Road**, lined with multimillion dollar townhouses, Victorian Italianate villas and wooden 'boatshed' homes leading down to the water.

Ironically, this finger of land was originally an abattoir of sorts, where Aborigines used to corner and kill kangaroos. Officially, the peninsula's name was changed from Long Nose Point to Yurulbin Point in July 1994 to reflect its Aboriginal heritage, but most people still refer to it by its former name.

Birchgrove also boasts the ramshackle **Sir William Wallace Hotel** (31 Cameron Street; 9555 8570), which features a large autographed poster of a kilted Mel Gibson in *Braveheart* mode. Locals claim that Gibson, who once lived in the area as an up-and-coming actor, was first inspired by the legendary Scot while drinking at its bar. Thursday night at the Wallace is '$5 roast night', when huge plates of lamb or beef smothered with vegetables are served up at the bar. On Sundays, the owners trundle their barbecue out into the street to cook lunch.

As Balmain was settled by burly boatbuilders and ships' captains in the late 1830s, pubs have always been a big draw. Yuppies seek out the **London Hotel** (234 Darling Street; 9555 1377) and the **Exchange Hotel** (corner of Beattie and Mullens Streets; 9810 1171), pool sharks the **Balmain Town Hall Hotel** (366 Darling Street; 9555 1894), serious punters the Balmain Leagues Club (*see p87*) and the **Sackville Hotel** (599 Darling Street; 9555 7555), musos the **Cat & Fiddle** (456 Darling Street; 9810 7931) and families the **Royal Oak** (36 College Street; 9810 2311) or **Dick's Hotel** (89 Beattie Street; 9818 2828). For years, legendary swimmer Dawn Fraser owned the **Riverview Hotel** (29 Birchgrove Road; 9810 1151), but now only the refurbished **Dawn Fraser Pool** (Elkington Park; 9555 1903) bears her name.

Balmain's spine is Darling Street, which starts at the Darling Street Wharf and curves up past the sandstone **Watch House** (once the police lock-up and now headquarters for the Balmain Historical Society and **St Andrew's Congregational Church** (Booth Street; 9810 3712), popular for Japanese weddings and the weekly venue for **Balmain Market**. Inside the church each Saturday stretch rows of food stalls – Thai, Himalayan, Lebanese and macrobiotic – while the churchyard

Balmain Market's broad church of bric-à-brac.

is crammed with stalls selling all sorts of bric-à-brac. Continue along Darling Street past hip cafés and jewellery shops, the expansive **Pentimento Bookshop** at number 275 (9810 0707), the stylish **Victoire Patisserie** at number 285 (9818 5529) and the artistically decorated **Emile's Fruit Store** at number 321 (9810 2759).

Lanes branch off Darling Street, crammed with cottages, each sporting its own idiosyncratic façade. Historical Society member Kath Hamey conducts guided tours of the area each Saturday at 11am from St Andrew's front gate (phone 9818 4954 for more details).

There are dozens of cuisines on offer in Balmain, from **Oporto Portuguese Style Chicken** (331 Darling Street) to the **Wok On In Noodle Bar** (Shop 3, 415 Darling Street; 9810 1399) and **Le Bich Vietnamese Restaurant** (386 Darling Street; 9555 1068). More serious foodies should head for the **Peninsula Restaurant** (264 Darling Street; 9810 3955) or **Gotham Bar & Brasserie** (135 Rowntree Street; 9555 8008). Queues are common for Sunday brunch at the **Tin Shed Cafe** (9555 1042), set in a junkyard at 148 Beattie Street. The owners recently opened the **Tin Shed Warehouse** (corner of Mullens and Roseberry Streets; 9555 1042), a massive shack crammed with everything from old railway benches to Chinese wooden screens.

It's all within easy walking distance, but if you're driving, let the overalled lads fill 'er up at Balmain's oldest service station **Bill's Garage** – est 1915 – at 418 Darling Street (9810 2611), complete with original fixtures and fittings.

Running along the top end of Darling Street is **Rozelle Market** (Darling Street; 9818 5373), held in the grounds of the High School each Saturday and Sunday from 9am to 4pm, where fossickers can ferret through stalls of discount CDs, plants, ceramics and collectibles. Also along this stretch are a smattering of cafés, plant nurseries, antique stores and gift shops, before Darling Street meets bustling Victoria Road. For years **Hylands Shoe Store**, a discount warehouse, stood on the corner of Victoria Road and Darling Street, but it recently shifted a few doors south to 104 Victoria Road (9555 1400). To the north is the **Balmain Leagues Club** (138 Victoria Road; 9555 1650) not only home to local rugby battlers the Sydney Tigers, but a place where punters can get cheap beer and play the pokies.

Just beyond the Darling Street-Victoria Road intersection, on the corner of Cambridge Street, is the famous Franco-Japanese **Tetsuya's** (9555 1017). Head deeper into Rozelle and you hit the former psychiatric hospital where part of the film *Cosi*, starring Toni Collette, was shot amid the stately sandstone buildings and manicured lawns overlooking Iron Cove. The area is now being renovated as the Sydney College of Arts.

Leichhardt

Called 'Little Italy' for no small reason (as well as 'Dykeheart' by its sizeable lesbian population), this working-class suburb's main thoroughfare, Norton Street, is always alive with the aroma of garlic and coffee. To get here from the city centre, take a 438, 468 or 470 bus. Studded with coffee shops, cafés and delicatessens, Norton Street serves up a smorgasbord of pasta, strong Italian coffee and Thai takeaways, but serious foodies can't go past **La Cremarie Sorbetteria Shop** (Shop 1, 110 Norton Street; 9564 1127) without stopping for a gelato or miss out on a latte at **Bar Italia** (169 Norton Street; 9560 9981). Nearby **Cafe Gioia & Pizzeria** (126A Norton Street; 9564 6245) is housed in a renovated service station.

A cluster of local heritage buildings includes the two-storey **Leichhardt Town Hall** (107 Norton Street; 9367 9222), built in 1888, which often houses visiting art exhibitions; the **Post Office** (109 Norton Street; 9569 2256); and **All Souls Anglican Church** (126 Norton Street; 9569 2646). **Leichhardt Market Place** (corner of Marion and Flood Streets; 9560 4488) is a modern shopping complex housing the usual supermarkets and chain stores as well as the odd 'seconds' store, while the **Norton Street Markets** (55 Norton Street; 9568 2158) is a warehouse with a sweeping array of fruit and veg plus other gourmet goodies from the Med.

Glebe

There are more holistic therapists and chiropractors per square metre in Glebe than anywhere else in Sydney, and an overpowering aroma of curries and clove cigarettes. This inner-western suburb is an incongruous but atmospheric mix of grand turn-of-the-century mansions flanking quaint terraces and drab 1970s flatlets, with most streets still sporting their original rusty street signs. The main bus from the city centre to Glebe, a 17-minute trip, is the 431.

All the action can be found along **Glebe Point Road**. One end joins up with the snarling traffic of Parramatta Road and the other tails off at Blackwattle Bay, where you'll find the Blackwattle Studios, a hotchpotch of artists' studios within an old factory complex featuring a tiny hip café (**Blackwattle Canteen/Studio 54**, 465 Glebe Point Road; 9552 1792) overlooking the Sydney Fish Markets across the bay in Pyrmont.

Glebe's film fans are well served by the legendary cult moviehouse, the **Valhalla** at 166D Glebe Point Road, while avid readers should head for **Gleebooks** at number 49, which is something of a literary institution dealing in both new and second-hand books, covering the mainstream

and the obscure. Or try **Cornstalk Books** (112 Glebe Point Road; 9660 4889/9552 1070) for antiquarian tomes. Those of a more cyber-minded disposition can mooch around the world wide web at the **Well Connected Coffee Shop** (35 Glebe Point Road; 9566 2655), one of the few Internet cafés in Sydney.

Heading south-west off Glebe Point Road towards Annandale, you'll find the infamous comedy/music venue, the **Harold Park Hotel** (115 Wigram Road), opposite the Harold Park Paceway. American comic Robin Williams has been known to pop into the hotel for an impromptu stand-up gig when visiting the Harbour City. The entertainment bill ranges from 'Comics in the Park' (three-minute opportunities for amateurs), 'Politics in the Pub' (debates) to boot-scootin' (line dancing).

On a turning off Wigram Road is **Tranby Aboriginal College** (13 Mansfield Street; 9660 3444). Housing books, music, reference material, clothing and artefacts, the college also runs an extensive mail order service (for Blackbooks, *see chapter* **Shopping & Services**).

Glebe is renowned for its wholesome food. Purveyors include **Iku Wholefood Kitchen** (25A Glebe Point Road); the cavernous **Russell's Natural Foods Market** (53 Glebe Point Road; 9552); **Demeter Food Products** (65 Derwent Street; 9660 2555), which holds bread baking classes; **Bad Manners** (37 Glebe Point Road; 9660 3797) and **Lolita's Coffee Lounge** (29 Glebe Point Road; 9692 0493).

For trinkets, try the fluoro-aluminium fronted gift store **Red Rock 7** (241 Glebe Point Road; 9566 4259) with its $7 banana candles and sterling silver Dalek salt and pepper shakers for $165. Or for a more eclectic choice, take a ramble through sprawling **Glebe Market** (*see chapter* **Shopping & Services**) on a Saturday.

Irish pub **The Friend in Hand Hotel** (58 Cowper Street; 9660 2326) has live crab races every Wednesday night and there's standing room only to hear the Irish bands on Sunday afternoons. As well as having the No Names

Restaurant under its roof, the hotel is a paraphernalia delight, stuffed with street signs, number plates from around the world and even a surfboat hanging from the roof in one room.

There's always a plethora of travellers around this area, thanks to several budget hotels including the leafy and large **Glebe Village Backpackers Hostel** (254-258 Glebe Point Road; 9660 8878/9552 4305), as well as earnest young students, due to the close proximity of the **University of Sydney**.

For guided walking tours of the area contact Maureen Fry at **Sydney Guided Tours** (9660 7157), who also runs similar tours in Balmain, Rozelle and Annandale, among other areas.

Annandale

Once earmarked as a 'model township' – hence the broad, tree-lined Johnston Street (named after handsome Lieutenant George Johnston, the first man to step ashore in 1788, albeit on the back of a convict) – Annandale quickly became a predominantly working-class area.

It is known today for its period architecture. A particularly fine example is the beautiful sandstone **Hunter Baillie Memorial Presbyterian Church** (80 Johnston Street; 9810 7869) whose spire is visible from the air as you fly into Sydney; it's also (yet another) favoured venue for Japanese tourists getting hitched. There's the ornate wrought-iron work on the **Goodwin Building** (corner of Johnston Street and Parramatta Road), while the towering pillars outside Annandale Primary School once guarded George Johnston's house, which stood where the **Stanmore Cinema Centre** serves today's cinema-goers. Beale's Piano Factory on Trafalgar Street was once the largest piano factory in the British Empire (Queen Mary had one of its pianos in Buckingham Palace), but it is now a storage warehouse. Along Johnston Street stand three huge homes with distinctive tall towers known as **The Witches' Houses** because from a distance they resemble witches' hats.

Like Leichhardt, Annandale is a mix of longtime residents and more recent yuppies who have chosen the inner west as an affordable area for buying and renovating a quaint terraced house. However, bisected by broad paved roads, Annandale lacks the brashness of Glebe, the self-consciousness of Balmain and the lively ethnicity of Leichhardt. Nevertheless, there is still a discernible village feel. The **Annandale Hotel** (corner of Parramatta Road and Nelson Street; 9550 1078) is known as a long-term hangout for up-and-coming bands; and dotted along a stretch of the Parramatta Road nearby, are dozens of antiques and second-hand furniture shops, a fertile haven for bargain-hunters.

Newtown & the South

Explore Newtown's multicultural buzz and the southern comforts of Botany Bay and the Georges River.

Although southern Sydneysiders are as loyally territorial as those living in the eastern suburbs, the truth is that few people from other parts of Sydney ever venture further south than Newtown. If they do, it's likely to be at 80 kilometres per hour along the Princes Highway as they head towards Wollongong or further on to out of town beaches. But southern suburbanites are quite happy to keep the secret attractions of the St George area and Sutherland to themselves. These southern reaches of the sprawling city epitomise the great Australian dream, with quarter-acre blocks of land surrounding each house, lawn-mowers droning all weekend and swimming pools galore.

Over the back fences are some of Sydney's most stunning waterways, also far less crowded and overpriced than the foreshores of Sydney Harbour. Among them are the Georges River, which flows into Botany Bay; and further south, the Port Hacking River, which borders the **Royal National Park**.

The real appeal of the southern suburbs, however, lies in their cultural diversity. The St George area, centred around Hurstville, reflects a range of influxes (Anglo, Greek, Italian, Chinese, Thai, Vietnamese, Croatian, Lebanese) and each district is scattered with delis, ethnic bakeries and restaurants representing every nationality – a microcosm of the multicultural make-up of Australia.

Newtown

In travel brochure-speak, Newtown would be dubbed 'gateway' to the southern suburbs. What was once a working-class district, crammed with terraced houses and semi-detached cottages, has gradually undergone a process of gentrification, as more affluent Sydneysiders covet Newtown's proximity to the city. The metamorphosis is particularly evident at the north end of King Street, where most of the houses have been groovily renovated and the laneways are dotted with BMWs. Newtown residents are quite clear about the appeal of their suburb: it is 'down-to-earth' – meaning that it is free of the perceived pretension of inner-city areas like Paddington.

Few other areas accommodate so many subcultures, and in such apparent harmony – grungy university students riddled with body piercings, yuppie professional couples, black-draped goths, and punks. You could easily spend a day wandering along King Street (and it's faster to stroll than drive, since the traffic is notoriously bad, particularly at weekends). Explore the intriguing – and often eccentric – specialist shops (there's one dedicated solely to buttons, another to ribbons and braids, another to arty candles).

Start at **Gould's Book Arcade** at number 519 King Street, one of the largest and most popular second-hand bookshops in Sydney (buses 422, 423 and 426 will get you there from the city). From there, you'll have no trouble finding somewhere to linger over a cappuccino and an obscenely generous slab of cake. Every second shopfront is a café or restaurant. Particularly numerous are Thai eateries, usually with joke names like Thai-Foon. One of the best is **Thai Pothong** (298 King Street; 9550 6277). New places seem to open every week and like all of Newtown's best cafés, these tiny establishments crammed with laminated tables are perfect for hiding out for a few hours. A popular spot is **The Old Fish Shop** (239 King Street; 9519 4295), an open-sided café with strings of garlic and chilli hanging from the roof. It's rare to score a table without having to queue, but that allows time to choose from the array of foccacia and cakes on offer.

A major newcomer in the area is the **Dendy Cinema**, also home to a great alternative music shop, **Fish Records**, at number 261 King Street. Of course, Newtown has no shortage of pubs, each with its own forte; among them are the **Sandringham Hotel** (live alternative music) and the **Newtown Hotel** (gay shows, *see chapter Queer Sydney*). Most have a restaurant tucked away at the back, often with an open-air courtyard. Recommended are the Thai restaurant at the **Bank Hotel** (324 King Street; 9557 1280), adjacent to Newtown Station. The decor is simple, with plastic green tables and long green railway station benches still marked with names like 'St Peters' and 'Macdonaldtown'. Such is the Australian passion for dining alfresco that even in winter the courtyard restaurant is often booked out at night.

The southern end of King Street becomes increasingly residential, with large apartment complexes, some of them still under construction. Many of the shopfronts are vacant, but there are still some interesting places to explore, notably the Pacific produce shops such as **Island Food Supplies** (565 King Street; 9519 1141) and **Fiji Market** (591 King Street; 9517 2054). To finish your travels on a suitably decadent note, sample some of the syrup-soaked Indian treats at **Maya Sweets** (642A King Street; 9550 6681).

South of St Peters Station, King Street becomes the Princes Highway, only of interest to plane-spotters: the aircraft roar perilously close overhead on their approach to Kingsford Smith Airport in nearby Mascot.

Botany Bay

When the British 'discovered' Sydney Harbour in 1770, they landed on the tip of the Kurnell Peninsula, in Botany Bay. Under the command of James Cook and with botanist Joseph Banks leading a party of scientists, the crew of HMS Endeavour spent a week exploring the area and recording information about the flora and fauna they found (hence the bay's name). Eighteen years later, when the newly appointed Governor of New South Wales, Captain Arthur Phillip, arrived with the First Fleet, he relinquished the base at Kurnell in favour of a deeper bay further north, which was named Sydney Cove. But Kurnell's historical significance was not forgotten, and in 1899 more than 100 hectares of land were set aside as a public area. **Captain Cook's Landing Place** is now a regular stop on the school excursion circuit, and on weekdays crowds of children visit the Cook Obelisk, Cook's Well and Landing Rock. At the weekend, it's a popular spot for family picnics. To find out more about the history of the area and the young colony, visit the Discovery Centre (Captain Cook Drive; 9668 9111).

On the far side of Botany Bay is Brighton-le-Sands, a grandiose name for a busy strip of cafés and restaurants dominated by an oversized, pyramid-shaped branch of the Novotel hotel chain (9597 7111). On Saturday nights and Sundays, the Grand Parade is choked with bumper-to-bumper traffic and crowds searching for somewhere to linger over a decent cappuccino for a few hours. The most upmarket restaurant in the area is Le Sands (The Parade; 9599 4949), which offers panoramic views of Botany Bay and its attractions: planes landing to the left, the pipes and towers of Kurnell oil refinery to the right. A more casual alternative is the nearby Signature Cafe (9599 3020), where you can enjoy the same view from an outdoor verandah.

Cronulla

A strange thing happens to Cronulla beach – Bondi of the south – every Sunday. The surfers seem to flee to its northern end (Elouera, Wanda and Green Hills Beaches) and are replaced by Greek, Italian and Arabic families approaching triple figures, who set about barbecuing delicious-smelling food so that garlic and onion mingle with the sea breeze.

Cronulla is a much longer beach than its more famous city counterparts (such as Bondi, Coogee, Clovelly and Maroubra). It takes at least 1½ hours to walk its length from South Cronulla to Green Hills to the north, which at weekends is busy with 4WDs churning up what remains of the sand hills. For those of a more pedestrian persuasion, there is a walking track that starts at South Cronulla, and wends it way around the cliff, past sea pools and picturesque coves, until you can gaze southwards across the water at the **Royal National Park**.

Cronulla Street, the area's shopping strip, features little more than surf shops, a few cafés and a quaint old cinema with seats like concrete. So if you find yourself at a loose end and hungry in Cronulla, **Jetz** (6 Surf Road; 9544 2709), hidden away in a quiet back street, could be your best bet. All hearty, wholesome and home-made, this is probably the only place in the area where you'll find Penelope Sach tea and decent coffee. Alternatively, you could try the **Hog's Breath Cafe** (18 The Kingsway; 9544 0644), part of a chain of American-style eateries that has recently set foot in Cronulla. Book a window seat: it's a nice spot to while away a few hours, eating upmarket nachos and burgers. Cheaper drinks can be had at the pub across the road, the **North Cronulla Hotel** (corner of The Kingsway and Elouera Road; 9523 6866) – fondly called 'Northies' by the locals. Have a drink out on the balcony so that you can gaze out to sea through the towering pine trees below. Of the few good restaurants in Cronulla, the best is Thy (57-61 Cronulla Street; 9527 1289), a tiny and always-crowded Vietnamese-Thai place.

Strangely absent from Cronulla are the good-quality fish and chip shops you would expect in a beachside suburb. The best in the south is **Smith's Seafoods**, with two outlets just north of Tom Ugly's Point in Blakehurst by the Georges River Bridge (430 Princes Highway, 9546 8043; and 727 Princes Highway, 9546 2843). At the weekend, people queue up to buy good-value fresh oysters and fried fish from them. Another great takeaway shop is south of the same bridge, in the suburb made famous by a less-than-flattering British television documentary. **Paul's Famous Hamburgers of Sylvania** (12B Princes Highway; 9522 5632) is often nominated as one of the best burger joints in Sydney.

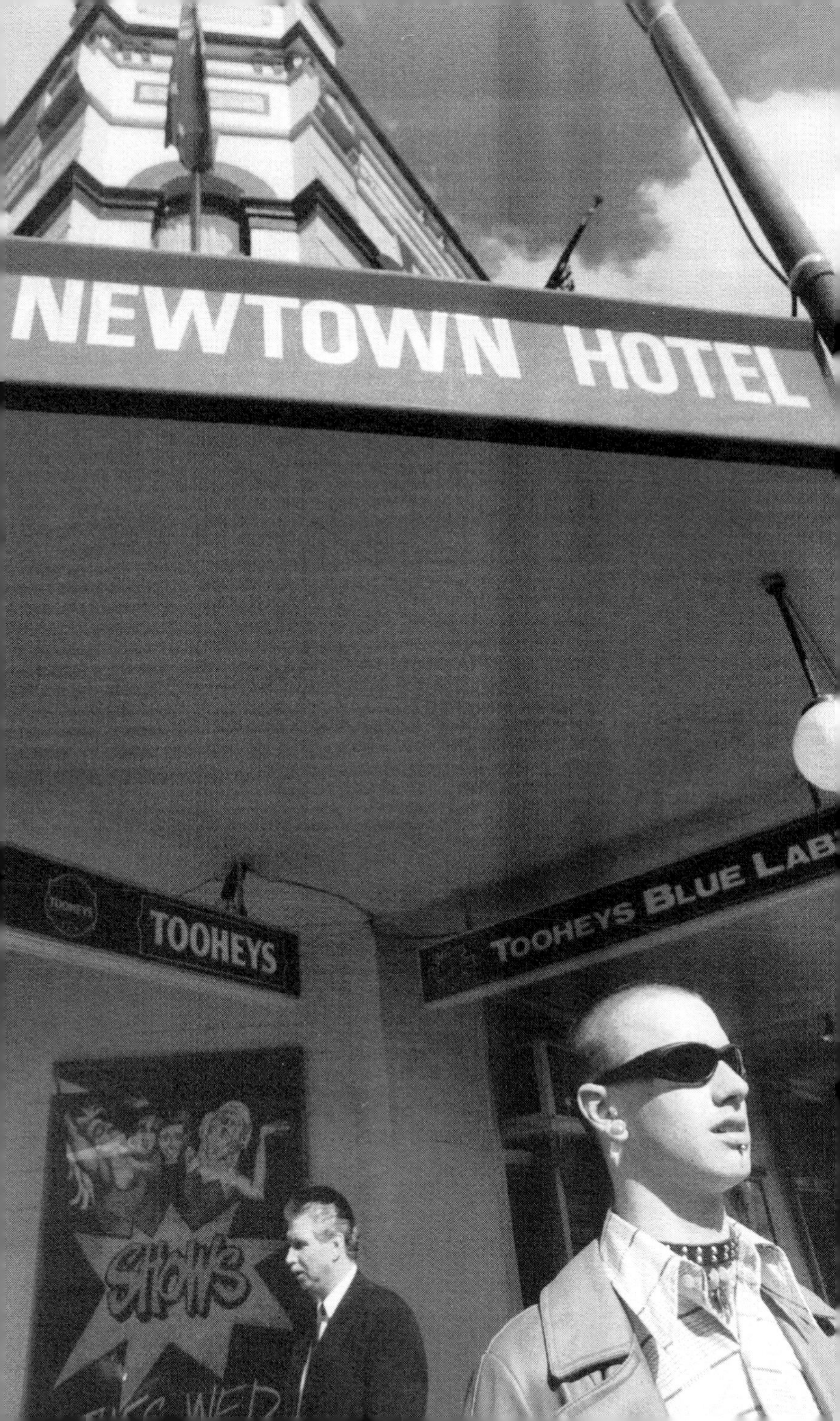
NEWTOWN HOTEL
TOOHEYS
TOOHEYS BLUE
SHOWS

*Bodies beautiful down **Cronulla** way. For the 'Bondi of the south', see page 90.*

Oatley & Como

Further inland, these two suburbs face each other across the Georges River and, not being on a route to somewhere else, they are sleepy backwaters, full of character. Oatley has its own national park. It may be only a fraction of the size of the Royal National Park, but the Oatley Reserve manages some great bushwalks, a children's playground constructed high in the gum trees, a small sandstone castle and a tidal pool (though this last attraction is too muddy for most people and more of a favourite with dogs on weekend mornings).

Oatley and Como are less than a kilometre apart as the crow flies, but driving between them takes about 30 minutes. A more enjoyable option is to stroll across the old railway bridge that links them. It runs alongside the existing rail line and at the weekend becomes a blur of cyclists and power-walkers. The Como side offers a tidal pool, a marina and the **Cafe de Como** (2 Cremona Road; 9528 3511), offering seafood and French cuisine. Just up the road, opposite the oval, is the restored **Como Hotel** (33 Cremona Road; 9528 5366), all wrought-iron trim and wraparound verandahs. The hotel's main claim to fame is that Australian poet Henry Lawson was a frequent visitor. The restaurant on the first floor is known for its reasonably priced seafood. Ask for a table on the verandah.

Around Sutherland

Sydney has an abundance of shopping malls, and the **Westfield Miranda** (*see chapter* **Shopping & Services**) has the dubious distinction of being the largest mall in the Southern Hemisphere. Inside, the architects have slyly provided only a handful of escalators, so that shoppers are forced to walk around and around, increasing the probability of them spending something. Not far from the biggest mall in the Southern Hemisphere is, reputedly, the biggest collection of azaleas in the Southern Hemisphere. **EG Waterhouse National Camellia Gardens** (corner of Kareena Road and President Avenue, Caringbah; 9710 0333) also has more than 1,500 camellias from all over the world, beautifully arranged around picnic areas, duck ponds, fountains and a tea house.

Some of the greatest treasures of the area lie further south, near the Royal National Park. Drive through the park to **Stanwell Tops**, where on a clear day there are spectacular (though not very picturesque) views down to Wollongong and the Port Kembla steelworks. Go on a Sunday, when the grassy clifftop is teeming with hang-gliders.

About five minutes' drive from Stanwell Tops is **Symbio Koala Gardens** (7-9 Lawrence Hargrave Drive, Stanwell Tops; 4294 1244), a small but popular animal park where you can get much closer to the wildlife than at, say, Taronga Zoo. There are koalas in a walk-through enclosure, as well as kangaroos, wombats, dingos and kookaburras.

A less obvious tourist attraction is the **Lucas Heights** nuclear reactor, now surrounded by housing estates as Sydney's population grows. According to the Australian Nuclear Science and Technology Organisation (ANSTO), it is used for medical and scientific research. Since ANSTO (New Illawarra Road, Lucas Heights; 9717 3168) offers tours of the reactor, you can have a look for yourself.

Parramatta & the West

The wilds of way out west – from the skyscrapers of Parramatta to the Cambodian caffs of Cabramatta.

When you visit Sydney's eastern suburbs, as all tourists inevitably do, you might hear a couple of pieces of shark bait – that is, surfies or waxheads – down at Bondi speaking disparagingly about 'westies'. Who are these dreaded creatures? The Macquarie Dictionary (Australia's answer to the Oxford) defines 'westie' as a colloquial and derogatory word describing 'someone from the western suburbs of Sydney; usually characterised as unsophisticated'. Many people in Sydney's more established and wealthier eastern suburbs have a morbid mix of fear and fascination when it comes to westies – the people who lay claim to the vast majority of Greater Sydney.

Occasionally a westie will bite back. Take this letter once printed in surfing bible *Tracks* magazine: 'As for the dickhead who thinks that westy girls are "bushpigs", we'd like to say "get fucked" and have a look at your own surfie chicks with their floppy brown tits trotting along behind you waxheads like drooling puppies.'

This rivalry between the people of Sydney's eastern and western suburbs has been going on almost since the day the First Fleet arrived in 1788. The convicts and their guards quickly realised that the land around the settlement at Sydney Cove (now the CBD) could not sustain them, despite its obvious real estate potential. Instead, they headed west and established a successful farming community at Parramatta – today the capital of western Sydney, and Australia's second oldest white settlement.

In the early years of the colony the two centres vied for supremacy, with Sydney Cove ultimately winning out. The current cultural war between east and west began in earnest after World War II, when the western suburbs changed from basically small rural villages to massive, sprawling suburbs housing the majority of Sydney's people and industry.

In many regards, Sydney is now a tale of two sometimes very different cities. The people of the eastern suburbs who try to stereotype the west, have almost invariably never been there. In reality it is an area far too large and diverse, culturally, economically and geographically, for derogatory generalisations – as a visit there will quickly prove.

Parramatta

To explore this 'other' half of Sydney, you should start with Parramatta, gateway to the west and its unofficial capital. While the CityRail network serves all the major suburban centres, Parramatta can be accessed by water by **Rivercat** from Circular Quay just as quickly, and the boat journey is far more scenic and relaxed.

Parramatta is an Aboriginal word said to mean a 'place where eels lie down' or 'head of the river', and it should be remembered that the land of western Sydney belonged to the Dharug, Dharawal and Gandangara people before white settlers took it from them in bloody warfare. The famous Aboriginal warrior, Pemulwuy, kept the people of Parramatta in fear of their lives for more than a decade before he was eventually killed in 1802 and his head sent off to England.

But the Aborigines of western Sydney were not driven to extinction. More than 1,000 descendants of the Dharug still live in western Sydney and there are more than 10,000 Aborigines altogether in the area – many others having moved in from rural areas.

As Australia's second oldest white settlement and Sydney's second largest business district, Parramatta holds a dynamic mix of the old and the new, with towering skyscrapers right next door to heritage-listed huts. **Elizabeth Farm**, built in 1793 by wool pioneer John Macarthur, and named after his wife, is the oldest home still standing in Australia and open for inspection. Also open to the public is **Old Government House** in the sprawling grounds of Parramatta Park.

Two things the people of western Sydney love are a beer and a bet. **Rosehill Gardens Racecourse** on Grand Avenue is a citadel to both pursuits, particularly during the Autumn Carnival when the $2 million **Golden Slipper** – the world's richest race for two year-olds – is held there.

One of Sydney's most marvellously restored movie theatres is the art deco **Roxy Cinema** (69 George Street), which has far more ambience than the mega-sized multiplexes found in most Sydney

A taste of local character at Parramatta's **Woolpack Hotel**.

suburban centres. The **General Bourke Hotel** (74 Church Street) prides itself on being the leading live music venue in the west, while other old Parramatta pubs with plenty of character include the **Woolpack** (19 George Street; 9635 8043), the **Albion** (135 George Street; 9891 3288) and the **Commercial** (corner of Hassall and Station East Street; 9635 8342).

And for children, in the nearby suburb of Merrylands, just south of the Great Western Motorway, there's the **Kidseum** (corner of Walpole and Pitt Streets; 9682 1907).

Around Blacktown

Blacktown earned its name from being home to the Native Institute, established by the early authorities to educate Aboriginal children. The area's premier attraction is **Australia's Wonderland** theme park (Wallgrove Road, Eastern Creek; 9830 9100), an American-style theme park and the largest in the country, featuring wild rides and Disney-style entertainment. Wonderland also boasts a native wildlife zoo where the main attraction is a five-metre saltwater crocodile from the Northern Territory called Maniac. Visit him at meal time, and you'll understand why. If you just want wildlife, nearby is an excellent family-run park in cut-throat competition with Wonderland called **Featherdale Wildlife Park** (217 Kildare Road, Doonside; 9622 1644).

Public transport tends to be poorer in the west than in the east, so westies like to have a special attachment to their cars. The real revheads love going to **Eastern Creek Raceway** (Horsley Road, Eastern Creek; 9672 1000), Sydney's biggest automotive venue, which regularly hosts touring cars, motorbikes and drag races

The Australian pub is a place of great mythology, but western Sydney is often dubbed 'club land'. Leagues clubs, golf clubs, bowling clubs, workers clubs, returned servicemen's clubs… they're everywhere, providing community services and cheap food, drink and entertainment subsidised by endless rows of poker machines, which pubs aren't allowed to have. Two of the biggest and the best are **Blacktown Workers Club** (Campbell Street; 9622 2355) and **Rooty Hill RSL Club & Resort** (corner of Sherbrooke and Railway Streets, Rooty Hill; 9625 5500).

Around Penrith

At the foot of the Blue Mountains and perched on the banks of the Nepean River, Penrith is a sprawling, modern city-suburb that boasts an impressive portfolio of beautiful rural and bushland scenery as well as history and modern culture. At the heart of Penrith is Panthers: Australia's largest licensed club, and the rugby league team it supports. Occupying over 80 ha (200 acres), like an antipodean Butlins resort, **Panthers World of Entertainment** (Mulgoa Road; 4720 5555) not only offers a vast array of bars, gaming facilities, restaurants, nightclubs and live music, but also has its own motel, swimming pools, water-skiing, waterslides, tennis courts, beach volleyball, a golf driving range and more.

Just across the road in **Penrith Park**, you can watch the Penrith Panthers go a round on winter weekends, perhaps against one of the western suburbs' three other first-class rugby league teams, the Parramatta Eels, the Canterbury-Bankstown Bulldogs or the Western Suburbs Magpies (based in Campbelltown).

If you're after a bet, Penrith has dogs and trots at **Penrith Paceway** (Penrith Showground, Station Street; 4721 2375). While on a more cultural note, there's the well respected **Q Theatre** (Belmore Street, Penrith; 4721 5735), the beautiful **Lewers Regional Art Gallery** (86 River Road, Emu Plains; 4735 1100) or the **Joan Sutherland Performing Arts Centre** (597 High Street, Penrith; 4721 5423).

On the river you'll find the historic paddlewheeler, **Nepean Belle** (The Jetty, Tench Avenue, Jamisontown; 4733 1274), which does lunch and dinner cruises up the spectacular Nepean Gorge.

The Penrith area is also home to several vineyards, including **Vicary's Winery** (The Northern Road, Luddenham; 4773 4161), which organises tastings and uses a converted woolshed to hosts rollicking bushdances every Saturday night.

North of Penrith, the Nepean River becomes the **Hawkesbury**, which forms the lifeline of another unique part of western Sydney. For the historic towns of Richmond, Windsor and Wilberforce, more on the delights of the Hawkesbury, *see* **Heading West** *in chapter* **Trips Out of Town**.

Bankstown, Liverpool & Fairfield

These city-suburbs and their neighbours are the country's multicultural heartland. Sydney is the most popular destination of migrants entering Australia and the vast majority of those go to live in the western suburbs. In some south-western suburbs, more than half the population was born overseas, in Italy, Greece, Vietnam, Cambodia, the Philippines, China, Serbia, Croatia, Poland, Latin America, the Lebanon and the Pacific Islands.

Cabramatta

Cabramatta, in particular, has developed a name for itself as the culinary centre of the western suburbs. It also suffers from a reputation as the heroin capital of Sydney, due to the presence of the Asian 5T gang, but its exotic mix of Aussie suburbia, Saigon, Shanghai and Phnom Penh shouldn't be missed if you like shopping and dining. For recommended eateries in the area *see chapters* **Restaurants** *and* **Cafés & Bars**. The best time to visit is when the Chinese and Vietnamese communities celebrate their New Years, with wild dragon parades and more firecrackers than you can shake a match at.

Due to the high level of immigration, soccer (or 'wog ball', as you may well hear local union and league supporters call it) is a bigger sport than rugby in this part of Sydney. And the Italian community-backed Marconi-Fairfield side is the region's representative in Australia's national soccer league, which is played during the summer (*see chapter* **Sport & Fitness**). Sydney soccer fans follow their teams with a sometimes fiery passion, based along ethnic lines, and the games can be boisterous and spectacular affairs. Club Marconi (Marconi Road; 9823 2222) is the biggest licensed club in the area with all the usual equipment, plus multicultural quirks such as *bocce* facilities.

Bankstown

Bankstown is the home suburb of the famous cricketing Waugh brothers and boasts a killer cricket team, which you can catch during the summer at weekends at the **Bankstown Oval** (Bankstown District Sports Club, 8 Greenfield Parade; 9709 3899).

Campbelltown & Beyond

Like the Hawkesbury River region, these areas of the far south-west are rich in colonial heritage, rural charm and rugged bushland, despite being part of Greater Sydney. There are still many historic and functioning farms in the area open for day visits or longer stays if you want to sample Australian rural life without straying too far from the big smoke. A good example is **Gledswood Homestead** (Camden Valley Way, Catherine Field; 9606 5111), built in 1827, where you can eat, drink, learn to throw a boomerang and ride a horse. The area's best pub is undoubtedly the **George IV Inn** (180 Old Hume Highway, Camden; 4677 1415), said to have been built in 1819. The beautiful sandstone building also houses its own boutique brewery, which produces such local delights as Burragorang Bock, packing a powerful 6.4 per cent alcoholic punch.

Geographically and in terms of climate, the Greater Sydney region is so diverse that it needs three botanic gardens to display the full range of local flora. One of these is **Mt Annan Botanic Gardens** (Mt Annan Drive, Mt Annan; 4646 2477), next to the Hume Highway (Route 31). Further south on Camden Valley Way, which becomes Remembrance Drive, underdog lovers can visit the **Dingo Sanctuary** (590 Arina Rd, Bargo; 4684 1156) to see Australia's much-maligned native critter and the world's oldest canine purebreed.

Beyond these south-western townships and farms, the rugged upper reaches of the Nepean River, Lake Burragorang and the Warragamba Dam (which provides Sydney's water supply) provide many beautiful lookouts, picnic spots, camping sites and walks.

North Shore

Who said money can't buy happiness? Sydney's northern residents seem to be pretty content with their lot.

The north shore is where Sydney's serious money lives, a sprawling *House & Gardens* confection of beautiful homes, tree-lined avenues, smart cars, chichi shops, swish restaurants and the occasional marina to park the boat which simply won't fit in the two-car garage. While Sydney's well-heeled eastern suburbs like to flaunt their social status, north shore residents go about their business in a far more discreet and understated manner.

Generations of breeding have taught the people of Mosman, Cremorne, Cammeray, Neutral Bay, Turramurra, St Ives and other 'silvertail' suburbs that rather than shout about their good fortune, they should just go out and live it. This they do in style, surrounded by some of Sydney's most beautiful urban scenery. And they're not the only ones.

One of the most surprising developments of recent years has been the north shore's embrace of Sydney's burgeoning multicultural character. What was once a bastion of Anglo-Oz WASP culture is now – as elsewhere – a melting pot of races and religions.

You need only spot the signs at Chinese-Catholic churches, the noticeboards at South African-Jewish schools, the menus at Thai restaurants and the billboards at Japanese supermarkets to see that the local culture is going through a dramatic change. Head for the leafy confines of Northbridge, for example, and you'll find a mock-gothic suspension bridge alongside a Tokyo Mart, which sells exclusively Japanese products. A version to change has given way to acceptance, all of which is good news for the visitor in search of a rich and diverse culture.

Kirribilli

The north shore starts at Kirribilli, nestled under the Harbour Bridge. With sweeping views of the city and Opera House, this tiny suburb is home to the official Sydney residences of the prime minister (**Kirribilli House**) and the governor-general (**Admiralty House**), where British royals and other foreign dignitaries stay when they're in town.

Its good-life, villagey atmosphere is fuelled by cafés such as **Billi's** (31A Fitzroy Street; 9955 7211) and **Freckle Face** (32 Burton Street; 9957 2116); fine restaurants like **The Fitzroy Cafe** (1 Broughton Street; 9955 3349); and the renowned **Kirribilli Hotel** (35 Broughton Street; 9955 1415).

Milsons Restaurant (corner of Broughton and Willoughby Streets; 9955 7075) is one of the best in Sydney, and the excellent **Ensemble Theatre**, built over the water at Careening Cove, is a leading local drama venue. All of which attracts a lively crowd of locals and visitors, especially at weekends.

With accommodation ranging from Housing Commission flats to $4 million mansions, Kirribilli has a wildly varied blend of residents, from well-heeled lawyers, chief executives and bankers to young families and cash-strapped pensioners.

Milsons Point & McMahons Point

On a sunny day, hop aboard a **Hegarty's Ferry** (9206 1167) at Circular Quay's Jetty 6 – the ride on the tiny, wood-panelled Twin Star or Leura is a delight in itself. This mini-voyage involves a glide past the Opera House to Jeffrey Street Wharf at Kirribilli, where you can take the harbourside walk which curls underneath the massive 'coathanger' span of the Harbour Bridge. The walk leads past the city's first Olympic swimming pool (next to the now defunct Luna Park funfair) and on to a wooden boardwalk winding around Lavender Bay – especially dazzling at sunset when the city lights shimmer in the golden glow.

Milsons Point and McMahons Point, flanking Lavender Bay, are home to an eclectic mix of architects, lawyers and media personalities. Blues Point Road, a café-lined avenue slicing through the heart of McMahons Point, is one of Sydney's great people-watching strips, and the coffee at **Blues Point Cafe** (9922 2064) is good, too. Allow yourself time to walk down to **Blues Point Reserve**, a swathe of open parkland at the south tip of Blues Point, providing great photo opportunities for that quintessential Sydney Harbour holiday snap.

The main commercial centre of the lower north shore is **Military Road**, a low-slung, bustling strip of shops, cafés and restaurants. The **Oaks Hotel** (118 Military Road; 9953 5515), with its tree-covered courtyard, is a favourite hangout for local groovers and shakers who order steaks and fish by the kilo and then make for the barbecue outside to cook up a storm for themselves.

Living on the edge: some prime perches overlooking Middle Harbour.

Fishy business at **The Spit**.

Cremorne & Mosman

Continuing east along Military Road brings you to Sydney's blue-ribbon suburbs: Cremorne, Mosman and Balmoral, where the heavily monied live in splendour with their double-incomes, trusty Volvos and neatly pressed children.

Cremorne Point, a sliver of a peninsula, offers one of the finest panoramas of Sydney Harbour. Once the setting for Sydney's raunchiest night spot, until scandal closed the pleasure grounds down in the 1850s, it is now the setting for a scenic harbourside walk. Take the ferry from Circular Quay to Cremorne Point Wharf, and you're at the gateway to **Robertsons Point**, with its white-washed lighthouse and a delightful walkway that leads around lush Mosman Bay – perfect for a peaceful picnic.

One of Sydney's great landmarks is **Taronga Zoo** (*see chapter* **Sightseeing**), which occupies a splendid vantage-point overlooking Bradleys Head. Take the ferry from Circular Quay to Taronga Zoo, Athol Wharf, and board the Aerial Safari cable car, which takes you up to the main zoo compound, where there are yet more splendid panoramic views across the harbour to the city.

Mosman's swanky commercial centre, which runs along Military Road (a continuation of the main route that links the suburbs of the lower north shore), is the place to shop. This is where designer women driving designer cars dine in designer restaurants before shopping for, well, designer clothes. Make a quick detour down Raglan Street, which leads down to Curraghbeena Point, for a magnificent view of Middle Harbour and then continue on to Balmoral, one of Sydney's prettiest harbour suburbs.

Balmoral

Blessed with not one but two beaches, lots of green space, a Romanesque bandstand (venue for many local events) and a couple of excellent restaurants – **The Watermark** (2A The Esplanade; 9968 3433) and **Bathers Pavilion** (*see chapter*

Restaurants *and* **Cafés & Bars**) – Balmoral offers a quintessential slice of Sydney life.

The two arcs of sand, Edwards and Balmoral Beaches, are separated by Rocky Point and part of Edwards is protected by a shark-proof net so you can swim in complete safety. Grab some fish and chips and a cool drink from one of the outlets on The Esplanade, and then dig your toes into the warm sand and watch the locals promenade. But remember: you're in the harbour, so there's no surf. The easiest way to get here from the centre is to take the ferry from Circular Quay to Taronga Park Wharf and take the 238 bus to Balmoral Beach.

The Spit to Manly

One of Sydney's best harbour foreshore walks starts at **The Spit Bridge**, which spans the narrowest section of Middle Harbour, and winds its way around Clontarf, Balgowlah Heights and Fairlight to Manly through part of the Sydney Harbour National Park.

Catch the 180 bus from Wynyard to The Spit Bridge, opt for a window seat on the left-hand side, and marvel as Spit Road races down Beauty Point, providing a dazzling view of million-dollar homes perched on tree-covered slopes plunging into the shimmering harbour, awash with motorboats and yachts. Alight at The Spit, walk across the bridge, and you'll find the start of the track at the first right-hand exit (just before Avona Crescent).

The easy, clearly marked trail leads across Sandy Bay, past Clontarf Beach, up to Castle Rock and then across the national park. It's a roller-coaster track, dropping deep into dense bushland before soaring up on to clifftop escarpments with breathtaking views of the main harbour and ocean beyond. The adventurous can clamber down to **Reef Beach**, a haunt for local nudists, or continue walking to **Forty Baskets Beach** and around North Harbour to Fairlight and, finally, Manly (*see page 100*). Allow at least a morning or afternoon for the walk – you need to be reasonably fit to tackle it – and avoid the hottest part of the day. A gentle ferry ride from Manly back to Circular Quay will ease those aching limbs.

Waverton

While the north shore's most spectacular vistas are to be found on the harbour foreshore, that's not to say other suburbs aren't worth visiting. A train ride across the Harbour Bridge to Waverton (one stop past North Sydney) will deliver you to **Balls Head Reserve**, a thickly wooded headland overlooking the start of the Parramatta River. There are free gas barbecues, so you can take your own lunch, cook up a feast and dine out at one of the best window seats in Sydney.

The *café-lined* **Blues Point Road** *in the heart of McMahons Point. See page 96.*

Northern Beaches

Pick a beach, any beach – from the madding crowd of Manly to the northern highlights of Palm, Whale and Avalon.

Manly's magical **Fairy Bower**.

If anything captures the essence of the northern beaches – golden sand, towering palm trees, casual restaurants, cool cafés, expansive golf courses and expensive houses – it's Palm Beach: stamping ground of Sydney's rich and famous, and arguably the most exclusive enclave in Australia. Basking on a narrow peninsula, the most northerly of the city's northern beaches is the social pinnacle of a community which stretches up from the leafy confines of the lower north shore, the yacht-lined waterways of Middle Harbour and the pleasure palaces of Manly.

Bondi may be Sydney's most famous beach, but it doesn't hold exclusive rights to the city's sun,

surf and sand culture. Head north from Manly, and you'll find a stretch of coastline that most European countries would sell their souls for.

Manly

A raffish resort town boasting both ocean and harbour aspects, Manly is as Sydney as the Opera House. Since its first days as a resort, Manly's catchcry has been 'Seven miles from Sydney and a thousand miles from care.' And after a relaxing ride across the harbour from Circular Quay on one of the four stately Manly ferries – named after the northern beaches of Freshwater, Narrabeen, Queenscliff and Collaroy – you can truly throw your cares to the salty sea breeze.

The suburb was given its name by Governor Arthur Phillip, when he sighted a number of 'manly' Aborigines on the shore of what he later called Manly Cove. Given that the beach suburb remains a centre for such macho pursuits as surf-lifesaving, bodysurfing and events like the Australian Ironman Championships, the name could not be more apt.

Sydneysiders have mixed feelings about Manly, but its perennial holiday atmosphere is overwhelmingly infectious. The main pedestrian precinct, **The Corso**, which links the ferry terminus with the oceanfront, is lined with tacky ice cream bars, fish and chip joints and tourist shops and is best avoided, but the laid-back bars and cafés of the North and South Steyne, with their panoramic ocean views, are idyllic spots from which to watch the world go by.

The walk around Fairy Bower, past some magnificent clifftop homes, to Shelly Beach is a must, and you can stop off for a cup of coffee at **The Bower** en route. Alternatively, hike up to **North Head**, the northern half of the gateway to Sydney Harbour (via Darley Road and North Head Scenic Drive), for the spectacular harbour panorama.

Manly's ocean beach, a long, pale crescent of sand and surf fringed by giant Norfolk Pines, is a weekend mecca for surfers, rollerbladers and sunbakers. The pines were planted by Henry Gilbert Smith in the 1850s, a wealthy English immigrant who decided to turn Manly from a tiny fishing village into a resort for the city. It was here, too, that WH Gocher, editor of the *Manly and North Sydney News,* flouted the law prohibiting daylight bathing in 1902, a symbolic act which probably marked the beginning of Manly's – and Sydney's – love affair with sun, sea, sand and surf.

If the crowds on the ocean beach get too much, sneak over to secluded **Manly Cove**, where you'll find a more peaceful patch of harbourside sand, though no surf, of course. Nearby, at the western end of the cove, is **Oceanworld**, which is worth a visit at shark-feeding time.

Freshwater to Whale Beach

From Manly, the northern beaches stretch out like a golden necklace and the names – Freshwater, Curl Curl, Dee Why, Collaroy, Narrabeen and Avalon – slip off the tongue like a surfer on the crest of a wave. This is Sydney's surf country, where the air smells of sea salt and coconut oil, and every second teenager hides under a mop of bleached-blond hair.

The easiest way to explore the northern beaches is by car, allowing you to stop and swim at leisure. Otherwise, the 190 bus from Wynyard will take you all the way to Palm Beach with stops at Dee Why, Narrabeen, Warriewood and Avalon (the whole journey takes about 1½ hours). You can hop off, catch a wave or two, and take the bus on to the next beach. The 180, 182 and 184 services from Wynyard run to Collaroy, Narrabeen and Mona Vale respectively.

The trip is a joy in itself: curling up past Long Reef and its palm-fringed headland golf course; dipping down alongside the tranquil Narrabeen Lakes; and up again to the clifftop twists of Bilgola, Avalon and Whale Beach.

Scattered communities of holiday homes and weekenders have grown into sizeable suburbs over the years, with increasing numbers of Sydney-siders opting to work in the city and put up with the long drive home for the sybaritic pleasures of living on the northern beaches.

Palm Beach

And so to Palm Beach, the end of the northern beaches line. If you haven't time for the road trip from the city, splash out and take a seaplane from Rose Bay to Pittwater, which lies on the sheltered western side of the Palm Beach peninsula. Try **Sydney Harbour Seaplanes** (1800 803 558) or **South Pacific Seaplanes** (9544 0077). Either way, it's a great day out, offering a soaring bird's-eye view of the northern beaches on the way there and back.

Palm Beach is worth at least a day's visit. Take the small ferry service across Pittwater to The Basin, where you can walk to some excellent Aboriginal rock carvings. If you've any energy left, the hike up **Barrenjoey Head** to the lighthouse offers superb gazing over the ocean, **Ku-Ring-Gai Chase National Park** (*see chapter* **The Great Outdoors**) and the golden swathe of Palm Beach. But maybe you should leave some time to indulge in that great northern beaches pastime of chilling out on the sand under a hot Sydney sun.

Manly Cove offers a change of pace on the flip side of Manly. For the Periwinkle, see page 21.

VETRO
Restaurant Wine Bar
Plaza Level, Grosvenor Place
225 George Street
Sydney NSW 2000
Ph: (02) 9247 8787

Monday & Tuesday   7.00am - 6.00pm
Wednesday - Friday   7.00am - late

Eating & Drinking

Eating & Drinking by Area

Central Sydney

CBD *Restaurants* BBQ King p115; Bodhi Vegetarian Restaurant p120; Brasserie Cassis p115; The Brooklyn p119; Capitan Torres p117; Casa Asturiana p117; CBD p111; Claudine's p115; Criterion p117; Edna's Table p117; Forty One p114; Gastronomia Chianti p117; Hellenic Club Restaurant p117; Kable's p106; Merrony's p116; Misto p113; Rock Fish Cafe p119; The Summit p114. *Cafés & Bars* Bambini Espresso Bar p122; Cigar Bar p130; The Forresters p129; George Street Bar p129; Hyde Park Barracks Cafe p125; Moretons p129; MOS Cafe p125. **Circular Quay** *Restaurants* Bennelong p106; Bilson's p113. **Darlinghurst** *Restaurants* Beppi's p116; Mario's p113; Oh! Calcutta! p116; La Pasquene p118. *Cafés & Bars* Bar Coluzzi p122; bills p122; Burdekin Hotel p130; Fu Manchu p127; Green Park Hotel p129; Judgement Bar p130; L'Otel p130; The Palace p129; Parmalat p126; Le Petit Crème p126; Taxi Club p130; Tropicana p127; Una's p127. **East Sydney** *Restaurants* The Edge p111. **Elizabeth Bay & Rushcutters Bay** *Cafés & Bars* The Penthouse Bar p129; Rushcutters Bay Kiosk p126; Vinyl Lounge p127. **Haymarket & Chinatown** *Restaurants* Chinatown Noodle Restaurant p115; Emperor's Garden Barbecue & Noodle Shop p115; Golden Century p115; Silver Spring p115; Superbowl Seafood p115. **Kings Cross** *Restaurants* Bayswater Brasserie p111; Cosmos p106; Darley Street Thai p106; Fishface p118; Lime & Lemongrass 119; Primadonna Restaurant & Oyster Bar p117. *Cafés & Bars* The Lounge Bar p130; Top of the Town p130. **Potts Point & Woolloomooloo** *Restaurants* Cicada p106; Edosei p116; Mezzaluna p114; Paramount p106; Morans p113; Pig & Olive p113; Wockpool p115. *Cafés & Bars* La Buvette p123; Minami p128; Wockpool Bar p128. **Redfern** *Restaurants* Andy's p119; Ericlyes p120; Sushi Suma p116. **The Rocks** *Restaurants* bel mondo p106; Palisade p114; Rockpool p106; Unkai p116; The Wharf p115. *Cafés & Bars* Hero of Waterloo p129; Horizons Bar p129; Lord Nelson Brewery Hotel p129; MCA Cafe p125; Mercantile Hotel p129; Sailor's Thai Canteen p128. **Surry Hills** *Restaurants* Divan p120; Mohr Fish p118; Prasit's p120; Riberries p118; Wood & Stone p118. *Cafés & Bars* Bizircus p122; Cafe Nikki p123; Chu Bay p127; The Dolphin p129; Metronome p125; Prasit's Northside Takeaway p128.

Eastern Suburbs

Bondi *Restaurants* Indochine p120. **Bondi Beach** *Restaurants* Biboteca p111; Hugo's p113; Onzain p114; Ravesi's p114; Raw Bar p116; Sean's Panorama p113; Sports Bar(d) p113. *Cafés & Bars* Beachwood Bar & Grill p129; Bondi Aqua Bar p122; Bondi Surf Seafoods p125; Burgerman p125; Digger's Café p123; Dip p123; Earth Food Store p125; Gusto p125; The Icebergs p130; Liberty Lunch p129; Oporto Portuguese Style Chicken p125; Ploy Thai p128; Red Kite p126. **Bondi Junction** *Cafés & Bars* Ju-Ju's p128. **Bronte** *Cafés & Bars* Sejuiced p126. **Coogee** *Restaurants* China Bowl p114. **Edgecliff** *Restaurants* A Flavour of India p116. **Kensington** *Restaurants* Ratu Sari p119. **North Bondi** *Restaurants* Savion p117. **Paddington** *Restaurants* Buon Ricordo p116; Four in Hand Hotel p111; Grand National p111; Grand Pacific Blue Room p111; La Mensa p113; Royal Bar & Grill p113; Verona p113. *Cafés & Bars* Centennial Park Café p123; Paddington Inn p129. **Rose Bay** *Restaurants* Catalina p113; The Pier p119. *Cafés & Bars* Bernasconi's p122. **Vaucluse** *Restaurants* Nielsen Park Kiosk p114. **Watsons Bay** *Restaurants* Doyles p118. **Woollahra** *Restaurants* Bistro Moncur p106; Claudes p106;

Prunier's Chiswick Gardens p116. *Cafés & Bars* Lord Dudley p129; Nostimo p126; The Woollahra p129.

Inner West

Balmain *Restaurants* Lennons p119. *Cafés & Bars* Chesters p123. **Glebe** *Restaurants* Iku Wholefood Kitchen p120. *Cafés & Bars* Rose Blues Cafe p126. **Leichhardt** *Restaurants* Frattini p117. **Rozelle** *Restaurants* Never on Sunday p117; Tetsuya's p106.

Newtown & the South

Dulwich Hill *Cafés & Bars* Minh p128. **Newtown** *Restaurants* Steki Taverna p117; Wedgetail p118.

Parramatta & the West

Bankstown *Restaurants* An Restaurant p120. **Cabramatta** *Restaurants* Tau Bay p120. **North Strathfield** *Restaurants* Abhi's p116.

North Shore

Balmoral *Restaurants* Bathers Pavilion p113. *Cafés & Bars* Bathers Pavilion Refreshment Room p125; Bottom of the Harbour p125. **Chatswood** *Restaurants* Fook Yuen p115. **Crows Nest** *Restaurants* Desaru p119; Sakana-ya p116; Sea Treasure p115. **McMahons Point** *Cafés & Bars* Thomas Street Cafe p127. **Neutral Bay** *Restaurants* Fiorentino p117. **North Sydney** *Restaurants* Armstrong's North Sydney p119; Plaza Grill p119; To's Malaysian Gourmet p119.

Northern Beaches

Manly *Restaurants* Armstrong's Manly p113; Brazil p113; Cafe Tunis p117; Le Kiosk p114. *Cafés & Bars* The Bower p123; Manly Fish Market & Cafe p125. **Palm Beach** *Restaurants* Jonah's p114. *Cafés & Bars* Ancora Cafe p122. **Whale Beach** *Cafés & Bars* Whaley's p127.

Further Afield

Blackheath *Restaurants* Cleopatra p115; Vulcan's p106. **Mascot** *Cafés & Bars* Caffe Italia p123.

Restaurants

From ModMed or ModOz to MidEast or Far East, there's many a twist in Sydney's culinary tale.

Where did all this good food in Australia – labelled 'upstart cuisine' by local writer and restaurateur Gay Bilson – come from? I mean, bloody Aussies, what a joke! Meat pies and Fosters and Bazza McKenzie pointing Percy at the porcelain wasn't that long ago. What happened?

Several things. Firstly, Australia was colonised by the English, who sent over their poor, tired, and disenfranchised – mainly Irish. Now, say what you like, but until recently the words 'good food', 'English' and 'Irish' rarely appeared in the same sentence. Alan Watkins, writing in the *Spectator*, said that his mother 'believed it ill-mannered to talk about food'. Well, you wouldn't have, would you? So when the huge influx of Mediterranean migrants began arriving after World War II, they found nothing to eat – Australia wasn't so much *terra nullus* as *tabula rasa*.

More importantly, they found people crying out for something decent to eat. George Haddad, credited with developing Lebanese-Australian food, remarked that although he was called a 'wog' (here meaning a Mediterranean) when he went to school, when he grew up and invited friends home, they were eager to try the strange food he was cooking.

It's one of the things about Australians: they're what the marketing people call 'early adopters'. Videos, mobile phones, electronic organisers – all are gobbled up. And so it was with the food of Australia's new residents. Then came the jumbo jet. 'My big hero in this story,' said Melbourne (and now Sydney) chef Bill Marchetti, 'is the Boeing 747. All of a sudden everybody can afford to get on a plane and fly to wherever they want and taste the food there.' When the travellers returned, they demanded the food they'd tasted in Europe.

And they began to get it. And as much as Sydneysiders hate to admit it, it probably began in Melbourne, with an institution known as the BYO (Bring Your Own – bottle). A change in licensing laws in the early 1970s saw an outbreak of such little restaurants, run by local heroes like Mietta O'Donnell, Stephanie Alexander, Tony and Gay Bilson, and Hermann Schneider. Then the revolution came to Sydney (as did Tony and Gay Bilson) and things began to hot up.

Although Australia had long been a farming country, it then began to think in terms of quality rather than quantity. As chefs demanded new produce, farmers learnt how to provide it. Today,

Bennelong. *ModOz at its best? See p106.*

there's a wider range of first-class ingredients available in Australia than almost anywhere in the world. Just look at the Sydney Fish Markets.

Finally, in 1972, the conservative (Liberal) government that had gazed fondly for 25 years into the distant colonial past (Asia was the place you flew over on the way to London) was replaced by a Labor government which, whatever its faults, taught Australians who they were – and where they were.

And so it was that the food of Australia's northern neighbours entered the mix. There may not actually be an identifiable Australian Cuisine yet – it's a controversial question – but who cares? Sydney has a world-beating choice of places to eat terrific, exciting and imaginative food.

The average price quoted in the listings below is for a three-course meal without drink. Many Sydney restaurants are BYO, which means that they aren't licensed to sell alcohol but you can bring your own. They usually charge a small corkage fee; licensed restaurants that are also BYO usually charge a higher fee.

Wizards of Oz

Here they are. The chefs from the front line of the revolution. In their diversity is strength. If you were keen enough and assiduous enough to eat your way around every one of these terrific places, you'd learn to unpick the strands that weave together to make up that elusive, multi-faceted, world-beating hybrid variously known as Australian Cuisine, Australian Contemporary Cuisine or just plain Modern Australian.

bel mondo

Level 3, The Argyle Department Store, 12 Argyle Street, The Rocks (9241 3700). CityRail/ferry Circular Quay. **Open** noon-3pm, 6-11pm, daily. **Average** $55. **Licensed. Credit** AmEx, BC, DC, MC, V.

The home of the best Italian food in Australia – previously called The Restaurant Manfredi – has moved from a back lane in Ultimo to grander premises in The Rocks. The quality remains constant in the kitchen, where Stefano Manfredi and mother Franca concoct classic northern Italian (and Italian-Australian) dishes using the best local ingredients.

Bennelong

Bennelong Point, Circular Quay (9250 7578/fax 9250 7993). CityRail/ferry Circular Quay. **Open** 6-11pm Mon-Sat. **Average** $75. **Licensed. Credit** AmEx, BC, DC, MC, $TC, V.

One of the world's most beautiful buildings now boasts one of the world's most beautiful restaurants. Inside, chef Janni Kyritsis and Sydney's first lady of food, Gay Bilson, combine their talents to offer food from the cutting edge of Australian Contemporary Cuisine – often challenging, always worth the effort – served with minimum fuss and maximum elegance. If you have time for just one night out in Sydney, this is it.

Bistro Moncur

116 Queen Street, Woollahra (9363 2782). Bus 378, 380, 382. **Open** 10.30am-10pm Tue-Sat; 9am-9pm Sun. **Average** $35. **Licensed. Credit** BC, DC, MC, $TC, V.

The satisfying food in this chic and buzzing see-and-be-seen room displays the deft touch and Gallic bent of chef and co-owner Damien Pignolet, one of Sydney's long-term civilising influences. He's now the city's leading purveyor of bistro classics. Lots of great bottles.

Cicada

29 Challis Avenue, Potts Point (9358 1255). Bus 311. **Open** 6.30-10pm Mon, Tue; noon-2.30pm, 6-10.30pm, Wed-Fri; 6.30-10pm Sat. **Average** $50. **Licensed. Credit** AmEx, BC, DC, MC, V.

Chef Peter Doyle and wife Beverley (front of house) offer a relaxed and already classic version of ModOz in a three-storey Victorian terrace, elegantly revamped in a breezy Italian manner. Fine sommelier Philippe Morin will guide you through an extensive and intelligent wine list.

Claudes

10 Oxford Street, Woollahra (9331 2325). Bus 378, 380, 382. **Open** 7.30-9.30pm Tue-Sat. **Average** $100. **BYO. Credit** AmEx, BC, MC, V.

The Australian phenomenon of the BYO finds its apogee here. Brilliant young chef Tim Pak Poy turns out intelligent and wonderful-tasting interpretations of (mainly) French classics with an elegant Australian twist.

Cosmos

185A Bourke Street, East Sydney (9331 5306). CityRail Kings Cross. **Open** 6.15-11pm Mon-Thur; noon-3pm, 6.15-11pm, Fri, Sat.* **Average** $35. **BYO. Credit** AmEx, DC.

Of course there's a Greek strand to ModOz, and in Sydney, it is provided by Peter Conistis (with assistance and spirit from mum Eleni) in an improbably tiny shopfronted room in East Sydney. Sure it's Greek food. It's just not the Greek food you've been conned into eating for years. Cosmos was due to move at the time of writing, so check its location first – but go.

Darley Street Thai

28-30 Bayswater Road, Kings Cross (9358 6530). CityRail Kings Cross. **Open** 6.30-10.30pm daily. **Average** $45. **Licensed. Credit** AmEx, BC, DC, MC, V.

David Thompson went to Thailand and fell in love. Ten years on, he dishes up new evidence of his ongoing love affair in this chic Kings Cross room. It's currently offering a seven-course fixed-price dinner from recipes collected and perfected by Thompson on his travels.

Kable's

The Regent Sydney, 199 George Street, Sydney (9238 0000/9255 0226/fax 9241 5397). CityRail/ferry Circular Quay. **Open** noon-3pm, 6-10.30pm, Tue-Fri; 6-10.30pm Sat. **Average** $42.50 lunch; $75 dinner. **Credit** AmEx, BC, DC, JCB, MC, TC, V.

Serge Dansereau came from Canada to discover a wonderland of fresh produce. The very best of that produce passes through the kitchen here, and appears, after minimum interference, in clever combinations on the plates in this quietly opulent setting. Way above the average hotel dining room. *Disabled: access; toilets.*

Paramount

73 Macleay Street, Potts Point (9358 1652). Bus 311. **Open** 6.30-11pm daily. **Average** $55. **Licensed. Credit** AmEx, BC, DC, MC, $TC, V.

In this chic and curvaceous room, Chrissie Manfield browses though the cuisines of Oz's Asian neighbours for her conception of ModOz, and creates her own intricate and layered dishes.

Rockpool

107 George Street, The Rocks (9252 1888). CityRail/ferry Circular Quay. **Open** noon-2.30pm, 6-11pm, Mon-Fri; 6-11pm Sat. **Average** $80. **Licensed. Credit** AmEx, BC, MC, $TC, V.

Sydney on a plate. The Asian influences; the more-than-a-passing nod towards the Mediterranean; the sleek and shiny city crowd in rooms to match; seafresh oysters shucked at the bar. Without even a glimpse of the harbour – but with a mainly marine menu – chef Neil Perry and his talented team have put this place four-square at the centre of the game. Go for the food. Go back for the experience.

Tetsuya's

729 Darling Street, Rozelle (9555 1017). Bus 440. **Open** 7pm-midnight Tue; noon-2.30pm, 7pm-midnight, Wed-Sat. **Average** $85. **Licensed & BYO. Credit** AmEx, BC, DC, MC, $TC, V.

What do you call a Japanese chef French-trained in Australia? Bloody brilliant, that's what. And unique. There is no one like Tetsuya Wakuda. Tetsuya's is where other chefs go to be amazed, dismayed and inspired. Place it on your must-visit list along with Uluru and the Barrier Reef.

Vulcan's

33 Govett's Leap Road, Blackheath (4787 6899). CityRail Blackheath. **Open** 9am-late Fri-Sun. **Average** $25. **BYO. No credit cards.**

When the history of Australian food is written, Phillip

East meets best at David Thompson's **Darley Street Thai.**

La Mensa: *designer diner. See page 113.*

Searle's name will be dotted throughout the book, especially under the heading 'Kangaroo'. Adelaidian Searle taught us how to put the 'roo into (or at least on top of) beetroot. Having moved with long-term partner Barry Ross to the Blue Mountains, he's taking it easier but still doing fine – if a little more relaxed – things in the kitchen of a tiny converted shopfront bakery. Aficionados please note: chequerboard ice-cream is always on the menu.

Hip

Be warned: what's hot today can go clammy without notice. Right now, these places are steaming.

Bayswater Brasserie

32 Bayswater Road, Kings Cross (9357 2177/fax 9358 1213). CityRail Kings Cross. **Open** noon-11pm Mon-Sat; 10am-10pm Sun. **Average** $35. **Licensed. Credit** AmEx, BC, DC, JCB, MC, $TC, V.
A long-time favourite hangout for glitterati, literati and arterati, which doesn't stop the food from being first-class and ever-changing, with a leavening of old favourites.

Biboteca

252 Campbell Parade, Bondi Beach (9300 9639/fax 9300 9633). Bus 380, 382. **Open** noon-3pm, 6-10pm, Mon-Fri; 10am-3pm, 6-10pm, Sat; 8am-3pm, 6-10pm, Sun. **Average** $30. **Licensed. Credit** AmEx, BC, DC, MC, $TC, V.
Bondi is home to a whole new wave of bars and restaurants, and Vince Trotta's Biboteca was one of the first off the mark. Trotta's Italian background and Roman wood-fired oven set the scene.

CBD

75 York Street, Sydney (9299 8911/9299 8292/fax 9299 8318). CityRail Wynyard. **Open** noon-3pm, 6-10pm, Mon-Thur; noon-3pm, 7-11pm, Fri. **Average** $40. **Licensed. Credit** AmEx, BC, DC, MC, V.

This eccentrically but comfortably renovated old bank building is home to a buzzy bar popular with local screen jockeys, a very good restaurant (Roux Brothers grad Luke Mangan is in the kitchen) and a private club for hand-picked members.

The Edge

60 Riley Street, East Sydney (9360 1372/fax 9380 5366). Bus 200, 323. **Open** noon-11pm daily. **Average** $40. **Licensed. Credit** AmEx, BC, JCB, MC, V.
No longer cutting but still hopping, after three years of wowing them with a surefire formula of wood-fired pizzas, Med-dish mains and desserts to drool for.

Four in Hand Hotel

105 Sutherland Street, Paddington (9326 2254/fax 9363 9543). Bus 380, 382. **Open** 11am-11pm Mon-Sat; noon-10pm Sun. **Average** $35. **Licensed. Credit** AmEx, BC, DC, MC, V.
One of the first trad Aussie pubs to fall victim to a smart publican, in this case Valdis Gravelis. It's now a favourite local watering and lunching spot for Paddo's DINKS.

Grand National

161 Underwood Street, Paddington (9363 4557/fax 9363 3542). Bus 378, 380, 382. **Open** noon-3pm Tue; noon-3pm, 6-10pm, Wed; noon-3pm, 6-10.30pm, Thur-Sat; noon-3pm Sun. **Average** $25. **Licensed. Credit** AmEx, BC, DC, MC, V.
Another old Paddo pub bites the dust, gets done over by an architect and pops up as a bright and comfortable bar/restaurant. Where does an old digger go for a drink these days?

Grand Pacific Blue Room

Corner of South Dowling and Oxford Streets, Paddington (9331 7108/fax 9331 6119). Bus 378, 380, 382. **Open** *restaurant* 6pm-midnight Mon-Sat; 6-10pm Sun; *bar* 11pm-1am Mon-Wed; 11pm-2.30am Thur; 11pm-3.30am Fri, Sat. **Average** $35. **Licensed. Credit** AmEx, BC, MC, $TC, V.
We wouldn't go here starving – although most of the crowd looks a bit that way – but it's a noisy, fun, hetero hangout on Oxford Street's gay way.

Buzzness as usual at **Bistro Moncur**. *See page 106.*

Winewise

The other important ingredient in the Australian food mix is, of course, Australian wine. An astonishing success story, both for the rapidity of its entry into international markets since the mid-1980s and for the quality of the product.

The good news for those travelling to Sydney is that, like the French, the Australians keep the best bottles for themselves. With over 600 winemakers and one leading wine cellar stocking over 1,000 products, the range is bewildering. But here are a few tips to help you make your choice.

Most good Australian wines are known by their varietal (grape) names, with a few exceptions – like Penfold's Koonunga Hill, a shiraz cabernet blend. So look for pinot noirs, rieslings and chardonnays, rather than Burgundy or Chablis. Secondly, until quite recently, the majority of wines were made as single varietals – using one grape variety – rather than as blends. This is now changing, and you can spot some interesting blends – among the more offbeat, Mitchelton's marsanne viognier roussanne.

Although wine is made throughout Australia (even in Alice Springs), different regions have different specialities. So try sémillon from the Hunter Valley; pinot from Tasmania; shiraz from the Barossa, north-eastern Victoria and the Hunter; fortified wines from north-eastern Victoria; chardonnay from the Adelaide Hills and the Yarra Valley; and riesling from the Clare Valley in South Australia. That said, you will also find excellent riesling from Tasmania; the shiraz (Hermitage) for the legendary Grange is grown all over South Australia; at least one very fine cabernet sauvignon (Lake's Folly) comes from the Hunter; and one winemaker in north-eastern Victoria, Brown Brothers, grows in excess of 20 different varietals.

But the experts are always in disagreement, or being confounded about *terroir*, so make your own discoveries – and seek guidance. In the grander restaurants that we have listed (for example, Cicada, bel mondo, Prunier's Chiswick Gardens or Merrony's), you'll find sommeliers, passionate professionals, only too pleased to help you – and to impart their own prejudices.

Then there are a couple of establishments which make a point of offering wide selections of excellent Australian wines by the glass (a practice which, thankfully, is spreading). Hazi's is a wine bar run by ex-wine merchant Chris Hayes, which has a permanent list of 30 mostly Australian offerings, including the best of the sparklers. In the CBD, Stan Sarris at Vetro, with the help of wine merchant Jon Osbieston, has put together a system of tasting with tapas-sized portions of food in 'flights' of three or five different wines – a system borrowed from professional wine-tasters.

Hazi's Wine Bar
45 Cross Street, Double Bay (9362 3733).

Vetro
Plaza Level, 225 George Street, Sydney (9247 8787).

BOTTLES & BOTTLE SHOPS

Finally, here's a list of retailers who are above average in their ability to help the inquisitive visitor, and for the width of their range, preceded by a list of bottles to watch out for. The Ultimo Wine Centre and the Wine Gallery are both a little off the beaten track, but they are impossible for the real wine lover to ignore.

Vine Distinctions

For each wine, the first suggestion is reasonably priced and commonly found, the second pricier and/or scarcer.
Chardonnay David Wynn Unwooded (Barossa/Eden Valley, SA); Bannockburn (Geelong, Victoria).
Sémillon Peter Lehmann (Barossa, SA); Lindemans Hunter River Classic Release 1986, Bin 6855 (Hunter Valley, NSW).
Riesling Brown Brothers (King Valley, Victoria); Paulette's Polish Hill River (Clare Valley, SA).
Stickies (dessert wine) De Bortoli Noble One botrytis (Riverina, NSW); Lillypilly Estate Noble Muscat of Alexandria (Leeton, NSW).
Shiraz Seaview (McLaren Vale, SA); Rothbury Estate Reserve (Hunter Valley, NSW).
Pinot noir Ninth Island (Piper's Brook, Tasmania); Salitage 1994 (Pemberton, WA).
Cabernet sauvignon Wilson Vineyard (Clare Valley, SA); Leeuwin Estate Art Series (Margaret River, WA).
Australian eccentrics Seppelts Show Sparkling Burgundy (Great Western, Victoria); Morris Very Old Liqueur Muscat (Rutherglen, Victoria).

Best Cellars
91 Crown Street, East Sydney (9361 5454).

Five Ways Cellars
4 Heeley Street, Paddington (9360 4242).

Kemeny's Food & Liquor
141 Bondi Road, Bondi (9389 6422).

Paddington Fine Wines
306 South Dowling Street, Paddington (9332 1811).

Ultimo Wine Centre
460 Jones Street, Ultimo (9211 2380).

Vintage Cellars
396 New South Head Road, Double Bay (9327 1333)

Wine Gallery
Shop 1, 211-219 Bulwara Road, Pyrmont (9552 2100).

Hugo's
70 Campbell Parade, Bondi Beach (9300 0900). Bus 380, 382. **Open** 6.30-10.30pm Mon-Fri; 9am-4pm, 6.30-10.30pm, Sat, Sun. **Average** $30. **Licensed. Credit** BC, DC, MC, V.
Spunky-looking staff and food are the big pulls at this newest of the Bondi hangouts. There's a big window – all the better to leer at the undulating scene along Campbell Parade.

Mario's
38 Yurong Street, Darlinghurst (9331 4945/fax 9360 9941). Bus 378, 380, 382. **Open** noon-3pm, 6-11pm, Mon-Fri; 6-11pm Sat. **Average** $30. **Licensed. Credit** AmEx, BC, MC, V.
Sit here long enough and *tout* Sydney (bizoids in the day-time, modelles and actrines after dark) will pass through in search of OK Italian and a hit of Mario's patented bright and noisy buzz.

La Mensa
257 Oxford Street, Paddington (9332 2963). Bus 378, 380, 382. **Open** 11am-9.30pm Mon-Fri; 9am-9.30pm Sat, Sun. **Average** $25. **Licensed. Credit** BC, DC, MC, V.
Here's the thing – a cafeteria. But wait: check the food. Smart, ModMed and Sydney south-east Asian with wines to match. There's produce (some of the best in Sydney) and La Mensa branded products (La Mensa rock candy) to go.

Misto
127 Kent Street, Millers Point (9251 9669). CityRail Wynyard. **Open** 7am-10pm daily. **Average** $40. **Licensed. Credit** AmEx, BC, DC, JCB, MC, $TC, V.
A sleek, all-white, stainless-steel café/restaurant and general shop offering a day-long ModMed, ModFrog mix.

Morans
61-63 Macleay Street, Potts Point (9356 2223/fax 9358 3035). Bus 311. **Open** *restaurant* 6.30-11pm Mon, Tue; noon-3pm, 6.30-11pm, Wed-Fri; 11.30am-3pm, 6.30-11pm, Sat, Sun; *café* 8am-midnight Mon-Fri; 8am-10pm Sun. **Average** *restaurant* $40; *café* $10. **Licensed. Credit** AmEx, BC, DC, MC, $TC, V.
There are two choices: a sleek, white, frosted-glass restaurant for swanky seating and superior eating; or slip round the corner for café-style lounging with the papers.

Pig & Olive
71A Macleay Street, Potts Point (9357 3745). Bus 311. **Open** 6-11pm Mon-Fri; 6-10pm Sun. **Average** $30. **BYO. Credit** AmEx, BC, MC, V.
The menus are these two noisy guzzling spots feature pizzas Pavarotti never sung for – sort of ModOz on a crust. There are other Italianate offerings as well, but it's the pizzas what drags 'em in.
Branch: 318A Military Road, Cremorne (9953 7512).

Royal Bar & Grill
237 Glenmore Road, Paddington (9331 2604). Bus 378, 380, 382. **Open** 10am-midnight Mon-Sat; noon-10pm Sun. **Average** $30. **Licensed. Credit** AmEx, BC, DC, MC, $TC, V.
Another Paddo pub but sticking to its Victorian roots, at least in decor. The food is clever modern bistro style, the bar is a scene, and upstairs the sofa-stuffed Elephant Bar is a well padded way to end the night.

Sean's Panaroma
270 Campbell Parade, Bondi Beach (9365 4924). Bus 380, 382. **Open** *summer* 7-10pm Mon-Thur; 8am-3pm, 7-10pm, Fri-Sat; 8am-3pm Sun; *winter* 7-10pm Wed, Thur; 8am-3pm, 7-10pm, Fri, Sat; 8am-3pm Sun. **Average** $45. **BYO. No credit cards.**
Ignore or enjoy the recycled decor and tuck into Sean Moran's home brand of clever comfort food – it's to go back for. Big on breakfasts.

Sports Bar(d)
32 Campbell Parade, Bondi Beach (9130 4582). Bus 380, 382. **Open** 6-11pm Mon; noon-11pm Tue-Fri; 9am-11pm Sat; 9am-10pm Sun. **Average** $20. **Licensed & BYO. Credit** AmEx, BC, MC, V.
Prevented by licensing laws from calling itself a bar, the Sports Bar(d) is good for just about anything: pool, break-fast, beer, coffee, onion soup, steak, potato wedges. Run by local Bondi boys and situated in the heart of Bondi, it represents that which is wholesome and good about Bondi: a healthy respect for food, surf and brown torsos.

Verona
17 Oxford Street, Paddington (9360 3266). Bus 378, 380, 382. **Open** noon-midnight daily. **Average** $20. **Licensed. Credit** AmEx, BC, DC, MC, V.
The designer café/bar attached to the new cinema complex offers a good selection of before and aftershow pizzas and pastas. Or there are more leisurely things for people who just want to hang out and enjoy the leafy view over Oxford Street. *Disabled: access; toilets.*

Views

Armstrong's Manly
Shop 213, Manly Wharf, Manly (9976 3835). Ferry Manly. **Open** 10.30am-11pm daily. **Average** $35. **Licensed. Credit** AmEx, BC, DC, MC, $TC, V.
Better-than-average food – everything from good steak to the expected seafood – with a view of the harbour side of Manly.

Bathers Pavilion
4 The Esplanade, Balmoral (9968 1133). Bus 257/ferry Mosman. **Open** noon-3pm, 6-11pm, Mon-Fri; 9am-3pm, 6-11pm Sat, Sun. **Average** $50. **Licensed. Credit** AmEx, BC, DC, MC, $TC, V.
This middle-class fantasy of a beach house on the calm beauty of Balmoral Beach is one of the three or four essential places for even the most hard-pressed Sydney visitor to sample. Food ranges from brilliant to well mannered (for local tastes) and tends to look north to Asia for flavours and inspiration. *See also chapter* **Cafés & Bars**.

Bilson's
Upper Level, Overseas Passenger Terminal, Circular Quay West, The Rocks (9251 5600). CityRail/ferry Circular Quay. **Open** noon-3pm, 6-10pm, Mon-Fri; 6-10pm Sat, Sun. **Average** $60. **Licensed. Credit** AmEx, BC, DC, MC, $TC, V.
This could just be the best view of Sydney Harbour (unlike Bennelong you can look back at the Opera House from here) with, finally, food (modern French) to match. *Disabled: access; toilets.*

Brazil
46 North Steyne, Manly (9977 3825). Ferry Manly. **Open** 8am-midnight daily. **Average** $20. **Licensed & BYO. Credit** AmEx, BC, DC, MC, $TC, V.
A long narrow room with an upstairs louvred view through Norfolk pines of the surfside of Manly, and a Sydney eclectic menu that encompasses everything from guacamole to Balinese spiced fish. There's also a street-level café.

Catalina
Lyne Park, off New South Head Road, Rose Bay (9371 0555). Bus 323, 324, 325. **Open** noon-11pm daily. **Average** $50. **Licensed. Credit** AmEx, BC, DC, MC, $TC, V.
The stark white curve of the building matches the languorous curve of Rose Bay, and somebody plopped Shark Island right in the middle of the view. The food ranges from excellent to indifferent, but go for the sheer glamour.

China Bowl

*169 Dolphin Street, Coogee (9665 3308). Bus 314, 315,
372, 373, 374.* **Open** 11am-10.30pm Mon-Fri; 10am-
11pm Sat, Sun. **Average** $15. **Licensed**. **Credit** AmEx,
BC, DC, MC, USTC, V.
Right in the heart of backpacker territory, the China Bowl
provides damn good Sunday yum cha (dim sum) – lots of
local Chinese eat here – and views of Coogee's fine beach.

Forty One

*Level 41, Chifley Tower, 2 Chifley Square, Sydney (9221
2500). CityRail Martin Place.* **Open** noon-4pm, 7pm-1am,
Mon-Fri; 7pm-1am Sat. **Average** $80. **Licensed**. **Credit**
AmEx, BC, DC, MC, $TC, V.
Top of the town for views, elegance, food and service, all the
more impressive an effort when you reflect that the team
could pack them in with the helicopter-height views alone.
Disabled: access; toilets.

Jonah's

*69 Bynya Road, Palm Beach (9974 5599/fax 9974 1212).
Bus 190.* **Open** noon-3pm, 6.30-9pm, Mon-Fri; 8-10am,
noon-3pm, 6.30-9pm, Sat, Sun. **Average** $55. **Licensed**.
Credit AmEx, BC, DC, MC, $TC, V.
Your chance to see how the other half lives. Admire sweeping views across Palm Beach and eat French-accented Med
food. You can stay the night (book well in advance) and
breakfast before a splash in the surf below.

Le Kiosk

*1 Marine Parade, Shelly Beach, Manly (9977 4122).
Ferry Manly.* **Open** noon-2.30pm, 6.30-9pm, Mon-Thur;
noon-2.30pm, 6.30-9.30pm, Fri; noon-3pm, 6.30-10pm, Sat;
11.30am-3.30pm, 6.30-9pm, Sun. **Average** $50.
Licensed. **Credit** AmEx, BC, DC, MC, $TC, V.
The first (it opened more than 20 years ago) of the beachside 'tearoom' conversions sits on the beach with a stunning view and up-and-down food – apparently up at the
time of writing.

Mezzaluna

*123 Victoria Street, Potts Point (9357 1988). CityRail
Kings Cross.* **Open** noon-3pm Mon; noon-3pm, 6-11pm,
Tue-Sun. **Average** $55. **Licensed**. **Credit** AmEx, BC,
DC, JCB, MC, $TC, V.
This is a second venture for the Polese family (*see*
Beppi's *under* **Italian**) and, subjectively, has the second-
best view in Sydney, offering more adventurous *cucina*
than pappa's place.

Nielsen Park Kiosk

*Greycliffe Avenue, Vaucluse (9337 1574). Bus 324,
325.* **Open** noon-3pm Tue-Sat; 8.30-11am, noon-3pm,
Sun. **Average** $45. **BYO**. **Credit** AmEx, BC, DC, MC,
$TC, V.
Walk through the park to this 1914 building that, for the
first time in recent years, appears to be in good (Italian) culinary hands. Go for a swim in the harbour pool, dry off, and
eat. There are good rolls and snacks to take away in the
adjoining canteen.

Onzain

*Second Floor, Bondi Digger's Club, 232 Campbell
Parade, Bondi Beach (9365 0763). Bus 380, 382.* **Open**
6-11pm Mon-Thur; noon-3pm, 6-11pm, Fri, Sat; 12.30-
9.30pm Sun. **Average** $30. **Licensed**. **Credit** AmEx,
BC, MC, $TC, V.
Despite the name, this is not the place for an old digger to
get a drink, unless he's a very switched on old digger indeed
and knows his rillettes from his andouillettes. Especially
good around dusk in summer for a grandly garish sunset
over Bondi – God bless that pollution. For **Diggers** *see*
chapter **Cafés & Bars**.

Not cutting but hopping at **The Edge**. *P111.*

Palisade

*35-37 Bettington Street, The Rocks (9251 7225).
CityRail/ferry Circular Quay.* **Open** noon-3pm, 6-10.30pm,
Mon-Fri; 6-10.30pm Sat. **Average** $30. **Licensed**.
Credit AmEx, BC, MC, $TC, V.
There are more of what Sydney real estate agents call 'har-
bour glimpses', but very interesting ones of the working end,
from the dining room of this ship-shape pub. The food is
equally fascinating.

The Pier

*594 New South Head Road, Rose Bay (9327 4187). Bus
323, 324, 325.* **Open** noon-3pm, 6-10pm, Mon-Sat; noon-
3pm, 6-9pm, Sun. **Average** $55. **Licensed**. **Credit**
AmEx, BC, DC, MC, $TC, V.
Sublime seafood on breathtakingly beautiful Rose Bay is
hard to beat – another one of those must-see-and-eat Sydney
spots for the visitor wanting to get to the essence.

Ravesi's

*Corner of Campbell Parade and Hall Street, Bondi Beach
(9365 4422/fax 9365 1481). Bus 380, 382.* **Open** 7.30-
11.15am, noon-10pm, daily. **Average** $30. **Licensed**.
Credit AmEx, BC, DC, MC, $TC, V.
An early high achiever in the neighbourhood, which has, of
late, dropped behind a bit, but is still good for gazing and
grazing, especially at breakfast time. It's also a good place
to stay (*see chapter* **Accommodation**).
Disabled: access; toilets.

The Summit

*264 George Street, Sydney (9247 9777). CityRail
Wynyard.* **Open** noon-3pm, 6-9.30pm, Mon-Thur; noon-
3pm, 6-10.30pm, Fri, Sat; noon-3pm, 6-9pm, Sun.
Average $45 buffet, $60 full menu. **Licensed**. **Credit**
AmEx, BC, DC, JCB, MC, V.

Included more for nostalgia than any other reason, the famous revolving restaurant here is a high point for those few remaining devotees of lobster thermidor. A landmark.

The Wharf
Pier 4, Hickson Road, Walsh Bay (9250 1761).
CityRail/ferry Circular Quay. **Open** noon-3pm, 6-10pm,
Mon-Sat. **Average** $30. **Licensed**. **Credit** AmEx, BC,
DC, MC, V.
At the end of a long wharf (and walk) that also houses the Sydney Theatre Company, the restaurant can look after you pre- or post-show, but is also a solo act with a clever collection of Sydney bistro food.

Chinese

The local Chinese was probably the first and only dining out experience for most Australians, pre-McDonald's. Then, as now, the majority of Australian Chinese were Cantonese. More recently, another influx of Cantonese – this time from northern China and Hong Kong – has created a second Chinatown in the northern Sydney suburb of Chatswood. The Australian version of dim sum is known as yum cha.

BBQ King
18-20 Goulburn Street, Sydney (9267 2433). CityRail
Town Hall. **Open** 11.30am-2am daily. **Average** $18.
Licensed. **Credit** AmEx, DC, MC, V.
Proudly grotty, and home to some of the best duck and pork in the city. This is where many ModOz chefs go after service.

Chinatown Noodle Restaurant
8 Quay Street, Haymarket (9281 9051). CityRail
Central. **Open** 11am-9pm daily. **Average** $28. **BYO**.
No credit cards.
A real find. A tiny corner of China's remote north-western Xinjiang province in south Chinatown. Noodlemeister Cin's handmade noodle and dumpling dishes are justly celebrated.

Emperor's Garden Barbecue
& Noodle Shop
213-215 Thomas Street, Haymarket (9281 9899).
CityRail Central. **Open** 9.30am-11pm daily. **Average**
$13.50-$30 BBQ; $9 noodles. **Licensed**. **Credit** AmEx,
BC, DC, MC, V.
Another BBQ joint with perhaps the edge over the King (*above*) in the suckling pig department. Pester the staff for a translation of the wall posters in Chinese, and you'll turn up some wonderful hot-pot dishes.
Branch: Emperor's Garden Seafood Restaurant, 100 Hay Street, Haymarket (9211 2135).

Fook Yuen
Level 1, 7 Help Street, Chatswood (9413 2688). CityRail
Chatswood. **Open** 11am-11pm daily. **Average** $16.
Licensed. **Credit** AmEx, BC, DC, MC, V.
The most visible evidence of the Hong Kongisation of Chatswood, this vast and noisy joint jumps with equally vast and noisy Chinese families lapping up yum cha by day and classic Cantonese banquets by night.

Golden Century
393-399 Sussex Street, Sydney (9212 3901). CityRail
Central. **Open** noon-4am daily. **Licensed**. **Credit** AmEx, BC, DC, JCB, MC, $TC, V.
Sydney's answer to Hong Kong's floating seafood restaurants – only the produce is better, and cheaper. You can try everything from finely sliced abalone to steamed whole parrot fish.

Sea Treasure
46 Willoughby Road, Crows Nest (9906 6388). Bus 273.
Open 11am-3pm, 6-11pm, daily. **Average** $28.
Licensed. **Credit** AmEx, BC, DC, MC, $TC, V.
Unprepossessing, but serving superior Cantonese seafood and daily yum cha, this place really is a treasure for hungry locals. Once again, push politely for daily specials often denied non-Chinese speakers.

Silver Spring
191 Hay Street, Haymarket (9211 2232). CityRail
Central. **Open** 10am-11pm Mon-Fri; 9am-11pm Sat, Sun.
Average $25. **Licensed**. **Credit** AmEx, BC, DC, MC, V.
On the right is the daytime yum cha area; on the left, under sparkling chandeliers, it's dinner-time eating, Hong Kong style. A great place to order perfect roast duck, choy sum lightly tossed in fragrant garlic, immaculate steamed prawns and salt-baked chicken.

Superbowl Seafood
39 Goulburn Street, Haymarket (9211 1568). CityRail
Central. **Open** 11am-11pm daily. **Average** $5 lunch; $10 dinner. **Licensed**. **Credit** AmEx, BC, DC, MC, $TC, V.
In addition to the usual (but excellent) array of Cantonese seafood dishes, this place offers an intriguing and changing selection of 'Provincial Specials': everything from pig-blood jelly to shredded jellyfish. Downstairs is cheap, upstairs swish.
Branch: Superbowl Restaurant, 41 Dixon Street, Haymarket (9281 2462).

Wockpool
155 Victoria Street, Potts Point (9368 1771). CityRail
Kings Cross. **Open** 6.30-11pm Mon-Sat; 6.30-10pm Sun.
Average $40. **Licensed**. **Credit** AmEx, BC, DC, MC, $TC, V.
It had to happen, and it had to be Neil (Rockpool) Perry who did it: ModOz Chinese – and it's good. Go for lots and lots of little things in this multilayered place to be scene in. For **Wockpool Bar** *see chapter* **Cafés & Bars**.

French

Originally the only food game in town, French cuisine is now in recovery after total rejection in the early heady days of ModOz (who needs 'em? was the attitude) and a more recent whammy thanks to M. Chirac's *Bombe Pacifique*. The more comfortable attitude acknowledges the debt to one of the great cuisines of the world.

Brasserie Cassis
Level 1, Chifley Plaza, Chifley Square, Sydney (9221
3500). **Open** 11am-9pm Mon-Fri. **Average** $55.
Licensed. **Credit** AmEx, BC, DC, MC, V.
One of Sydney's slickest lunch spots manages to serve fair dinkum Frog food (with ModOz twists) with real flavours and textures – inside one hour. Some feat.
Disabled: access; toilets.

Claudine's
151 Macquarie Street, Sydney (9241 1749). CityRail/ferry
Circular Quay or Martin Place. **Open** noon-2pm, 6-8.30pm,
Mon-Fri. **Average** $40. **BYO**. **Credit** AmEx, MC, V.
A long-running act that manages to stay fresh, friendly and even fairly French amidst mounting competition in the CBD. A favourite with the French community.

Cleopatra
Cleopatra Street, Blackheath (4787 8456). CityRail
Blackheath. **Open** 7.30-9.30pm Mon-Sat; 1-3pm, 7.30-9.30pm, Sun. **Average** $65. **BYO**. **Credit** BC, MC, V.

A superb out-of-towner, a guest house with a dining room of rare quality. This is one for a weekend of indulgence and culinary pleasure – especially in winter when long walks give your hunger an edge for the pleasures of Dany Chouet's table. Opening times may vary so it's advisable to phone in advance.

Merrony's

2 Albert Street, Sydney (9247 9323). CityRail/ferry Circular Quay. **Open** noon-2.30pm, 5.45-11.30pm, Mon-Fri; 5.45-11.30pm Sat. **Average** $55. **Licensed.** **Credit** AmEx, BC, DC, MC, $TC, V.

Solid, well crafted but never boring Gallocentric tucker from the hands of a ModOz master. Paul Merrony does duck as well as anyone in town. A comforting, vaguely Manhattanish room with harbour glimpses through the Cahill Expressway. Good before the opera.

Prunier's Chiswick Gardens

65 Ocean Street, Woollahra (9363 1974). Bus 200, 327. **Open** noon-3pm, 6.30-9.30pm, Mon-Fri; 6.30-9.30pm Sat. **Average** $55. **Licensed.** **Credit** AmEx, BC, DC, MC, $TC, V.

A Sydney landmark in a gracious garden setting and now in the hands of two professionals delivering what is the Frenchest food in town – with service to match. Francophiles have been known to rave.

Indian

The reverse of London, Sydney lacks that general high standard in local curry houses. The few exceptions are listed below.

Abhi's

163 Concord Road, North Strathfield (9743 3061). Bus 458, 461. **Open** noon-3pm, 6-10pm, Mon-Fri; 6-10pm Sat. **Average** $25. **BYO.** **Credit** AmEx, BC, MC, V.

If you're really hot for heat, you might as well schlep out here. Locals and curry fiends from further afield have an almost fetishistic relationship with this place.

A Flavour of India

120 New South Head Road, Edgecliff (9326 2659). Bus 323, 324, 325, 327. **Open** 6-11.30pm Mon, Tue, Sat, Sun; noon-3pm, 6-11.30pm, Wed-Fri. **Average** $25. **Licensed.** **Credit** AmEx, BC, DC, MC, V.

Another fancied purveyor of above-average Indian food.

Oh! Calcutta!

251 Victoria Street, Darlinghurst (9360 3650). CityRail Kings Cross. **Open** noon-3pm, 6-11pm, daily. **Average** $15. **BYO.** **Credit** AmEx, BC, MC, V.

Right in the heart of caffeine alley. Worth special note here are the specialities from the North-West Frontier, reflecting the origins of the owners. There's a good selection of vegetarian food and a bow in the direction of ModOz.

Japanese

Close trade relations with Japan have meant a long tradition of very good Japanese food on all levels in Sydney.

Edosei

22 Rockwall Crescent, Potts Point (9326 9108). Bus 311. **Open** 6-11pm daily. **Average** $45. **Licensed.** **Credit** AmEx, BC, DC, JCB, MC, $TC, V.

Sushi and sashimi lovers swear by this old favourite on the edge of the Cross. It's not all that swish to look at – more your Tokyo neighbourhood sushi bar.

Raw Bar

Corner of Warners and Wairoa Avenues, Bondi Beach (9365 7200). Bus 380, 389. **Open** noon-midnight daily. **Average** $30. **BYO.** **Credit** BC, MC, V.

Good sushi – for Bondi, not known for raw fish out of the water – combines with good espresso in this dark green corner spot.

Sakana-ya

336 Pacific Highway, Crows Nest (9438 1468). Bus 288, 289, 290, 291, 292. **Open** noon-2.30pm, 6-10.30pm, Mon-Fri; 6-10.30pm Sat, Sun. **Average** $15. **BYO.** **Credit** AmEx, DC, JCB, MC, V.

It's almost a tautology to call this a Japanese seafood restaurant, but they do a lot more here than the standard sushi/sashimi. There's fish and seafood raw, boiled and pickled – even sea urchin roe – in this simply laid-out but dead serious place.

Sushi Suma

421 Cleveland Street, Redfern (9698 8873). Bus 372, 393, 395. **Open** noon-2pm, 6-10pm, Tue-Fri; 6-10pm Sat, Sun. **Average** $25. **BYO.** **Credit** AmEx, BC, MC, $¥TC, V.

Tiny and incongruously tucked in amid all the Indian and Turkish joints. Service is from groovy Japanese kids with earring overload, and the food's good.

Unkai

Level 36, ANA Hotel, 176 Cumberland Street, The Rocks (9250 6123). CityRail/ferry Circular Quay. **Open** 6.30-10am, noon-2.30pm, 6-10pm Mon-Fri, Sun; 6.30-10am, 6-10pm, Sat. **Average** $50. **Licensed.** **Credit** AmEx, BC, DC, JCB, MC, $TC, V.

Now we're not talking serious Japanese. Forget *Tampopo*: in this eyrie, with a sublime view over Sydney Harbour, they do the style of food called kaiseki, which is, like haiku poetry, dictated by the seasons. And unless you know better, let the experts dictate what you eat. Undoubtedly Sydney's best Japanese.

Disabled: access; toilets.

Italian

Italian (and, even earlier, Greek) food led the democratisation of dining in Sydney, with Beppi's (which celebrated it's fortieth birthday in 1996) the Godfather of the pack. Leichhardt – Sydney's Little Italy – can provide some pretty average and very good experiences, but on the whole excellence resides elsewhere.

Beppi's

Corner of Yurong and Stanley Streets, Darlinghurst (9360 4558). CityRail Museum. **Open** noon-3pm, 6-11.30pm, Mon-Fri; 6-11.30pm Sat. **Average** $55. **Licensed.** **Credit** AmEx, BC, DC, JCB, MC, TC, V.

Beppi Polese and staff have survived through changes in fashion and fortune by providing the sort of service and hospitality which have all but disappeared from Sydney dining. Which is why it remains the favourite of so many of the city's rich and powerful. To say that Beppi's is old-fashioned is not to disparage the food (which at its best is very good), but to praise the ambience.

Buon Ricordo

108 Boundary Street, Paddington (9360 6729). Bus 378, 380, 382. **Open** 6-11pm Tue-Thur; noon-3pm, 6-11pm, Fri, Sat. **Average** $80. **Licensed.** **Credit** AmEx, BC, MC, V.

Naples and Tuscany meet with a bang and a song in the kitchen of this hugely enjoyable restaurant run by the ebullient Armando Percuoco who you will, no doubt, meet.

Fiorentino

Corner of Young and Grosvenor Streets, Neutral Bay (9908 1320). Bus 228, 229, 230. **Open** noon-3pm, 6-11pm, Mon-Fri; 6-11pm Sat. **Average** $45. **Licensed.** **Credit** AmEx, BC, DC, MC, TC, V.

An elegant dining room, Fiorentino offers superior northern Italian food in a Milanese minimal space surrounded by the unrelieved blandness of Neutral Bay.

Frattini

122 Marion Street, Leichhardt (9569 2997). Bus 468. **Open** 11am-3pm, 6-10pm, Mon-Fri; 6-10pm Sat, Sun. **Average** $30. **BYO.** **Credit** AmEx, BC, DC, MC, V.

Not your trad Leichhardt eaterie (more Milan than Naples), Frattini still manages to pop out enough fresh and hearty flavours to keep local Italians – and Italophiles – happy.

Gastronomia Chianti

44 Elizabeth Street, Sydney (9319 4748). CityRail Martin Place. **Open** 10.30am-4.45pm Mon-Thur; 10.30am-10.30pm Fri; noon-10pm Sat. **Average** $20. **Licensed.** **Credit** AmEx, BC, DC, MC, $TC, V.

Not as much of a gastronomia as it was when it opened (it still sells the odd salami or two), Chianti is more of a friendly downtown trat – busy and buzzy by day, relaxing by night, and offering easygoing rather than flashy food.

Primadonna Restaurant & Oyster Bar

33 Bayswater Road, Kings Cross (9358 5582). CityRail Kings Cross. **Open** noon-3pm, 6-11pm, daily. **Average** $35. **Licensed.** **Credit** AmEx, BC, DC, JCB, MC, $TC, V.

The big man of Melbourne Italian food, Bill Marchetti, has made his first foray into the Sydney market in this light and attractive room, promising his 'unique brand of Italian soul food'. Though not yet open when we went to press, with Marchetti involved it'll be worth a visit.

Mediterranean

In here is everything from Lebanese to Spanish, with Israeli, Tunisian and Greek for good measure.

Cafe Tunis

30 South Steyne, Manly (9976 2805). Ferry Manly. **Open** 7am-10.30pm daily. **Average** $25. **Licensed & BYO.** **Credit** AmEx, BC, DC, MC, V.

Sydney's only Tunisian restaurant happens to be a ripper, as anyone who knows this very fine cuisine will agree. Chef Jamil Ben Hassine does not stick strictly to the canon, but experiments deftly with the style, and is introducing Sydneysiders to increasingly exotic fare, like lamb casserole with melokhia.

Capitan Torres

73 Liverpool Street, Sydney (9264 5574). CityRail Town Hall. **Open** noon-3pm, 6-11pm, daily. **Average** $25. **Licensed.** **Credit** AmEx, BC, DC, JCB, MC, $TC, V.

Set in the heart of Sydney's Little Spain, Torres specialises in seafood, and if you stick to the grilled fish, prawns, octopus and other simple fodder, it isn't half bad. The garfish, when it's on, is wonderful. Good for pre-theatre quickie snacks. *Disabled: access; toilets.*

Casa Asturiana

77 Liverpool Street, Sydney (9264 2805). CityRail Town Hall. **Open** 5.30-10.30pm Mon, Sat; noon-3pm, 5.30-10.30pm, Tue-Fri, Sun. **Average** $15. **Licensed.** **Credit** AmEx, BC, DC, MC, V.

Spanish food doesn't travel well. That said, this homely place – also on the *Calle* Liverpool – does a damn good job (the best in town) of recreating the flavours of the Iberian Peninsula, especially those of the province of Asturia.

Criterion

Lobby Level, MLC Centre, Martin Place, Sydney (9264 5574). CityRail Martin Place. **Open** noon-3pm, 6-10pm, Mon-Fri; 6-10pm Sat. **Average** $55. **Licensed.** **Credit** AmEx, BC, DC, MC, $TC, V.

The Criterion is a cut above the lukewarm bunch of Lebs scattered around Sydney (mainly Elizabeth Street). The owners are becoming bolder and bolder in choosing to serve the real thing as well as interesting MidEast/ModOz crossovers.

Hellenic Club Restaurant

251 Elizabeth Street, Sydney (9264 5128). CityRail Museum. **Open** noon-3pm, 5-9pm, Mon-Fri; 5-9pm Sat. **Average** $25. **Licensed.** **Credit** BC, DC, MC, $TC, V.

The views over Hyde Park and the unchanging menu – slow-cooked lamb, baked snapper – keep regulars coming back here. Some have been coming for 30 years. Recently a couple of Greek regional dishes, such as souzoukavia pilaf, have crept on to the menu, but nothing too alarming.

Never on Sunday

576 Darling Street, Rozelle (9810 2411). Bus 440. **Open** 6-11pm Mon-Sat. **Average** $25. **BYO.** **Credit** AmEx, BC, DC, MC, $TC, V.

Everything Greek food should be: simple, fresh and unpretentious, with ModMed touches to keep everyone happy.

Savion

Shop 1, 38 Wairoa Avenue, North Bondi (9130 6357). Bus 389. **Open** 9am-10pm Mon-Thur, Sun; 9am-3pm Fri. **Average** $10. **Licensed.** **No credit cards.**

A fair dinkum Israeli snack bar in Bondi already. This is Sephardic and not Ashkenazi Jewish – falafel, houmous, baba ganouj, chicken schnitzels and the incredibly edible Savion tomato salad. It's kosher.

Steki Taverna

2 O'Connell Street, Newtown (9516 2191). Bus 422, 423, 426, 428. **Open** 6.30-11pm Wed-Sun. **Average** $20. **Licensed.** **Credit** BC, MC, V.

Food is not the point at Steki, it's the music – live, Greek and sweaty. On any given Friday or Saturday night, come 11pm, the joint is jumping with gyrating Greeks and their more obstreperous Aussie mates. Stick to the meze, and hit that tiny floor.

Native Produce

Curious though it may seem, it has taken two centuries for Oz chefs to begin using the food products that sustained the Aboriginal people for at least 50,000 years. In most Australian states, it wasn't even legal to eat kangaroo until the law changed in 1993. Consequently, there are only a handful of restaurants seriously and consistently using these ingredients. Here are the best two.

Edna's Table

Lobby Level, MLC Centre, Martin Place, Sydney (9231 1400). CityRail Martin Place. **Open** noon-3pm Mon; noon-3pm, 6-10pm, Tue-Fri; 6-10pm Sat. **Average** $50. **Licensed.** **Credit** AmEx, BC, DC, MC, $TC, V.

The most Australian experience you'll have in Sydney. Not only for chef Raymond Kersh's skilful and fascinating use of native produce and cooking techniques (baking in paperbark is one), but also for the warmth of service and the arresting 'Aboriginalesque' decor, complete with boomerang-backed chairs.

Doyles: *the fisher king of Watsons Bay.*

Riberries

411 Bourke Street, Surry Hills (9361 4929). Bus 390,
391, 392. **Open** 7-9.45pm Tue-Sat. **Average** $48. **BYO.**
Credit AmEx, BC, DC, MC, V.
French-born chef Jean Paul Bruneteau is a pioneer in
integrating the flavours of Australia's native produce into a
classical European context. He taught himself – and then the
rest of us – how to use ingredients like riberries, Illawarra
plums and Tasmanian pepperberries. A unique experience.

Pizza

See also **Bibotecca** *and* **Pig & Olive** *under* **Hip.**

La Pasquene

324A Victoria Street, Darlinghurst (9331 4287).
CityRail Kings Cross. **Open** 8am-1am Mon-Thur, Sun;
8am-2am Fri; 8am-3am Sat. **Average** $20. **BYO.**
No credit cards.
Lines local stomachs on Friday and Saturday nights with
traditional, unpretentious pizzas of the slim, sleek variety.

Wedgetail

1A Bedford Street, Newtown (9516 1568). CityRail
Newtown. **Open** 4-10pm Tue-Thur, Sun; 4-11pm Fri, Sat.
Average $20. **BYO. No credit cards.**
This is nowhere near a view, but it's close to the best pizza
in Sydney. Another wood-fired joint with thin-based pizzas
of traditional and 'Hellfire' combinations.

Wood & Stone

559 Crown Street, Surry Hills (9319 0757). Bus 301,
302, 303. **Open** 11.30am-10pm Mon, Tue, Sun; 11.30am-
10.30pm Wed, Thur; 11.30am-11pm Fri, Sat. **Average**
$25. **Licensed. Credit** AmEx, BC, MC, V.
Has gourmet pizza gone too far? Tandoori, chicken satay,
rare roast beef, lamb vindaloo and Thai fish are all very
well, but this may be the only safe place to order a
Skippy pizza.

Seafood

There's a surprising lack of solely seafood places
in Sydney – probably because you will find
seafood, expertly handled, in most of the best
restaurants.

Doyles

11 Marine Parade, Watsons Bay (9337 1572). Bus 324,
325. **Open** *beach restaurant* noon-3pm, 6-9.30pm, daily;
wharf restaurant 5.30-9.30pm Wed-Sat. **Average** $40.
Licensed. Credit BC, DC, MC, $TC, V.
The Doyle family has done more than any other in Sydney
to promote and publicise the rich variety and excellent quality of Australian fish and seafood. The restaurant in
Watsons Bay is the original fish restaurant (it's been in the
family since 1885) and is a quintessentially Sydney place to
eat fish and chips.
Disabled: access; toilets.

Fishface

132 Darlinghurst Road, Kings Cross (9332 4803).
CityRail Kings Cross. **Open** 6-11pm Mon-Thur; noon-
3pm, 6-11pm, Fri, Sat; noon-3pm, 6-10pm, Sun. **Average**
$28. **BYO. No credit cards.**
This smart little hole-in-the-wall in Darlinghurst, owned by
a chef and a wholesale fishmonger, offers some of the most
interesting and unusual fish on Sydney menus. It's always
packed, so you might have to wait for a table in the pub across
the road, but it's worth the wait and it's not a bad pub, either.

Mohr Fish

202 Devonshire Street, Surry Hills (9318 1326). CityRail
Central. **Open** 7am-10pm Mon-Fri; 9am-10pm Sat, Sun.
Average $22. **BYO. No credit cards.**
Another popular hole-in-the-wall with a pub waiting room, but
here is where you come for unbeatable fish and chips and other
smacking fresh fish treated more than fairly by specialist staff.
Branch: 527 Crown Street, Surry Hills (9319 5682).

The Pier
*594 New South Head Road, Rose Bay (9327 6561). Bus
324.* **Open** noon-3pm, 6-10pm, Mon-Sat; noon-3pm, 6-
9pm, Sun. **Average** $60. **Licensed**. **Credit** AmEx, BC,
DC, MC, $TC, V.
Sydney's winning entry in the best fish and chips with the
flashest view in town competition. Chefs Greg Doyle and
Steve Hodges preside over a kitchen from which emanates
not only superbly handled seafood dishes but deadly
desserts to drool over.

Rock Fish Cafe
*14 Loftus Street, Sydney (9252 3114). CityRail/ferry
Circular Quay.* **Open** *summer* noon-3pm, 5.30-9.30pm,
Mon, Tue; noon-3pm, 5.30-10pm, Wed-Fri; *winter* noon-
3pm, 5.30-9pm, Mon, Tue; noon-3pm, 5.30-9.30pm, Wed-
Fri. **Average** $30. **Licensed**. **Credit** AmEx, BC, DC,
MC, $TC, V.
More than competent seafood in the centre of the city, buzz-
ing with bizoids by day, quiet by night for a pre-theatre meal.

South-east Asian
If Indian is lacking, south-east Asian is booming.
The centre for Indonesian restaurants is Kensington, with its big student population; the others are
more aimlessly scattered. This is chilli territory,
where restaurants make abundant use of the tiny
variety known to addicts as scuds. *See also page
127* **Oodles of Noodles**.

Andy's
*658 Bourke Street, Redfern (9319 6616). Bus 372, 393,
395.* **Open** 6-10.30pm Tue-Fri; noon-3pm, 6-10.30pm, Sat,
Sun. **Average** $15. **BYO**. **Credit** AmEx, BC, DC, MC, V.
Andy's could equally be listed under Indian – this is Indian
via Malaysia – but you haven't lived until you've tried a
murtabak, and you won't get murtabak in your average
Indian restaurant.

Desaru
*407 Pacific Highway, Crows Nest (9439 2559). Bus 288,
289, 290, 291, 292.* **Open** noon-3pm, 6-10pm, Mon-Fri;
6-10pm Sat. **Average** $20. **Licensed**. **Credit** AmEx, BC,
DC, MC, $TC, V.
It calls its food 'eclectic' – you'll find a touch of Thai in some
dishes – but Desaru still serves one of the best laksas in town.

Pondok Buyung
*124 Anzac Parade, Kensington (9663 2296). Bus 390,
391.* **Open** noon-9pm Mon, Tue, Thur-Sun. **Average**
$10. **BYO**. **No credit cards**.
Reportedly the best place in town for the legendary nasi
Padang-style food, the pinnacle of Indonesian cuisine ema-
nating from Sumatra. Disregard the placcy tablecloths, and
ask for beef (or beef heart) rendang, the holy grail of this
style. They're halal here – no pork, no prawns, but plenty of
Muslim students and clientele.

Ratu Sari
*476 Anzac Parade, Kensington (9663 4072). Bus 390,
391.* **Open** noon-10pm Tue-Sun. **Average** $20. **BYO**.
Credit AmEx, BC, DC, MC, V.
Another student special, long on flavours, short on flash.
Once more, don't forget to ask many questions and uncover
the secrets of the house.

To's Malaysian Gourmet
*181 Miller Street, North Sydney (9955 2088). Bus 202,
203, 205, 207.* **Open** 11am-6pm Mon-Wed; 11am-7pm
Thur, Fri; 11.30am-3pm Sat. **Average** $10. **Unlicensed**.
No credit cards.

Nothing much more than a tiny takeaway with a few tables
but, according to addicts both Oz and Malaysian, a place that
serves one of the best chicken laksas in town.

Steak
There's been a curious resurgence of steakhouses
in Sydney recently. One theory (this reviewer's)
being that Sydneysiders are eating light at home
– pasta and couscous – and ripping into the red
meat when they go out. Steak as a treat: a turn-
around for a country which used to eat steak and
eggs for breakfast.

Armstrong's North Sydney
*1-7 Napier Street, North Sydney (9957 3011/9955
2066). CityRail North Sydney.* **Open** noon-4pm, 6-11pm,
Mon-Fri; 6-11pm Sat. **Average** $55. **Licensed**. **Credit**
AmEx, BC, DC, MC, V.
One of the earliest of the new-wave steakhouses and, for
some time, the only game in North Sydney. A clubby haunt
for local suits who want to drink red wine and chew red
meat along with some interesting offerings from the
ModOz canon.

The Brooklyn
*225 George Street, Sydney (9247 6808). CityRail
Wynyard.* **Open** 7.30-11am, noon-3pm, 6-10pm, Mon-
Thur; 7.30-11am, noon-3pm, Fri. **Average** $50.
Licensed. **Credit** AmEx, BC, DC, MC, V.
A snazzy refurbishment of a landmark city pub by top chef
Greg (The Pier) Doyle together with superb beef from a
consortium of farmers previously only selling to Japan, has
ensured this is a favourite with the local screen jockeys and
money market hustlers. Don't let that put you off.

Lennons
105 Victoria Road, Drummoyne (9819 7511). Bus 500.
Open noon-3pm, 6-10pm, Tue-Fri; 6-10pm Sat. **Average**
$45. **Licensed**. **Credit** AmEx, BC, DC, MC, $TC, V.
A little out of town, but if you're headed Balmain way, this
smart, well run place gives good beef and more. The rump
is served with such smart accompaniments as roast spring
onions and baked potato flan.

Plaza Grill
*36 Blue Street, Greenwood Plaza, North Sydney (9964
9766). CityRail North Sydney.* **Open** noon-3pm Mon-
Wed; noon-3pm, 6.30-10pm, Thur, Fri. **Average** $40.
Licensed. **Credit** AmEx, BC, DC, MC, $TC, V.
Mark Armstrong's other joint (*see above* **Armstrong's
North Sydney**) is also big on beef – housed in vaguely
south-west American-themed rooms – and does good freshly shucked oysters and lots of char-grilled things as well.

Thai
Thanks to the gods of gastronomy, Sydney is
blessed with more Thai restaurants than a
medium-sized town in Thailand. Most of them are
of fair to average quality, a handful are excellent
and of those, two have an Australian Thaiophile
presiding over the kitchen. Don't argue, enjoy. *See
also page 127* **Oodles of Noodles**.

Lime & Lemongrass
*42 Kellett Street, Kings Cross (9358 5577). CityRail
Kings Cross.* **Open** 6.30-10.30pm daily. **Average** $20.
Licensed. **Credit** AmEx, BC, DC, MC, V.

Ericiyes
*409 Cleveland Street, Redfern (9319 1309). Bus 372,
393, 395.* **Open** 10am-midnight daily. **Average** $12.
BYO. Credit BC, MC, V.

Girne Pide
*427 Cleveland Street, Redfern (9319 4307). Bus 372,
393, 395.* **Open** 11am-11pm Tue-Sun. **Average** $8.
BYO. No credit cards.

Vegetarian

See also **Red Kite** *in chapter* **Cafés & Bars.**

Bodhi Vegetarian Restaurant
187 Hay Street, Sydney (9281 9918). CityRail Central.
Open 7am-3pm, 5-10pm, daily. **Average** $2.20-$5 yum
cha per dish; $18 full menu. **Licensed. No credit cards.**
The Asian vegetarian option – including vegan yum cha.
Starters can be disappointing, but the clay pots of hokkein
noodles, vegetables and miso, the curd dishes and rice com-
bos are as cheap as they are flavoursome. The newer Wild
Foods Cafe goes in for organic grub and bush tucker.
Branch: Central Station, Sydney (9281 6162).

Iku Wholefood Kitchen
*25A Glebe Point Road, Glebe (9692 8720). Bus 431,
434.* **Open** noon-9pm daily. **Average** $11. **BYO. No
credit cards.**
You don't have to be vegan to enjoy the food from this macrobiotic, meat, sugar and dairy-free eatery. It's a tiny haven for
health fiends, where deep-fried rice balls, tofu fritters, laksa,
salads, musubi and veggie pies actually taste good.
Branch: Shop 2, The Grove, 176-178 Military Road, Neutral
Bay (9953 1964).

Vietnamese

There are now a lot of Vietnamese (or ethnic
Chinese from Vietnam) in Australia, due to that
little stoush a few years back. Whole suburbs have
been transformed – Cabramatta in the west is
known as Vietnamatta. *See also page 127* **Oodles
of Noodles.**

An Restaurant
*29-31 Greenfield Parade, Bankstown (9796 7826).
CityRail Bankstown.* **Open** 7am-8pm daily. **Average** $6.
Unlicensed. No credit cards.
This is a Vietnamese noodle restaurant specialising in the
fresh rice noodles (usually in soup) known as pho – there's
a sign in the window offering pronunciation help: 'So pho,
so good.' Everything about this place smells terrific and it's
worth a pilgrimage.

Indochine
99 Bondi Road, Bondi (9387 4081). Bus 380, 382.
Open 5.30-10.30pm daily. **Average** $15. **BYO. Credit**
AmEx, BC, DC, MC, $TC, V.
This place gets an entry because of the enthusiastic long-
term patronage of a well known (and very good) Sydney chef.
Others find it far from appealing. Make up your own mind.

Tau Bay
*Shop 15, 107 John Street, Cabramatta (9724 7162).
CityRail Cabramatta.* **Open** 7.30am-7.30pm daily.
Average $9. **BYO. No credit cards.**
Another pho-away Vietnamese noodle joint in the middle of
bustling Cabramattta, this is the phavourite of all the
phoodies – chicken soup (Vietnamese penicillin) is very big
here, but go and make your own discoveries as well.

For the best yum cha, head for Chinatown.

Good solid trad Thai around the corner from the **Darley
Street Thai** *(see p106)* in a street full of houses with red
lights at the front door. Big on duck.

Prasit's
*413 Crown Street, Surry Hills (9319 0748). Bus 301,
302, 303.* **Open** 6-10pm Mon-Wed, Sat; noon-3pm, 6-
10pm, Thur, Fri. **Average** $25. **BYO. Credit** AmEx, BC,
DC, MC, $TC, V.
The chef/owner behind these two clever places, Prasit
Prateeprasen, opens and closes restaurants faster than most
of us open and close fridge doors. But there'll always be a
Prasit's somewhere, and they'll always be worth going to for
smart and satisfying OzThai. For **Prasit's Northside
Takeaway** *see p127.*
Branch: 77 Mount Street, North Sydney (9957 2271).

Turkish

For an alternative, cheap but healthy pig-out,
think Turkish. There's a small Turkish belt in
Surry Hills where the restaurants are loud,
relaxed, BYO and great for a gang (belly-dancing
always fills a lull in the conversation). Meze plates
of beetroot, aubergine and cacik (cucumber and
yoghurt) come with kebabs and pide (pitta) bread,
and plenty of unpronounceable dips. Turkish
bread pizzas are sensational.

Divan
*577 Crown Street, Surry Hills (9698 4434). Bus 301,
302, 303.* **Open** 10am-midnight daily. **Average** $20.
BYO. No credit cards.

Cafés & Bars

Sydney is a latte lover's paradise and pub culture runs deep, though the city has yet to experience a bar-room blitz.

You won't need your cossie at the nostalgic **Bathers Pavilion**. *See pages 113 and 122.*

It seems that every week a new café opens in Sydney, each one more groovy, more designed, more novel than the last. But don't be fooled. Halogen lights and stainless-steel benches don't guarantee a good cuppa. There are four major café

Don't miss

Best breakfast
bills *p122*, Sean's Panaroma *p113*, Una's *p127*

Best views
Bernasconi's *p122*, The Bower *p123*, Sejuiced *p126*

Best gutter scene
Bar Coluzzi *p122*, Bondi Aqua Bar *p122*, Parmalat *p126*

Best boozing
Bayswater Brasserie *p111*, The Icebergs *p130*, Lava Bar *p130*

belts in the city, where competition is stiff and standards are high: Darlinghurst, Potts Point, Surry Hills and Bondi. Outside these areas, if you find a good café it's, well, a find.

There are nearly as many brands of coffee as there are cafés. Illy and Grinders are the best. Vittoria, Segafredo, Primo and Robert Timms also turn up frequently. If the person operating the machine can't tell you which brand they use, it's probably time to walk out. Very few cafés have table service or printed menus, so here's the deal: check the blackboard and go up to the counter to order; stay as long as you like, and keep ordering juice, or biscotti, or food; when you have finished, go back to the counter, tell them what you had, and pay before leaving.

THE FOCCACIA FACTOR

You can expect to eat foccacia made from Italian or Turkish bread, stuffed with any number of antipasto fillings, and toasted. You may also find rosetta rolls, wood oven-fired Italian bread, bagels, Polish rye, brioche, croissants and crusty baguettes, but it's hard to ignore the foccacia.

Larger cafés like to think they have a way with caesar salad, nachos, pasta, pizza, Thai beef salad, stuffed (any vegetable that can accommodate some stodgy rice) veggie things, poached and scrambled eggs, and sticky date pudding. Some do. Some don't.

Non-coffee drinkers shouldn't demur. Fresh juice is a huge fad, especially in Bondi. So a beetroot, carrot, apple and ginger juice is surprisingly readily available, along with herbal teas, fruit smoothies and an endless range of bottled water.

Cafés

Ancora Cafe

1112 Barrenjoey Road, Palm Beach (9974 5969). Bus 190. **Open** *Dec-Jan* 11am-3pm, 7-11pm, Tue-Sat; 9.30am-3.30pm Sun; *Feb-Nov* 11am-3pm Tue-Thur; 11am-3pm, 7-11pm, Fri, Sat; 9.30am-3.30pm Sun. **Average** $16 breakfast; $35 lunch/dinner. **BYO**. **Credit** AmEx, BC, MC, $TC, V.
The café is situated on the Pittwater side of the peninsula, and there's no view to speak of, but the atmosphere is friendly, the apple juice comes out of apples and the poached eggs come out perfect every time. Locals dressed in beach towels start here at breakfast and drop in and out all day.

Bambini Espresso Bar

299 Elizabeth Street, Sydney (9261 3331). CityRail Town Hall. **Open** 7am-5pm Mon-Fri. **Average** $13. **Licensed**. **Credit** AmEx, BC, MC, V.
This tiny tot opposite the law courts is full of stand-up suits. They are usually full of sweet potato and Illy coffee. Foccacia comes packed with gusty ingredients like salami, avocado and Spanish onion, and the place is packed all day long.

Bar Coluzzi

320 Victoria Street, Darlinghurst (9380 5420). CityRail Kings Cross. **Open** 5am-7.30pm daily. **Average** $6. **Unlicensed**. **No credit cards**.
A Sydney institution, this is one of the oldest and arguably best cafés in town. Its position on Victoria Street may have set off a chain reaction, because the street's gutters are now lined with little stools and café lizards. It's a plain Italian café, frequented by boxers, politicians and taxi drivers at dawn. The mix of strange characters, family continuity and Robert Timms special Coluzzi blend makes for a café which nearly defies description.
Branch: 99 Elizabeth Street, Sydney (9233 1651).

Bathers Pavilion Refreshment Room

4 The Esplanade, Balmoral (9968 1133). Bus 257/ferry Mosman. **Open** 7am-10.30pm daily. **Average** $15. **Licensed**. **Credit** AmEx, BC, DC, MC, $TC, V.
Balmoral Beach is almost too picturesque, and this rather gala whitewashed building houses a truly fine café. The position is sublime, overlooking glittering north Balmoral. Atmospherically, this is a trip back in time, but with a mercifully all-mod-cons menu: sourdough fruit toast, oysters and dipping sauce, ham and cheddar baguettes, eight different Twining teas by the pot, low-fat decaffs for mad people, and Stella Artois for the sane. *See also chapter* **Restaurants**.

Bernasconi's

Corner of O'Sullivan and Plumer Roads, Rose Bay (9327 5717). Bus 323, 324, 325. **Open** 8am-6pm daily. **Average** $12. **BYO**. **Credit** BC, MC, $TC, V.

Caffeine culture

Sydney's first cool cafés were opened by Italians, who set the pace and the blackboard menus. So if you're not familiar with the lingo, here's a rough guide to what you can order.

An **espresso** is a shot of strong black coffee, also known as a **short black**. A **doppio** is a double strength espresso. **Caffè latte** is half coffee, half steamed milk, served in a glass. **Cappuccino** is an espresso topped up with steamed milk, froth and powdered chocolate, served in a cup. A **flat white** is a cappuccino – hold the froth and the chocolate. **Macchiato** is an espresso with a 'stain' of steamed milk. A **skinniccino** is made with skimmed milk. And for the bambini, there's the **baby 'cino** – a froth-only version of the grown-up cappuccino, served in a tiny glass.

Opposite the golf course, this is a comfy, sunny space (indoors and out) with superior food. Smoked salmon bagels, steak and kidney pies, cakes and rip-snorting Illy coffee. There's no attitude here, just old-fashioned friendly service.

bills

433 Liverpool Street, Darlinghurst (9360 9631). Bus 389. **Open** 7.30am-4pm Mon-Sat. **Average** $25. **BYO**. **No credit cards**.
Just off the major café strip on Victoria Street, bills delivers just about everything you could want in a café: good Grinders coffee, imaginative fresh food, a great space, human service, superior magazines and very tasty vibes. It could take you a few ricotta hot cakes, a sunrise drink, toasted coconut bread, a rest, a steak sandwich, a pastry and about three lattes to eat your way through this month's *New Yorker*. Frequented by Jane Campion and George Miller (actually, all of Australia's Academy Award winners), the café offers plenty of people-watching opportunities for non-readers.
Branch: bills 2 355 Crown Street, Surry Hills (9360 4762).

Bizircus

67 Albion Street, Surry Hills (9211 3294). CityRail Central. **Open** 7.30am-10pm Mon-Sat. **Average** $10 breakfast/lunch; $30 dinner. **BYO**. **No credit cards**.
Is this a sandwich shop or a fabulous restaurant in disguise? You can get a baguette, as fine as any, stuffed with ham and semi-dried tomatoes and good cheese. Or you can concentrate on a huge bowl of clear wanton soup with shiitake, or a salad of plump Yamba prawns and green papaya. Cheap, clean, fun and groovy at night.

Bondi Aqua Bar

266 Campbell Parade, Bondi Beach (9130 6070). Bus 380, 382. **Open** *summer* 7am-8.30pm daily; *winter* 7.30am-6pm daily. **Average** $10 breakfast; $14 lunch. **BYO**. **No credit cards**.
From the rich pickings along the northern reaches of Bondi Beach, there are no bad choices. The Aqua Bar delivers with the view, the juices, the coffee, jams, toast, service and the magazines. A bracing run and a swim at Bondi should always be rewarded with an Aqua Bar breakfast and a cup of the ubiquitous Grinders coffee.

The Bower

7-9 Marine Parade, Manly (9977 5451). Ferry Manly.
Open 8am-10.30pm, noon-3.30pm, daily. **Average** $30.
BYO. Credit AmEx, BC, MC, V.
Sit by the sea and gaze at Shelley Beach over scrambled eggs, thick toast, freshly squeezed orange juice and Illy coffee. On a clear day there is no better breakfast or photo opportunity.

La Buvette

2 Challis Avenue, Potts Point (9358 5113). Bus 311.
Open 7am-6pm Tue-Fri; 8am-8pm Sat, Sun. **Average** $10. **Unlicensed. No credit cards.**
This is a non-cutlery café: no scrambled eggs, no salads. No drama. La Buvette is a Mecca for pâtisserie purists. The fruit tarts. The chocolate cakes. Savoury morsels are cheap and good: smoked salmon brioche with ricotta, dill and watercress costs three bucks fifty. Overcome your fear of sexual stereotyping with the little quiches: they are worth it.

Cafe Nikki

544 Bourke Street, Surry Hills (9319 7517). Bus 301, 302, 303. **Open** 7am-10pm Mon-Fri; 8am-10pm Sat; 8am-4pm Sun. **Average** $15. **BYO. No credit cards.**
Of all the sunny-side walks in Surry Hills, Cafe Nikki has the edge. You can ignore the healthy-hippie attitude which prevails in the neighbourhood and go for orange-glazed walnut snails or raspberry bagels, baked on the premises. The bacon and egg breakfasts are justly legendary and the triple berry frappés are irresistible. The coffee isn't half bad, either.

Caffe Italia

Shop 23, Departure Level Terminal, Kingsford Smith Airport (9669 6434). Bus 400/Airport Express. **Open** 7.30am-5pm Mon-Wed, Fri; 7.30am-9pm Thur, Sat, Sun. **Average** $10. **Licensed. Credit** BC, MC, $TC, V.
Leaving our fair shores? Torture yourself with one last creamy, steamy Grinders coffee before you go. Caffe Italia looks and feels like a bustling Italian railway station, which

is about the last thing you'd expect on your hunt for duty free. Stash some orange coconut tarts for the journey.
Disabled: access; toilets.

Centennial Park Cafe

Corner of Grand and Parks Drives, Centennial Park (9360 3355). Bus 380. **Open** 8.30am-4pm daily.
Average $17. **Licensed. Credit** AmEx, BC, MC, V.
All duck ponds, Dalmatians and Frisbees. The open café-in-the-round is brunch central at weekends, so go early or prepare to queue. If you sit at an outdoor table, a cantering pony may well kick a divot into your scrambled eggs.

Chesters

148 Beattie Street, Balmain (9555 2185). Bus 441, 442.
Open 8am-4pm daily. **Average** $12. **BYO. Credit** BC, DC, JCB, MC, V.
Enjoy a hearty breakfast surrounded by distressed doors, tin buckets and battery acid vases. This is Balmain, so poached eggs, local butcher beef sausages and coffee are available in this quaint antique junk yard. A good place to fossick for arty types and the odd bargain.

Digger's Cafe

Bondi Digger's Club, 232 Campbell Parade, Bondi Beach (9365 4958). Bus 380, 382. **Open** 7am-sunset daily.
Average $15. **BYO. No credit cards.**
Digger's delivers consistently, on both coffee and food. It's not a glamorous little space, and sometimes the pavement breeze can blow your brains out (not entirely a bad thing), but the breakfasts are among the best in Bondi. Scrambled eggs, skinny sausages, vine-ripened tomatoes, home-made relish, four kinds of toast, and jams in latte glasses. For **Onzain** *see chapter* **Restaurants**.

Dip

8 Lamrock Avenue, Bondi Beach (9130 8075). Bus 380.
Open 6.30am-7pm daily. **Average** $7. **BYO.**
No credit cards.
The models' bodies packing this stylish sardine can may be a testament to the food. Banana coconut porridge, scrambled

bills: *just about everything you could want in a café. See page 122.*

Food to go

For every glorious Sydney seaside location, there's a horrible tourist-trap restaurant. However, you need not fall into their clutches every time you want to eat with a view. The myriad takeaway alternatives include hamburgers, fish and chips, pizza, Portuguese chicken and deli cafés. *See also* **Savion** *in chapter* **Restaurants**.

Bondi Surf Seafoods

128 Campbell Parade, Bondi Beach (9130 4554). Bus 380, 382. **Open** 9am-9pm daily. **No credit cards**.
Pick up a dozen cheap Wallis Lake oysters, some king prawns and a few fillets of grilled baby Dory or a grilled salmon steak. Deep-fried chips are mandatory. Stroll across to the road to the beach, and be amazed.

Bottom of the Harbour

21 The Esplanade, Balmoral (9969 7911). Bus 238, 257. **Open** 9am-8pm daily. **No credit cards**.
Balmoral is not a cheap suburb, nor is this a cheap fish shop. Huge chunks of blue-eye cod, John Dory or snapper are fried in a secret house batter and served on a bed of chips.

Burgerman

249 Bondi Road, Bondi Beach (9130 4888). Bus 380, 382. **Open** 5-10pm Mon-Fri; noon-10pm Sat, Sun. **No credit cards**.
Eat in or take away a dream burger of lamb fillet and marinated aubergine, chicken breast and rocket, or beef and everything you can get in a burger.
Branch: 116 Surrey Street, Darlinghurst (9361 0268).

The Earth Food Store

81 Gould Street, Bondi Beach (9365 5098). Bus 380, 382. **Open** 8am-7.30pm daily. **No credit cards**.
An organic fruit and veg shop which stocks millet balls and musubi (Japanese rice balls) from Iku Wholefoods (*see chapter* **Restaurants**). The Earth Food Store makes up organic salads and plenty of sugar- and gluten-free desserts.

Manly Fish Market & Cafe

Shops 1 and 2, Ocean Beach end of Wentworth Street, Manly (9976 3777). Ferry Manly. **Open** *shop* 8am-9pm daily; *café* noon-3pm, 5.30-9pm, daily. **Credit** AmEx, BC, DC, MC, $TC, V.
Dine in the café or take away some John Dory, snapper, jewfish or flathead, crumbed and deep-fried in 100% corn oil. A stone's throw from that beach you've heard so much about.

Oporto Portuguese Style Chicken

Unit 1, 36 Campbell Parade, Bondi Beach (9365 1177). Bus 380, 382. **Open** 11am-9pm Mon-Fri; 10am-9pm Sat, Sun. **No credit cards**.
Whole flattened chickens – with crispy chilli sauce skins and juicy flesh – come with tubs of coleslaw, potato salad and tabouleh, and fluffy white buns. Cheapest feast you can find.
Branches: 3C Roslyn Street, Kings Cross (9368 0257); 331 Darling Street, Balmain (9810 1555); 944 Anzac Parade, Maroubra (9314 1002); 127-128 Willoughby Road, Crows Nest (9906 6050); 19 Howard Avenue, Dee Why (9982 9222).

tofu and Turkish bread veggie burgers (tofu, polenta, pine nuts, capsicum, cheese, greens) with all the flavour of much less healthy competition. This café is not vegetarian, but it's not a bad place to pretend you are.

Gusto

16 Hall Street, Bondi Beach (9130 4565). Bus 380, 382. **Open** 6.30am-7.30pm Mon-Fri; 6.30am-6pm Sat, Sun. **Average** $10. **Unlicensed**. **No credit cards**.
More like a deli with good coffee, Gusto in Bondi does great baguettes and has nice flower beds to sit in. Don't go with a burning desire for a table or comfort. This is some of Sydney's best gutterside Grinders.
Branch: 2A Heeley Street, Paddington (9361 5640).

Hyde Park Barracks Cafe

Hyde Park Barracks, Queens Square, Macquarie Street (9223 1155). CityRail Martin Place or St James. **Open** 10am-4pm Mon-Fri; 11am-3pm Sat, Sun. **Average** $20. **Licensed**. **Credit** BC, MC, $TC, V.
Ah, historic Sydney! Inside or out of this beautiful sandstone building, you can't really go wrong. The food is all fresh, cheap and good. Soups, salads, pasta, cake, onion tarts, even bangers and mash. You can get wine by the glass (which may not be a bad idea, because the coffee is less than thrilling). *See also chapters* **Museums & Galleries** *and* **Sightseeing**.
Disabled: access; toilets.

A Bondi deli where good coffee is served with **Gusto**.

MCA Cafe

Museum of Contemporary Art, 140 George Street, The Rocks (9241 4253). CityRail/ferry Circular Quay. **Open** 11am-5pm Mon-Fri; 9am-5pm Sat, Sun. **Average** $45. **Licensed**. **Credit** AmEx, BC, DC, JCB, MC, $TC, V.
Cafés at major cultural institutions are usually dogs. This smart café is the exception that proves the rule. Another establishment in the Neil Perry stable (*see* **Rockpool** *and* **Wockpool** *in chapter* **Restaurants**), it's always packed with local business types at lunchtime. In the mornings, on a calm and sunny day, it's just about the perfect place to sit outside for cake and coffee. *See also chapter* **Museums & Galleries**.
Disabled: access; toilets (via 140 George Street entrance).

Metronome

413 Bourke Street, Surry Hills (9361 5015). Bus 301, 302, 303. **Open** 7.45am-5pm Mon-Sat; 9.30am-3.30pm Sun. **Average** $8. **BYO**. **No credit cards**.
Just off the busy nightmare that is Taylor Square, Metronome provides something of a haven (well, at least a quiet backyard with a fish pond). The all-day breakfast menu is worth a look. The toasted baguettes stuffed with nearly too much pastrami never fail to satisfy and the Portuguese custard tarts are addictive.

MOS Cafe

Museum of Sydney, 37 Phillip Street, Sydney (9241 3636). CityRail/ferry Circular Quay. **Open** 7.15am-10pm Mon-Fri; 9.15am-6pm Sat, Sun. **Average** $42. **Licensed**. **Credit** AmEx, BC, MC, V.

Discover Zen and the art of noodle consumption at the funky **Fu Manchu.** *See page 127.*

The ancient red gum and steel giant tables provide a good Lonely Guy space in the middle of town. The menu has a bit of everything, including eggs Benedict made with light, dry brioche and no stinting on the hollandaise. The coffee isn't as good as the eggs or the room.

Nostimo

113 Queen Street, Woollahra (9362 4277). Bus 389. **Open** 7am-10pm Mon-Sat. **Average** $10. **BYO. No credit cards.**
Too bright, too vivid and nearly too much, but this is Queen Street and Nostimo is a current café with a Greek twist. There's a good mixed plate of dolmades, black olives, tsatsiki, aubergine and ricotta, and impressively expensive well stuffed pide (pitta) sandwiches.

Parmalat

320B Victoria Street, Darlinghurst (9331 2914). CityRail Kings Cross. **Open** 6am-7.30pm daily. **Average** $7. **Unlicensed. No credit cards.**
It's narrow. It's noisy. The orange juice is full of pips and sometimes you can't get a seat, even in the gutter. But the coffee, the food and the stupid three-legged chairs are addictive. Competition with neighbouring Bar Coluzzi (*see p122*) exists more in the minds of the patrons than the proprietors. The food here (especially the Turkish bread foccacia) may have the edge, and a Parmalatte certainly rivals a Coluzzitatte.

Le Petit Crème

118 Darlinghurst Road, Darlinghurst (9361 4738). CityRail Kings Cross. **Open** 7am-4pm Mon-Fri; 7am-5pm Sat; 8am-5pm Sun. **Average** $7. **BYO.**
In the only strictly French café in Victoria Street, regulars bog into bols and croques mesdames as if foccacia had never been invented. The big breakfasts of bacon, scrambles and brioche are cheap and popular. At the weekend, customers seem to hang from the ceiling, and the staff manage crowd control brilliantly. Particularly charming on a rainy day.

Red Kite

Corner of Roscoe and Gould Streets, Bondi Beach (9365 0432). Bus 380, 382. **Open** *summer* 8am-midnight daily; *winter* 8am-6pm daily. **Average** $15. **BYO** (evening only). **No credit cards.**
A vegetarian café that is so good, it can make you forget to miss bacon. Really. There's no view or flash decor, but there are some rather impressive chilli corn cakes, fab omelettes, Polish rye toast, and the Red Kite blend of Grinders coffee.

Rose Blues Cafe

23 Glebe Point Road, Glebe (9552 2105). Bus 431, 434. **Open** 8am-10pm Mon; 8am-11pm Tue-Thur; 8am-midnight Fri, Sat; 8.30am-10pm Sun. **Average** $8 breakfast, $25 lunch/dinner. **BYO. Credit** AmEx, BC, MC, $TC, V.
Glebe is a little lost in the 1970s and, happily, so is the price list at this long-time favourite neighbourhood café. Only $2 for a croissant or toasted damper with proper jam. Seriously! This is one of those breakfast, burgers, pasta, caesar salad, sticky date pudding cafés – but it is a fine one. The courtyard is as good a place as any to drink white wine in Glebe.

Rushcutters Bay Kiosk

Rushcutters Bay Park, New Beach Road, Rushcutters Bay (9331 3119). Bus 327. **Open** 8.30am-4.30pm daily. **Average** $10. **Unlicensed. No credit cards.**
This park is famous for its joggers, junkies, Frisbee dogs and tethered yachts. Recently, the old toilet blocks have been nicely converted into a café serving great coffee, simple crusty baguettes stuffed with everything you want, pastries and cold drinks.
Disabled: access; toilets.

Sejuiced

472 Bronte Road, Bronte (9389 9538). Bus 378. **Open** *summer* 7am-9.30pm daily; *winter* 7am-5pm daily. **Average** $10. **BYO. No credit cards.**
More than a jumped-up juice bar, this is the place to come for freshly shucked oysters in summer and a fab view of

Bronte Beach all year round. There's great Turkish bread foccacia, health-fiend muesli, better-than-Bronte-average coffee and good sidewalk sunlight. A fine place to sit in a towel with a beetroot juice.

Thomas Street Cafe
2 Thomas Street, McMahons Point (9955 4703). CityRail North Sydney. **Open** 8am-3pm Mon-Sat. **Average** $12 breakfast; $20 lunch. **BYO. Credit** AmEx, BC, MC, V.
When it's perfect leafy courtyard weather, Thomas Street has just the right courtyard. Beyond the usual baked beans, eggs and the broad breakfast menu, it's also worth remembering this suburban hideaway for the pies and cakes served all day long.

Tropicana
227B Victoria Street, Darlinghurst (9360 9809). CityRail Kings Cross. **Open** 5am-11pm daily. **Average** $10. **BYO. No credit cards.**
Is this a café or a movie set? There's something not quite down and never completely out about Trop customers which keeps them pinned to exactly the same stools for about a decade. Another Sydney institution, the café provides a home/office for so many independent film-makers, that it became host to the country's most popular short film festival. Not the best coffee or food on the strip, but probably the nicest natured.

Una's
340 Victoria Street, Darlinghurst (9360 6885). CityRail Kings Cross. **Open** 6.30am-11pm Mon-Sat; 8am-11pm Sun. **Average** $7 breakfast; $15 lunch/dinner. **BYO. No credit cards.**
This does one of the biggest breakfasts in Sydney. Yes, it is possible to fit scrambled eggs, sausages, mushrooms, tomatoes, bacon and potatoes on one plate. Beyond breakfast, Una's schnitzel is good, huge, cheap and, well, huge. A Sydney institution to rival Bar Coluzzi (*see p122*) in terms of legend and clientele.

Vinyl Lounge
17 Elizabeth Bay Road, Elizabeth Bay (9326 9224). CityRail Kings Cross. **Open** 8am-5pm daily. **Average** $10. **BYO. No credit cards.**

Breakfast choice for tired and emotional locals. Big breakfasts, juices, baguette toast, comfy vinyl seats and mostly vinyl music make this converted shopfront an ideal recovery stop.

Whaley's
231 Whale Beach Road, Whale Beach (9974 4121). Bus 193. **Open** 7.30am-7pm daily. **Average** $8. **Unlicensed. No credit cards.**
This is The Peninsula, and a Peninsula Boy's body is a temple at which he regularly worships with a Whaley's burger, made from a local Avalon Bakery bun, home-made soy or beef patties, beetroot, chilli sauce, melted cheese and/or tahini. You can get a pretty good espresso here, but a milk shake is more culturally correct.

Oodles of Noodles

Perhaps the only thing more plentiful in Sydney than cafés or sickeningly good views is the Asian restaurant. The ready availability of good Thai, Vietnamese, Chinese, Japanese and Korean food has educated Sydney folk to eat Asian at every opportunity. In recent years a new hybrid form, the noodle bar, has all but replaced the faithful old bowl of pasta for a cheap quick snack.

Chu Bay
312A Bourke Street, Surry Hills (9331 3386). Bus 377, 390, 391, 392. **Open** 5.30-11pm daily. **BYO. Credit** BC, MC, V.
Not strictly a noodle joint, but if you are roaming the streets with a huge desire to spend about $7.50 on prawn noodles, mixed Asian veg and a chilli chicken dish, you can't go wrong.

Fu Manchu
249 Victoria Street, Darlinghurst (9360 9424). CityRail Kings Cross. **Open** noon-10.30pm Mon-Sat; 5.30-10pm Sun. **BYO. No credit cards.**
This stylishly redesigned chemist's is all stainless steel and lipstick-red pillow stools. The char siew wanton egg noodle soup is a great solo dish. Warm duck noodles and char kway teow are house favourites for sharing.

There's no view, but the food's fab at the **Red Kite.** *See page 126.*

Lighting-up time at the **Paddington Inn**. *See page 129.*

Ju-Ju's
76 Spring Street, Bondi Junction (9389 7905). CityRail Bondi Junction. **Open** *noon-2.30pm, 5.30-9.30pm, Mon-Sat.* **BYO. No credit cards.**
Tiny and strictly Japanese. Beef teriyaki, shabu shabu and tempura are nearly as popular as the soba noodle dishes.

Minami
87C Macleay Street, Potts Point (9357 2481). CityRail Kings Cross. **Open** *noon-1am Mon-Sat; noon-midnight Sun.* **BYO. No credit cards.**
A laminated hole-in-the-wall in the middle of the serious restaurant belt. The soups are a little oily, but you can't argue with the flavour or the quantity. Cha shu men (egg noodles in a miso-flavoured stock topped with slices of pork) is nearly unfinishably large and costs about $9.

Minh
508 Marrickville Road, Dulwich Hill (9560 0465). Bus L23, 423, 426. **Open** *10am-10pm daily.* **Licensed & BYO. Credit** AmEx, BC, MC, V.
You shouldn't make the pilgrimage out to Dulwich Hill just for this Vietnamese favourite, but if you're in the area... There's more on offer, but the beef pho made with noodles, onion, mint, chilli and bean sprouts is the original and best, and costs about $6.

Ploy Thai
132 Wairoa Avenue, Bondi Beach (9365 1118). Bus 380, 382. **Open** *noon-10pm Mon, Tue, Thur-Sun.* **BYO. No credit cards.**
This Thai joint has been popular with Bondi foodies for years. It's not just a noodle bar, but the roast duck noodle soup rivals all comers for quality and value.

Prasit's Northside Takeaway
395 Crown Street, Surry Hills (9332 1792). Bus 301, 302, 303. **Open** *11am-3pm, 5-10pm, Tue-Sun.* **BYO. No credit cards.**
Prasit's is not on the Northside, nor is it strictly takeaway. It is, however, one of the best cheap Thai feeds going. These are superior Thai noodles.

Sailor's Thai Canteen
106 George Street, The Rocks (9251 2466). CityRail/ferry Circular Quay. **Open** *noon-8pm daily.* **Licensed. No credit cards.**
A curiously named (it's in the old Sailor's Home) second venture for David Thompson of Darley Street Thai fame (*see chapter* **Restaurants**). On the ground floor is a Thai noodle bar, complete with long communal table; downstairs is a less formal version of the Darley Street experience. A gem.

Wockpool Bar
155 Victoria Street, Potts Point (9368 1771). CityRail Kings Cross. **Open** *6.30-11pm Mon-Sat; 6.30-10pm Sun.* **Licensed. Credit** AmEx, BC, DC, MC, $TC, V.
Neil Perry, one of the kings of the restaurant scene, turned the bar of his latest restaurant into a noodle quickie, specialising in laksa, pho and amazing caramelised poached eggs. For the **Wockpool** *see chapter* **Restaurants**.

Bars & Pubs

Visitors could be forgiven for thinking Sydney is a barless town. Its rich pub history and weird liquor laws have conspired against a good bar culture. Most bars live in disguise – the renovated saloon at an old pub, the annex or courtyard of a big restaurant, an old fogies' club which is overcome by hipsters one night a week, the room of an international hotel which operates independently. A liquor licence is cheaper if customers approach the bar with 'an intention to eat'. God help you and the management if you just turn up with 'the intention to drink'.

Hotel Bars

The international hotel is the most sophisticated (read expensive) of the myriad watering holes. Killer view bars at the **Gazebo** and the **ANA** have a great after-work following among suits. Nobody hovers for too long because the sun goes down and the drinks get no cheaper. A welcome new addition is the **George Street Bar** at the Regent Hotel. With renovations including a giant pizza oven and a smart menu from Regent-trained Greg Bookalill, the GSB fills the 'tween martini gap.

George Street Bar
Ground floor, Regent Hotel, 199 George Street, Sydney (9238 0000). CityRail/ferry Circular Quay or Wynyard. **Open** noon-10pm Mon-Thur; noon-11.30pm Fri. **Credit** AmEx, BC, DC, JCB, MC, $TC, V.

Horizons Bar
ANA Hotel, 176 Cumberland Street, The Rocks (9250 6000 ext 4310). CityRail/ferry Circular Quay or Wynyard. **Open** noon-1am Mon-Sat; noon-11pm Sun. **Credit** AmEx, BC, DC, JCB, MC, $TC, V.

The Penthouse Bar
17th floor, Gazebo Hotel, 2 Elizabeth Bay Road, Elizabeth Bay (9358 1999 ext 315). CityRail Kings Cross. **Open** 5-11.30pm Tue, Wed; 5pm-12.30am Thur-Sat. **Credit** AmEx, BC, DC, JCB, MC, TC, V.

Restaurant Bars
The restaurant bar is a local favourite. Sydney-siders do love to eat. Bondi's **Beechwood** and **Liberty Lunch** are packed with intended diners by the end of the week. For more than a decade, the **Bayswater Brasserie** has provided the answer for the genuinely undecided drinker; after a few Stoli crushes it's a sensible idea to eat (the bar is meant for diners only). The **Sports Bar(d)** in Bondi operates the same way (*see chapter* **Restaurants** for both).

Sydney's newest restaurant/bar success is the **Grand Pacific Blue Room** on Oxford Street. The crowd is hip, brown and pierced. The booths are for eating. The bar is for drinking and, before the last plate is spirited from the tables, there's live music and lusty pick-ups for the young and… young (*see chapter* **Restaurants**).

Beechwood Bar & Grill
100 Campbell Parade, Bondi Beach (9365 5986). Bus 380, 382. **Open** 8am-midnight daily. **Credit** AmEx, BC, MC, V.

Liberty Lunch
106 Campbell Parade, Bondi Beach (9365 1628). Bus 380, 382. **Open** noon-10.30pm Mon-Thur; noon-11pm Fri, Sat; 10am-10pm Sun. **Credit** AmEx, BC, MC, $TC, V.

Pubs
Drinkers in for the long haul still choose the gentrified pub. You'll recognise it by the slightly dated *trompe-l'œil* paint finishes, the jugs of illusions and the marked absence of disenfranchised locals. Girls in pastel suits feel comfortable in a gentrified pub. The **Green Park Hotel**, the **Four in Hand** (*see chapter* **Restaurants**), the **Paddington Inn**, the **Lord Dudley**, **The Woollahra**, **The Forresters**, **The Dolphin** and **The Palace** all have dedicated

tribal followers, as does the new and groovy **Moreton's**. It's not mandatory to play pool, but it doesn't hurt.

The closest you'll get in Sydney to a traditional British boozer is probably the **Lord Nelson**, which brews its own beer. Otherwise, try the determinedly ancient **Hero of Waterloo** or Molly Bloom's at the **Mercantile Hotel** in The Rocks.

The Dolphin
412 Crown Street, Surry Hills (9331 4800). CityRail Central. **Open** 10am-midnight Mon-Sat; noon-10pm Sun.

The Forresters
336 Riley Street, Sydney (9211 2095). CityRail Central. **Open** 11.30am-midnight Mon-Sat; noon-10pm Sun.

Green Park Hotel
360 Victoria Street, Darlinghurst (9380 5311). CityRail Kings Cross. **Open** 10am-1am Mon-Sat; 11am-midnight Sun.

Hero of Waterloo
81 Lower Fort Street, Millers Point (9252 4553). CityRail/ferry Circular Quay. **Open** 10am-11pm Mon-Sat; 10am-10pm Sun.

Lord Dudley
236 Jersey Road, Woollahra (9327 5399). CityRail Edgecliff. **Open** 11am-11pm Mon-Wed; noon-midnight Thur-Sat; noon-10pm Sun.

Lord Nelson Brewery Hotel
19 Kent Street, The Rocks (9251 4044). CityRail/ferry Circular Quay. **Open** 11.30am-11pm daily.

Mercantile Hotel
25 George Street, The Rocks (9247 3570). CityRail/ferry Circular Quay. **Open** 10am-11.45pm Mon-Wed, Sun; 10am-12.45am Thur-Sat.

Moreton's
20 Sussex Street, Sydney (9262 6988). CityRail Wynyard. **Open** 10.30am-9pm Mon, Tue; 10.30am-midnight Wed-Fri.

Paddington Inn
338 Oxford Street, Paddington (bar 9380 5277/bistro 9361 4402). Bus 380, 382. **Open** *bar* noon-1am daily; *bistro* 6.30-10.30pm Mon-Sat; noon-2.30pm Sun.

The Palace
122 Flinders Street, Darlinghurst (9361 5170). Bus 339, 372, 373, 397, 398, 399. **Open** 4pm-midnight Mon-Wed; 4pm-1am Thur-Sat; 4-11pm Sun.

The Woollahra
116 Queen Street, Woollahra (9363 2782). Bus 389. **Open** *back bar* (pool room, pinball, card tables) 10am-midnight Mon-Sat; noon-9pm Sun; *front bar* (jazz) noon-midnight Mon-Sat; noon-9pm Sun.

See also **Lookout Theatre Club** *in chapter* **Theatre & Dance**.

Bars for Lounge Lizards
The **Lounge Bar** (at the Piccadilly Hotel) is an enormous new space on the site of an old Korean restaurant. All pale timber and wide windows, it transports the average pool player to the lounge of a grand hotel somewhere in the Blue Mountains before the war.

The **Burdekin Hotel** is many bars rolled into one. Downstairs in the **Dug Out Bar**, Kim of the Killer Martini still works her magic with a perfume atomiser of vermouth. Upstairs, the **Lava Bar** has been renovated and overrun by the **Q Bar** crowd (feral pool players, *see chapter* **Nightlife**). With comfy lounges and dark nooks, we have a bar where Q meets **Gilligan's** (*see chapter* **Queer Sydney**).

Burdekin Hotel
Dug Out Bar & Lava Bar, 2 Oxford Street, Darlinghurst (9331 3066/Lava Bar 9331 8065). Bus 378, 380, 382. **Open** *street bar* 11am-12.30am Mon-Thur; 11am-3.30am Fri, Sat; *Dug Out Bar* 4pm-12.30am Mon-Thur; 4pm-3.30am Fri, Sat; *Lava Bar* 5pm-12.30am Wed, Thur; 5pm-3.30am Fri, Sat; 7pm-1am Sun.

The Lounge Bar
Above the Piccadilly Hotel, 171 Victoria Street, Kings Cross (9358 6511). CityRail Kings Cross. **Open** 6pm-midnight Mon-Thur, Sat, Sun; 5pm-midnight Fri.

Stars & Bars

If you like a little entertainment with your ale, there are a number of reliable venues. For stand-up comedy head for the Harold Park Hotel; jazz can be found at The Basement, Zeibar and Round Midnight; cabaret flourishes at The Tilbury; and there is regular live music at the Annandale, Coogee Bay and Sandringham Hotels, as well as at the Harbourside Brasserie.

For details of these places, as well as other places with live music, s*ee chapters* **Nightlife** *and* **Music: Rock, Folk & Jazz**.

Niche Bars

Finally, bars with a mission. For big-haired models, **L'Otel**. For cheap beer with a view, **The Icebergs**. For drunken money market boys on a Friday night, the **CBD** (*see chapter* **Restaurants**). For the bar that time forgot (red-buttoned vinyl, killer view), **Top of the Town**. For sheer contrariness, the **Cigar Bar** at the Inter-Continental Hotel. For late-night insanity, the **Judgement Bar** of the Courthouse Hotel and **Taxi Club**.

Cigar Bar
Inter-Continental Hotel, 117 Macquarie Street, Sydney (9232 1199). CityRail/ferry Circular Quay. **Open** 5.30pm-1am Mon-Sat.

The Icebergs
Bondi Icebergs Club, Notts Avenue, Bondi Beach (9130 3120). Bus 380, 382. **Open** 9am-8.30pm Mon-Thur; 9am-1am Fri, Sat; 9am-9pm Sun.

Judgement Bar
Courthouse Hotel, 189 Oxford Street, Darlinghurst (9360 4831). Bus 378, 380, 382. **Open** 11am-3am Mon-Thur; 24 hours Fri, Sat; 11am-midnight Sun.

L'Otel
114 Darlinghurst Road, Darlinghurst (9360 6868). CityRail Kings Cross. **Open** 7am-midnight daily.

Taxi Club
40-42 Flinders Street Darlinghurst (9331 4256). Bus 378, 380, 382. **Open** 9am-6am Mon-Fri; 24 hours Sat, Sun.

Top of the Town
227 Victoria Street, Kings Cross (9361 0911). CityRail Kings Cross. **Open** 11.30am-midnight Mon-Sat; noon-10pm Sun.

*Booze with a view at **Top of the Town**.*

Shopping & Services

Shopping & Services by Area

Central Sydney

CBD ABC Stores p136; Angus & Roberston p136; Ashwoods p152; Ava & Susan's Records p152; Aveda Esthetiqe p147; Birdland p152; Black Vanity p140; Blockbusters p153; Body Shop p147; Brashs p153; Brave Women p139; Clarence Street Cyclery p154; David Jones p135; Chifley Plaza p135; Country Road p140; Dinosaur Design p150; Dioptics p152; Dymocks p136; Evelyn Miles p154; Fairfax & Roberts p150; Fletcher's Photographic p137; Florida p139; Foto Riesal Camera House p137; GC's p154; General Pants p153; Glasshouse p135; Glenn A. Baker's Time Warp p152; Gowing Brothers p135; Grace Bros p135; Hardy Bros p150; HMV p153; Hunting World p151; Hunt Leather p151; Ian McMaugh p139; IM Lingerie p151; Inski p154; Jaye M Underfashion Boutique p151; Jurlique p148; Love & Hatred p150; Madame Korner p147; Marcs p141; Michael's Music Room p152; Mick Simmon's p154; Mid City Centre p135; Moray p145; MLC Centre p135; Mollini p154; Morrissey Edmiston p139; OPSM p152; Paddy Pallin p154; Paraphernalia for Gifts p145; Paspaley Pearly p150; Queen Victoria Building p135; Ray Costarella p139; Rebel p154; Red Eye p152; Rex p150; RM Williams p141; Saba p139; Skygarden p136; Sock Shop Australia p151; Sportsgirl p141; Strand Arcade p136; Strand Hatters p145; Surf Dive 'n' Ski p153; Ted's Camera Store p137; Third Millenium p140; Tony Barlow p137; Tony Barlow p137; Utopia Import Records p152; Vintage Clothing p142; Waterfront Records p152; Zomp p154.
Darlinghurst Art House p143; The Book Shop p136; Central Station Records & Tapes p152; Fish p152; Kookaburra Kiosk p141; Helmet p148; Route 66 p142; Sax p151; Synergy p148; Tony & Guy p148; Zoo p142.
Darling Harbour & Pyrmont Simon Johnson Quality Foods p143; Sydney Fish Markets p143.
Haymarket & Chinatown Paddy's Market p147.
Kings Cross Bliss p137; Relaxation Centre p147.
Potts Point & Woolloomooloo Grandiflora p142.
Redfern Designer discounts: Redfern p140.
The Rocks The Rocks Market p147.
Surry Hills Beauty on Crown p145; The Costume Shop p137; The Golf Shop p154.

Eastern Suburbs

Bondi Beach Bondi Beach Market p147; Bondi Beach One Hour p137; Bondi Surf Co p153.
Bondi Junction Bondi Junction Plaza p151; Heaven Scent p145.
Bronte Isabella Klompe p145.
Double Bay Belinda p140; Caralyn Taylor p148; Edward Mellor p154; Jane Lambert p145; Joh Bailey p148; Lesley McKay p136; Mondo p145; Nicholas Pounder p137; Raymond Castle p154; Smyth & Fitzgerald p147; White Ivy p151.
Paddington Alison Coates p142; Amazing Hire Company p137; Antony Whitaker p148; Ariel p136; Berkelouw Book Sellers p136; Bibelot p143; Bracewell p140; Collette Dinnigan p150; Coo-ee Aboriginal Emporium & Art Gallery p143; Family Jewels p150; Five Way Fusion p140; Folkways Music p152; Fuss p148; La Gerbe d'Or p143; Hot Tuna p153; Jane Stoddart p145; Jodie Boffa p139; The Look p148; Loyal Florist p142; Mambo p153; Mexico p145; New Edition p136; Nice Things p141; Paddington Market p147; Robbie Ingham p141; Sanctum p148; Scanlan & Theodore p139; Venustus p142; Victoria Spring p151; Vivid p142; Willis p151; Woolys Wheels p154; Zambesi p141.
Rose Bay Parisi's of Rose Bay p143.

Woollahra Liza Ho p140; Orson & Blake p145; Riada p141; Surfection p153; Zimmerman p140.

Inner West

Balmain Balmain Market p147; Victoire French Bakery p143.
Drummoyne Designer discounts: Birkenhead Point p140.
Glebe Glebe Market p147; Gleebooks p136; Half a Cow p152; Interim p145; Recycled p152; Reincarnation p142.
Leichhardt Caffe Bianchi p142.

Newtown & the South

Miranda Westfield Miranda p151.
Newtown Afrique Ali p147; iiii p152; Goulds p137; The Look p141; Scraggs p142.

Parramatta & the West

Penrith Penrith Plaza p151.

North Shore

Chatswood Chatswood Chase p151; Clinique p148; Lemon Grove p151; Westfield Chatswood p151.
Crows Nest Five Star Gourmet Foods p142; Goodman Bros Photo Retail p137.
Gore Hill ABC TV Costume Department p137.
Kirribilli Kirribilli Market p147.
Milsons Point Baltronics p137.
Mosman The Cheese Shop p142.
Neutral Bay Blue & White p137.
Northbridge Antico's p142.

Northern Beaches

Manly Aloha Manly p153.
Newport Quicksilver p153.

Further Afield

Mascot Beach Culture p153.

Shopping & Services

Whether you're tackling the tourist shops of The Rocks or taking time out from the surf at the Bondi Beach market, shopping in Sydney is an easygoing experience.

Shopping in Sydney is not the contact sport that it is in New York, where you need a booster shot to battle the crowds at Macy's on a Saturday, or Hong Kong, where you require the cunning of a fox to bargain with a stallholder in Stanley Market. Rare is the sales assistant who works on commission, and the price you pay is the one you see on the price ticket.

Recently, the city has experienced an influx of international fashion names like DKNY, Armani and Versace. When added to stayers like Chanel, Moschino and Gucci, there's plenty to keep the big spenders spending. However, a lot of Sydney's strength in fashion comes from young local designers. As many of them are now selling in Asia and the US, visiting shoppers can return home with a wardrobe of clothes that are a full season ahead. For fast and forward fashion don't leave town without a visit to the Strand Arcade.

Sale time is generally at the end of summer and winter, but department and larger stores also hold sales to coincide with public holidays, like Easter. The big ones to watch out for are David Jones' Twice Yearly Clearance at the end of June and after Christmas (they have no other sales) and Grace Bros' Boxing Day Sale. The best savings are made at the designer level.

OPENING HOURS
Store hours are generally 9am-5.30pm Monday-Friday. Thursday is late shopping night, when most stores stay open till 9pm. At the weekend anything goes. Increasingly, shops are trading on Sundays, but most that do won't open their doors until 11am or noon. During the summer months, most shops outside the CBD stay open at least an hour later than in winter, particularly in beachside areas.

SHOPPING AREAS
It is possible to walk from the Town Hall end of the **CBD** to Martin Place during a downpour without ever needing to flex a brolly. A system of arcades, malls and department stores connected by tunnels and overhead walkways provides continuous cover. But this doesn't mean you should save an expedition here for a rainy day. Then you'd miss the streetside cafés that are popping up all over the place and... Chanel.

The shops in **Darlinghurst**, particularly around the 'Golden Mile' on Oxford Street, reflect that suburb's role as centre of queer Sydney. You can take a break from the camp merchandise by nipping into **Crown Street** to check out the young designer stores, vintage clothing and cool record shops.

Paddington locals avoid their area on Saturdays because of the crowds, but the market (*see page 147*

Markets) is justifiably popular. However, if it's small fashion shops that you want to check out, do Paddo on a weekday. Most of the shops are on Oxford Street, but don't ignore side streets like Glenmore Road and William Street. Some people lament the opening of chain stores such as Jigsaw and General Pants because of their effect on local rents, but the area still offers the best selection of small- and medium-sized designer shops outside the CBD.

Home to ex-prime minister Paul Keating, **Woollahra's** quiet and leafy Queen Street is also known for its many antique shops, which range from art deco to antique wine wares.

The first thing to do in **Double Bay** is get off the New South Head Road and plunge in among the Rolls Royces and BMWs in Bay, Cross and Knox Streets. This really is one of those places where you can settle down in a café after exploring the designer outlets and watch the world go by; in this part of town the world is blond, tanned and wearing shades.

On the west side of the CBD lie the suburbs of **Balmain**, **Rozelle** and **Glebe**. Unlike its surrounding maze of tiny lanes, Darling Street in Balmain makes shopping a leisurely activity, especially on Saturday market days.

Heading south, studenty **Newtown's** King Street was once a downbeat suburban shopping strip, and parts of it still are. But other stretches are home to some of the quirkiest furniture shops and coolest cafés in Sydney. The area also boasts more vintage clothing shops than any other in the city.

The **north shore's** prime shopping strip, **Military Road**, runs from Neutral Bay, where you'll find lots of smaller arcades and malls interspersed with restaurants and recycled designer labels stores, to Mosman, with its homewares, kids clothing and new classic fashion labels.

Department Stores

David Jones
65-77 Market Street & 86-108 Castlereagh Street, Sydney (9266 5544). CityRail Martin Place, St James or Town Hall. **Open** 9am-6pm Mon-Wed, Fri; 9am-9pm Thur; 9am-5pm Sat; 11am-5pm Sun. **Credit** AmEx, BC, DC, JCB, MC, TC, V.
The advertising claims David Jones is the most beautiful store in the world and at Christmas its window displays really are something special. The seventh floor is international designer heaven – home to Donna Karan, Calvin Klein and labels not found elsewhere in Sydney. Cross underground to the Market Street branch and enter the food hall – the Harrods meets Balducci's of Sydney – which stocks anything: meat, poultry, deli items, imported and local delicacies, tea and coffee, fruit and veg. There's also a food hall in the Bondi branch (*see p151* **Bondi Junction Plaza**). *Disabled: access; toilets.*

Gowing Brothers
Corner of Market and George Streets, Sydney (9264 6321). CityRail Town Hall. **Open** 8.30am-6pm Mon-Wed, Fri; 8.30am-8.30pm Thur; 9am-5pm Sat; 11am-5pm Sun. **Credit** AmEx, BC, DC, MC, TC, V.

The department store especially for the fellas. A three-storey emporium full of those boys own essentials like Hard Yakka overalls, King Gee workshorts, RM Williams moleskin and Blundstone boots. Now moving from bloke classics to supertrendy gear.

Grace Bros
436 George Street, Sydney (9238 9111). CityRail Town Hall. **Open** 9am-6pm Mon-Wed, Fri; 9am-9pm Thur; 9am-6pm Sat; 11am-5pm Sun. **Credit** AmEx, BC, DC, JCB, MC, TC, V.
The down-to-earth chain is in the midst of a state-wide renovation programme and, unfortunately, the city store is last on the list. Judging by the others, though, it will be worth the wait. Unlike its television namesake, this department store runs to Anne Klein, DKNY and CK sections; it's also strong on European labels. *Disabled: access.*

City Shopping Centres

For the 200 or more shops – from tourist outlets to designer stores – that make up the Harbourside Shopping Centre *see* **Darling Harbour** *in chapter* **Sightseeing**.

Chifley Plaza
2 Chifley Square, Sydney (9221 4500). CityRail Martin Place.
This building could be an empty cave housing only Tiffany & Co and a lot of people wouldn't mind. Fortunately, for the keen shopper, there are other stores here. Apart from the internationals, local names are well represented too: RM Williams for the essential riding boot; Oroton for accessories; and Makers Mark for beautiful jewellery and pieces made by local craftspeople. See below for listings of individual shops. *Disabled: access; toilet.*

Glasshouse
Bridge Level, 135 King Street, Sydney (9223 8533). CityRail Martin Place or Town Hall.
Lacking its own identity, this centre has fallen prey to the spread of the outlet store – already it has three (Jeans West, Portmans and Calvin Klein). There are a couple of well priced shoe shops for men and women, but the best thing about the Glasshouse is the overpass linking it with the MLC Centre. See below for listings of individual shops. *Disabled: access; toilets (level 3).*

Mid City Centre
197 Pitt Street, Sydney (9221 2422). CityRail Martin Place or Town Hall.
There's a big HMV store, a large sports shop (Rebel Sports) and a great fashion store (Marcs) at the front. You can skip the rest. See below for listings of individual shops. *Disabled: access; toilets.*

MLC Centre
19-29 Martin Place, Sydney (9224 8333). CityRail Martin Place.
Not a big place, but what a sweet place. This is where you will find Moschino, Gucci et al. Also part of the same building are the Theatre Royal and Dendy Cinema, which has a great film bookshop. See below for listings of individual shops. *Disabled: access; toilets.*

Queen Victoria Building (QVB)
455 George Street, Sydney (information 9264 1955; tours 9264 9209). CityRail Town Hall.
For full details of the best-looking of the city shopping centres, *see chapter* **Sightseeing**.

Skygarden

*77 Castlereagh Street, Sydney (9231 1811). CityRail
Martin Place.*
One of the newer centres, this one houses Sportsgirl over two
levels and a large Country Road branch. Men are well catered
for and there is an upper level almost entirely devoted to
homewares. If you need some sustenance before you shop,
take the express elevator from the Pitt Street entrance
straight to the rooftop food hall. See below for listings of individual shops.
Disabled: access; toilets.

Strand Arcade

*412 George Street, Sydney (9232 4199). CityRail Martin
Place or Town Hall.*
As beautiful as the QVB but a hundred times cooler. Don't
be fooled by the opals and koala sweaters on the ground
floor, the best fashion is to be found upstairs. Just don't trip
over the too-groovy shopgirls sharing ciggies and gossip on
the balcony. See below for listings of individual shops.

Books

ABC Stores

*Shop 48, 1st Floor, QVB (9333 1635). CityRail Town
Hall.* **Open** 9am-5.30pm Mon-Wed, Fri; 9am-9pm Thur;
9am-5pm Sat; 11am-4.30pm Sun. **Credit** AmEx, BC, DC,
MC, $TC, V.
As the name suggests, most titles here bear some relation to
ABC television and radio programmes.

Angus & Robertson

*Imperial Arcade, 168 Pitt Street, Sydney (9235 1188).
CityRail Martin Place or Town Hall.* **Open** 8.30am-6pm

For the QVB, see pages 35 and 135.

Mon-Wed, Fri; 8.30am-9pm Thur; 9am-5.30pm Sat;
10.30am-5pm Sun. **Credit** AmEx, BC, DC, MC, TC, V.
A mega-store catering to a broad market. Check the front
tables for big mark-downs. The magazine selection is vast.

Ariel

*42 Oxford Street, Paddington (9332 4581). Bus 378,
380, 382.* **Open** 10am-midnight daily. **Credit** AmEx,
BC, DC, MC, TC, V.
More than just a bookshop. A couple of well placed sofas
make it hard to remember that this is a shop and not a
friend's living room. Good art/photography and Australian
fiction sections.

The Book Shop

*207 Oxford Street, Darlinghurst (9331 1103). Bus 378,
380, 382.* **Open** 10am-10pm Mon-Wed, Fri; 10am-
midnight Sat; noon-10pm Sun. **Credit** AmEx, BC, MC,
$TC, V.
These stores specialise in gay and lesbian material. They
also stock a range of rare imported books.
Branch: 186 King Street, Newtown (9557 4244).

Dymocks

*424-428 George Street, Sydney (9235 0155). CityRail
Town Hall.* **Open** 9am-6pm Mon-Wed, Fri; 9am-9pm
Thur; 9am-5pm Sat; 10am-5pm Sun. **Credit** AmEx, BC,
DC, MC, TC, V.
An all-purpose chain of superstores with a large stationery
department. This branch also hosts regular literary luncheons
with well-known writers as guests. Branches are too numer-
ous to list here: check the phone book for your nearest.

Gleebooks

*49 Glebe Point Road, Glebe (9660 2333). Bus 431, 432,
433, 434.* **Open** 8am-9pm daily. **Credit** AmEx, BC, DC,
JCB, MC, TC, V.
Gleebooks has two branches on Glebe Point Road and was
Bookseller of the Year in 1995. No 49 sells new titles while
no 191 specialises in second-hand and children's books as
well as more esoteric books on the humanities.
Branch: 191 Glebe Point Road, Glebe (9442 2526).

Lesley McKay

*346 New South Head Road, Double Bay (9327 1354).
Bus 323, 324, 325.* **Open** 9am-10pm Mon-Sat; 10am-
10pm Sun. **Credit** AmEx, BC, DC, MC, TC, V.
Experienced staff and 28 years in the business go a long way
towards making this bookshop one for the connoisseur.
Particularly good are the design, art, history, biology and
literature sections, and there's Doctor Seuss and other kids'
books at the sister store across the street.
Branch: 401 New South Head Road, Double Bay (9363 0374).

New Edition

*328A Oxford Street, Paddington (9360 6913). Bus 378,
380, 382.* **Open** 9.30am-9pm daily. **Credit** AmEx, BC,
DC, MC, TC, V.
There's not really room to swing a backpack in this tiny
shop, but the selection is good and the service excellent.

Second-hand

See also above **Gleebooks**.

Berkelouw Book Sellers

*19 Oxford Street, Paddington (9360 3200). Bus 378,
380, 382.* **Open** 10am-midnight daily. **Credit** AmEx,
BC, DC, MC, TC, V.
This emporium has an interesting selection of antique
Australiana and assorted rare books, mostly new but also
second-hand – not the musty variety, though; most are
plastic-wrapped. There is also a café upstairs with a great
view of Oxford Street.

More than just a bookshop: **Ariel***, page 136.*

Goulds
32 King Street, Newtown (9519 8947). Bus 422, 423. **Open** *7am-midnight daily.* **Credit** *AmEx, BC, MC, TC, V.*
Around 9,000 square feet of books make this the largest second-hand bookshop in Sydney. There are new books, too.

Nicholas Pounder
346 New South Head Road, Double Bay (9328 7410). Bus 323, 324, 325. **Open** *10am-6pm Mon-Sat; noon-6pm Sun.* **Credit** *AmEx, BC, DC, MC, TC, V.*
Although most business is through its mail order catalogue, the shop in Double Bay has a varied selection of modern first editions, letters, twentieth-century literature and rare titles.

Cameras & Photo Developing

Baltronics
3 Northcliff Street, Milsons Point (9959 5200). CityRail/ferry Milsons Point. **Open** *8.30am-5.30pm Mon-Fri.* **Credit** *AmEx, BC, MC, TC, V.*
If you're here for work, not play, but left your flash pack/medium format camera/reflector at home, this is where to hire it.

Bondi Beach One Hour
25 Hall Street, Bondi Beach (9300 9577). Bus 378, 380, 382. **Open** *8.30am-6pm Mon-Wed, Fri; 9am-6pm Sat, Sun.* **Credit** *BC, MC, V.*
Want to send snapshots home that look like postcards? When you leave your film to be processed here, the photos come back with those old-fashioned white borders around them.

Fletcher's Photographic
317 Pitt Street, Sydney (9267 6146). CityRail Town Hall. **Open** *8.30am-5.30pm Mon-Wed, Fri; 8.30am-7.30pm Thur; 9am-1.45pm Sat.* **Credit** *AmEx, BC, DC, MC, TC, V.*
The camera superstore. A good place to start for duty free because you'll get the best advice (you'll can still shop around). It has a great professional department that students utilise. Want your friends to think you windsurfed with Brad Pitt on your hols? Take in your holiday snaps and a pic of him and let Fletcher's do the rest: the digital imaging services are the best in town.

Foto Riesal
Camera House
364A Kent Street, Sydney (9299 6746). CityRail Town Hall. **Open** *9am-5.30pm Mon-Fri; 9am-3pm Sat.* **Credit** *AmEx, BC, DC, JCB, MC, TC, V.*
For the serious snapper. The kind of place where, if you're not a professional or at least an advanced amateur, you probably won't speak the same language.

Goodman Bros Photo Retail
121 Alexander Street, Crows Nest (9439 3666). Bus 288, 289, 290, 291, 292. **Open** *8.30am-5.30pm Mon-Fri; 9am-noon Sat.* **Credit** *AmEx, BC, DC, MC, V.*
A good stopover for pros, advanced amateurs and students.

Ted's Camera Store
254 Pitt Street, Sydney (9264 1687). CityRail Town Hall. **Open** *9am-5.30pm Mon-Wed, Fri; 9am-7pm Thur; 9am-5pm Sat; 11am-5pm Sun.* **Credit** *AmEx, BC, DC, MC, TC, V.*
Good for the happy snapper to buy film, have it processed and get expert advice.

Costume Hire

ABC TV Costume Department
221 Pacific Highway, Gore Hill (9950 4284). Bus 288, 289, 290, 291, 292. **Open** *8am-5pm Mon-Fri; 10am-3pm Sat.* **Credit** *BC, DC, MC, V.*
More conducive to wardrobe stylists but if you're in the area, definitely worth a try, especially for period outfits.

Amazing Hire Company
112 Oxford Street, Paddington (9361 3878). Bus 378, 380, 382. **Open** *10.30am-6pm Mon-Wed, Fri; 10.30am-7pm Thur; 10am-5pm Sat.* **Credit** *AmEx, BC, DC, MC, V.*
During Mardi Gras week, every queen in town fights it out over sequin bra-tops and Lurex hotpants in the hire department. At any other time of the year, the selection of vintage dresses, suits and hats is good, if a little pricey.

The Costume Shop
7th floor, 61 Marlborough Street, Surry Hills (9318 2511). CityRail Central. **Open** *9.30am-6.30pm Mon-Wed, Fri; 9.30am-8pm Thur; 9am-4pm Sat.* **Credit** *BC, MC, $TC, V.*
If the person or character you want to dress up as has appeared in a recent Australian Opera production, chances are you'll find the costume here. It also has some great contemporary pieces for bad-taste parties, as well as your classic Roman centurion and medieval princess numbers.

Tony Barlow
Shop 2, Strand Arcade (9232 1159). CityRail Martin Place or Town Hall. **Open** *9am-5.30pm Mon-Wed, Fri; 9am-9pm Thur; 9am-4pm Sat; 11am-4pm Sun.* **Credit** *AmEx, BC, DC, JCB, MC, TC, V.*
If the costume you're after is a penguin suit, try the hire department here. But don't leave it till the day of the 'do', because adjustments will probably have to be made to trouser hems and so on.

Dry Cleaners

Bliss
9 Ward Street, Kings Cross (9358 6510). CityRail Kings Cross. **Open** *8am-6pm Mon-Sat.* **No credit cards.**
This is where your Gucci leather and Prada suede will receive the very best of care.

Blue & White
180-182 Military Road, Neutral Bay (9909 2235). Bus 228, 229, 230. **Open** *7am-7pm Mon-Fri; 8am-5pm Sat; 10am-4pm Sun.* **Credit** *AmEx, BC, MC, V.*
The drive-thru facility makes dropping off your dirty duds almost as much fun as ordering a Big Mac and fries from a fibreglass hamburger. Blue & White will also hand-dye leather coats, shoes and bags. A big plus is this establishment's eco-friendliness – even the coathangers are recycled. **Branch:** Corner of West and Falcon Streets, Crows Nest (9955 6044).

Florida

Carlton Arcade, 55 Elizabeth Street, Sydney (9231 1309).
CityRail Martin Place. **Open** 7.30am-5.30pm Mon-Fri.
Credit AmEx, BC, MC, V.
A mini-chain but with a personal touch.
Branches: 10 Cross Street, Double Bay (9327 5594);
7 Newland Street, Bondi Junction (9387 1747); 221
Maroubra Road, Maroubra Junction (9349 3176).

Fashion

Shopping centres and malls are great for access to
affordable fashion, but when it comes to international prestige labels (and bigger duty free savings) it's often better to get off the beaten track.
Fear not, though, if you just need need your regular fix of Gucci or Chanel – most of the biggest
names are conveniently grouped together in the
CBD around Castlereagh and Elizabeth Streets.

Hardest to miss is the area at the corner of King
and Castlereagh Streets. Not that most fashion punters couldn't find the interlocked 'Cs' with their eyes
closed anyway (**Chanel** 70 Castlereagh Street; 9233
4800). On King you'll also find **Christian Lacroix**
at number 63 (accessories only, but keep your fingers crossed; 9223 4311/9236 9617). Diagonally
opposite from Chanel is **Louis Vuitton** (9223
4311/9236 9605) and further along Castlereagh on
either side of the street there's **Hermès** (9233 4007),
Céline (9223 4209) and **Loewe** (9236 9625).

On the corner of Elizabeth Street opposite David
Jones is **Giorgio Armani** (137 Elizabeth Street;
9283 5562). Right around the corner is **Bulgari** for
seekers of serious jewels. Most recently opened in
this newly developed fashion corner is **Gianni
Versace** in the Sheraton on the Park (128
Elizabeth Street; 9267 3232).

Gucci, **Ferragamo** and **Moschino** can all be
tracked down to the MLC Centre (*see page 135*) as
can **Adrienne Vittadini** and **Walter Steiger**.
For the more casual end of the international market – like groovy **Guess!** – head for the QVB (*see
page 135*) and for the brights of **Kenzo**, the coats
of **MaxMara** and the classics of **Nina Ricci**, the
Chifley Plaza is the place (*see page 135*).

The Designers

Brave Women

Shop 78, Strand Arcade (9221 5212). **Open** 9.30am-
5.30pm Mon-Wed, Fri; 9.30am-8.30pm Thur; 10am-5pm
Sat. **Credit** AmEx, BC, DC, JCB, MC, TC, V.
If you're bigger than an Australian/UK size 12 (US 10), give
this store a miss. Hemlines are high and sideseams severe.
Always very current fashion. The men's shop is nearby.
Branch: Brave Men, Shop 69, Strand Arcade (9221 5292).

Ian McMaugh

Shop 71, Strand Arcade (9221 3357). **Open** 10am-
5.30pm Mon-Wed, Fri; 10am-8.30pm Thur; 10am-4.30pm
Sat. **Credit** AmEx, BC, DC, MC, TC, V.
Previously, McMaugh has done womenswear, but for now
he's concentrating on cool menswear. Lurex shirts and net
tops nestle amongst rugged knits and jeans.

Jodie Boffa

26 Glenmore Road, Paddington (9361 5867). Bus 378,
380, 382. **Open** 10am-6pm Mon-Sat; 11am-4pm Sun.
Credit AmEx, BC, MC, V.
Flawless fashion from exquisite fabrics: beautiful soft suiting.

Morrissey Edmiston

Shop 63, Strand Arcade (9221 5616). **Open** 9.30am-
5.30pm Mon-Wed, Fri; 9.30am-8.30pm Thur; 10am-5pm
Sat. **Credit** AmEx, BC, DC, MC, TC, V.
Fast, fun, inexpensive fashion. Too busy creating their own
styles to waste time copying others', these guys also have
great sales (much later in the season than the rest).

Ray Costarella

Shop 70, Strand Arcade (9221 1153). **Open** 10am-
5.30pm Mon-Wed, Fri; 10am-8.30pm Thur; 10am-4.30pm
Sat. **Credit** AmEx, BC, DC, JCB, MC, TC, V.
Fine suits and special frocks free of superfluous details.

Saba

Shop P3, Pitt Street Level, Skygarden (9231 2183).
Open 9.30am-6pm Mon-Wed, Fri; 9.30am-9pm Thur;
9.30am-5pm Sat; noon-4pm Sun. **Credit** AmEx, BC, DC,
JCB, MC, TC, V.
Great for suits that don't scream 'woman in the boardroom!'
Good fabrics combined with a perfect cut. Look out also for
the soft knits and casual linens.

Scanlan & Theodore

443 Oxford Street, Paddington (9381 6722). Bus 378,
380, 382. **Open** 10am-6pm Mon-Sat; noon-5pm Sun.
Credit AmEx, BC, DC, JCB, MC, TC, V.
Definitely one of the better young Australian designers. More
original than most, with great fabrics, colours and quality.

Designer discounts

Factory outlet shopping anywhere is a tricky business. Not every visit will reap the same rewards. Some stores might be having their equivalent of a bad hair day, while others will seem to be giving the stuff away. In either case, don't forget to try things on (sizes may not be on the garment, or they may not be correct) and check for faults.

Bargain Buyers Bus Tours
(9310 1088). **Prices** $21-$39. **No credit cards**.
Though you can find some good bargains at the relatively central Redfern and Birkenhead Point outlets, some equally great bargains are spread around Sydney in warehouses and factory-attached outlets. These require not only transport to get around, but also an insider to gain entry. Bargain Buyers Bus Tours gives you both, with the choice of half- and full-day shopping trips.

Birkenhead Point
Cary Street, Drummoyne (9181 3922). Bus 500, 501, 506/ferry Birkenhead Point.
None of the stores here are at the 'designer' end of the market, but they do represent a good portion of the

Australian clothing market. **Country Road** is definitely the drawcard and the discounts on men's/women's clothes and homewares are worth the trip from the city centre. You'll also find **Esprit**, **Osh Kosh**, **Footlocker**, **Timberland** and **Howard Showers** among a lot of shops that you didn't think could get any cheaper anyway. The shopping complex overlooks Iron Cove, so you can lunch here at one of the alfresco cafés or grab some fish and chips and head for the water's edge.

Redfern
Corner of Redfern and Regent Streets. CityRail Redfern or Central.
This area has been growing over the last ten years to the point where, now, virtually every shop is a designer outlet store. The only difference between the places is their interpretation of the words 'designer' and 'discount'. One shop where you'll get both is **Marcs**. It has good labels, imports and own-label stuff at up to 75% off – though the mix leans towards menswear. Another is **Italian Designer Clearance**, which has more Italian men's labels than you'll find on the Via Condotti. The **Adam Bennett** store is worth crossing the street for. If you're after swimwear try **Seafolly** and **Howard Showers** does some sizeable discounts too.

Third Millenium
Shop 65, Strand Arcade (9221 4089). **Open** 9.30am-5.30pm Mon-Wed, Fri; 9.30am-8.30pm Thur; 9.30am-4.30pm Sat. **Credit** AmEx, BC, MC, TC, V.
Selling only its own label in each of the stores, Third Millenium supplies groovy young things with affordable but cool basics as well as some amazing special-occasion frocks.
Branch: 328 Crown Street, Darlinghurst (9331 2490).

Zimmerman
24 Oxford Street, Woollahra (9360 5769). Bus 378, 380, 382. **Open** 10am-6pm Mon-Wed, Fri; 10am-8pm Thur; noon-5pm Sat. **Credit** AmEx, BC, MC, TC, V.
Really fun fashiony togs with a difference. In summer the pieces get especially cute.

The Stores

Belinda
8 Transvaal Avenue, Double Bay (9328 6288). Bus 323, 324, 325. **Open** 10am-6pm Mon-Fri; 10am-5pm Sat; noon-5pm Sun. **Credit** AmEx, BC, DC, MC, TC, V.
Sells the pick of the crop, both locally and from overseas, selected by the store's stylish namesake. This is the place for exquisite fashion enhanced with beautiful accessories and jewellery.

Black Vanity
Shop 29, Strand Arcade (9233 6241). **Open** 9.30am-5.30pm Mon-Wed, Fri; 9.30am-8.30pm Thur; 9.30am-4.30pm Sat; 11am-4pm Sun. **Credit** AmEx, BC, DC, JCB, MC, TC, V.
This store has been solving the wardrobe crises of Sydney women for over 20 years from the small-ish Strand Arcade location. Now it also serves them from the huge Surry Hills store that also has a café at the back.
Branch: 182 Campbell Street, Surry Hills (9331 4801).

Bracewell
264 Oxford Street, Paddington (9360 6192). Bus 378, 380, 382. **Open** 10am-6pm Mon-Wed, Fri, Sat; 10am-8.30pm Thur; 11.30am-5.30pm Sun. **Credit** AmEx, BC, DC, JCB, MC, TC, V.
Sophisticated merchant of imports (Demeulemeester, Patrick Cox), local designers (Susan Nurmsalu, Bisonte) and its own label. Wander a few doors down and you'll find the equally impressive men's store.
Branch: 274 Oxford Street, Paddington (9331 5844).

Country Road
142-144 Pitt Street, Sydney (9232 6299). CityRail Martin Place or Town Hall. **Open** 9am-5.30pm Mon-Wed, Fri; 9am-9pm Thur, 9am-5pm Sat; 11am-5pm Sun. **Credit** AmEx, BC, DC, JCB, MC, TC, V.
The good basics here rarely change: pleated and flat-front trousers, suits, shirts, knits etc. But each season they throw in a few frontline pieces which are worth keeping an eye out for.

Five Way Fusion
205-207 Glenmore Road, Paddington (9360 2572). Bus 378, 380, 382. **Open** 10am-6.30pm Mon-Wed, Fri, Sat; 10am-8.30pm Thur; noon-5pm Sun. **Credit** AmEx, BC, DC, MC, TC, V.
For the party girl in all women, this small boutique off the beaten track purveys a mix of Lacroix, Versace, Moschino and Issey Miyake. Next door is the men's store with more of the same – but not so many dresses.

Lisa Ho
2A-6A Queen Street, Woollahra (9318 0233). Bus 378, 380, 382. **Open** 10am-6pm Mon-Wed, Fri; 10am-7pm Thur; noon-4pm Sun. **Credit** AmEx, BC, DC, MC, V.
Less expensive and a little less fashionable than most of the fashion stores on Oxford Street, but Lisa Ho is still worth a look.
Branch: 82 Devonshire Street, Surry Hills (9281 7520).

Marcs

Shop P228, Pitt Street Mall (9221 4583). CityRail Martin Place or Town Hall. **Open** 9.30am-6pm Mon-Wed, Fri; 9.30am-9pm Thur; 9am-5pm Sat; noon-4pm Sun. **Credit** AmEx, BC, DC, JCB, MC, TC, V.

Although you can choose from a selection of the better imports, the strength of Marcs lies in its own-label merchandise – good basics and some quirky styles. Once known for men's shirts, with the recent addition of a new designer, its womenswear has improved. *See also above* **Designer Discounts**.

Nice Things

276 Oxford Street, Paddington (9331 2830). Bus 378, 380, 382. **Open** 10am-6pm Mon-Wed, Fri, Sat; 10am-8.30pm Thur; 10am-5pm Sun. **Credit** AmEx, BC, DC, JCB, MC, TC, V.

This was the teenager's 'toy' shop in the 1980s. Now, Nice Things stocks a good range of local young designer labels and it's the only place in Sydney where you'll find Anna Sui.

Riada

Queens Court, 11 Queen Street, Woollahra (9363 0654). Bus 378, 380, 382. **Open** 10am-6pm Mon-Fri; 10am-5pm Sat. **Credit** AmEx, BC, DC, MC, TC, V.

The Harbour Tunnel was built to cope with the flow of eastern suburbs women making the trip north to the original Mosman store. Now the women have one of their own in Woollahra, it has been decided to keep the Tunnel anyway.

Branch: Shop 6, 81A Military Road, Mosman (9969 4269).

RM Williams

389 George Street, Sydney (9262 2228). CityRail Martin Place or Town Hall. **Open** 9am-5.30pm Mon-Wed, Fri; 9am-9pm Thur; 9am-4.30pm Sat; 11am-4pm Sun. **Credit** AmEx, BC, DC, JCB, MC, TC, V.

Stop by at the 'bushman's outfitters' for the real thing in moleskins and riding boots – accept no substitutes. You'll also find all the other outdoor essentials that every jack and jillaroo needs.

Robbie Ingham

422 Oxford Street, Paddington (9361 3221). Bus 378, 380, 382. **Open** 10am-6pm Mon-Wed, Fri, Sat; 10am-9pm Thur; 11am-5pm Sun. **Credit** AmEx, BC, DC, MC, TC, V.

What started out as a single men's store is slowly building up into a small empire. Now there are individual shops catering to men, women and jeans-wearers. Local labels include Jodie Boffa and knitwear from Anne McKay, while other countries are represented by Corinne Cobson, Romeo Gigli, CP Company and Katharine Hamnett.

Sportsgirl

Shop C12, Skygarden (9233 8255). **Open** 9am-6pm Mon-Wed, Fri; 9am-9pm Thur; 9am-5pm Sat; 11am-5pm Sun. **Credit** AmEx, BC, DC, JCB, MC, TC, V.

Where a lot of young girls spend their first pay cheque. They soon graduate from the young Sportsgirl label to the more grown-up Elle B and David Lawrence. Can't be beaten for bright T-shirts, canvas sneakers and packaged undies. Check the phone book for the nearest of the numerous branches.

Zambesi

452 Oxford Street, Paddington (9331 3999). Bus 378, 380, 382. **Open** 10am-6pm Mon-Wed, Fri, Sat; 10am-8pm Thur; noon-5pm Sun. **Credit** AmEx, BC, DC, MC, $TC, V.

Ethereal, deconstructed clothing from New Zealand and the rest of the world (Jean Paul Gaultier, Martin Margiela and Helmut Lang).

Vintage & Second-hand Clothing

See also page 137 **Amazing Hire Company**.

Kookaburra Kiosk

112 Burton Street, Darlinghurst (9380 5509). Bus 378, 380, 382. **Open** 10am-6pm Mon-Sat. **Credit** AmEx, BC, MC, V.

For a vintage clothing store – and they can be a bit of a mess sometimes – this one always looks gorgeous. It's light, so

*Touching up the paintwork at **The Look**. See page 148.*

you can see the clothes properly, and it doesn't smell like the recycling bin outside an old peoples' home.

The Look

230 King Street, Newtown (9550 2455). Bus 422, 423. **Open** 10am-6pm Mon-Thur; 10am-10pm Fri, Sat. **Credit** BC, MC, V.

Getting back to the idea of the second-hand shop as a fund-raiser for charities, all money made here goes to the Wesley Central Mission. There's a really good selection of stuff, which is reasonably priced, but they're not giving it away.

Reincarnation

169 Glebe Point Road, Glebe (9660 2092). Bus 431, 432, 433, 434. **Open** 10am-6pm Mon-Fri; 9am-5pm Sat. **Credit** AmEx, BC, MC, V.

This shop is a distillation of what was once at least three shops. What's left is an interesting and ever-changing collection, including some really old items not found in the groovier stores. Again, though, it's not cheap.

Route 66

255 Crown Street, Darlinghurst (9331 6686). Bus 378, 380, 382. **Open** 10.30am-6pm Mon-Sat; 10.30am-8pm Thur. **Credit** AmEx, BC, MC, $TC, V.

Rockabilly heaven. A huge range of second-hand Levi's, 1950s chintz frocks and more Hawaiian shirts than you can shake a hula skirt at.

Scraggs

551E King Street, Newtown (9550 4654). Bus 422, 423. **Open** 10.30am-5.30pm Mon, Wed-Sun; 10.30am-5pm Tue. **Credit** BC, MC, V.

Even if furniture shops aren't your thing, don't give up as you're walking down King Street. Scraggs has some of the prettiest 1950s and 1960s dresses, and some of the bigger 1970s flares and caftans.

Vintage Clothing

147 Castlereagh Street, Sydney (9267 7135). CityRail St James or Town Hall. **Open** 10.30am-6pm Mon-Wed, Fri; 10.30am-7pm Thur; 10.30am-4pm Sat. **Credit** AmEx, BC, DC, MC, TC, V.

This is an emporium for the serious fashion collector. Not the kind of stuff that you might dye next season when you get over the ivory colour of the 1940s chemise, or cut the hem off to make the 1930s dress into a mini. The array of *bijouterie*, bags and other bits and pieces are extremely covetable.

Zoo

332 Crown Street, Darlinghurst (9380 5990). Bus 378, 380, 382. **Open** 11am-6pm Mon-Wed, Fri; 11am-8pm Thur; noon-5pm Sat. **Credit** AmEx, BC, MC, TC, V.

Definitely the best-edited collection of 1970s stuff. Not just clothing but little bits of ephemera too. If the Roxy was still a roller-disco, this is where you would get your gear.

Florists

Alison Coates

92 William Street, Paddington (9360 2007). Bus 378, 380, 382. **Open** 9am-4pm Mon-Fri. **Credit** AmEx, BC, MC, V.

Distinctive arrangements with a sculptured look are the speciality at Alison Coates. Unusual native fruits, pods and leaves are used, which last a lot longer than the average pansy. And you won't find printed cellophane here either – arrangements are wrapped in beautiful ink-blue paper and tied with rope.

Grandiflora

Shop 1, 12 Macleay Street, Potts Point (9357 7902). CityRail Kings Cross/311 bus. **Open** 8.30am-6pm Mon-Fri; 8.30am-4pm Sat. **Credit** AmEx, BC, MC, V.

The latest of the designer florists to spring up, its popularity matched by its originality.

Loyal Florist

284 Oxford Street, Paddington (9360 4794). Bus 378, 380, 382. **Open** 8am-8pm Mon-Sat; 8am-6pm Sun. **Credit** AmEx, BC, DC, JCB, MC, V.

Don't want to arrive at a barbecue empty-handed? Grab a bunch of gerberas or sunflowers from here and you'll still have enough money for a six-pack and some chardonnay.

Vivid

56 Oxford Street, Paddington (9361 3277). Bus 378, 380, 382. **Open** 8am-7pm Mon; 8am-8pm Tue-Fri; 10am-6pm Sat, Sun. **Credit** AmEx, BC, MC, $TC, V.

No pale pink posies from this place. As the name suggests, Vivid deals in strong colours and is well known for its magnificent, unusual floral arrangements.

Food & Drink

For **Burlington Centre Supermarket**, *see page 77*; for **La Mensa**, the cafeteria-cum-restaurant which also sells an alluring range of jams, preserves and pasta sauces, *see page 113*. For the food hall in **David Jones**, *see page 135*.

Antico's

Shop 24, Northbridge Plaza, Northbridge (9958 4725). Bus 202, 208. **Open** 8am-5.30pm Mon-Wed; 8am-7pm Thur, Fri; 7am-5pm Sat; 9am-4pm Sun. **Credit** AmEx, BC, DC, MC, $TC, V.

Located at the back of the Northbridge Plaza which also houses the amazing **Tokyo Mart** (everything you need to cook Japanese and then some) and **Costi's** fish shop (one of the best). Antico's is the saviour of the north shore: pristine produce with exotic essentials like galangal and soursop, white asparagus in season.

Caffe Bianchi

6 Leichhardt Market Place, Leichhardt (9745 2391). Bus 436, 437, 438, 470. **Open** 9.30am-5.30pm Mon-Sat. **Credit** AmEx, BC, MC, V.

An astonishing range of coffee machines and coffee. Alvaro Bianchi probably knows more about coffee than anyone in Sydney other than Andrew Gross at Coffee 'n' Things (123 Belmore Road, Randwick; 9399 3008). Like Gross, Bianchi roasts his own beans.

The Cheese Shop

797 Military Road, Mosman (9969 4469). Bus 228, 229, 230. **Open** 8.30am-6pm Mon-Wed, Fri, Sat; 8.30am-7pm Thur; 11am-5pm Sun. **Credit** AmEx, BC, DC, MC, $TC, V.

Australian and imported cheeses, speciality cheeses and the best range outside Simon Johnson (*see p143*). Pyengana cloth-wrapped mature Cheddar (the only real one in Australia at the moment), Milawa Gold (washed-rind, love that smell), and Heidi Gruyère and Raclette.

Five Star Gourmet Foods

13 Willoughby Road, Crows Nest (9438 5666). CityRail St Leonards. **Open** 9am-9pm daily. **Credit** AmEx, BC, DC, MC, V.

A huge space with a deli section, butcher, the longest cheese counter in Australia and a gourmet supermarket and bakery where they sell about 30 different breads including bread from the Haberfield Bakery, cakes and strudels. There is also a flower shop and coffee shop, and it's open late.

Dress well at **Bracewell**. *See page 140.*

La Gerbe d'Or
255 Glenmore Road, Paddington (9331 1070). Bus 378, 380, 382. **Open** *8am-7pm Tue-Fri; 8am-4pm Sat; 8am-1pm Sun.* **No credit cards.**
Wonderful cakes and pastries, breads and quiches made by a master baker who has been here for 15 years or more.

Parisi's of Rose Bay
15 Dover Road, Rose Bay (9371 8732). Bus 323, 324, 325. **Open** *8am-6pm Mon-Wed; 8am-7pm Thur, Fri; 8am-4pm Sat; 9am-3pm Sun.* **Credit** BC, DC, MC, V.
If Antico's is the place for fresh fruit and veg northside, this is the eastern suburbs' mecca. The warehouse-height building houses choice produce, freshly squeezed juices and a salad counter. Be warned, though: this quality doesn't come cheap.

Simon Johnson Quality Foods
181 Harris Street, Pyrmont (9552 2522). Bus 21, 443. **Open** *9.30am-4pm Mon-Wed, Fri, Sat; 9.30am-6.30pm Sun.* **Credit** AmEx, BC, MC, V.
You have just died and gone to foodie heaven. Mariage Frères tea, Valrhona chocolate, Martelli pasta, Gay Kervalla chèvre, Duchy of Cornwall biscuits, the best olive oils, wonderful balsamic vinegars and the only place in Sydney that sells clotted cream. SJ also specialises in an incredible range of Australian and imported cheeses. This trade and retail outlet also supplies the best restaurants around town.

Sydney Fish Markets
Pyrmont Bridge Road, corner of Bank Street, Pyrmont (9660 1611). Bus 500, 501. **Open** *7am-4pm daily.* **No credit cards.**
Only the ones in Japan are better than this. Sydney Harbour prawns in season are a rare delicacy but you will find them here, as well as black squid ink for your pasta nera. The best fish in Australia ends up on the auction floor and on the counters of the more than a dozen retail outlets that make up the complex down at Blackwattle Bay. Good prices, outdoor eating (fish and chips, of course), takeaway sushi, a deli, florist and good fruit and veg shop make this a one-stop shopping stop.

Victoire French Bakery
385 Darling Road, Balmain (9818 5529). Ferry Darling Street/433 bus. **Open** *8am-7pm Mon-Fri; 7.30am-6pm Sat; 7.30am-4pm Sun.* **No credit cards.**
This is the real thing, much sought after in a town not noted for its bread. Famous for its lightly yeasted pain au levain (light sourdough) and croissants made by a master French *pâtissier* who does divine cakes. There is also a small but good cheese shop run by the owner's daughter.

Gifts

Don't miss the groovy gifts on sale at the **Museum of Sydney**, **Museum of Contemporary Art** and **Powerhouse Museum** (*see chapter* **Museums & Galleries**).

Art House
66 McLachlan Avenue, Darlinghurst (9332 1019). Bus 323, 324, 325, 327. **Open** *9.30am-5.30pm Mon-Fri; 11am-4pm Sat.* **Credit** AmEx, BC, DC, MC, TC, V.
A huge space devoted to unique contemporary artwork by Australian artists. Apart from operating as a shop, the showroom has an ever-changing exhibition space which constantly shows new pieces by a roster of local talent.

Bibelot
445 Oxford Street, Paddington (9360 6902). Bus 378, 380, 382. **Open** *10am-6pm Mon-Wed, Fri, Sat; 10am-8pm Thur; 11am-5pm Sun.* **Credit** AmEx, BC, MC, V.
Top-end, glossy corporate-style pieces. Always original.

Coo-ee Aboriginal Emporium & Art Gallery
98 Oxford Street, Paddington (9332 1544). Bus 378, 380, 382. **Open** *10am-6pm Mon-Wed, Fri, Sat; 10am-8pm Thur; 11am-5pm Sun.* **Credit** AmEx, BC, DC, MC, TC, V.

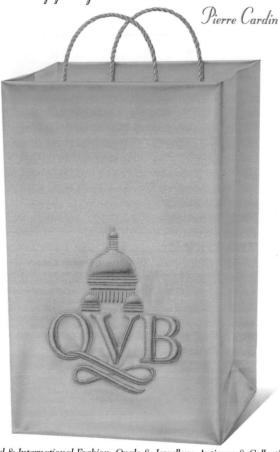

*The **Strand Arcade**. See page 136.*

You've got to get your fix of Aboriginal culture from some-where, and if Ayers Rock is not on the itinerary, Coo-ee is the place to go.

Interim
47 Glebe Point Road, Glebe (9552 2045). Bus 431, 432, 433, 434. **Open** 10am-6.30pm Mon-Wed, Fri; 10am-7.30pm Thur; 10am-6pm Sat; noon-5pm Sun. **Credit** AmEx, BC, MC, V.
Trendy (the ubiquitous Alessi), useful (plain white English porcelain mugs) and chic (Japanese-designed, Italian-made make-up bags).

Mexico
92 Oxford Street, Paddington (9360 7283). Bus 378, 380, 382. **Open** 10.30am-6pm Mon-Fri; 11am-5pm Sat; 11am-5pm Sun. **Credit** AmEx, BC, MC, TC, V.
Bright pieces for the home and some interesting silver work.

Mondo
27 Bay Street, Double Bay (9362 4964). CityRail Edgecliff. **Open** 10am-5.30pm Mon-Fri; 10am-5pm Sat; noon-4pm Sun. **Credit** AmEx, BC, MC, TC, V.
From the TSE cashmere at the back to the handsome, mod-estly priced umbrellas and leatherbound concertina files at the front, Mondo is a smart package. Check out the won-derful silver and museum repro jewellery, covetable bags and briefcases.

Orson & Blake
83-85 Queen Street, Woollahra (9326 1155). Bus 378, 380, 382. **Open** 9.30am-5.30pm Mon-Sat; noon-4pm Sun. **Credit** AmEx, BC, DC, MC, TC, V.
A very tasteful selection of homewares, including hand-shaped iron flatware.

Paraphernalia for Gifts
Shop 22, Strand Arcade (9231 2474). CityRail Martin Place or Town Hall. **Open** 9am-5.30pm Mon-Wed, Fri; 9am-8.30pm Thur; 9am-4.30pm Sat. **Credit** AmEx, BC, MC, TC, V.
Groovy watches, Itaala glass candleholders, the odd Asian antique and clever jigsaw puzzles mixed with basics like wooden soap dishes.

Hats

Isabella Klompe
19 Evans Street, Bronte (9387 3897). Bus 378. **Open** 9am-5pm Mon-Sat; by appointment Sun. **No credit cards.**
Working frequently with couturier Jonathan Ward, Klompe creates unusual yet glamourous *chapeaux*.

Jane Lambert
Shop 1, 23-25 Bay Street, Double Bay (9327 8642). Bus 330. **Open** 9.30am-6pm Mon-Fri; 9.30am-4pm Sat; 1-4pm Sun. **Credit** AmEx, BC, DC, MC, V.
From her light-filled studio-cum-store in affluent Double Bay, Lambert covers the heads of Melbourne Cup-goers more than any other Sydney milliner. Purchase off the stand or wait a little longer for a special order.

Jane Stoddart
58 William Street, Paddington (9360 5508). Bus 378, 380, 382. **Open** 10am-5pm Tue, Wed, Fri, Sat; 10am-6pm Thur. **Credit** AmEx, BC, MC, $TC, V.
Tucked away on a road off Oxford Street, this artisan creates quirky but comfy hats that don't make you feel as if you're wearing a watermelon on your head.

Moray
Shop 306, Strand Arcade (9223 1591). **Open** 9.30am-4pm; by appointment Sat. **No credit cards.**
Those who are serious about their headgear make the trip to the top of the Strand Arcade to track down the illusive David Moray, hidden beneath new and vintage tulle, gross grain, felt and flowers.

Strand Hatters
Shop 8, Strand Arcade (9231 688). CityRail Martin Place or Town Hall. **Open** 8.30am-5.30pm Mon-Wed, Fri; 9.30am-8.30pm Thur; 9.30am-4.30pm Sat; 10.30am-3.30pm Sun. **Credit** AmEx, BC, DC, MC, $TC, V.
When it's time to fill all the shopping orders for Akubra hats, this is the place to do it. The Wright brothers know their stuff.

Health & Beauty
Beauty Salons & Body Treatments
Beauty on Crown
Shop 2, 355 Crown Street, Surry Hills (9361 4363). Bus 374, 376, 391. **Open** 9am-7pm Mon-Fri; 9am-4pm Sat. **Credit** BC, MC, V.
Although it's on a busy street, this salon is surprisingly quiet and the muddy-cement walls create a cool, cavelike feeling. Beauty on Crown's forte is the body salt scrub – a necessity before unpeeling at Bondi.

Heaven Scent
243 Oxford Street, Bondi Junction (9369 3372). CityRail Bondi Junction. **Open** 9am-7pm Mon-Sat; 10am-5pm Sun. **Credit** AmEx, BC, MC, V.
The speciality here is the marine algae bath. Soak for 25 minutes to detoxify and enjoy brunch with a glass of cham-pagne. The bath's high frizz factor means you'll probably need to book a hair appointment at the salon afterwards.

Markets

Most of Sydney's markets are held in local schools or church grounds. Be prepared to try things on in the toilets and leave the credit cards at home – cash is preferred and you're more likely to get a bargain that way. Most of the markets have a variety of new and old clothing, craft and artwork, home-baked confectionery, and new and used furniture, as well as take-away foodstalls. For **Sydney Fish Markets**, *see page 143*.

Balmain

Corner of Darling Street and Curtis Road, Balmain (9818 2674). Bus 441, 442, 443/ferry Darling Street or Thames Street. **Open** 8.30am-4pm Sat.
There's an international food hall in the church. Baby wear and handmade homewares predominate – a reflection of the area's yuppification (*see also p86*).

Bondi Beach

Bondi Beach Public School, Campbell Parade, Bondi Beach (9398 5486). Bus 380, 382. **Open** *summer* 10am-5pm Sun; *winter* 10am-4pm Sun.
It's a good idea to use this market for a respite from the midday rays of Bondi. Not a big gathering, but the range of stalls is good, selling mainly crafts and second-hand clothes.

Glebe

Glebe Public School, Glebe Point Road, Glebe (4237 7499). Bus 431, 432, 433, 434. **Open** 10am-4pm Sat.
The most feral of them all. Second-hand clothes are good here and there's a big playing field for picnic lunches.

Kirribilli

Bradfield Park North, Alfred Street, Milsons Point (9922 4428). CityRail Milsons Point. **Open** 7am-3pm last Saturday of the month.
Specialises in 'upmarket' bric-à-brac and antiques.

Paddington

2 Newcombe Street, Paddington (9331 2646). Bus 378, 380, 382. **Open** *summer* 10am-5pm Sat; *winter* 10am-4pm Sat.
Probably the best of the suburban markets. Many a big-name fashion designer began by selling to the crowds that swarm here. A word of warning: parking is well nigh impossible on a Saturday and packs of promenading fashion victims turn the footpath into a claustrophobic's worst nightmare.

Paddy's

Corner of Hay and Thomas Streets, Haymarket (9319 2374). CityRail Central/monorail Haymarket. **Open** 9am-4.30pm Sat, Sun.
Different from the others, in that it's fully under cover in a large pavilion and there's nary a second-hand frock or recycled-paper book in sight. Mostly inexpensive clothing, shoes, CDs and electrical goods.

The Rocks

George Street, The Rocks (9255 1717). CityRail/ferry Circular Quay. **Open** 10am-5pm Sat, Sun.
Here you'll find mainly arts, crafts, homewares, antiques and collectibles. It's a piece of cake to hoof it from here to Kirribilli on the north shore, making a perfect day for the active tourist – just make sure it's the last Saturday of the month (for Kirribilli's market) before you leave the south bank.

Madame Korner

Shop 614A, Royal Arcade, 482 George Street, Sydney (9264 1241). CityRail Town Hall. **Open** 8am-5.30pm Mon, Fri, Sat; 8am-8pm Wed. **Credit** AmEx, BC, MC, TC, V.
Muddy pores? Legs hairier than King Kong's? Visit this time-warped salon for 'one of everything' and enjoy the 1970s (but not shabby) decor.

Relaxation Centre

1st floor, Hotel Capital, 111 Darlinghurst Road (9358 2755). CityRail Kings Cross. **Open** 10am-10pm daily. **Credit** AmEx, BC, DC, JCB, MC, TC, V.
French Polish for the body Korean-style, with some oriental wisdom administered via steam, ginseng baths, scrubs and masterly massage. There are separate baths for men and women.

Smyth & Fitzgerald

Shop 17-19, Ritz-Carlton Promenade, 33 Cross Street, Double Bay (9326 1385). Bus 323, 324, 325. **Open** 9am-6pm Mon, Tue, Sat; 9am-7pm Wed; 9am-8pm Thur. **Credit** AmEx, BC, MC, TC, V.
French manicure is the house speciality. To get a Saturday appointment with Christina you'll have to scan the obituary columns for the death of a regular client.

Venustus

381 Oxford Street, Paddington (9361 4014). Bus 378, 380, 382. **Open** 10am-9pm Mon-Wed; 10am-9pm Thur; 9am-8pm Fri; 9am-6pm Sat; 10am-8pm Sun. **Credit** AmEx, BC, MC, TC, V.

As all treatments are aromatherapy-based, you'll smell the lavender, frankincense and sandalwood oils long before you enter the salon. If you don't want to hear the social plans of all of Oxford Street, ask for a back room.

Cosmetics

Afrique Ali

Shop 7, 324 King Street, Newtown (9557 3574). Bus 422, 423. **Open** 9.30am-6pm Mon-Sat; 9.30am-9pm Thur. **Credit** AmEx, BC, DC, MC, V.
Specialists in hair and skin of all different ethnic types. If you fancy some Coolio dreads or Queen Latifah braids, this is the place to go.

Aveda Esthetique

Shop 16, Lower Ground Walk, QVB (9264 8925). **Open** 9am-6pm Mon-Wed, Fri; 9am-9pm Thur; 9am-6pm Sat; 11am-5pm Sun. **Credit** AmEx, BC, MC, V.
Selling skincare and haircare products, and cosmetics based on plant extracts, this is a relatively tranquil spot in a busy part of the CBD. The salon does complimentary mini-facials, hand treatments and makeovers as demonstrations in the front of the store. For paying customers there is a quiet room at the back.

Body Shop

Shop G48, George Street Level, QVB (9264 1796). **Open** 8.30am-6pm Mon-Wed, Fri; 8.30am-9pm Thur; 8.30am-5pm Sat; 10am-5pm Sun. **Credit** AmEx, BC, DC, JCB, MC, TC, V.

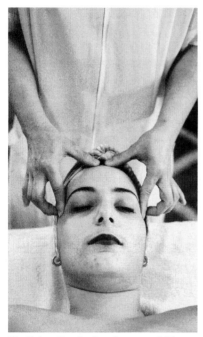

The **Relaxation Centre**. See page 147.

It's comforting to know that no matter where you are in the world you can always buy your Peppermint Foot Lotion or Mango Body Butter. Sydney is no exception.

Clinique
Shop K305 Westfield Chatswood (9415 3377). CityRail Chatswood. **Open** 9am-5.30pm Mon-Wed, Fri; 9am-9pm Thur; 9am-5pm Sat; 10am-4pm Sun. **Credit** AmEx, BC, DC, MC, V.
Keep an eye out for the bargain table in front of this tiny cosmetics kiosk and ask about their 'frequent flyer' points scheme. Best of all is the play table, which is set up like a kid's Lego centre. Men can slide in, purchase their Scruffing Lotion, and slide out, without being spotted by their footie team mates.

Jurlique
Shop 1, Strand Arcade (9231 0626). **Open** 9am-5.30pm Mon-Wed, Fri; 9am-9pm Thur; 9am-4pm Sat; 11am-4pm Sun. **Credit** AmEx, BC, DC, MC, TC, V.
Already selling in the States, this small company based in South Australia does a range of Oz aromatherapy products. The rose water freshener is perfect for weary travellers.

The Look
74 Oxford Street, Paddington (9331 1417). Bus 378, 380, 382. **Open** 10am-6.30pm Mon-Sat; noon-5pm Sun. **Credit** AmEx, BC, DC, MC, $TC, V.
Unlike most beauty stores, which centre more around skin-care products, this one is almost 100% colour cosmetics. Napoleon can mix foundations and powders for any skin tone, which is great news for those that don't fit into the commercially preferred peaches 'n' cream type.

Sanctum
446 Oxford Street, Paddington (9360 3895). Bus 378, 380, 382. **Open** 10am-6pm Mon-Wed, Fri; 10am-8pm Thur; 9.30am-6pm Sat; 11am-5pm Sun. **Credit** AmEx, BC, DC, MC, V.
At the back of the store there is a sanctum where you can have stress-relieving mini-massages and facials. At the front you can purchase skin and haircare products based on natural ingredients and spring water from Byron Bay.

Hairdressers

Antony Whitaker
10 Oxford Street, Paddington (9360 9411). Bus 378, 380, 382. **Open** 9am-7.30pm Mon-Wed, Fri; 9am-9pm Thur; 9am-6pm Sat; 10.30am-6pm Sun. **Credit** AmEx, BC, MC, TC, V.
A happy medium between traditional good service and cutting-edge fashion.

Caralyn Taylor
5 Transvaal Avenue, Double Bay (9363 1771). Bus 323, 324, 325. **Open** 9am-5pm Mon-Wed, Fri; 9am-9pm Thur; 8am-noon Sat. **Credit** AmEx, BC, MC, TC, V.
For those who don't like to take risks with their tresses. Ms Taylor favours a natural look, and that's how she retains her loyal thirty- and fortysomething (female) following.

Fuss
447 Oxford Street, Paddington (9331 7166). Bus 378, 380, 382. **Open** 8am-8pm Mon-Wed, Sat, Sun; 8am-10pm Thur, Fri. **Credit** AmEx, BC, DC, MC, TC, V.
Fuss will always fit you in – even outside their regular hours. Sometimes service can be a bit 'wham bam'. Ask for a room upstairs to avoid salon chatter.

Helmet
49-51 Flinders Street, Darlinghurst (9380 5103). Bus 377, 390, 397, 398. **Open** 9am-4.30pm Tue-Sat; 9am-7.30pm Thur. **Credit** AmEx, BC, MC, TC, V.
The grooviest salon in Sydney; there's little chance that you'll escape with anything other than the style or the colour.

Joh Bailey
7 Knox Street, Double Bay (9363 4111). Bus 323, 324, 325, 327, 330. **Open** 9am-6pm Mon-Wed, Fri; 9am-8.30pm Thur; 8am-5pm Sat. **Credit** AmEx, BC, DC, MC, TC, V.
The Double Bay salon has dripping chandeliers, gilt chairs and *Mittel* European etched mirrors so that eastern suburbs matrons can feel at home. The back entrance means that even on a bad hair day you can sneak in unseen. For the best blow-ups ask for Bailey himself. Chifley Plaza is suit city. **Branch**: Shop 30, Chifley Plaza (9223 7673).

Synergy
44 Oxford Street, Darlinghurst (9360 7739). Bus 378, 380, 382. **Open** 9am-5pm Mon-Wed, Sat; 9am-8pm Thur, Fri. **Credit** AmEx, BC, DC, MC, $TC, V.
Another hair joint for groovesters. This one has its own café.

Tony & Guy
35 Oxford Street, Darlinghurst (9267 6299). Bus 378, 380, 382. **Open** 10am-6pm Mon-Wed; 10am-8.30pm Thur, Fri; 9am-5pm Sat. **Credit** AmEx, BC, DC, MC, V.
Fast and friendly two-storey salon that provides services other than hair-related ones. Think of it as a 'one-stop get-gorgeous shop'.

Luminous objects of desire at **Dinosaur Design**. *See page 150.*

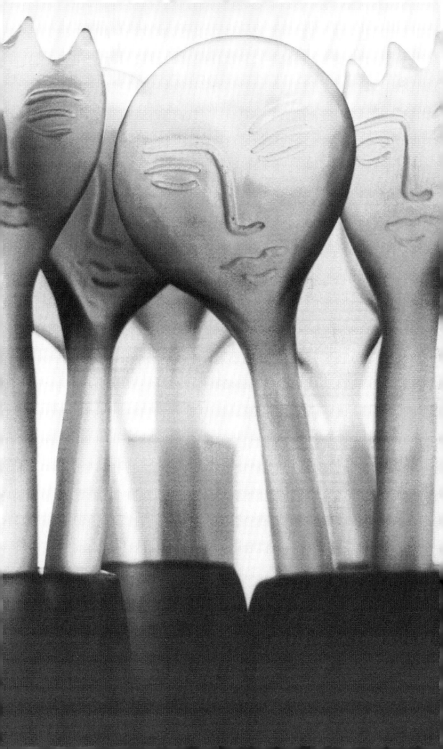

*Getting to the roots of the matter at **Synergy**. See page 148.*

Jewellery

For less expensive jewellery, explore Sydney's many markets, where local craftspeople sell their wares (*see page 147* **Markets**). For **Tiffany**, head for the Chifley Plaza (*see page 135*); and **Cartier**, that world-wide constant, is at 43 Castlereagh Street (9235 1322).

Dinosaur Design

Shop 77, Strand Arcade (9223 2953). **Open** 9.30am-5.30pm Mon-Wed, Fri; 9.30am-8.30pm Thur; 10am-4pm Sat. **Credit** AmEx, BC, MC, $TC, V.
It has been said that this is a gallery of beautiful objects rather than just another jewellery store, partly because it now sells homewares too. The beautifully lit translucent resin objects seem to emit a glow of their own.
Branch: 339 Oxford Street, Paddington (9361 3776).

Fairfax & Roberts

44 Martin Place, Sydney (9232 8511). CityRail Martin Place. **Open** 10am-6pm Mon-Wed, Fri; 10am-7pm Thur; 10am-3pm Sun. **Credit** AmEx, BC, DC, JCB, MC, TC, V.
Wonderful silver, gold, pearls. Classics but fashionable.

Family Jewels

46 Oxford Street, Paddington (9331 6647). Bus 378, 380, 382. **Open** 10am-6pm Mon-Sat; 11am-6pm Sun. **Credit** AmEx, BC, JCB, MC, TC, V.
Need something to go with that black velvet push-up corset? You'll find it at Family Jewels – just don't believe them when they tell you that it's Swarovsky. The $39.95 price tag doesn't lie.

Hardy Bros

77 Castlereagh Street, Sydney (9232 2422). CityRail Martin Place or St James. **Open** 9.30am-5pm Mon-Wed; 9.30am-6pm Thur; 9.30am-5.30pm Fri; 9.30am-4pm Sat. **Credit** AmEx, BC, DC, JCB, MC, TC, V.
Exclusive jewellers with a strong line in South Sea pearls, opals and Argyle diamonds. This is timeless family heirloom stuff.
Branch: 2 Guilfoyle Avenue, Double Bay (9327 1366).

Love & Hatred

Shop 70, Strand Arcade (9233 3441). CityRail Martin Place or Town Hall. **Open** 10am-5.30pm Mon-Wed, Fri; 10am-9pm Thur; 10am-4.30pm Sat. **Credit** AmEx, BC, DC, MC, V.
Beautiful pieces from local designers – and they'll do just about anything to order.

Paspaley Pearls

142 King Street, Sydney (9232 7633). CityRail Martin Place. **Open** 10am-5.30pm Mon-Fri; 10.30am-3.30pm Sat. **Credit** AmEx, BC, DC, JCB, MC, TC, V.
Specialists in South Sea pearls, drawn mainly from the area around Broome in Western Australia. These pearls are bigger, brighter and better than Japanese ones, and they're not necessarily white, coming also in pink, gold, blue or silver.

Rox

Shop 31, Strand Arcade (9232 7828). **Open** 9.30am-5.30pm Mon-Wed, Fri; 9.30am-9pm Thur; 10am-4pm Sat. **Credit** AmEx, BC, DC, JCB, MC, TC, V.
Although they do smaller, more discreet pieces (delicate earrings, for example), it's the big silver bracelets, rings and necklaces filled with precious and semiprecious stones that have been bringing in the fashion editors for years.

Victoria Spring
33 William Street, Paddington (9331 7862). Bus 378,
380, 382. **Open** 10am-6pm Mon-Sat. **Credit** AmEx, BC,
MC, $TC, V.
There was a time when Victoria only did jewellery. Now
her found-object style is available in flatware, candlesticks
and anything else that will hold a burnished leaf chain and
a few pearls.

Leather Goods

Hunting World
199 George Street, Sydney (9241 3762). CityRail/ferry
Circular Quay. **Open** 10am-6.30pm Mon-Fri; 10am-6pm
Sat, Sun. **Credit** AmEx, BC, DC, JCB, MC, TC, V.
Luxurious jackets and bags made in England from Italian
leather. Duty free on presentation of an airline ticket.
Branch: Shop 701A, MLC Centre (9223 8870).

Hunt Leather
Shop 704, MLC Centre (9233 8702). **Open** 9am-5.30pm
Mon-Wed, Fri; 9am-8pm Thur; 9.30am-4.30pm Sat. **Credit**
AmEx, BC, DC, JCB, MC, TC, V.
Good-quality, lasting luggage and bags. No clothes or shoes.

Sax
110A Oxford Street, Darlinghurst (9331 6105). Bus
378, 380, 382. **Open** 10am-6pm Mon-Wed, Fri; 10am-
7pm Thur; 10am-5pm Sat; noon-5pm Sun. **Credit** AmEx,
BC, DC, JCB, MC, TC, V.
This place goes to show that there's more to leather than
bags, belts and shoes. Browse among the bras and bondage
gear. Got a penchant for paddles? Like to hang in a harness?
Or maybe you just fancy being whipped, clad in nowt but a
leather G-string. Whatever your fetish, you can get the gear
from the shop or through their mail order service.

Lingerie

Collette Dinnigan
39 William Street, Paddington (9360 6691). Bus 378,
380, 382. **Open** *summer* 10am-6pm Mon-Sat; noon-4pm
Sun; *winter* 10am-6pm Mon-Sat. **Credit** AmEx, BC, DC,
JCB, MC, TC, V.
For the most exquisite Australian-made (with imported
fabrics) lingerie you need go no further than Collette's shop.
Most special of all are her corsets.

IM Lingerie
Shop 18, First Floor, QVB (9261 2180). **Open** 9.30am-
6pm Mon-Wed, Fri, Sat; 9.30am-9pm Thur; 11am-5pm
Sun. **Credit** AmEx, BC, DC, JCB, MC, $TC, V.
Tucked away at the top of the QVB, amid the opals and the
koala-print T-shirts, is this little pocket of luxury lingerie.
Be prepared to spend, big time.

Jaye M Underfashion Boutique
Shop 62, Strand Arcade (9231 2796). **Open** 9.30am-5pm
Mon-Wed, Fri; 9.30am-6.30pm Thur; 9.30am-2pm Sat.
Credit AmEx, BC, MC, TC, V.
Come here for the best selection of good-brand bras. Try
them all until you find the one that fits – there are no pass-
ing 'spectators on the second floor of the Strand Arcade.

The Sock Shop Australia
227A Pitt Street, Sydney (9221 5389). CityRail Town
Hall. **Open** 8.30am-6pm Mon-Wed, Fri; 8.30am-9pm
Thur; 8.30am-6pm Sat; 10am-4pm Sun. **Credit** AmEx,
BC, DC, MC, TC, V.
Cheap and cheerful. These stores have socks, tights, bras
and knickers in brights, solid colour and the odd basic black.
Check the phone book for your nearest branch.

White Ivy
Shop 2, 365 New South Head Road, Double Bay (9326
1830). Bus 323, 324, 325. **Open** 10am-6pm Mon-Fri;
10am-4.30pm Sat. **Credit** AmEx, BC, DC, JCB, MC, TC, V.
Not just naughty bits of lace, but beautiful cotton pieces of
exquisite quality as well. You'll have no need to blush if your
bag is inspected going through customs on the way home.

Willis
386 Oxford Street, Paddington (9360 7266). Bus 378,
380, 382. **Open** 9.30am-6pm Mon-Wed, Fri, Sat; 9.30am-
9pm Thur; 11am-5pm Sun. **Credit** AmEx, BC, DC, JCB,
MC, TC, V.

Malls

Nearly every mall in Sydney is owned and
operated by Westfield. Which has its good
points (you always know what you'll find
inside) and its bad (you always know what
you'll find inside). The only thing that differs
from mall to mall is the location of the
carparks. Each mall is usually anchored by a
branch of David Jones and/or Grace Bros;
beyond that you'll usually find a mixture of
the practical and cheap kitsch, padded out
with fashion chain outlets and branches of K-
mart. The massive Westfield Miranda also
houses an eight-screen cinema complex.

Bondi Junction Plaza
500 Oxford Street, Bondi Junction (9387 3333).
CityRail Bondi Junction. **Open** 9am-5.30pm Mon-
Wed, Fri; 9am-9pm Thur; 10am-4pm Sun.

Chatswood Chase
345 Victoria Avenue, Chatswood (9411 2122).
CityRail Chatswood. **Open** 9am-5.30pm Mon-Wed,
Fri; 9am-9pm Thur; 9am-5pm Sat; 10am-4pm Sun.
Disabled: access; toilets.

Lemon Grove
441 Victoria Avenue, Chatswood (9411 2122).
CityRail Chatswood. **Open** 9.30am-6pm Mon-Wed,
Fri; 9.30am-9pm Thur; 9am-4pm Sat; 11am-4pm
Sun.
Disabled: access; toilets.

Penrith Plaza
585 Henry Street, Penrith (4721 4354). CityRail
Penrith. **Open** 9am-5.30pm Mon-Wed, Fri; 9am-
4pm Sat; 10am-4pm Sun.
Disabled: access; toilets.

Westfield Chatswood
1 Anderson Street, Chatswood (9412 1555).
CityRail Chatswood. **Open** 9.30am-6pm Mon-Wed,
Fri; 9am-9pm Thur; 9am-5pm Sat; 10am-4pm Sun.
Disabled: access; toilets.

Westfield Miranda
600 Kingsway, Miranda (9525 6344). CityRail
Miranda. **Open** 9am-5.30pm Mon-Wed, Fri; 9am-
9pm Thur; 9am-5pm Sat; 10am-4pm Sun.
Disabled: access; toilets.

This shop started out selling just lingerie. Now they do clothes too, but it's the bras and knickers that get the young girls in. Lots of pretty florals, with a good range in stretch cotton.

Opticians & Eyewear

iiii's
316 King Street, Newtown (9557 4542). Bus 422, 423. **Open** 9am-6pm Mon-Wed, Fri; 9am-8pm Thur; 9am-5pm Sat. **Credit** AmEx, BC, DC, MC, V.
Cool and quirky styles plus some nifty titanium frames.

Dioptics
Shop 320, Mid City Centre (9221 0049). CityRail Martin Place or Town Hall. **Open** 9am-5.30pm Mon-Wed, Fri; 9am-9pm Thur; 9am-4pm Sat. **Credit** AmEx, BC, DC, MC, TC, V.
Has a good range, with some more obscure names among the well-knowns.

OPSM
383 George Street, Sydney (9299 3061). CityRail Martin Place. **Open** 9am-5.30pm Mon-Wed, Fri; 9am-8pm Thur; 9am-3pm Sat. **Credit** AmEx, BC, DC, MC, TC, V.
Essential eyewear with a fast prescription service.

Records, Tapes & CDs

Ashwoods
376 Pitt Street, Sydney (9267 7745). CityRail Museum. **Open** 9am-6pm Mon-Wed, Fri; 9am-7pm Thur; 9am-5pm Sat; 11am-4pm Sun. **No credit cards.**
The second-hand market is centred on this block of Pitt Street, with shops clustered around Ashwoods. Here is the place to find that obscure piece of vinyl or unloved (by its first owner anyway) CD.

Ava & Susan's Records
Shop 7, Town Hall Arcade, Sydney (9264 3179). CityRail Town Hall. **Open** 9am-5.30pm Mon-Wed, Fri; 9am-7pm Thur; 9am-4pm Sat. **Credit** AmEx, BC, DC, MC, V.
Specialists in soundtracks of films and stage musicals.

Birdland
3 Barrack Street, Sydney (9299 8527). CityRail Wynyard or Martin Place. **Open** 9am-6pm Mon-Wed, Fri; 9am-7pm Thur; 9am-4pm Sat. **Credit** AmEx, BC, DC, MC, V.
The purists might argue, but Birdland is the best jazz shop in the city, the place to go for new and exciting Australian sounds, as well as old favourites. The staff give good tips.

Central Station Records & Tapes
46 Oxford Street, Darlinghurst (9361 5159). CityRail Museum. **Open** 10am-6pm Mon, Tue, Sat; 10am-7pm Wed, Fri; 10am-9pm Thur; noon-6pm Sun. **Credit** AmEx, BC, DC, JCB, MC, TC, V.
Purveyor of take-home groove to Sydney's clubbers, this Oxford Street institution has seen more dance fads come and go than any of them. And still manages to keep up.

Fish
33 Oxford Street, Darlinghurst (9267 5142). CityRail Museum. **Open** 10am-midnight Mon-Sat; 10am-9pm Sun. **Credit** AmEx, BC, DC, JCB, MC, V.
Just down the road from Central Station Records. Caters for clubbers, but leans closer to the Top 40.

Folkways Music
282 Oxford Street, Paddington (9361 3980). Bus 380, 382. **Open** 9am-6pm Mon-Wed, Fri; 9am-9pm Thur; 9.30am-6.30pm Sat; 11am-6pm Sun. **Credit** AmEx, BC, DC, MC, JCB, TC, V.
The name gives you a good hint. Standard-bearer for folk and ethnic music.

Glenn A. Baker's Time Warp
289 Clarence Street, Sydney (9283 1555). CityRail Wynward. **Open** 9am-6pm Mon-Wed, Fri; 9am-9pm Thur; 9am-4pm Sat. **Credit** AmEx, BC, MC, V.
Mercifully, it has nothing to do with The Rocky Horror Picture Show. Time Warp is a collector's shop in the centre of the city and specialises in vinyl rarities.

Half A Cow
74 Glebe Point Road, Glebe (9660 6084/9552 1734). 431, 432, 433, 434. **Open** 10am-6pm Mon-Wed, Fri, Sat; 10am-9pm Thur; noon-6pm Sun. **Credit** AmEx, BC, DC, MC, V.
A record label which is also a music shop, which is also one of the most eclectic and interesting bookshops in town.

Michael's Music Room
Shop 19, Town Hall Arcade, Sydney (9269 1351). CityRail Town Hall. **Open** 9am-6pm Mon-Fri; 9am-2pm Sat. **Credit** AmEx, BC, MC, V.
One of the best shops in Sydney for classical CDs.

Red Eye
Tankstream Arcade, Corner of King and Pitt Streets, Sydney (9233 8177). CityRail Wynyard. **Open** 9am-6pm Mon-Wed, Fri; 9am-9pm Thur; 9am-5pm Sat; 11am-5pm Sun. **Credit** AmEx, BC, MC, TC, V.
The biggest of the indie stores, this underground shop has an excellent selection of Australian bands and labels, as well as British, American, German and Japanese imports. There's a well-stocked second-hand branch, also in the Tankstream Arcade.

Recycled
Shop 2, 37 Glebe Point Road, Glebe (9660 1416). Bus 432, 432, 433. **Open** 10.30am-6pm Mon-Wed, Fri, Sat; 10.30am-9pm Thur; noon-6pm Sun. **Credit** AmEx, BC, MC, V.
A pair of CD boutiques owned by the same people, in different areas. Both carry a curious mix of current releases with world music, jazz and dance. There's always a gem waiting to be uncovered, and the owners often import titles others don't.
Branch: **Parade Music & Wear** 68 Campbell Parade, Bondi Beach (9365 1248).

Utopia Import Records
636 George Street, Sydney (9283 2423). CityRail Town Hall. **Open** 10am-7pm Mon, Wed; 10am-8pm Tue; 10am-9pm Thur; 10am-10pm Fri, Sat; noon-7pm Sun. **Credit** AmEx, BC, DC, MC, V.
Like, this shop really rocks, dude. Long hair and loud guitars are the motifs of Utopia Records. Metal, grunge, thrash and any number of other terms for ear-shattering volume.

Waterfront Records

89 York Street, Sydney (9262 4120). CityRail Town Hall.
Open 10am-6pm Mon-Wed, Fri; 10am-9pm Thur; 10am-6pm Sat; noon-4pm Sun. **Credit** AmEx, BC, CD, MC, TC, V.
Another indie bastion, this shop carries a small but interesting stock of what is currently cool in seedy pubs and university dorms. It keeps a great collection of fanzines and underground books, and is a good place to buy tickets for local gigs.

Megastores

There are three city megastores. If you believe that big is better, these are the places to go. Their size and buying power usually guarantees discounts, but don't expect a lot of imported stock. They also have classical and world music sections. Check the phone book for their suburban branches.

Blockbuster

162 Pitt Street Mall, Sydney (9223 8488). CityRail Town Hall. **Open** 9am-6.30pm Mon-Wed, Fri; 9am-9pm Thur;
9am-6pm Sat; 10am-5pm Sun. **Credit** AmEx, BC, DC, JCB, MC, TC, V.

Brashs

244 Pitt Street, Sydney (9261 2555). CityRail Town Hall.
Open 9am-5.30pm Mon-Wed, Fri; 9am-9pm Thur; 9am-6pm Sat; 11am-4pm Sun. **Credit** AmEx, BC, DC, MC, V.

HMV

Shop 1, Mid City Centre (9221 2311). **Open** 9am-6pm Mon-Wed, Fri; 9am-8pm Thur; 9am-5.30pm Sat; 11am-5pm Sun. **Credit** AmEx, BC, MC, TC, V.

See also page 141 **RM Williams**.

Shoes

Donna-May Bolinger

379 South Dowling Street, Darlinghurst (9360 7898).
Bus 380, 382, 396, 398. **Open** 10am-6pm Mon-Fri; 10am-5pm Sat. **Credit** AmEx, BC, MC, TC, V.
Order off the shelf or have the shoe you want, made in the size you need, in the leather of your choice.

Surf gear

Aloha Manly

44 Pittwater Road, Manly (9977 3777). Bus 155, 157 159, 169/ferry Manly. **Open** 9am-7pm Mon-Wed, Fri-Sun; 9am-9pm Thur. **Credit** AmEx, BC, DC, MC, TC, V.
One of the best ranges of boards in Sydney and they come with sound professional advice. Between sets you can chill out in the cosy café.

Beach Culture

Shop 8, International Terminal, Kingsford Smith Airport (9317 3668). Bus 400/Airport Express.
Open 6am-10.30pm daily. **Credit** AmEx, BC, DC, JCB, MC, TC, V.
Left your brand-new boardies under the shower at Bondi? Well, it's not too late to make a last-minute grab here. Lots of labels and not at inflated airport prices. Even if you forget to make the stop before going through customs, there are two more chances on the other side.

Bondi Surf Co

Shop 2, 72-76 Campbell Parade, Bondi Beach (9365 0870). Bus 380, 382. **Open** 9.30am-6pm Mon-Wed, Fri; 9.30am-7pm Thur; 9am-6pm Sat, Sun. **Credit** AmEx, BC, JCB, MC, $TC, V.
If you're interested in the fact that Jason Donovan had one of his infamous collapses outside, you're probably not a potential customer anyway. The Surf Co is well located, stocks wetsuits available for hire and also offers boardriding lessons for beginners.

General Pants

391 George Street, Sydney (9264 2311). CityRail Town Hall or Wynyard. **Open** 9am-6pm Mon-Wed, Fri; 9am-9pm Thur; 9am-5pm Sat; 10am-5pm Sun.
Credit AmEx, BC, DC, JCB, MC, TC, V.
Less surf, more street, but good for the skatey crew – lots of denim, Stüssy, Mossimo. Gear for the skatey chick too.

Hot Tuna

180 Oxford Street, Paddington (9361 5049). Bus 378, 380, 382. **Open** 10am-6pm Mon-Sat; noon-5pm Sun.
Credit AmEx, BC, DC, MC, $TC, V.
Known for prints that are less Ken Done sweetness and more post-apocalyptic darkness, Hot Tuna does authentic surf gear from the Central Coast of New South Wales. Great for tough canvas boardies.

Mambo

17 Oxford Street, Paddington (9331 8034). Bus 378, 380, 382. **Open** 9am-6pm Mon-Wed, Fri; 9am-9pm Thur; 9am-5pm Sat; 11am-5pm Sun. **Credit** AmEx, BC, MC, $TC, V.
A shrine to the farting dog, violent hen and naked emperor, the Mambo emporium attempts to 'transcend the frivolous world of art'. Here you'll find offensive graphics on everything from surfboards to the Time Lord range of watches, and also on the odd pair of boardshorts. A unique showcase of Australian culture, art and humour.

Quiksilver

303 Barrenjoey Road, Newport (9997 8833). Bus 187, 188, 189, 190. **Open** 9am-6pm Mon-Fri; 9am-5pm Sat, Sun. **Credit** AmEx, BC, DC, MC, $TC, V.
It's a long trip but chances are, if you're serious about the surf, you're going to head up to the northern beaches anyway. Like Mambo and Hot Tuna, Quiksilver sells only its own label. Check out the range of wetsuits.

Surf Dive 'n' Ski

464 George Street, Sydney (9267 3408). CityRail Town Hall. **Open** 8.30am-5.30pm Mon-Wed; 8.30am-9pm Thur; 8.30am-6pm Fri; 9am-5pm Sat. **Credit** AmEx, BC, DC, JCB, MC, TC, V.
As the name suggests, this store caters to more than just the waxhead. Practitioners of other sports like snow and skateboarding will find their needs met equally well here.

Surfection

308 Oxford Street, Woollahra (9387 1413). Bus 378, 380, 382. **Open** 9am-6pm Mon-Wed, Fri; 9am-9pm Thur; 9am-5pm Sat; 10am-4pm Sun. **Credit** AmEx, DC, MC, $TC, V.
Sells a wide variety of brands from all over Australia with a good stock of surfboards.

Edward Meller
37 Knox Street, Double Bay (9327 7197). Bus 323, 324, 325, 327, 330. **Open** 9am-5.30pm Mon-Wed, Fri; 9am-7pm Thur; 9am-6pm Fri; 9am-5pm Sat; noon-5pm Sun. **Credit** AmEx, BC, DC, MC, TC, V.
A good selection of fashion footwear.

Evelyn Miles
Shop 7/05, MLC Centre (9233 1569). **Open** 9am-5.30pm Mon-Wed, Fri; 9am-8pm Thur; 9.30am-5pm Sat. **Credit** AmEx, BC, DC, MC, $TC, V.
One-stop shopping for those with a true Imelda Marcos complex. Michel Perry, Robert Clergerie, Patrick Cox.

GC's
Shop 30, Strand Arcade (9232 6544). **Open** 9am-5.30pm Mon-Wed, Fri; 9am-8.30pm Thur; 9.30am-5pm Sat. **Credit** AmEx, BC, DC, JCB, MC, TC, V.
The Castles' (*see below* **Raymond Castle**) offspring, Gary is now soothing the shoeless souls of the daughters of that establishment's clientele with new styles at bearable prices in beautiful environs.

Mollini
Shop 4R01 Glasshouse (9232 5191). **Open** 9am-5.30pm Mon-Wed, Fri; 9am-9pm Thur; 9am-4pm Sat. **Credit** AmEx, BC, DC, MC, TC, V.
Reasonably priced shoes 'inspired' by more expensive overseas designer styles.

Raymond Castle
19-27 Cross Street, Double Bay (9232 6780). CityRail Edgecliff. **Open** 9am-6pm Mon-Wed, Fri; 9am-9pm Thur; 9am-5pm Sat; 11am-5pm Sun. **Credit** AmEx, BC, DC, JCB, MC, TC, V.
Raymond Castle has been putting famous-name imported leather on the soles of establishment matrons for years. However, after a parting of the ways, Mrs Castle is now in charge and Mr C is doing his own thing. *See above* **GC's** for their son's activities.

Zomp
Shop 303, Mid City Centre (9221 4027). **Open** 9am-5.30pm Mon-Wed, Fri; 9am-9pm Thur; 9am-5pm Sat; 11.30am-4pm Sun. **Credit** AmEx, BC, DC, JCB, MC, TC, V.
Fun, up-to-the-minute and inexpensive. Check the phone book for your nearest branch.

Sport

Clarence Street Cyclery
104 Clarence Street, Sydney (9299 4962). CityRail Wynyard. **Open** 8.30am-5.30pm Mon-Wed, Fri; 8.30am-8.30pm Thur; 8.30am-4pm Sat; 10am-4pm Sun. **Credit** AmEx, BC, DC, MC, TC, V.
Stocking a good range of models at most price levels, this shop is so environmentally conscientious that, according to their leaflet (printed on 100% recycled stock, of course): 'Should you choose to travel in by train instead of car, we will deduct that fare from your purchase.'

The Golf Shop
250 Riley Street, Surry Hills (9212 7212). CityRail Central. **Open** 9am-5pm Mon-Fri; 10am-3pm Sat. **Credit** AmEx, BC, DC, MC, TC, V.
For all golfers, from professionals to simple pleasure-seekers.

Inski
46 York Street, Sydney (9233 3200). CityRail Wynyard. **Open** 9am-5.30pm Mon-Wed, Fri; 9am-8pm Thur; 9am-5pm Sat; 11am-4pm Sun. **Credit** AmEx, BC, DC, JCB, MC, TC, V.
For snow bunnies, ski instructors and those who just like to lounge around the chalet log-fire, all ski requirements can be met here.

Mick Simmon's
478 George Street, Sydney (9264 2744). CityRail Town Hall. **Open** 8.45am-5.30pm Mon-Wed, Fri; 8.45am-8.30pm Thur; 9am-5pm Sat; 11am-4pm Sun. **Credit** AmEx, BC, DC, MC, TC, V.
Carries equipment for all track and field sports.

Paddy Pallin
507 Kent Street, Sydney (9264 2685). CityRail Town Hall. **Open** 9am-5.30pm Mon-Wed; 9am-9pm Thur; 9am-6pm Fri; 10am-4pm Sat, Sun. **Credit** AmEx, BC, DC, JCB, MC, TC, V.
Equipment shop catering for all your climbing and outdoor needs.

Rebel
Shop 401, Gallery Level, Mid City Centre (9221 8633). CityRail Martin Place or Town Hall. **Open** 9am-6pm Mon-Wed, Fri; 9am-9pm Thur; 9am-5pm Sat; 11am-5pm Sun. **Credit** AmEx, BC, MC, TC, V.
All-purpose store for the non-specific sportspeople. Rebel's got it all at a basic level.

Woolys Wheels
82 Oxford Street, Paddington (9331 2671). Bus 378, 380, 382. **Open** 7am-6pm Mon-Wed, Fri; 9am-8pm Thur; 9am-4pm Sat; 11am-5pm Sun. **Credit** AmEx, BC, DC, MC, TC, V.
If a store that sells push-bikes can be fashionable, this is the one. It's pretty pricey too. Speciality lines include casual beachcruisers and hi-tech mountain bikes. The workshop service is reliable.

Saddle up at **Woolys Wheels**.

Museums & Galleries

Explore Sydney's **PAST**

Rediscover the daily lives of convicts at the
HYDE PARK BARRACKS MUSEUM,
Macquarie St, Sydney. Open daily 10am-5pm.

Stroll through 27 acres of grounds and glorious
gardens at **VAUCLUSE HOUSE**,
Wentworth Rd, Vaucluse.
Open Tue-Sun 10am-4.30pm.

Explore the world of crims and coppers at the
JUSTICE AND POLICE MUSEUM,
Cnr Phillip and Albert Sts, Circular Quay. Open
daily 10am-5pm and Sun-Thu throughout January.

See Australia's oldest European building,
ELIZABETH FARM,
set in a magnificent 1830s garden.
70 Alice St, Rosehill. Open daily 10am-5pm.

Take in the splendour of
ELIZABETH BAY HOUSE, known as
the 'finest house in the colony'. 7 Onslow Ave,
Elizabeth Bay. Open Tue-Sun 10am-4.30pm.

Shop in a turn-of-the-century store at
SUSANNAH PLACE,
58-64 Gloucester St, The Rocks.
Open Sat-Sun 10am-5pm and daily in January.

Embark on a journey of discovery at the
state-of-the-art **MUSEUM OF SYDNEY**
on the site of first Government House,
Cnr Bridge and Phillip Sts, Sydney.
Open daily 10am-5pm.

Visit **MEROOGAL** with its rich and fascinating
history. Cnr West and Worrigee Sts, Nowra.
Open Sat 1pm-5pm and Sun 10am-5pm.

Contrast all of these with the uncompromising
modernist style of **ROSE SEIDLER HOUSE**,
71 Clissold Rd, Wahroonga.
Open Sun 10am-5pm.

*You can visit all of these individually
or with the value added*
TICKET THROUGH TIME

For further information or a brochure, telephone the
HISTORIC HOUSES TRUST OF NEW SOUTH WALES
on 02 9692 8366.

Museums & Galleries

Interested in surfboard canvases, contemporary Aboriginal art or echoes of the colonial past? Sydney has galleries galore, with plenty of hands-on museums in between.

For the exhibition-obsessive, this city is a treat. As the site of the first phase of British colonisation of Australia, Sydney has a number of museums relating to the country's days as a penal outpost. For instance, the **SH Ervin Gallery** on Observatory Hill was initially the colony's first military hospital, while the **Hyde Park Barracks** in Macquarie Street was built to house convicts.

The brutality of the colonisation process led to the massacre of thousands of Australian Aborigines and the desecration of local Aboriginal cultures and lifestyles. The **Museum of Sydney** is one of the few mainstream museums to address some of the difficult and discomforting issues this history raises.

Possibly Sydney's best house museum is a building by internationally acclaimed architect Harry Seidler, the man many Australians love to hate. **Rose Seidler House**, tucked away in one of the city's sedate northern suburbs, is a wonderful time capsule and important repository of 1950s design. Another of the city's more eccentric museums calls for a trip across Sydney Harbour to **Mary MacKillop Place**, which pays surreal homage to Australia's first saint.

Of the Sydney galleries, the **Art Gallery of New South Wales** provides the best general round-up of local artistic traditions, and its Yiribana Gallery offers a vivid introduction to the world of Aboriginal art. At the **Museum of Contemporary Art** you are likely to find more fabulous Aboriginal pieces, along with a mixture of both obscure and accessible exhibitions of international and local contemporary work.

With a wide spectrum of high quality commercial spaces and a number of vital artist-run galleries, Sydney is blessed with the liveliest contemporary art circuit in the country. And, like any pulsing contemporary scene, it is prey to an impressive range of fads and trends. At galleries such as the **CBD** and **Artspace** you will often find exhibitions of installation-based work – art you're unlikely to be able to buy and cart home to decorate your walls.

Many Sydney galleries do a good trade in art that is often described as vernacular. The **Ray Hughes Gallery** in Surry Hills shows a stable of visibly Aussie artists, such as Robert Moore who has been known to use that icon of Ozdom, the surfboard, as his canvas. In recent years corrugated iron, an important element of Australian rural and outback architecture, has become a favourite material in contemporary work, as has recycled wood. But Australia's queen of recycled materials is the redoubtable Rosalie Gascoigne, (represented by the **Roslyn Oxley9 Gallery** in Paddington). Gascoigne, a fascinating character who only started exhibiting in her sixties, constructs works that give the viewer a glimpse of the Australian landscape in uniquely poetic abstracts.

As you trundle around the Sydney contemporary art scene, you're likely to notice the recurrence of a painting style that could loosely be described as lyrical abstraction – something of a Sydney house style. Sparkling sunshine and the spectacular harbour go a long way towards explaining this preference for a painterly, lyrical daub.

Don't miss

Art Gallery of New South Wales
For the colonial perspective.

Hogarth Galleries
Where the serious collectors go.

Museum of Contemporary Art
From funky animation to fabulous Aboriginal art.

Museum of Sydney
Can archaeology be this chic?

The Powerhouse
Hands-on and huge.

Rose Seidler House
An architectural time capsule.

Roslyn Oxley9 Gallery
For the big names and the bad boys of contemporary art.

At the **Boomalli, Hogarth** and **Utopia** galleries, you can see first-rate contemporary Aboriginal art, from the rich figurative works of Harry Wedge and Ian Abdulla to the magnificent paintings of such desert artists as Emily Kame Kngwarreye (from Utopia, Northern Territory) and Rover Thomas (from Turkey Creek, Western Australia).

Public Galleries & Museums

Central Sydney

Art Gallery of New South Wales

Art Gallery Road, The Domain, Sydney (9225 1700/9225 1744). CityRail Martin Place or St James/888 bus (Mon-Fri). **Open** 10am-5pm daily. **Admission** *gallery* free; *exhibitions* from $7 adults; $4 concessions. **No credit cards.**
Has a solid collection of nineteenth- and twentieth-century Australian artists, as well as a few European masters and international contemporary art stars. However, the gallery has a tendency to exhibit its holdings of established names, rather than tantalise the public with some of its marvellous pieces by lesser-known artists. Interestingly, the collection's plethora of second- and third-rate nineteenth-century English and European works was acquired during the gallery's early years and are typical of the colonial institution's obsessive imitation of the mother country. There is a fine Asian art collection and the temporary exhibition programme features established contemporary artists as well as regular 'blockbuster' shows of overseas collections. One of its most popular exhibitions is the Archibald Prize, an annual portraiture competition, which is complemented by the Wynne Competition (for landscape and sculpture) and the Sulman (covering the somewhat archaic category of 'subject pictures'). *Café. Disabled: access; toilets. Library. Restaurant. Shop. Tours. Website at: http://www.ozemail.com.au/~agnsw/*

Australian Museum

6 College Street, Sydney (9339 8111). CityRail Museum, St James or Town Hall. **Open** 9.30am-5pm daily. **Admission** $5 adults; $2-$3 concessions; $12 family ticket. **Credit** AmEx, BC, DC, JCB, MC, V.
Has a very large natural history collection covering the prehistory, biology, botany and geology of Australia, Papua New Guinea and the Pacific region. The permanent display includes some impressive examples of those museum staples, skeletons. Any serious museum-tripper should see a few of the local stuffed animals and the display here will answer all your questions about Australian mammals. On a more serious note, much of the museum's vast collection of early, rare Aboriginal artefacts is not on public display and can only be accessed with special permission. *Disabled: access; toilets.*

Australian National Maritime Museum

2 Murray Street, Darling Harbour (Mon-Fri 9552 7777/Sat, Sun 9552 7500/recorded information 0055 62002). Bus 443/ferry Aquarium Wharf/monorail Harbourside. **Open** 9.30am-5pm daily. **Admission** $7 adults; $4 concessions; $18.50 family ticket. **Credit** AmEx, BC, DC, MC, $TC, V.
In the heart of Darling Harbour is this museum built around Australia II, the yacht which won the Americas Cup in 1983. Built to a revolutionary design by Ben Lexcen and owned by the (since disgraced) Perth-based tycoon Alan Bond, Australia II was the first challenger to take the Cup in the race's 132-year history. Moored outside the Maritime Museum is a range of working vessels, including a Vietnamese fishing boat. Inside there are exhibitions on Aboriginal maritime culture, the history of sea travel to Australia and the story of the Australian navy, as well as exciting video footage of the 1983 Americas Cup, and of Sydney's flying 18-footers. Among the many maritime art treasures are rare pieces of sailors' scrimshaw and whalers' mats. *Café. Disabled: access; toilets. Shop.*

The **Art Gallery of NSW** – *for Oz Masters and harbour views.*

Public art

Several government buildings in the city centre feature statuary that reflects Sydney's colonial beginnings. Near Circular Quay in Bent Street is the Italian Renaissance-style **Department of Lands** building designed by colonial architect James Barnet. James White, William P MacIntosh and Tommaso Sani carved the 23 sandstone sculptures that adorn the niches – at ground and first-floor level are sculptures of local politicians and botanists, while the top level is reserved for explorers.

Some of the more charming sculptures to emerge from this phase of public works are Sani's spandrels and keystones adorning the Pitt Street and Martin Place façades of the **General Post Office**. The Pitt Street keystones show the four seasons, surrounded by various professions and trades, and where possible Sani has incorporated postal activities. Summer is flanked by a telegraph operator reading a telegram and a printer working a press; spring is accompanied by a farmer at his plough, reading a letter by the setting sun, and an astronomer pointing to Sydney on a chart. But Sani's wry, unpretentious approach did not appeal to the mass of Sydneysiders in the 1880s. The spandrels only narrowly escaped removal after much parliamentary discussion.

Outside the **Queen Victoria Building** on George Street is a sculpture of the *grande dame* herself (*pictured*) by Irish sculptor John Hughes. Executed in 1908, this massive bronze was originally installed at Leinster House in Dublin, but in 1947 was put into storage. It was not until the 1980s that the piece once more saw the light of

day, when it was installed in its present location.

Hyde Park is home to two handsome pieces of early twentieth-century public art which commemorate Australia's war efforts: the **Archibald Fountain** and the **Anzac Memorial**. The fountain, by French sculptor Françoise Leon Sicard, was commissioned in celebration of 'Australia and France fighting side by side for the liberties of the world in World War I'. Nevertheless, it features Apollo, Pan, Theseus and Diana. The academic neo-classicism of Sicard's work contrasts strongly with the surprising sensuality of the single soldier prostrate in the Anzac Memorial, sculpted by Sydney artist Rayner Hoff, who had himself served in the trenches.

At the corner of Darlinghurst Road and Macleay Street in Kings Cross is another war memorial – this time commemorating World War II. Like the Archibald Fountain, the **El Alamein** fountain, made in 1961 to a design by architects Woodward and Taranto, bears little obvious relationship to those it commemorates, but the dandelion clock spherical structure is a welcome feature of the Cross cityscape.

Behind the Art Gallery of New South Wales, facing the Cahill Expressway is a sculpture **Almost Once 1968-91** by Brett Whiteley, who since his death of a heroin overdose has been transformed into a tragic junkie-genius figure of mythic proportions. The fibreglass sculpture of an unlit match and a burnt one is usually seen as some kind of metaphor for potential, and since Whiteley's death has been interpreted as an ironic reflection on the artist's own life.

Hyde Park Barracks

Queens Square, Macquarie Street, Sydney (9223 8922). CityRail Martin Place or St James. **Open** 10am-5pm daily. **Admission** $5 adults; $3 concessions; $12 family ticket. **Credit** AmEx, BC, DC, MC, V.

Designed by colonial architect Francis Greenway in 1817-1819, Hyde Park Barracks was initially a jail and was then used for a range of purposes, including immigration depot and government offices, before its conversion to a museum. The Greenway Gallery on the ground floor shows temporary exhibitions, usually related to some aspect of Australian social history. The first floor exhibit is essentially about the building's history, featuring painstaking displays of archaeological discoveries. The top floor houses an evocative exhibition about barracks life. *See also chapter* **Sightseeing**. *Café. Disabled: access; toilets. Shop.*

Museum of Sydney

Museum of Sydney, 37 Phillip Street, Sydney (9251 5988). CityRail/ferry Circular Quay. **Open** 10am-5pm daily. **Admission** $6 adults; $4 concessions; $15 family ticket. **Credit** AmEx, BC, MC, $TC, V.

This modern building stands on one of the most historic spots in the city, the site of the first Government House. And the concept of contemporaneity meeting history is key to the philosophy of the MOS. Exhibits concentrate on the period 1788-1850, but the material is presented with the very latest museum methodology and technology. Just outside the entrance is a sculpture by Fiona Foley and Janet Laurence, *Edge of the Trees*, a rare instance of collaboration between an Aboriginal artist and a non-Aboriginal artist. It's worth visiting the museum just to see its state-of-the-art and extremely chic display cases: visitors can pull open the

The **Museum of Sydney**: *where the past meets the fashionable present. See page 159.*

elegant chrome-edged drawers containing exquisite displays of archaeological finds illuminated by tiny halogen lights. The trendy shop is worth a visit in its own right.
Café (see chapter **Cafés & Bars**). *Disabled: access; toilets.*

Powerhouse Museum

500 Harris Street, Ultimo (9217 0111). CityRail Central/ monorail Haymarket/501 bus. **Open** 10am-5pm daily. **Admission** $8 adults; $2-$3 concessions; $18 family ticket. **No credit cards**.
The Powerhouse is the largest museum in Australia. Its exhibitions concentrate on the areas of science, technology, creativity, decorative arts and Australian popular culture. Taking a fresh hands-on approach with banks of computers and interactive video screens, the Powerhouse is a joy to visit. Its democratic celebration of material culture has resulted in exhibitions on such diverse topics as Aussie pop music and the history of contraception.
Disabled; access; hearing loops; toilets. Restaurant. Shop.

SH Ervin Gallery

National Trust Centre, Watson Road, Millers Point (9258 0135). CityRail/ferry Circular Quay or Wynyard. **Open** 11am-5pm Tue-Fri; noon-5pm Sat, Sun. **Admission** $6 adults; $3 concessions. **Credit** AmEx, BC, DC, MC, V.
This National Trust gallery, spectacularly situated on Observatory Hill, specialises in Australian art and has a small but very good collection of Australian works on paper. Popular annual exhibitions include the 'Salon des Refuses', an alternative selection of some of the rejects from the Archibald and Wynne competitions; the Portia Geach Award, a national portraiture exhibition for Australian women artists; and the Australian Watercolour Institute exhibition, a suburban display for sale of some of the country's most competent, if dreary, watercolourists. These exhibitions punctuate a more scholarly programme based on the study of Australian art and architecture.
Disabled; access.

State Library of New South Wales

Macquarie Street, Sydney (9230 1414). CityRail Martin Place. **Open** 9am-9pm Mon-Fri; 11am-5pm Sat, Sun. **Admission** free.
Houses one of the country's largest and most fascinating collections of historical paintings, manuscripts, photographs and rare books. The exhibition programme is almost entirely drawn from the collection, and as the staff curators are lauded experts in their respective fields, this programme is of a consistently high quality. The historic Mitchell Wing is worth a visit in itself, with fine bronze bas-relief doors, a grand mosaic and terrazzo vestibule, stained-glass windows and extensive amounts of Australian stone and timber. The Mitchell's Shakespeare Room is a wonderful piece of pseudo-Tudor style, and legend has it that Sir Laurence Olivier once studied there. *See also chapter* **Sightseeing**.
Café. Disabled: access; toilets. Shop.

Eastern Suburbs

See also **Elizabeth Bay House** *and* **Vaucluse House** *in chapter* **Sightseeing**.

Bondi Pavilion Gallery

Bondi Pavilion Community Cultural Centre, Queen Elizabeth Drive, Bondi Beach (9130 3325). Bus 380, 382. **Open** 10am-5pm daily. **Admission** free.
This community access space is housed in the Bondi Pavilion, which itself organises a fun and energetic programme of festivals and activities all year round. The gallery programme is refreshingly quirky and sometimes political, with a good dose of local artists as well as thematic exhibitions which complement the Pavilion's calendar – such as the Festival of the Winds (a breathtaking annual event held on the second Sunday in September, when kites of all descriptions fill the Bondi sky) and the South American Festival.
Disabled: access; toilets.

Ivan Dougherty Gallery

Corner of Selwyn Street and Albion Avenue, Paddington (9385 0726). Bus 380, 382. **Open** 10am-5pm Mon-Fri; 1-5pm Sat. **Admission** free.

This art school gallery, specialising in international and Australian contemporary art, shows some of the most fascinating exhibitions in Sydney. Here you'll find enquiring thematic exhibitions, new media displays, solo shows and, occasionally, a mediocre exhibition of work by art school staff. *Disabled: access.*

North Shore

Mary MacKillop Place

7 Mount Street, North Sydney (9954 9688). CityRail North Sydney. **Open** 10am-4pm Mon-Fri; noon-4pm Sat. **Admission** $5 adults; $2-$4 concessions; $10 family ticket. **Credit** BC, MC, V.

Mary MacKillop (1842-1909) founded the Sisters of Saint Joseph, an order initially devoted to educating the poor children of the Australian outback. The 1994 beatification of the founding sister gave Australia its first official saint, and sparked a new industry, the crowning glory of which is Mary MacKillop Place. It was developed on the site of MacKillop's North Sydney convent, and is a mind-boggling mix of some very humble nineteenth-century objects and late twentieth-century hi-tech wizardry. A nun who took a vow of poverty leaves behind few conventional treasures. The motley assortment of crucifixes, rosary beads, a few small figurines and scraps of MacKillop's habits is jazzed up with talking dioramas, videos and various other special effects. One of the highlights is 'Nuns on the Run', a model mountain populated with dolls dressed as nuns engaged in a range of strenuous activities including swinging Tarzan-style from vines, riding bicycles and driving cars. As the banners adorning the exterior tell you, this vernacular Vatican is 'more than a museum, it's a journey'. So you may regard Mary MacKillop Place as a site of pilgrimage. And in true Catholic style, there are plenty of holy souvenirs on sale. *Disabled: access; toilets; wheelchairs. Shop.*

Rose Seidler House

71 Clissold Road, Wahroonga (9487 1771). Bus 575. **Open** 10am-4.30pm Sun; by appointment at other times. **Admission** $5 adults; $3 concessions. **No credit cards**.

This is the first house that Viennese-born architect Harry Seidler built in Australia. It was constructed in 1951, four years after his arrival in Australia with his parents. As the first local instance of the International style, Rose Seidler House caused a sensation (something for which the architect has never lost his knack) and a spate of imitations. In essence the house is a box on pipe columns based on a rocky slope in the leafy north shore bush, with sandstone blade walls forming the carport and the entrance. Seidler used lots of glass and painted the walls of the house off-white, with black and primary-coloured accents. Inside the open-plan living area there is a Mondrianesque feature wall and wonderful 1950s furniture. The young Seidler dictatorially refused to allow his parents to furnish his masterpiece with any items from their old world except his mother's floral dinner set. *Disabled: access; toilets.*

Parramatta & the West

Campbelltown City Gallery

Art Gallery Road, Campbelltown (4620 1333). CityRail Campbelltown. **Open** by appointment Mon; 10am-4pm Tue-Sat; noon-4pm Sun. **Admission** free.

This purpose-built gallery is made from that icon of suburban mediocrity, the blond brick. Despite its unprepossessing appearance, Campbelltown City Gallery is thriving, with a popular exhibition programme and a vigorous range of activities offered in extensive workshops. The permanent collection has a regional emphasis: historical paintings and prints relating to the settlement of the Campbelltown area and works by contemporary artists from the locale. Nearby Wedderburn is home to several significant contemporary artists including Joan Brassil, Suzanne Archer, Elizabeth Cummings, John Peart and Roy Jackson, and Savanhdary Vongpoothorn. *Disabled; access; toilets.*

Casula Powerhouse

1 Casula Road, Casula (9824 1121). CityRail Casula. **Open** 10am-4pm daily. **Admission** free.

Casula Powerhouse, opened in 1994, is one of the most exciting museum spaces in Australia. The converted electricity generating station has been transformed by three artworks which are incorporated into the fabric of the building. The concrete floor bears a huge-scale painting by Judy Watson, the windows are the work of Robyn Backen, and Nicole Ellis has created a dado honouring the men and women who worked at the power plant. The public toilets are another high point – fitted out with beautiful tiles which were the result of a workshop with Tom Strachan. Casula Powerhouse runs a lively exhibition programme with a strong emphasis on community and contemporary arts. *Disabled: access; toilets.*

Experiment Farm Cottage

9 Ruse Street, Harris Park (9635 5655). CityRail Harris Park or Parramatta. **Open** 10am-4pm Tue-Thur; 11-4pm Sun. **Admission** $4 adults; $2-$2.50 concessions; $10 family ticket. **Credit** BC, MC, V.

This modest cottage is on the site of the colony's first land grant, which was given to convict farmer James Ruse in 1792. Ruse sold the land to a surgeon, John Harris, who built the house the following year. Although few items in the house can be provenanced to Surgeon Harris, the cottage has some

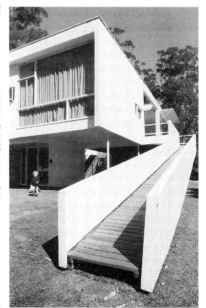

Rose Seidler House.

very good pieces of Australian colonial furniture and the museum displays some early farming implements.
Disabled: access.

Old Government House
Parramatta Park, Parramatta (9635 8149). CityRail Parramatta. **Open** 10am-4pm Tue-Fri; 11am-4pm Sat, Sun. **Admission** $5 adults; $3 concessions; $12 family ticket. **No credit cards.**
Previously a Vice Regal residence, Old Government House was built on the foundations of Governor Arthur Phillip's 1790 cottage. Its classic Georgian façade looks on to pleasant lawns and hides the nation's most important collection of Australian colonial furniture. One of many treasures is the Packer Cabinet. Its inscription – 'James Packer Sydney New South Wales an a Prentice 1815' – marks it as the earliest known piece of Australian furniture signed and dated by an Australian-born maker.

Rouse Hill House
980 Windsor Road, Rouse Hill (information 9627 5108/booking 9692 8366). CityRail Riverstone or Scofield then 740, 745 bus. **Open** by appointment only 10am-1pm first Thur of month. **Admission** $10 adults; $8 concessions. **Credit** BC, MC, $TC, V.
This two-storey Georgian house, set in a 15-ha (37-acre) estate, has the longest period of unbroken family occupancy of any house in Australia. Free settler Richard Rouse built the house in 1813-18, and direct descendants of Rouse are still in residence. As a result, Rouse Hill is an authentic reflection of Australian taste from the early nineteenth to the twentieth century.

Contemporary Art
Central Sydney

Artspace
Ground floor, The Gunnery, 43-51 Cowper Wharf Road, Woolloomooloo (9368 1899). Bus 311. **Open** 11am-6pm Mon-Sat. **Admission** free.
Located opposite the finger wharfs of Woolloomooloo, Artspace is a government-funded contemporary art gallery for local and international artists. Experimental and challenging are the key words here and the exhibitions are often very good. The gallery is complemented by an artist's studio programme.
Disabled: access; toilets.

CBD Gallery
62 Erskine Street, Sydney (9290 3076). CityRail Wynyard/ 202, 207, 263, 272 bus. **Open** 1-6pm Wed-Sat. **Admission** free.
In a current gallery listing, CBD describes itself as 'an artists' project gallery that provides a professional and critical venue for the exhibition of contemporary and experimental art practice'. Got the picture? Some of the finest – and, occasionally, some of the most vacuous – of local cutting-edge work can be seen here. But the exhibition programme is always dotted with impressive international names too. Preferring cool installation-based work, CBD is unique in its relentless schedule of one-week exhibitions, putting on 50 a year.
Disabled: access.

Ken Done Gallery
1 Hickson Road, The Rocks (9247 2740). CityRail/ferry Circular Quay. **Open** 10am-5.30pm daily. **Admission** free.
In his previous career Ken Done was an extremely successful

*For planes, trains and automobiles, head for the **Powerhouse Museum**. See page 160.*

*Modern times at the **MCA**. See page 164.*

advertising man, and he hasn't lost his marketing flair. With wife Judy he heads a design empire of bed linen, clothing, dinnerware – and the list goes on. In Japan he is phenomenally popular. Indeed, it is a rare stroll through The Rocks that does not yield the sight of at least one Japanese tourist sporting a Ken Done bag. His brightly coloured beach scenes, flower paintings and interiors have led some to call him Australia's Matisse, but he is yet to be accepted by the serious art scene.
Disabled: access.

Legge Gallery
183 Regent Street, Redfern (9319 3340). CityRail Redfern. **Open** 11am-6pm Tue-Sat. **Admission** free.
Legge Gallery's artists are mostly painters and sculptors, and they are generally young. The most charming exception to the rule is Beryl Wood, who was in her sixties when she began painting naive scenes of football games and other essentially Aussie subjects. There is often a tone of whimsy in Legge Gallery shows, for example in Brian Doar's ceramic Asian-inspired sculptures of intricate towers of elephants, or in Bruce Howlett's Australian landscapes which incorporate corrugated iron in the painting's surface.

Mori Gallery
168 Day Street, Sydney (9283 2903/fax 9283 2909). CityRail Town Hall/monorail Darling Park. **Open** 11am-6pm Wed-Sat. **Admission** free.
Mori Gallery has a well-earned reputation for showing fine contemporary artists. As well as representing an impressive stable of established young names – including photographer

Tracey Moffatt, painters Susan Norrie, Louise Hearman, Tim Johnson and Judy Watson, and *petit point* artist Narelle Jubelin – gallery director Stephen Mori is always receptive to new artists and his choice of 'unknowns' demonstrates that his is a remarkably discerning eye.
Disabled: access.

Museum of Contemporary Art

140 George Street, The Rocks (9252 4033/24-hour recorded information 9241 5892). CityRail/ferry Circular Quay. **Open** 10am-6pm daily. **Admission** $8 adults; $5 concessions; $18 family ticket. **Credit** AmEx, BC, DC, JCB, MC, $TC, V.
The MCA's exhibition programme is a balance of the esoteric and the accessible: from funky animation to sexy Mapplethorpe blockbusters to surveys of Russian and Japanese art. This stylish museum is a must for anyone with a serious interest in contemporary art and it has established a reputation for particularly fine shows of Aboriginal works. Exhibitions include selections from the permanent collection of international and Australian art, touring shows from museums around the world, and curated temporary exhibitions developed by the MCA.
Café (see chapter **Cafés & Bars**). *Disabled: access; toilets. Shop.*

The Performance Space

199 Cleveland Street, Redfern (9698 7235). CityRail Central. **Open** noon-8pm Wed-Sat. **Admission** free.
If you like challenging, innovative contemporary art forms, The Performance Space – with its versatile gallery, studio and theatre spaces – is for you. Exhibitions here specialise in installations involving sound, video and multimedia techniques. The events programme is an energetic menu of interesting and cutting-edge performance art (*see chapter* **Theatre & Dance**).

Ray Hughes Gallery

270 Devonshire Street, Surry Hills (9698 3200). Bus 301. **Open** 10am-6pm Tue-Sat. **Admission** free.
Many of Ray Hughes' artists have a very Australian flavour, whether it's the fierce light and resplendent colours of painters like William Yaxley and William Robinson, the thongs and faded driftwood which feature in the sculptures of Tom Risley or the surfboards onto which Robert Moore has been known to paint. Hughes, himself one of the most colourful characters in the Sydney art world, also shows some tribal and indigenous art from places like Africa and the Cook Islands.

Watters Gallery

109 Riley Street, Surry Hills (9331 2556). CityRail Museum. **Open** 10am-5pm Tue, Sat; 10am-8pm Wed-Fri. **Admission** free.
In the 1970s Watters was one of the most experimental spaces in town, earning a reputation for supporting not only innovative art but also human rights issues. These days, it represents a number of significant artists who have stayed loyally with the gallery throughout their careers – a rare thing in the fickle world of art. As a result, the majority of Watters artists are at the mid-to-late stage of their careers; for example, acclaimed sculptor Robert Klippel, master surrealist painter James Gleeson, Tuscany-based painter Ken Whisson and the inimitable Vivienne Binns.

Eastern Suburbs

Rex Irwin Art Dealer

1st floor, 38 Queen Street, Woollahra (9363 3212). Bus 380, 389. **Open** 11am-5.30pm Tue-Sat. **Admission** free.
This smallish but smart gallery represents several of Australia's most bankable artists, including painting heavyweight Peter Booth, much-loved virtuoso print-maker Cressida Campbell and landscape artist John Wolseley. Rex Irwin also

deals in works by Frank Auerbach, Lucien Freud, David Hockney and Picasso.

Roslyn Oxley9 Gallery

Soudan Lane (off 27 Hampden Street), Paddington (9331 1919). Bus 378, 380, 382. **Open** 10am-6pm Tue-Fri; 11am-6pm Sat. **Admission** free.
Roslyn Oxley's gallery is one of the most beautiful spaces in town. She represents some of the biggest local contemporary art names, such as Rosalie Gascoigne, Ken Unsworth, Julie Rrap, Lindy Lee and Fiona Foley – and two of the bad boys of Australian contemporary art, Juan Davila and Dale Frank. Oxley has established a tradition of showing infamously appropriate artists to coincide with Sydney's Gay & Lesbian Mardi Gras, and these flamboyant exhibitions are always accompanied by a great opening party.

Sherman Galleries Goodhope

16-18 Goodhope Street, Paddington (9331 1112). Bus 378, 380, 382. **Open** 11am-6pm Tue-Sat. **Admission** free.
Sherman Goodhope is something of a local 'tall poppy'. When this place opened in 1993, a number of Sydney's most highly regarded artists 'migrated' to it; to the continued irritation of some local dealers, this migration process, while having slowed, has not stopped. What's more, the gallery boasts a spectacular space designed by celebrated architect Andrew Andersons and a beautiful sculpture garden. The 'migratory' stars of this gallery include Yorkshire-born sculptor Hilarie Mais, whose ongoing preoccupation with the grid form has compelled Sydney viewers for almost a decade, and conceptual heavyweight Mike Parr.

Inner West & South

Annandale Galleries

110 Trafalgar Street, Annandale (9552 1699). Bus 470. **Open** 11am-5.30pm Tue-Sat. **Admission** free.
Annandale Galleries represents a stable of mostly mid-

SH Ervin Gallery. *See page 160.*

*Contemporary Australian photography shows at the **Stills Gallery** in Paddington.*

careerish artists, many of whom are highly regarded. One of its most exceptional regulars is Jennifer Turpin, who creates beguiling water sculptures. This space also shows contemporary international artists such as Paula Rego and Rebecca Horn, as well as graphic exhibitions by saleable masters including Marc Chagall and Joan Miró.

Sarah Cottier Gallery
36 Lennox Street, Newtown (9516 3193). CityRail Newtown. **Open** 11am-6pm Wed-Sat. **Admission** free.
Sarah Cottier's name appeared near the top of Australian fashion mag *Mode*'s latest list of the country's best dressed women, and her gallery also gleams with expensive chic. This converted small-goods factory is one of the slickest spaces on the contemporary art circuit. A high proportion of Cottier's artists are chosen to represent Australia in trendy international biennales and triennales, and in groovy local museum exhibitions. The one gallery in town that can claim Kylie Minogue as a visitor.

Photography

Australian Centre for Photography
257 Oxford Street, Paddington (9332 1455). Bus 378, 380, 382. **Open** *gallery* 11am-6pm Tue-Sat; *workshop* noon-6pm daily. **Admission** *gallery* free; *workshop* members only.
This public gallery presents Australian and international photography, photomedia work and new image technologies within a scholarly, critical context. The complex also houses darkrooms and there is a workshop programme. *Photofile*, a contemporary photography journal, is published by the centre. The centre shares premises with hip canteen La Mensa (*see chapter* **Restaurants**).

Byron Mapp Gallery
178 Oxford Street, Paddington (9331 2926). Bus 378, 380, 382. **Open** 10am-6pm Mon-Sat; noon-5pm Sun. **Admission** free.
Prior to this commercial venture, Sandra Byron and Penny Mapp were, respectively, curator and assistant curator of photography at the Art Gallery of New South Wales. And it seems they have brought a scholarly touch to their current enterprise, representing some of the country's most celebrated

photographers including Judith Ahern, Max Pam and Gerrit Fokkema. The gallery also has access to inventories of such international stars as Man Ray, Cecil Beaton and Herb Ritts.

Stills Gallery
16 Elizabeth Street, Paddington (9331 7775). Bus 378, 380, 382. **Open** by appointment Tue; 11am-6pm Wed-Sat. **Admission** free.
The Stills Gallery shows a variety of contemporary Australian photographers and is headed by Sandy Edwards, who produces lyrical, documentary-style pieces. The spectrum of work you'll find here includes the photomontages of George Schwarz, the photojournalism of Lorrie Graham and the large-scale theatrical constructions of Suellen Symons.

Other Art Dealers

Eva Breuer Art Dealer
83 Moncur Street, Woollahra (9362 0297). Bus 380, 382, 389. **Open** 11am-6pm Tue-Sun. **Admission** free.
Although it's the size of a chocolate box, Eva Breuer's gallery shows Australian art of a consistently high standard. The exhibition programme is a mix of solo shows by contemporary artists, mini-surveys of historical artists and interesting thematic shows incorporating both contemporary and historical works.

Josef Lebovic Gallery
34 Paddington Street, Paddington (9332 1840). Bus 378, 380, 382. **Open** 1-6pm Tue-Fri; 11am-5pm Sat. **Admission** free.
Deals primarily in works on paper, prints and photographs, both Australian and international. Lebovic's stimulating and insightful exhibitions are usually based around a theme, rather than an individual artist. Each exhibition is accompanied by a scholarly catalogue.

Martin Browne Fine Art
13 Macdonald Street, Paddington (9360 2051). Bus 389. **Open** 10am-6pm Tue-Sun. **Admission** free.
Martin Browne is a dealer who always has an impressive selection of major pieces by significant contemporary Australian and New Zealand artists, as well as earlier twentieth-century pieces and more historical works.

Aboriginal art

Today many agree that Aboriginal art is the most vital area of contemporary Australian art. Gone are the days when people equated Aboriginal art with rock carvings and painted bark. Since the first desert artists adapted their traditional techniques to the modern medium of acrylic paint on canvas, at Papunya in the Northern Territory in 1971-2, there has been a veritable explosion of Aboriginal dot painters from the Northern Territory and Western Australia. This phenomenon has created a new field in contemporary Australian art, overwhelming the local and international markets. Twentieth-century viewers, well versed in the joys of abstraction, have heartily embraced these paintings, but it has taken some time for people to understand them.

In fact, Aboriginal dot paintings are never – well, very rarely – abstract. They tend to be a description of the artist's country, of their traditional lands. And, generally, the casual viewer will only be allowed access to certain layers of

Turkey Tolson at **Utopia Art Sydney**.

information contained in such paintings. Sacred or secret areas and stories are simply not explained. In traditional Aboriginal culture, knowledge must be earned. Of course, there is a whole lexicon of symbols, the meanings of which are freely available to non-Aborigines. For instance, concentric circles denote a significant area (often a waterhole) and a horseshoe shape refers to a seated person (from the mark someone makes when sitting on the soil).

The desert painting phenomenon is not restricted to central Australia. From Turkey Creek in northern Western Australia comes another internationally celebrated school of painting in which flat areas of black and brown are delineated by white dots, again a description of country. Undoubtedly, the most celebrated exponent of this style is Rover Thomas. From Balgo in Western Australia come wildly colourful dot paintings – collectors fight to get works by senior Balgo woman Eubena Nampitjin. (A word of warning to buyers: do not purchase paintings by desert artists which are unaccompanied by basic biographical information. Apart from limiting your knowledge of the work, the absence of such details would suggest that it was acquired hastily and unethically.)

In more recent years, the contemporary Australian art scene has witnessed the emergence of an amazing number of Aboriginal artists working in non-traditional media. Harry Wedge and Ian Abdulla are fine exponents of a narrative figurative style, both artists working from their own very unique perspectives. Wedge has created series such as *Captain Cook Con Man*, which present a potent and ironic perspective on the usually celebrated Botany Bay landing. Abdulla's largely autobiographical paintings provide compelling insights into the experience of Aborigines growing up on missions.

There is a tradition of very fine Aboriginal photographers from Mervyn Bishop (one of the first Aborigines to work as a professional photographer in Australia) to film-makers/photographers such as Tracey Moffatt and Michael Riley. Brook Andrew and Rea both combine photography with computer technology.

It is important to realise that some of the most exciting Aboriginal artists are not represented by specialist galleries. Tracey Moffatt, whose films *Night Cries* and *Bedevilled* were highly acclaimed and whose photographs have received international recognition, is represented by the Mori Gallery (*see page 163*), as is 1995 Moët et Chandon

Representing NSW artists: **Boomalli Aboriginal Artists' Co-op**.

Fellow, painter Judy Watson. Likewise, Fiona Foley, who has featured in many national surveys, and the late Robert Campbell Junior are represented by the Roslyn Oxley9 Gallery (*see page 164*).

Boomalli Aboriginal Artists' Co-op
27 Abercrombie Street, Chippendale (9698 2047). CityRail Central. **Open** (during exhibitions only) 10am-5pm Tue-Fri; 11am-5pm Sat. **Admission** free.
Boomalli's exhibition programme ranges from single artist shows and thematic curated exhibitions to all-inclusive surveys. Similarly, the media used range from traditional to very contemporary. Many of Australia's most highly regarded Aboriginal artists have been or are closely associated with Boomalli. You are less likely to find desert artists from Western Australia and the Northern Territory here: Boomalli has a commitment to New South Wales Aboriginal artists.

Hogarth Galleries/ Aboriginal Arts Centre
7 Walker Lane, Paddington (9360 6839). Bus 380, 382. **Open** 11am-5pm Tue-Sat. **Admission** free.
Hogarth is patronised by serious collectors, as gallery director Ace Bourke has a long acquaintance with Aboriginal art and his exceptional eye ensures that his stock passes muster with even the fussiest connoisseurs. Hogarth's exhibitions cover the gamut of contemporary Aboriginal arts and crafts – from Maningrida bags and weavings, Tiwi poles and paintings by Balgo and Utopia artists, to colour photocopies by the witty and iconoclastic Melbourne-based Destiny Deacon.

Utopia Art Sydney
50 Parramatta Road, Stanmore (9550 4609). Bus 436, 438, 440, 461. **Open** 10am-4pm Wed-Fri; noon-5pm Sat. **Admission** free.

This gallery (*pictured below*) specialises in Aboriginal artists from Utopia and Papunya Tula in the Northern Territory, with two exceptions: proprietor Christopher Hodges, himself an artist, shows at Utopia, as does Western Australian John R Walker. This is a good place to pick up works by the celebrated Emily Kame Kngwarreye and other Utopia artists such as Gloria Petyarre. Stock ranges from museum-standard pieces to affordable and charming small-scale works.

Where do you find out what's happening in London?

http://www.timeout.co.uk

Time Out

Your weekly guide to the most exciting city in the world

Arts & Entertainment

Literary Sydney

Read all about the Harbour City, in fact and fiction.

Sydney's rich tradition as literary capital of Australia probably had its origins with **Watkin Tench** (1858-1833), born in Chester, England, who joined the Marine Corps and travelled with the First Fleet to Botany Bay. His accounts of the establishment of the colony, republished recently as *1788*, give colourful and often brutal descriptions of the beginnings of Sydney and its outer suburbs. Tench's reworked journals have since been appraised as perhaps the start of a national literature.

It wasn't until poet and short story writer **Henry Lawson** emerged in the late-nineteenth century that Sydney was truly celebrated as a significant backdrop for fiction. While Lawson is widely known for his 'bush' ballads and comic narratives, his later work draws extensively on inner-Sydney life. Much of his work was published in the famous *Bulletin* magazine, and he was a familiar and often drunken figure in the periodical's George Street offices. By the time of his death in

September 1922, Lawson had become a household name. His modest grave can be found in Waverley Cemetery, which overlooks the sea beyond Bronte.

Sydney's inner suburbs, particularly Redfern, Surry Hills, Chinatown and the area around Central Station were the subject of **Louis Stone**'s novel *Jonah* (1911), which details the 'larrikin' pushes at the turn of the twentieth century. His only other novel was *Betty Wayside* (1915), about the Sydney musical world.

Poet **Christopher Brennan**, who for a time lived in the Glen Hotel in Paddington, centred much of his work on city life. Brennan lectured at Sydney University and became known as the city's pre-eminent Symbolist poet. Towards the end of his life he lived in obscurity in Crown Street, Woolloomooloo, near the docks, and would take 'breakfast' (in a bottle) at the Prince Albert Hotel.

A contemporary of Brennan and Stone – **Norman Lindsay** – shocked Australia with his graphic paintings and illustrations as well

as his prose. An early novel, *Redheap* (1930), was banned. Lindsay later settled at his studio in Springwood in the Blue Mountains, where his home is now a museum (*see pages 43 and 249*).

Miles Franklin, author of *My Brilliant Career* (1901), also spent time in Sydney, writing her other classic, *All That Swagger* (1936) in the south-western suburb of Carlton. Australia's most prestigious literary award now bears her name.

Perhaps the first writer to authentically capture the beauty of Sydney's meandering harbour was poet **Kenneth Slessor**, culminating in his classic 'Five Bells', first published in 1939. A former journalist, Slessor spent most of his life in Sydney and recorded its lively flavour and many of the local characters, particularly around the suburbs of Kings Cross and Potts Point, an area he lived in for over 40 years. His distinctive turreted house in Billyard Avenue, Elizabeth Bay, has become a landmark.

In a late memoir, Slessor wrote of Sydney: '... the grumble of the flying boats climbing down to their nests in Rose Bay; the crowds in the streets of Kings Cross waiting for the strokes of midnight to ring in the New Year; Macquarie Street and its brass plates; Macleay Street; Potts Point; St James Church in King Street, riding aloofly on the clouds, its lovely scales of verdigris giving the copper a green like

tarnished snow, an old, dim, decayed, peeling almond-green, but indubitably green, as if to honour its eighteenth century architect Mr Francis Greenway.'

His work celebrated, above all, the harbour and its unique bridge, of which he had a permanent view from his home. 'The Harbour has never been out of my window,' he once said.

Similar terrain was also mined by novelist **Christina Stead**, her most famous work being *The Man Who Loved Children* (1940), since regarded as a twentieth-century classic. Stead spent much of her childhood in Pacific Street, Watsons Bay, one of Sydney's prettiest and most exclusive harbourside suburbs. The bay entered much of her work, becoming the fictional 'Fisherman's Bay' in her early novel, *Seven Poor Men of Sydney* (1934). Her later novels had international settings.

Australia's only recipient of the Nobel Prize for Literature, **Patrick White**, spent a year at Sydney's Cranbrook School before being moved to a college in Mossvale, southern NSW, where the climate eased his chronic asthma. White later lived in England and Europe before settling back in Australia after the Second World War.

He initially took up a small farm in Castle Hill, north-west Sydney, and later moved to the fringe of inner-Sydney's Centennial Park, where he lived for the rest of his life. Sydney featured

in much of White's work, particularly *Riders in the Chariot* (1961) and *The Eye of the Storm* (1973). In the latter work, White's main character, the bitchy Mrs Hunter, is dying in her rambling home in Centennial Park.

White was particularly active in protecting the park against development, and was a visible presence at many public protests during the 1970s.

The inner-Sydney suburb of Balmain, a narrow peninsular overlooking the city and the Harbour Bridge, became something of a literary enclave during the late 1970s and 1980s, and gained a reputation as a 'writer's ghetto'. The leading figures of this period were writers **Frank Moorhouse**, **Peter Carey** and **Michael Wilding**. Moorhouse, in his many 'discontinuous narratives', has documented much of the era. His collection of essays, interviews and articles, *Days of Wine and Rage* (1980), is an invaluable document of this 'bohemian' period, which featured epic 24-hour readings as well as the publication of seminal magazines such as *Tabloid Story*. Many of the writers of this group were considered politically radical and sexually experimental, and their exploits in Balmain's numerous pubs and hotels have become legendary.

Sydney today has a lively and active literary community and a continuous calendar of readings by local and international writers. The primary venues are **Gleebooks**, in Glebe Point Road, and **Ariel** in Oxford Street, Darlinghurst. For these, and other major bookshops, including **Dymock's** in the city, and **Nicholas Pounder's** excellent outlet specialising in second-hand works as well as first editions, *see chapter* **Shopping & Services**.

The city's pre-eminent literary festival, incorporated within the Sydney Festival, is held in the last week of January (*see* **Sydney Writers' Festival** *in chapter* **Sydney by Season**). A smaller festival, the Spring Writer's Festival, is usually held in October. Sydney also has a writer's centre in Rozelle.

Visitors to Circular Quay will find the **Writer's Walk** (*pictured*), a series of plaques that circumvent the Quay from The Rocks to the Sydney Opera House. The plaques bear quotes about Sydney from some of Australia's best-known writers, as well as international visitors who have written about the city over the century, including Robert Louis Stevenson, Jack London and DH Lawrence. Lawrence spent a short time in Sydney before retreating to the tiny seaside hamlet of Thirroul, south of the city, where he wrote his novel *Kangaroo*.

For more on many of the works mentioned here, together with a useful list of other Sydney-related reading, *see page 266* **Further Reading**.

C.J. DENNIS
1876–1936

It 'appened this way: I 'ad jist come down,
After long years, to look at Sydney town.
An' 'struth! Was I knocked endways? Fair su'prised?
I never dreamed! That arch that cut the skies!
The Bridge! ...

'I DIPS ME LID' (1936)

C.J. DENNIS WON GREAT POPULARITY FOR HIS RACY, VERNACULAR
VERSE, WHICH CAPTURED THE ESSENTIAL AUSTRALIAN SPIRIT OF
HIS DAY. HIS BEST KNOWN CHARACTER, GINGER MICK, WAS
IMMORTALISED IN *THE SONGS OF A SENTIMENTAL BLOKE* (1915).

NSW MINISTRY FOR THE ARTS
WRITERS WALK

Media

M is for Murdoch, as Oz's most influential export continues his plans for domination of the world media.

Like London, Sydney is a media city. Melbourne may fool itself that there is a rivalry, but really, the dollar deals are done in the harbour city, and most of the media is based there. And like all media cities, a lot of Sydney's media is about nothing much more than other media – it's obsessed with itself and the little bubble world it lives in. Media panics and bushfires are quickly started, but rarely put out with the same energy. In the 1990s, the climate of hysteria that has surrounded many issues, from drugs to gun control, has been largely of the media's making. The government-funded Australian Broadcasting Corporation sets the standard in radio and TV but though everybody will swear otherwise, the newspapers really run the show. The morning fish and chip wrappers effectively set the agenda for almost all of the radio and television news services, which tend to be lazy when it comes to breaking their own news.

Boss of News Corporation, Rupert Murdoch.

Newspapers

The first problem of the Australian media is lack of population. Unlike London, Sydney has only a handful of papers serving four million people. The market won't bear any more, as the 1980s proved with the closure of afternoon tabloids like the *Sun* and the *Mirror*, and the gradual sinking of upmarket weekly the *National Times*. Sydney is a very tight newspaper town. The second problem, exacerbated by the low number of papers, is the lack of diversity in ownership. This is a problem throughout the media, but if you work in newspapers, you work for one side of the street or the other, for Rupert Murdoch's News Corporation or Conrad Black's Fairfax.

Dailies

The *Sydney Morning Herald* (Black) is the only quality broadsheet in the Sydney market. The paper is a local institution – it could hardly avoid being one. Its only broadsheet competition is the *Australian* (Murdoch), a national paper run from Sydney, which has been sharpening its act up in the 1990s, losing a lot of its conservative starch and giving the Herald a run for its money, especially at the weekends. The *Daily Telegraph*, a morning tabloid, is closer to Murdoch's traditional sensationalism, but is much more sedate than its London tabloid counterparts – the Page Three girl died in Australia a decade ago. The *Australian Financial Review* (Fairfax), also run from Sydney, covers the business community.

Weekend Papers

The *Sydney Morning Herald* and the *Australian* both have Saturday editions, ever-expanding as expensive new presses have allowed both to add sections in the hope of attracting more circulation. You need a wheelbarrow to get them home from the newsagent. The *Sun Herald* (Fairfax) and the *Sunday Telegraph* (Murdoch) are bulging Sunday tabloids, crammed with sport, lifestyle and all the old fashioned stuff (gardening columns, recipe swaps etc).

Suburban

There are 42 smaller suburban papers in the Sydney metropolitan area, covering many and various communities, enclaves and fiefdoms, from the *St George and Sutherland Shire Leader* in the south to the *Wentworth Courier* in the east (think property ads), the *North Shore Times* across the Harbour Bridge and the *Fairfield City Champion* out west (well, southwest). These are often free and widely circulated. They're useful for all sorts of highly localised information.

Ethnic

There are also more than 50 daily and weekly ethnic newspapers being produced in Sydney for the consumption of individual communities. Sydney's Chinese population, for example, have half a dozen to choose from. There are also official organs for everyone from the French to the Lithuanians to the Filipinos. The *Irish Echo* is a popular read for Sydney's sizeable community of Emerald Isle expats.

Magazines

Australians read more magazines per head than any other people in the world. No one is quite sure why. Perhaps it's because the public transport is pretty lousy and you have to have something to do at the bus stop. The 1996 edition of Margaret Gee's *Media Guide* lists 968 different local mags available to the public (with a further 691 trade publications). On top of that, container ships full of imported magazines arrive in the city every month. The biggest local producer is Australian Consolidated Press, owned by Australia's richest man, Kerry Packer.

Women's

The crunch end of the market. Also the most crowded. The Australian *Women's Weekly* (a monthly) sells more than a million copies of each issue, extraordinary figures for a country of this size. *Woman's Day* (a weekly), sells slightly more. Its opposition, *New Idea*, only sells three quarters of a million a week. The glossy mag market is dominated by **Cleo**, which knocks off *Cosmo*, with various local versions of *Elle*, *Marie Claire*, *Vogue* and others fighting for the rest of the market. The most interesting of the lot is *HQ*, which attempts to be a mag for humans high in both oestrogen and brain matter. Now there's a novel idea.

Men's

Sorry gals, but men's mags in Oz still mostly means Australian *Playboy* and Australian *Penthouse*. *Inside Sport*, a successful monthly foray into the world of blood and liniment, may present itself as analytical and serious, but it still puts girlies in bikinis on the cover of every issue. And don't bother looking for a local version of *Esquire*, *Arena* or *GQ* – they're not there.

Coffee-table

One of the magazine trends of the 1990s has been the large, lavishly tooled, gorgeously photographed magazine. Titles such as *Black & White*, *Australian Style* (no, that's not an oxymoron) and *Blue* are self-consciously arty (and walk all over the line between soft porn and erotica).

News & Issues

The *Bulletin* has been running for more than a century and has a fine tradition of political criticism, though it has lost much of its humorous edge. The more recent *Independent Monthly* is a welcome addition to the scene, a crusading and intelligent magazine offering in-depth analysis of current events and issues.

Freebies

The city is awash with weekly free mags, mostly entwined with the rock culture of teens and twenty-somethings. *Drum Media* and *On The Street* are the old competitors, but they have been joined over the last few years by the *City*, *Beat*, club mag *3D*, the *Hub* and others. Free queer papers the *Star Observer* and *Capital Q* are also easily found, particularly in the eastern suburbs. You never have to pay to find something to read in Sydney, though the quality of some of the journalism unfortunately helps to explain the cover price.

Humour

A lot of people don't think they're funny in the slightest, but *People* and *Picture* magazines, both part of the ACP stable, manage to cross the tits and bums aesthetic of certain English papers with the 'Photo of Elvis cured my cancer' lunacy of certain American mags, refusing to take anything seriously. The stupider the idea, the more likely it is to get a run. The result is not often pretty, and pushes the boundaries of taste and decorum every week of the year, but there are curious and idiosyncratic successes.

Radio

AM

Radio National
(ABC) 576AM
The thinking person's radio station. At its talk end, stalwarts like Phillip Adams are almost always intelligent and provocative, and often deal with complex, non-soundbite ideas. At its creative end, programs such as *The Listening Room* explore the artistic possibilities of the medium.

Parliamentary News Network
(ABC) 630AM
Someone thought it would be a good idea for the whole country to be able to listen to what goes on in Parliament. On paper, of course, this is a good idea – an informed public makes a better democracy and all that. However, the removal

from office of Paul Keating has somewhat flattened the tone of debate. When not concerned with the goings on in the Houses, it's a full-time news network.

2BL

(ABC) 702AM
Talk radio of the non-commercial, non-ranting kind. The most popular of the ABC stations, built on a diet of morning news and current affairs, with the gradual inclusion of lifestyle issues as the day goes on. Probably the best way to keep up with what's going on in the minds of (sane) Sydneysiders.

2GB

873AM
This was a force to be reckoned with in the 1970s and 1980s, but has seen its listeners dwindle in the last few years. A revolving door lineup and management problems have not helped either. The station has changed hands recently and has been revamped, hiring a lot of names of the 1970s and 1980s. Time will tell if the gambit works.

2UE

954AM
The Theatre of Ego. Home to the radio demagogues. Be they smooth salesman or riled-up ranters, the jocks at 2UE command attention. Their extraordinary power over a huge and devoted listening public is often remarked upon, particularly by politicians, who are forced to break bread with them. The King of Radio, the honey-tonsilled John Laws, broadcasts each weekday morning from his self-described 'Fortress of Arrogance', sending out his message (his fortune cookie philosophy and his unbelievably awful poetry) via a solid gold microphone. It's utterly compelling, and a couple of hours of his show will tell you as much about a certain part of Australian culture as you could ever want to know.

2KY

1017AM
Racing, racing and more racing, with a little non-threatening music and chat when the horses aren't running.

2CH

1170AM
Easy listening. So inoffensive it could be invisible.

2RPH

1224AM
Radio for the print handicapped.

KICK AM

1269AM
They play both kinds of music. Yep, country and western. The owners were convinced that kerntry myoosak was the next big thing. We're still waiting.

SBS Radio

1386AM
Specialises in ethnic radio programs, in their own languages, for Sydney's many and varied communities.

FM

Sydney Information Radio

87.8FM
For tourists. Broadcasts in the city area only.

ABC Classic FM

92.9FM
Since its 1990s revamp, purists claim this is now the Idiot's Guide to Classical Music. The station says it has simply become more consistent. Listenership has risen.

SBS Radio 2

97.7FM
Special interest ethnic programs.

2000FM

98.5FM
Another ethnic specialist, with various community groups putting together programs. Homesick Brits might enjoy the BBC feed from midnight to dawn.

Cyber surf

If you want to get on-line in Sydney, try the **Well Connected Coffee Shop** (*above*, 35 Glebe Point Road; 9566 2655), or the **Internet Café** in the Hotel Sweeney (corner of Druitt and Clarence Streets; 9261 5666). Meanwhile, here are a few useful addresses to check out.

ABC Online
http://www.abc.net.au/
Ansett Schedules
gopher://cis.anu.edu.au:70/11/FAQ-ext/Airlines/
Art Gallery Of NSW
http://www.ozemail.com.au/~agnsw/
Australian Financial Review
http://www.afr.com.au
Australian Museum
http://www.nma.gov.au/AMIS/am/home1.html
Australian Opera
http://www.ausopera.org.au/sydney/index.html
Australian Rugby League
http://www.arl.org.au/
Australian Stock Exchange
http://www.asx.com.au/
Beat Magazine
http://www.ozonline.com.au/beat/
Kick AM
http://www.kick-am.com.au/
Macquarie University
http://www.mq.edu.au/
Museum of Contemporary Art
http://www.mca.com.au/
On the Street
http://www.real.net.au/ots/
Oxford Net (Guide to Oxford Street)
http://www.toolkit.com.au/OxfordNet/
Powerhouse Museum
http://www.mov.vic.gov.au/powerhse/index.html
QANTAS
http://www.anzac.com/qantas/qantas.html
State Library of NSW
http://www.slnsw.gov.au/slnsw.html
State Transit (Harbour Ferries)
http://www.anzac.com/aust/nsw/stnsw4.html
Sydney Cam
http://spectrum.com.au/citycam.html
Sydney Convention & Exhibition Centre
http://www.scec.com.au/
Sydney Cricket Ground
http://www.scgt.oz.au/
Sydney Film Festival
http://www.sydfilm-fest.com.au/
Sydney For Visitors
http://www.magna.com.au/~michaelb/sydney.html
Sydney Gay & Lesbian Mardi Gras
http://www.geko.com.au/~mardigras/
Sydney Morning Herald
http://www.smh.com.au
Sydney Opera House
http://www.sydneyoperahouse.nsw.gov.au/
Sydney Restaurant Search
http://garnet.kcs.com.au:8001/restaurant/showrest.html
Sydney Swans
http://www.sydneyswans.com.au
Sydney Tourist Guide
http://www.ida.com.au/sydney/
Sydney Tower
http://www.centrepoint.com.au/
Sydney Turf Club
http://www.stc.com.au/
Sydney 2000 Olympics
http://www.sydney.olympic.org/
Sydney Television Guide
http://www.sofcom.com.au/TV/Sydney.html
Sydney Theatre Guide
http://www.eventnet.aust.com/theatsyd.html
Sydney University
http://www.usyd.edu.au/
Sydney Weather Forecast
gopher://babel.ho.BoM.GOV.AU:70/11/Australian%20Weather%20Information/New%20South%20Wales
Telstra White and Yellow Pages
http://www.telstra.com.au/
University of NSW
http://www.unsw.edu.au/
University of Technology
http://www.uts.edu.au/
University of Western Sydney
http://www.uws.edu.au/

2WS
101.7FM
That's 2-Western-Suburbs, a station set up to keep the good people of Sydney's great western spread informed and entertained. It joined the rush to FM at the start of the decade, with yet another hits and memories playlist. Safe and middle of the road.

2MBS
102.5FM
The other classical station. This one now prides itself on being a little more highbrow than Classic FM, and has a slightly wider brief. If you wade through its schedule, you'll find jazz, funk and all manner of contemporary experimental music.

2CBA
103.2FM
Christian Broadcasting Association. What, you don't like marching bands and Andy Lloyd-Webber? Shame on you.

2DAY
104.1FM
Made a name for itself by being the first of the big FM stations to actually consider that women might be part of the audience, and that they wouldn't necessarily want to listen to AC/DC all day and night. Currently riding high. Check out the phenomenally popular Martin and Molloy on the afternoon drive shift, if they haven't been lured to bigger pastures.

MMM
104.9FM
Rock, rock, rock, rock and, after the ads, more rock. White, male, suburban, guitar rock. It's narrow, it's predictable and by golly, it rates its long-haired, Spinal Tap ass off. Sigh.

Triple J
105.7FM
Was the *enfant terrible* of Australian radio in the 1970s as Double J, an AM station with dope-smoking, irreverent (and occasionally nude) DJs who played whatever they loved. Yeah man, more Captain Beefheart. For 20 years, it has been the station most devoted to the discovery and spread of new music, in all its forms. It goes through periods of being conservative in its taste, but is still so much better than most of the competition in Sydney, and overseas, that it deserves its landmark status.

MIX
106.5FM
Is your definition of music Billy Joel, Whitney Houston, Phil Collins et al? Then do we have the station for you!

Public Broadcasters

In the last two decades, dozens of public radio stations have sprung up around Australia, supported by the government and various educational institutions. These stations often have a very limited transmission range, and they cater for the interests of specific community groups within their areas. Their output may be a little rough around the edges, but it is eclectic, unrestrained by commercialism and able to explore issues and sounds other stations don't get near. There are 16 public radio stations in Sydney. The biggest of the pack, **2SER** (107.3FM), broadcasts from the University of Technology, near the Central Railway Station.

ABC
The government station, Australia's own 'Aunty', has no commercials and exists on the high moral ground of 'quality' programming. Almost nothing American ever makes it to air, aside from the occasional documentary. A large percentage is local content, with emphases on comedy, drama (the Brit stuff seems to arrive later and later), natural history, news and current affairs. Can be a little stuffy in places, but the ABC also makes a safe harbour for most of the risk-taking and innovative local fare. Typical programs: *Frontline, Pride and Prejudice*.

Seven
Perennial bridesmaid threatens Nine's supremacy every year, but never seems to topple it from the perch. Solid in local comedy and in drama, Seven is also willing to entertain the occasional foray into risky (for commercial channels) programming. It just can't seem to find the winning news and current affairs combination to kick off prime time. Typical programs: *Home and Away, Blue Heelers*.

Nine
The juggernaut of commercial television. Has been the number one station for a decade or, if you believe the self-image, forever. Unashamedly populist (it hates coming second in any timeslot), Nine also has a tendency, in its weaker moments, to be overly blokey and dumb. Does game shows and lifestyle programs well, but has a strange habit of choking on drama and comedy. Sport obsessed. Believes it has the best current affairs and news on offer, but the jury is permanently out on that one. A big chequebook helps it buy overseas hits. Typical programs: *The Footy Show, ER*.

Ten
In the early 1990s, Ten changed direction, abandoning the race with the other commercial stations for the biggest market. The station now concentrates on the 18-39 year olds and is home to virtually every American show for groovy young things there is, from *The Simpsons* to *Melrose Place* to *The X Files*. Tries its heart out but falls down on local content – though *Neighbours* winds ever onwards, and *Heartbreak High* was braver than anything the others have tried in recent years. Typical programs: *Seinfeld, 90210*.

SBS
A real first for Australia, SBS begun in the early 1980s. The network broadcasts a diet of mostly foreign fare, with a few local programs thrown in. Movies, documentaries and soap operas from around the globe make up most of its time schedule. It doesn't have a huge audience, but its supporters are vocal and passionate. The most eclectic of the bunch, SBS is also the best place to find European sport and is the traditional host channel of the football (soccer) World Cup. Typical programs: *The Movie Show, Eat Carpet*.

Pay Television
Most of the best Pay TV action hasn't been on screen. The battle of the corporate titans, Kerry Packer versus Rupert Murdoch, has been fought in court and on the streets. Packer is aligned with Pay TV operator Optus Vision, while Murdoch has Foxtel. The market is big enough to support two cable providers, so they've been duking it out in public. In 1995, Murdoch tried to bolster his chances by buying Rugby League, Sydney's favourite sport. His plans to set up a Super League were initially foiled in a courtroom battle against Packer, but in 1996 the ruling against him was overturned. Meanwhile, channels appear left, right and centre. The first arrived in late 1995. A year later there were more than 30, with all the usual staples: sport, music, movies, cartoons, old TV shows and home shopping. The subscription rate has so far been disappointing, but these are early days. Murdoch and Packer have only just begun their fight.

Nightlife

Club culture is alive and groovin' but if dancing's not your thing, there are pool halls, comedy clubs and a casino to keep you up all night.

The epicentre of Sydney nightlife is Oxford Street, an eclectic, mile-long strip running out of the city's corporate and commercial centre. It is here, amid the cafés and all-night pubs, that you'll find the essence of Sydney's club culture. And it's alive and kicking. Since the early 1980s, when Sydney first felt the shock waves of a world turning on to dance music, things have grown steadily. Today, dance is fast becoming the dominant force, luring kids from the warm stability of the pubs to the sweaty, frenetic world of all-night clubbing.

Musically, this culture is diverse. Pop-techno sounds are in abundance, but those with a taste for soul, hip hop and house will also find plenty of joy out there.

In terms of venue size, however, the city is still in its infancy. While special events held sporadically throughout the year can attract huge crowds, you won't find regular clubs the size of London's Ministry of Sound or New York's The Tunnel here. Venues tend to be cosy rather than colossal, often restricted to one or two floors. Accordingly, the vibe is generally laidback and friendly. Alcohol is readily available, but not the preferred choice of intoxicant for many club-goers, so obvious drunkenness is mostly confined to the pubs.

For those used to regular pat-downs on arrival at a club, security levels will come as a pleasant surprise. To date, Sydney clubs haven't attracted much violence, and door staff are primarily employed to enforce dress codes, not to grope around in your personal effects. On the whole, door policy is fairly liberal. Dress as if you're out for a good time, and you're unlikely to have a problem.

INFORMATION

Of course, as with any healthy scene, things are changing constantly. New venues pop up weekly and one-off events are perennially popular. Details can be found in local free sheets such as *3D World* and *Beat* or on fliers, most commonly handed out along Oxford Street and stacked in record shops and cafés in the area.

Bars & Clubs

Banta Room

163 Oxford Street, Darlinghurst (9360 2528). Bus 378, 380, 382, L82. **Open** 6pm-3am Thur-Sat. **Admission** free Thur; $10 Fri, Sat. **Credit** AmEx, BC, MC, TC, V.
This well established upstairs venue has gone through more

incarnations than any other in the city, so don't be at all surprised to find it has changed again when you turn up. Standard glitterball-and-mirrored decor lends the place a late 1970s atmosphere. What you can count on is plenty of house, techno and soul spurring on an eager crowd of tourists and local clubbers.

The Basement

29 Reiby Place, Sydney (9251 2797). CityRail/ferry Circular Quay. **Open** noon-2am Mon-Thur; noon-4am Fri; 7pm-4am Sat; 7pm-2am Sun. **Tickets** $7-$25. **Credit** AmEx, BC, DC, MC, TC, V.
Despite a solid reputation as Sydney's premier jazz venue, the Basement has recently bowed to the changing times. Warm lighting and stageside dinner tables jostle for supremacy with the newer dance crowd. You can expect anything from hip hop and soul to jazz fusion in this attitude free, feel-good dance space. It has a fun clientele to match. *See also chapter* **Music: Rock, Folk & Jazz**.

Bentley Bar

320 Crown Street, Surry Hills (9331 1186). Bus 378, 380, 382, L82. **Open** 2pm-2am Mon; 2pm-3am Tue-Thur; noon-5am Fri, Sat; 10am-10pm Sun. **Admission** free. **No credit cards**.
Small, dark, very noisy and extremely sweaty, the Bentley is a mainstay of the Sydney club scene, attracting DJs keen to experiment with the latest sounds. The place started life as a pub and has evolved accordingly, with its pool tables still the centre of attention on most nights. Bentley-goers are typically locals on a week-long bender or early-morning refugees from the later Oxford Street venues. Musically, expect anything that's new and can be played loud.

Byblos

169 Oxford Street, Darlinghurst (9331 7729). Bus 378, 380, 382, L82. **Open** phone for details.
Despite its prime Oxford Street position, Byblos is a bit of a wasted opportunity for a premier dance venue. The unimaginative decor reflects the clientele: at its weekend best, the place attracts a safe, well-heeled lot who share a taste for hard house. Midweek nights see a mix of laid-back bar-hangers and slower grooves on the dancefloor. Expect to find the odd suit mingling with the Lycra-and-tan set in a mainly straight, twentysomething crowd.

Club 77

77 William Street, Woolloomooloo (9361 4981). Bus 323, 324, 325. **Open** 6pm-6am Fri-Sun. **Admission** $7-$10. **No credit cards**.
Outside the Darlinghurst scene, and a favourite of those who wouldn't be caught dead in Darlo anyway, Club 77 is an underground venue covering a broad range of musical styles: funk, hip hop, trance and jungle to name a few. This tiny space is low on attitude (and often oxygen), big on fun and proudly alternative.

DCM

31-33 Oxford Street, Darlinghurst (9267 7380). Bus 378, 380, 382. **Open** 11pm-5am Thur; 11pm-6am Fri; 11pm-9am Sat; 10pm-8am Sun. **No credit cards**.
Undoubtedly the best known dance club on the Oxford Street

strip, DCM (Don't Cry Mama) caters for serious clubbers who like their music hard and fast. The mixed gay/straight crowd loves to get near-naked and sweat it out. Lycra and highly toned flesh abound amid the dedicated party people dancing till the wee small hours to a frantic mix of house and Hi-NRG. *See also chapter* **Queer Sydney**.

The Exchange
34 Oxford Street, Darlinghurst (9331 1936). Bus 378, 380, 382. **Open** *Street bar* 9pm-3am Mon-Wed; 5pm-3am Thur, Fri; 5pm-6.30am Sat; 9am-2am Sun. *Lizard Lounge* 5pm-midnight Mon-Wed; 5pm-2am Thur; 5pm-3am Fri-Sun. *Phoenix* 10pm-4am Tue-Thur; 10pm-3am Fri; 10pm-noon Sat-Sun; 10pm-2am Sun. **Admission** free Mon-Thur, Sun; $5 Fri, Sat. **No credit cards**.
This Darlinghurst triple-deckered landmark devotes itself to slow groove on week-nights and Hi-NRG at the weekend. A favourite gay hangout, though these days the crowd tends to be more mixed. *See also chapter* **Queer Sydney**.

Kinsela's
383 Bourke Street, Darlinghurst (9331 3299). Bus 378, 380, 382, L82. **Open** 8pm-3am Tue-Sat; 7pm-midnight Sun. **Admission** ground level free; upper levels $5-$10. **No credit cards**.
At one time an inner-city funeral parlour, today Kinsela's is distinguished by its shiny deco lounge bar on the ground floor, which regularly plays host to funk bands (*see chapter* **Music: Rock, Folk & Jazz**). Upstairs, two cavernous levels are purpose-built for dancing: a small bar area makes way for the dancefloor and an impressive light show – first floor, funk; second floor, mostly house with local big-name DJs. All comers are generally welcomed midweek, but at the weekends the door policy can be tough. Dress to impress.

The Metro
624 George Street, Sydney (9264 2666). CityRail Town Hall. **Open** phone for details of dance nights. **Credit** AmEx, BC, MC, $TC, V.
Though better known as a live rock venue, this large coliseum-style theatre has played host to some of Sydney's best dance parties in recent times. While there are no regular nights, an excellent sound system and room to move ensure that many a successful one-off is held here. Check the local papers or phone for details of what's coming up. *See also chapter* **Music: Rock, Folk & Jazz**.

Mister Goodbar
11A Oxford Street, Paddington (9360 6759). Bus 378, 380, 382, L82. **Open** 4pm-3am Mon, Tue; 4pm-4am Wed, Thur; 4pm-5am Fri; 4pm-7am Sat. **Admission** by donation Mon; free Wed; $8 Thur, Sun; $10 Fri, Sat. **Credit** BC, MC, V.
Mister Goodbar is a dimly lit, warehouse-style space that refuses to allow itself any particular classification. Thursday to Sunday tends towards slow grooves with an abundance of soul, while Monday's **Brackets and Jam** is a live, folksy, amateur night that attracts the crusty crowd. For funklovers, Wednesday's **Warm Up**, often featuring live music, is the only place to be.
Disabled: access; toilets.

Q Bar
Level 2, 44 Oxford Street, Darlinghurst (9360 1375). Bus 378, 380, 382, L82. **Open** 4pm-3am Mon, Tue; 4pm-4am Wed, Thur; 4pm-5am Fri; 4pm-7am Sat. **Admission** free. **Credit** BC, DC, JCB, MC, V.
More of a pool hall than a club (*see p183*), but if you're torn between dancing and playing the tables, this is the place to go. Despite the restrictions of the postage stamp of a dancefloor, Q still manages to attract the weekend punters with a reasonable sound system, pumping out mainly funk and hip hop. A stronger draw, perhaps, is the fact that there is no door charge and there's a late licence at the weekend.

Retro
Angel Place Brasserie, 1 Angel Place, between Pitt and George Streets, Sydney (9223 2220). CityRail Martin Place. **Open** phone for details.
A relatively new club whose name is on everyone's lips thanks to the rebirth of glam. A hefty $15 cover charge gets you in to three large rooms. Expect a young crowd, packed wall-to-wall, and DJs spinning the best and worst of the 1970s and 1980s.

Riva
130 Castlereagh Street, Sydney (9286 6666). CityRail St James or Town Hall. **Open** 10pm-4am Thur-Sat. **Admission** $8 Wed; $12 Thur, Fri; $15 Sat. **Credit** BC, MC, V.
If DCM occupies one end of the spectrum, Riva sits right at the other. Located beneath the Sheraton on the Park in the CBD, this place tends to attract very straight, label-conscious office types who are mostly looking to pull. Commercial dance music is favoured above all else and deviants are discouraged. Swanky.

The Rooftop
Kings Cross Hotel, corner of Victoria Street and William Street, Kings Cross (9368 1486). CityRail Kings Cross. **Open** 11pm-6am Fri, Sat. **Admission** $15-$20. **No credit cards**.
For sweeping views of Kings Cross and the city, the top floor of this Hotel is hard to beat. In previous incarnations a regular venue for indie rock followers, the Rooftop now tends to play host to one-off weekend parties, drawing the dance crowd for liberal helpings of house and hip hop. There's always a door charge and the 100-step climb to the roof is a chore, but usually worth it.

Soho
171 Victoria Street, Potts Point (9358 4221). CityRail Kings Cross. **Open** noon-2am Mon-Thur, Sun; noon-5am Fri, Sat. **Admission** free. **No credit cards**.
From its heyday as an indie rock venue in the 1980s, the small, elegant Soho bar has metamorphosed beautifully to become a hot spot for local clubbers of all denominations. Monday night is **Sight**, favouring laid-back beats from dub to trip hop, while weekend DJs favour house.

Taxi Club
40-42 Flinders Street Darlinghurst (9331 4256). Bus 378, 380, 382. **Open** 9am-6am Mon-Fri; 24 hours Sat, Sun. **Admission** (after midnight Fri-Sun) $2 members; $5 non-members. **No credit cards**.
To experience Sydney in all its glorious diversity the Taxi Club is the first place to head for. Where else can you find pokie-playing seniors and wayward suburbanites mixing it with high-camp disco bunnies, trannies and drag queens? The sounds of disco divas from past to present reverberate through a new sound system over two levels. There's no door policy and it's open till late morning (and sometimes beyond). *See also chapter* **Queer Sydney**.

Underground Cafe
22 Bayswater Road, Kings Cross (9358 4676). CityRail Kings Cross. **Open** *café* 6pm-11pm Thur-Sat; *dance club* 11pm-dawn Thur-Sat. **Admission** free Thur; $6 Fri; $12 Sat. **Credit** AmEx.
As the name suggests, this is a dark and brooding establishment that's solely dedicated to joys of the serious all-night house party. The crowd is young and energetic, the music loud and fast, and it's open till 7am most days of the week. The door can be pricey for weekend events and one-offs, but it's free on Thursdays.

Disco divas dance their socks off at **DCM**.
See page 179.

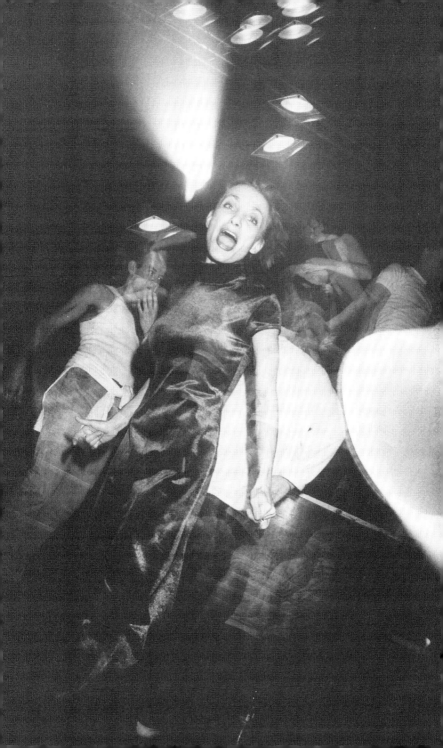

Comedy & Cabaret

Despite a lack of regular venues, the local comedy scene has struggled along bravely for the past decade or so. And it hasn't been an easy task: if you're talking tough audiences, Sydneysiders are up there with the worst of them.

More a subculture than an entertainment force, comedy in Sydney is pretty much confined to a couple of specific, dedicated venues that do their utmost to support the fledgling scene. At these places the bill is varied enough to include the occasional international star as well as a novice braving hecklers for the first time.

The best known and most accessible of the venues is the **Harold Park Hotel** in Glebe. A simple, no-frills, suburban pub, this place has long been a supporter of both local and interstate comic talent. It's also a favourite of US comic Robin Williams, who has graced the place with his powerful presence twice in recent years. A regular session on Mondays is **Comics in the Park**, a stand-up night (admission $5) with an open-mike section for talented (and not so talented) nobodies, which has launched many a successful Australian career. Seasonal shows are advertised, cost between $12 and $15, and generally run for a few weeks at a time.

Alternatively, there's **The Comedy Store**, in Petersham. This place is Sydney's original cabaret-style comedy nightclub and punters are encouraged to take up the dinner-and-show deals that are available six nights a week.

Another venue to keep an eye on is the **Harbourside Brasserie**, a jazz and cabaret venue at Pier 1, overlooking Walsh Bay near the Harbour Bridge. The L-shaped room can make for odd viewing angles, so book a table with a clear view of the stage.

The Comedy Store

450 Parramatta Road, Petersham (9564 3900). CityRail Petersham. **Open** *Front bar* 5pm-midnight Tue-Thur, Sun; 5pm-1am Fri, Sat. **Performances** from 8.30pm Tue-Sun; *extra shows* from 11pm Fri, Sat. **Admission** $6-$25; $21-$40 (incl dinner). **Credit** AmEx, BC, MC, V.
Disabled: access; toilets.

Harbourside Brasserie

Pier 1, Hickson Road, Walsh Bay (9252 3000). CityRail/ferry Circular Quay then 15-minute walk. **Open** 6pm-midnight Mon-Fri; 6pm-2am Sat, Sun. **Tickets** $6-$25. **Credit** AmEx, BC, MC, V.

Harold Park Hotel

115 Wigram Road, Glebe (9552 2999). Bus 433. **Open** *hotel* 11am-midnight daily; *theatre* 8-11pm Mon, Wed-Sat. **Tickets** $5-$15. **Credit** AmEx, BC, MC, V.

The Tilbury

Corner of Forbes Street and Nicholson Street, Woolloomooloo (9368 1955). Bus 311. **Open** 11am-11pm Mon-Sat; noon-10pm Sun. **Performances** 9-11pm Mon-Fri; 2-4pm, 8-10pm, Sun. **Admission** (booking essential) $25 Mon-Thur; $27 Fri, Sat; $15-$20 Sun. **Credit** AmEx, BC, MC, V.

Pool Halls

In recent years, Sydney has gone pool mad. When you walk into a Sydney pub, chances are the centre of attention, apart from the alcohol, is going to be a rectangle of green baize.

Anyone is welcome to play, but competition, even over friendly games, is intense, especially in the inner-city pubs. Beginners are barely tolerated when the tables are full, particularly on Fridays, which is universally regarded as pub night.

Accordingly, competitions abound – often for cash prizes. For a couple of dollars you can try your hand, but unless you're an accomplished player, the thrill of competition is about all you'll get out of it. There are some pool sharks around, but not too many. Although it's not unheard of for regular games to be played for cash in some joints, it's probably a good idea to get to know a place before putting your money on the line.

As with most pub games, rules vary from place to place, and are usually displayed near the tables. Don't make the mistake of assuming international rules: in most cases, it's the regulars who decide what's what on their tables.

For the dedicated player, a smattering of purpose-built pool halls can be found throughout the inner-city areas, typically identified by a steep set of stairs with a cheap neon sign at the front. While the standard can be high in these places, they are often not the best venues in which to play: the

atmosphere is less than electric, the music is bad, and you can't drink. A better bet is to check out one of the pub-based pool halls. Though they tend to be a little more expensive, you're sure of finding a livelier crowd and having a better time all round.

Palace Hotel

122 Flinders Street, Surry Hills (9361 5170). Bus 339, 372, 373, 397, 398, 399. **Open** 4pm-midnight Mon-Wed; 4pm-1am Thur-Sat; 4-11pm Sun. **Credit** AmEx, BC, MC, $TC, V.

One of the best pool halls in the city, this two-storey Surry Hills pub is perfect for a quiet drink and a game. The place has been recently renovated, the equipment's brand new, there's plenty of space, and at the time of writing the tables still cost just two dollars a game.

Pavilion Bar at the Beach Road Hotel

71 Beach Road, Bondi (9130 7247). Bus 389. **Open** noon-midnight Mon-Thur; noon-1am Fri, Sat; 10.30am-10pm Sun. **No credit cards**.

For great atmosphere, cheap drinks and quality pool, it's hard to go past the upstairs bar of the Pavilion Hotel at Bondi Beach. It's a favourite of young indie types all through the week, and for obvious reasons: the combination of a great sound system, occasional bands and pool tables to spare makes this the best bar in Bondi. Week-nights tend to be

calm, while Saturdays are lively, but it's Sunday night (and the added attraction of live music) that really packs them in.

Planet Pool

Corner of Regent and Broadway Streets, Sydney (9211 2321). CityRail Central. **Open** 10am-midnight Mon-Sat. **Admission** free. **No credit cards**.

Just a few minutes from the city centre, Planet Pool is the newest of the inner-Sydney pool halls. A cavernous old pub, it was recently decked out with new tables to cater for the swelling numbers of pool devotees. A favourite with students from the nearby universities.

Q Bar

See page 180 for listings.

Pay a deposit for a pair of cues, and a designated table is yours for a while – how long exactly depends on how busy the place is. On the up side, you're always assured of getting a game. On the down side, the cues are shabby and the tables are old, looking better designed for snooker than pool.

Soho

See page 180 for listings.

At $3 a game, Soho is always going to be a pretty expensive night of stick. What makes up for the cost, is a couple of dozen new tables, good cues and great music. The popularity of this place means there can be long queues on Friday and Saturday nights, leading to a crush inside. Arrive early.

Place your bets

As has been said, Australians are consummate gamblers (*see chapter* **Sport & Fitness**). If you've got the inclination, and the money to spare, the casino can provide a great night out, as even if you don't intend to gamble, it's the perfect place to observe a broad cross-section of Sydneysiders at play.

Currently, the Sydney Harbour Casino is housed in a temporary space by Darling Harbour, a modest 150-table affair sitting on an old finger wharf that reaches out into Pyrmont Bay. As yet, there's little Vegas-style glitz in evidence. Apart from the mandatory neon signage at the front, it's a relatively conservative structure as far as casinos go.

But this is set to change dramatically. Even at the time of writing, the new permanent site was beginning to take shape across the road and, given the $867 million being poured into the project (which will include a theatre, ten restaurants and bars, and a five-star hotel), it promises to be one of the most imposing landmarks in the area.

And probably the tackiest. Not content with being second best to the Americans, the casino's owners announced grand plans for a series of themed rooms, bars and restaurants – inspired by a fact-finding visit to Las Vegas and Atlantic City in 1996. From what are being described as 'desert-style' interiors and giant glass waterfalls to a 'rainforest lobby', these lavish interiors are supposed to reflect Australia's native flora and fauna in all its diversity, over several floors. 'Gobsmackingly gaudy' is how one city newspaper has described the plans.

Until then, though, visitors will have to be content with something a little less adventurous. The temporary site, to give it credit, is fully functional and can be fun. While the decor is dull – standard hotel lighting and fixtures – all the usual gaming tables are present: blackjack, baccarat, roulette, plus some more unusual ones like Sic Bo and Pai Gow (Chinese card games that cater for the city's large Sino-presence). Then there's the traditional Aussie coin game, Two Up, previously only legal on Anzac Day, a public holiday, but now allowed in casinos as well. For the less savvy gambler there's even a simple chocolate wheel.

A handful of tables play a $5 limit, but most bets are set at $10 and over. There are four bars well-stocked bars, but, unlike Vegas practice, you must pay for every drink you order here. On the weekends, live music is a plus, although most acts tend to be straight-up rock 'n' roll or gimmicky cover bands.

And remember, if your luck's down on the tables, there's always the horses: a separate TAB area allows visitors to bet on races being run all over the country.

Sydney Harbour Casino

Wharves 12 & 13, Pyrmont Bay, next to Darling Harbour (9777 9079/1300 300 711). CityRail Town Hall/monorail Exhibition Centre then free shuttle bus every 10 min). **Open** 24 hours daily. **Admission** free. **Credit** AmEx, BC, DC, JCB, MC, TC, V. *Disabled: access, toilets.*

Film

From blockbusters on George Street to Jackie Chan in Chinatown or arthouse flix in Paddington, movie-going in Sydney is just fine and Dendy.

Sydney is a great town for going to the movies. Everything is available and in abundance, with both arthouse and mainstream films easily accessible within a small area. However, despite the arthouse explosion of the late 1980s, there is no 'scene', no coterie of hardcore enthusiasts who congregate on a regular basis at a particular venue to discuss the medium they love. This is probably because there is no national film theatre or large film society that encourages the appreciation of film and its history. If there is a gaping hole in Sydney's film scene, it's the fact that none of the film organisations take responsibility for importing curated seasons of classic, genre or national cinema. Most of the work in this area comes from the limited though excellent resources of the National Film Library.

However, as you'll see from our guide below, most 'marginal' areas of contemporary cinema are well represented – from gay to foreign or cult or classic, you'll find it here somewhere. And as in most large cities there's a movie strip. In Sydney it's George Street, just south of the Town Hall, where the three major chain multi-screens sit side by side, surrounded by huge amusement arcades, pool halls and bars. Across the road is Planet Hollywood. It's a tacky, run-down bit of town – but hey, once you're inside a darkened auditorium it doesn't really matter, right?

First Run

There are a lot and they're everywhere. If you're hankering after the latest from Tom, Arnie or Jim, it's best to stay close to the city centre and sample one of several multi-screens there. Sydney's endless suburban sprawl is to be avoided, especially if you're new to the city and all that is required is a modest, mainstream night at the flicks. And besides, the handkerchief-size screens that plague the heavily populated shopping-malls in the suburban centres are no fun.

TICKETS & INFORMATION

First-run movies open on Thursdays. Ticket queues in the city cinemas tend to be orderly and brisk. Prices are usually $12 for adults with concessions for children, senior citizens, students and the unemployed. Tuesday night is bargain

night, when adult tickets cost $8.50 and concessions are generally reduced to $4.50.

To find out screening times, phone the venue or look in the Metro supplement of the *Sydney Morning Herald* (out on Friday), or one of the weekly listings freebies like *Drum* or *Beat*. There is a saturation of movie reviewing in Sydney: you'll be bombarded with opinions in the daily press, free sheets or on television and radio.

Bondi Plaza Cinema

500 Oxford Street, Bondi Junction (9389 5877). CityRail Bondi Junction. **Tickets** $6-£10 adults; $4-$7.50 concessions. **No credit cards.**
Suburban multi-screen situated amid the shopping malls of Bondi Junction.
Disabled: access; toilets.

Greater Union on George Street

525 George Street, Sydney (9267 8666). CityRail Town Hall. **Tickets** $12 adults; $7-$9 concessions. **Credit** AmEx, BC, MC, V.
This six-screen, noisy, cavernous and generally packed multiplex offers an ambience akin to a shopping mall – complete with fairy lights and shiny surfaces. The latest releases get the big digital sound treatment, but presentation quality of sound and image is erratic. On a good night, though, it's the best of the city centre bunch.
Disabled: access; toilets.

Hoyts

505 George Street, Sydney (information 13 2700/box office 9267 9877). CityRail Town Hall. **Tickets** $12 adults; $7.50-$9 concessions. **Credit** AmEx, BC, MC, V.
The first of the city's multi-screen centres, and boy does it show. Aircraft hangar-like and antiseptic, Hoyts has hardly touched the sprayed-concrete decor and carpet that must have looked très chic in 1977, and now just looks… dated. It's all here: the video games; the poster shop; the expensive ice cream; and, best of all, the overwhelming aroma of popcorn that hits you as soon as you enter one of its seven darkened, cacophonous auditoriums. It's a great place to see a blockbuster because the screens on the mezzanine level are huge. Presentation, however, is a bit hit-and-miss. The fare on view ranges from B-movie horror to *Braveheart* to the latest Bertolucci. Friday/Saturday-night late shows of Jackie Chan and action cinema are a speciality.
Disabled: access; toilets.

IMAX

Darling Harbour, Pyrmont. Information from Darling Harbour Visitors Centre (9286 0111).
The bumblebee yellow and black chequerboard bulk of the new IMAX centre hadn't yet opened when we went to press. The $20 million complex boasts a 540-seat theatre and a movie screen eight-storeys high, as well as a restaurant (under the aegis of Neil 'Rockpool' Perry), a theatre and a

function centre. Phone the visitors centre or check the local press for more details.

Pitt Centre
232 Pitt Street, Sydney (9264 1694). CityRail Town Hall. **Tickets** $12 adults; $7.50-$9 concessions. **Credit** BC, MC, V.
Located opposite the Hilton Hotel, this is one of the city's best cinemas in every respect. It offers the latest in 'quality commercial cinema' (recent showings include *Quiz Show* and *Ed Wood*) and difficult-to-market art movies. It is also the second major venue for the Sydney Film Festival. There is excellent presentation in terms of sound, image quality and screen size, with comfortable seating in all three cinemas and polite service. The crowd is middle-brow to grunge, depending on the picture.

Randwick Ritz
43 St Paul's Street, Randwick (9399 9840). Bus 314, 372. **Tickets** $7 adults; $3-$5 concessions. **No credit cards**.
A beautiful old art deco cinema scheduled to be turned into a suburban four-screen multiplex. It currently shows mostly first-run material.
Disabled: access; toilets.

Stanmore Cinema Centre
200 Parramatta Road, Stanmore (9569 0488). CityRail Stanmore. **Tickets** $10 adults; $6.50-$7 concessions. **No credit cards**.
A favourite with inner-city yuppies in spite of poor sound and picture quality, and seats that are a tad uncomfortable. There are bargain-priced Sunday double bills.

Village Cinema
545 George Street, Sydney (9264 6701). CityRail Town Hall. **Tickets** $12 adults; $7.50-$9 concessions. **No credit cards**.
A centre for blockbusters with six screens and 1970s decor (the 'giant's acne' ceiling finish in Cinema Two has to be seen to be believed). The women's toilets are too few and the queues are long, but the seating is comfortable. Presentation in both sound and image, as with the other George Street centres, varies. Don't go and see anything screening in Cinema Six – it's no better than watching a large TV.
Disabled: access; toilets.

Walker Cinema
121 Walker Street, North Sydney (9959 4222). CityRail North Sydney. **Tickets** $12 adults; $7.50-$9 concessions (all tickets $7.50 Mon). **No credit cards**.
A tiny screen in the heart of one of Sydney's most boring suburbs (which doubles as the city's major business centre), with a programme brief similar to that of the Village Double Bay Twin (*see p189*).
Disabled: access.

(*see p189*)

Arthouse

Academy Twin Cinema
3A Oxford Street, Paddington (9361 4453). CityRail Museum. **Tickets** $12 adults; $9 concessions. **No credit cards**.
One of the city's longest-running art cinemas, situated in the heart of Sydney's 'pink strip', the Academy is fittingly home to the Gay and Lesbian Film Festival, held every year during Mardi Gras (*see chapter* **Sydney by Season**). With an excellent array of restaurants nearby, it's perfect for a night out. Recently refitted with comfortable seats, the main screen is quite simply one of the best in Sydney. Programming comprises 'quality' cinema and foreign-language films.

Chauvel Cinema
Paddington Town Hall, corner of Oatley Road and Oxford Street, Paddington (9361 5398). Bus 380, 382. **Tickets** $11.50 adults; $6.50-$8.50 concessions. **Credit** BC, MC, V.
Once considered the doghouse of Sydney's cinema scene, the Chauvel, situated in the beautiful Paddington Town Hall, has become a superb provider of arthouse and quality mainstream presentations. Refitted and renovated in 1995, it now offers a spacious foyer and a fine bar (though small). It's the venue for the Australian Film Institute's (AFI) screenings, so for an annual membership fee of around $60, you can see the year's new Australian films in a matter of weeks during August and September. As in the old days, when the theatre was managed by the AFI, the programme still includes 'marginal' fare – recent seasons include an enormously successful night of shorts from indigenous directors. Projection and seating is fine in the main cinema. The theatrette is very small but comfortable, and has excellent sound. As the Chauvel is still home to Sydney's National Cinematheque (*see p189*), it attracts plenty of crusty, not-so-old cineastes; eavesdropping on ferocious arguments is recommended.
Disabled: access; toilets.

(*see p189*)

Cremorne Orpheum
380 Military Road, Cremorne (9908 4344). Bus 228, 229, 230, 257. **Tickets** $12 adults; $7.50-$9 concessions. **Credit** BC, MC, V.
The jewel in the crown of Sydney cinemas? Possibly. Certainly there is nothing like it anywhere else in the city. For sheer chutzpah, grace and style the Cremorne is outstanding and it's worth crossing town to see its glittering art deco splendour. The main cinema features a huge organ (played before the main evening show at the weekend) and offers great sightlines and seating design. The screen is big and so is the sound. A new screen, called the Vergona, recently opened in the complex and follows the main

---

Hong Kong viewing

Chinatown is centred around the pedestrianised Dixon Street, south of Liverpool Street in Haymarket. This compact area boasts five excellent cinemas that feature the latest in Hong Kong mainstream cinema. Look out for the Hoover on Goulburn Street, one of the oldest cinemas in Sydney. This is where the Jackie Chan/John Woo cult started in Australia. New films arrive thick and fast from Hong Kong – and depart almost as quickly, so it's worth going every week if you're into that sort of thing. Viewing is scheduled by the double feature with older material filling out the bill, which is great because you can catch up on current releases or just enjoy an old favourite. And after the pictures, a night out in Chinatown awaits.

Newest of the art cinemas is the chic **Verona**. *See page 188.*

See page 188.

*For giant screens and wrap-around sound, head for the **Hoyts Centre**. See page 185.*

auditorium's art deco style. The other two cinemas are good, but aim for a Saturday evening session in the Big One. The programme is based on quality arthouse output, but the 'nostalgia seasons' are a blast – recent hits include *All About Eve* and *An Affair to Remember*. It also screens 70mm specials at weekends, and occasionally breaks ground: in August 1995 it made a hit out of Philip Kaufman's *The Right Stuff*, a flop in Australia on its initial 1984 release.

Dendy Cinema

19 Martin Place, Sydney (9233 8166). CityRail Martin Place. **Tickets** $11.50 adults; $7-$8.50 concessions. **Credit** AmEx, BC, DC, MC, V.
Once upon a time (well, in the 1980s) this was something of a risk-taker and a trend-setter. These days the Dendy's programme of mostly foreign-language Film Festival prizewinners looks positively *de rigueur*. The Dendy brought a new, aggressive style of marketing to the Sydney film scene – closer to rock 'n' roll cool than the slightly cerebral atmosphere that most arthouses try to cultivate. The Martin Place location, recently renovated, offers a trendy bar/restaurant full of beautiful people and equally breath-taking prices. Inside, the cinema is small, but the sound and image are fine and the seats are great.
Disabled: access; toilets.

Dendy Cinema

624 George Street, Sydney (9264 1577). CityRail Town Hall. **Tickets** $11.50 adults; $7-$8.50 concessions. **Credit** AmEx, BC, DC, MC, V.
Opposite the Hoyts Centre and in the same building as the city's top music venue, the Metro, this is the best of the Dendys. Its decor is the bastard son of 1970s futurism and 1930s art deco. The roomy foyer, with bar and lounge, is at the top of very steep stairs. The auditorium is wonderful, with a sharp incline providing excellent sightlines to the big screen and good sound. Programming tends to be more accessible than at other Dendy sites – *Reservoir Dogs* played here.
Disabled: access; toilets.

Dendy Cinema

261 King Street, Newtown (9550 5699). CityRail Newtown. **Tickets** $11.50 adults; $7-$8.50 concessions. **Credit** AmEx, BC, DC, MC, V.
A former supermarket in one of Sydney's best inner-city

suburbs which has been converted into a complex housing a bar, restaurant, music shop and cinema. Newtown is a potent mix of yuppie and grunge, working-class pensioners, poor students and gay/lesbian chic. So naturally the Dendy programmes accordingly. Its well placed for a night out, nestled among excellent pubs and some of the best cheap restaurants – especially Thai – around. Inside, the cinemas are smallish, with multiplex-size screens and OK sound and projection.
Disabled: access; toilets.

Valhalla

166D Glebe Point Road, Glebe (9660 8050). Bus 431, 433, 438. **Tickets** $11.50 adults; $6-$8 concessions. **No credit cards**.
Smack in the middle of one of the leafiest inner-city suburbs and surrounded by good cafés and bookshops. What was once an outstanding, outsized single-screen repertory cinema, retaining faded 1930s glory, has been converted into an excellent, two-screen, first-run theatre. The repertory stuff has been sidelined to Sundays, late-night screenings and Saturday matinées (at the latter, admission includes an orange drink and a bag of sweets). Managed and programmed by a hardline movie buff, the Valhalla is one of the few risk-taking cinemas in Sydney: it dares to run feature documentaries. Mostly, though, it programmes first-run material, which can be safely hip or just plain off-the-wall, for a largely youthful audience (recent titles include *Trainspotting, Richard III* and *Suture*). Repertory here tends to cover the more predictable cult films with such chestnuts as *Eraserhead, A Clockwork Orange* and *Harold and Maude* haunting the screening list year after year. Inside, the cinemas are comfortable with fittings that include lovely hand-carved armrests on well padded, 1930s-style seats. Good screen size, fine projection and (particularly downstairs) BIG sound. Arrive early, as big queues are another feature. Also on offer are bargain nights and subscriber discounts.
Disabled: access; toilets (Cinema One only).

Verona

17 Oxford Street, Paddington (9360 6099). Bus 378, 380. **Tickets** $12 adults; $7.50-$9 concessions. **No credit cards**.
Despite some impressively designed decor, the newest of the art cinemas is a disappointment in many respects. For

a start, you have to queue on the street for tickets, unprotected from noisy traffic, the cold and, in summer, the heat. Once inside, the foyer is up several steep flights of stairs. On the second floor, there is a bar/café packed to the rafters with beautiful people who aren't there for the movies (*see* chapter **Restaurants** for more details). The screens in all four cinemas are no bigger than you'd find in a good local. The high-backed seats feel comfortable for about 20 minutes. The films tend to be standard arthouse fare mixed with more schmaltzy, middle-brow Hollywood stuff. Monday is cheap night.
Disabled: access; toilets.

Village Double Bay Twin Cinemas

377 New South Head Road, Double Bay (9327 1003). CityRail Edgecliff. **Tickets** $12 adults; $4.50-$9 concessions. **No credit cards.**
If you can drag your eyes off the price tags in the boutiques that line the main drag of this pretty neighbourhood, try this cinema duo for the 'soft' end of the market – the latest Woody Allen or sweet-natured French flicks – that its middle-brow, largely middle-aged audience seem to love. It is also technically one of Sydney's best cinemas with fine sound and image, and comfy seating.
Disabled: access (Cinema Two only).

Classic, Cult & Experimental

Third Eye Cinema

64 Devonshire Street, Surry Hills (9281 1191). CityRail Central. **Tickets** $11.50 adults; $6-$8.50 concessions. **Credit** AmEx, BC, DC, MC, TC, V.
A pokey little theatrette in a grungy part of town just outside Central Station. It runs Asian softcore porn and recently introduced a programme of cult classics ranging from Tarkovsky and Godard to Warhol and Waters. Beware: battered prints are a feature. Upstairs is Govinda's Movie Room, which shows arthouse flicks; punters lounge on beanbags and share a fixed-price buffet ($13.50 per person).

National Cinematheque

Chauvel Cinema (see p186 for listings). **Shows** 7.30pm Mon. **Tickets** four-night pass $15 adults; $12 concessions. **Credit** BC, MC, V.
A year-long programme on Monday nights. Hardcore cineastes mix with curiosity-seekers and would-be cultists as they soak up an enormous range of important films from all eras. There are plans to introduce talks and special screenings.

Festivals

Festival of Jewish Cinema

Academy Twin Cinema (see p186). **Date** November.
Annual gathering of international Yiddish fare.

Flickerfest

Box 52, Sydney, NSW 2000 (9262 4777/9331 4547/ fax 9262 4774). **Date** January.
An outdoor travelling film festival of international and Australian shorts held every summer. The venue is usually Bondi Pavilion, but phone to check first.

Gay & Lesbian Mardi Gras Film Festival

Information from Queer Screen, PO Box 1081, Darlinghurst, NSW 2010 (9332 4938/fax 9331 2988/email info@queerscreen. com. au). **Date** February.
Queer Screen organises the annual Gay & Lesbian Film Festival as part of the month-long Mardi Gras festival. For more on Gay and Lesbian Mardi Gras, *see chapters* **Sydney by Season** *and* **Queer Sydney.**

Sydney Film Festival

405 Glebe Point Road, Glebe, NSW 2037 (9660 3909/9660 3844/ticket enquiries 9320 9000). **Date** June.
One of the oldest movie fests in the world, the Sydney Film Festival was started in the 1950s by buffs hungry for foreign cinema. It has evolved into a slick, high-profile, two-week orgy of international film, which screens up to 250 movies in two venues every winter (beginning on the Queen's Birthday weekend in early June). Because it began as a purely cultural, non-profit event there is a good feeling of camaraderie about it. It is an audience-oriented festival (non-competitive in the features section and generally marketing-free) so the programming can be freewheeling and is heavily dependent on the tastes or prejudices of the Festival Director, whose only brief is to 'find great cinema'. The Festival includes the Dendy Awards, which are open to Australian short film-makers working in all genres. Regular highlights include a major retrospective and meet-the-film-maker forums. There are also seminars on issues of film culture. The major screening venue is the State Theatre (*see chapter* **Theatre & Dance**), one of the world's last remaining picture palaces – all magnificent marble and chandeliers, and with the best seats in town.

Tropfest: The Tropicana Film Festival

Suite 24, 2A Bayswater Road, Kings Cross, NSW 2011 (9368 0434/fax 9356 4531). CityRail Kings Cross. **Dates** February.
A free, one-night, outdoor festival held every February outside one of the hippest Darlinghurst cafés (the Tropicana, *see chapter* **Cafés & Bars**). It's frequented by actors, directors and writers – the sort of place where the patrons dive *en masse* for their mobiles at the faintest electronic tinkle. The event features short films made specially for the festival; it's full of industry heavies and great fun. Approximately 300 shorts are also screened in various cafés along Victoria Street throughout March.

Women on Women

PO Box 552, Paddington, NSW 2021 (9332 2408/9332 4584/fax 9331 7145).
Women in Film & Television (WIFT) organises the annual Women on Women film festival, featuring short and feature-length work by new and established talent. Membership of WIFT costs $60 (adults) or $40 (concessions). The festival is held at the Chauvel (*see p186*). Contact WIFT for more details.

Organisations

Alliance Française

257 Clarence Street, Sydney, NSW 2000 (9267 1755/ fax 9283 2549). CityRail Town Hall. **Open** 9.30am-7pm Mon-Thur; 9.30am-5pm Fri; 9am-3pm Sat.
An institution that aims to encourage French culture and has helped organise the French Film Festival in the past.

Filmwest

PO Box 153, Milperra, NSW 2214 (9774 2043).
A community screening programme designed to bolster film culture in Sydney's heavily populated western suburbs, which are well served by multiplexes but not much else. Filmwest has run a small festival since 1994, combined with fortnightly community screenings.
Website at: http://www.mcarthur.uws.edu.au/filmwest

Goethe Institute

90 Ocean Street, PO Box 37, Woollahra, NSW 2025 (9328 7411). CityRail Edgecliff. **Open** noon-3pm, 5-8pm, Mon, Tue; noon-3pm Wed-Fri.
The institute encourages appreciation of German culture and has an excellent record in promoting the study of German film-makers.

Matinaze

First floor, 168 Day Street, Sydney, NSW 2000 (9264 7225/fax 9267 8539/email sinsite@ozemail.com.au).
The Sydney Intermedia Network (SIN) is a community-based group of hardcore enthusiasts, film-makers and technicians working in experimental alternative film and video, and multimedia. It puts on two or three shows or exhibitions a year.

Education & Information

In addition to the Museum of Contemporary Art (*see below*), other museums that screen films are the Australian Museum and the Art Gallery of NSW (*see chapter* **Museums & Galleries**).

Australian Film Institute

Information (9332 2111/fax 9331 7145).
The AFI programmes screenings of Australian shorts and documentaries at the Chauvel and runs the National Cinematheque (*see above for both*). It also organises film discussion evenings and the Australian version of the Academy Awards (AFI Awards).

Australian Film TV and Radio School

Corner of Epping and Balaclava Roads, North Ryde (9805 6611/fax 9887 1030). CityRail Epping.
Holds special talks and screenings involving both local and overseas directors, writers, producers and technicians. Recent highlights include visits by Mike Leigh, Jane Campion, Chris

Noonan and Joel Coen. The school also has an excellent library of books, tapes, laser discs and CD-ROMs.

The Cinestore

37 Liverpool Street, Sydney (9283 3049/fax 9283 3035). CityRail Town Hall. **Open** 9.30am-5pm Mon-Fri; 11am-4pm Sat, Sun. **Credit** AmEx, BC, MC, $TC, V.
It looks a little ropey, but there is no other bookshop like it in the world. The excellent library specialises in technical film texts, scriptwriting 'how to' books and film fanzines. There is a huge range of original Hollywood scripts on sale – many of them new releases. Scriptwriting software is also available. And it all comes with expert advice.

Museum of Contemporary of Art

140 George Street, The Rocks (9252 4033/fax 9252 4361). CityRail Circular Quay. **Open** 10am-6pm daily.
Admission $8 adults; $5 concessions. **Credit** AmEx, BC, DC, MC, $TC, V.
Recent events held at the MCA have included The Dawn of Cinema, a superbly curated, comprehensive look at early cinema. The museum's major long-term project is the establishment of a permanent National Cinematheque based on the Parisian model. Funds are currently being raised to establish a purpose-built cinema for it.

WEA Film Group

72 Bathurst Street, Sydney, NSW 2000 (9949 1613).
Runs film appreciation study groups that overflow with aggressive opinions, and it regularly screens difficult or rarely obtainable material.

Sydney, camera, action!

Sydney has a wonderful Harbour, a big bridge and a magnificent Opera House – but you won't see them on the big screen very much (the small screen is a different matter).

Film production in Sydney tends to be low-key, with most of the high-budget activity in advertising. The feature film and TV production industry is still mainly funded through government tax concessions and the support of federal government bodies such as the Film Finance Corporation and the Australian Film Commission, which means the films are usually low-budget. Filming in a major city is notoriously expensive and logistically difficult. For that reason – unless it's something to do with cultural cringe or sheer modesty – Sydney's tourist spots and man-made wonders don't get much of a celluloid look-in. If you want to make a movie in Sydney, contact the state's major funding body, the NSW Film and TV Office, Level 6, 1 Francis Street, Sydney NSW 2000 (9380 5599/fax 9360 1090).

Once in a while, though, Sydney does get to star in the movies. The following are some of the city's recent bit-parts:

In 1981 the streets of Kings Cross, Woolloomooloo and the Harbour Bridge formed the backdrop to Phillip Noyce's conspiracy

thriller and urban horror movie **Heatwave**, starring Judy Davis. The leafy Royal Botanic Gardens featured in Ray Lawrence's 1985 adaptation of Peter Carey's novel **Bliss**. It's still good for a stroll. Central Station and a rain-soaked, hard-to-recognise Harbour Bridge put in a brief appearance before Billy Zane storms on board in **Dead Calm** (Phillip Noyce again, 1988), whilst the altogether more civilised terraces and Victorian mansions of Glebe are where Lisa Harrow and Kerry Fox reside in **The Last Days of Chez Nous** (Gillian Armstrong, 1991).

Sydney's larger-than-life Newtown drag scene opens and closes the **Adventures of Priscilla, Queen of the Desert** (Stephan Elliott, 1994), while Toni Collette dreams of **Muriel's Wedding** (PJ Hogan, 1994) in a video shop on Oxford Street. The old quadrangle of Sydney University doubles as a mental institution in the 1996 Oz hit **Cosi**, whose inmates witness a memorably bad performance at the open-air Bondi Beach Pavilion; and finally, if you're travelling out of town, you can check out Norman Lindsay's house in the Blue Mountains, setting for John Duigan's 1994 *Sirens* (*see* **The Far Side** *in chapter* **Sightseeing** *and chapter* **Trips Out of Town**.

Music: Classical & Opera

Performers and venues are few and far between, but the city's classical music fans are many and keen.

Given that Australians fancy themselves as sports-mad, outdoors types, stoked by myths of soldiering, sheep farming and generally rugged behaviour, they are surprisingly enthusiastic about the rarefied pleasures of classical music. On any given evening, the sweet strains of a symphony orchestra, choir or opera production can be heard issuing out across the harbour from Sydney's iconic Opera House, the principal classical venue.

Venues

Classical music in Sydney is provided by a handful of key organisations, all of which have a keen following in the city. They concentrate on the halls of the **Opera House**, fanning out to smaller venues around the city when the occasion arises. Because Australia is such a massive continent and so distant from overseas centres, national tours are expensive and promoters operate on the principle of 'the bigger, the better' when it comes to choice of concert hall.

That Sydney doesn't have a recital space – quartets usually have to make use of the 2,700-seat Concert Hall of the Opera House – is a cause for constant political agitation on the part of music-lovers. The **Eugene Goossens Hall**, a less awesome space in the Australian Broadcasting Corporation's (ABC) Ultimo headquarters, is often used for smaller ensembles playing contemporary music. **Sydney Town Hall** (*see chapter Sightseeing*) is also used for contemporary music and for some recitals. **Churches** are popular venues for recitals, but are pressed into secular service irregularly; a guide to church music can be found in the *Sydney Morning Herald* Metro supplement, published on Fridays. Surprisingly, in a city as balmy as Sydney in summer, there are few outdoor performances. The main ones to look out for are the Australian Opera's **Opera in the Park** and the Sydney Symphony Orchestra's **Symphony in the Park**, which take place in January. And in September, watch out for the Spring Festival of New Music, run by Australian

Rehearsing in **Sydney Town Hall**.

pianist Roger Woodward (*see chapter* **Sydney by Season** for details of all three).

Eugene Goossens Hall

ABC Ultimo Centre, 700 Harris Street, Ultimo (9333 1500/fax 9333 1104). CityRail Central.

Sydney Opera House

Bennelong Point, Circular Quay (box office 9250 7777/information 9250 7111/fax 9251 3943). CityRail or ferry Circular Quay/438 bus. **Open** *box office 9am-8.30pm Mon-Sat; 2 hours before show Sun.* **Credit** AmEx, BC, DC, MC, V.
Carpark. Disabled: access; toilets; hearing loop; information (9250 7185); TTY for hearing impaired (9250 7347). Shuttle bus from The Domain carpark.

Information

Advertisements for concerts are run in the *Sydney Morning Herald* Entertainment Guide published on Saturdays. ABC TV and ABC FM often broadcast live relays of opera performances, usually on Sunday nights; it's worth keeping an eye on the papers for details. Leaflets listing forthcoming events are also available from the Opera House box office. For details of ticket agencies that also deal with classical performances, *see chapter* **Theatre & Dance**.

Australian Chamber Orchestra

Under the flamboyant artistic directorship of high-profile young violinist Richard Tognetti, the Australian Chamber Orchestra (ACO) has brought excitement back into classical music. The Sydney-based orchestra is youthful – most of the performers are under 35 – and Tognetti's programming is always provocative. The ACO gives 16 concerts a year in the Concert Hall of the Opera House. Tognetti likes to mix periods, offer rarely heard works and even blend period instrument-playing soloists with the contemporary instruments of the orchestra. A typical night at the concert hall, Tognetti-style, might involve him lulling the audience with some nice Mozart, before hitting them with something obscure and 'difficult', and then sending them home humming Haydn. International soloists accompany the ACO on its national tours – usually ones who are in accord with Tognetti's iconoclastic views. For tickets and information on their programming phone the ACO (9357 4111/fax 9357 4781) or contact the Opera House; ticket prices range from $22 to $44.

Australian Opera

Australian divas are disproportionately represented in the ranks of world opera stars – Nellie Melba, Joan Hammond, Joan Sutherland and Yvonne Kenny, to name but a few. The Australian Opera is based in the inner-Sydney suburb of Surry Hills (enquiries 9319 6333/24-hour booking 9319 1088; *see p194* **Opera Centre**). It performs in the Opera Theatre of the Opera House for nine months of the year (January, February and the first weeks of March, then from June to November) and has the third largest programme, after Covent Garden and the Vienna Staatsoper, of any opera company in the world. Between March and May it disappears to Melbourne for a southern season. Despite a strong penchant for nineteenth-century Italian works, the

The Concert Hall of the Opera House: brilliant for Bruckner, but too big for recitals. See page 191.

Australian Opera is one of those very contemporary companies that fogies criticise for being 'director-led'. Staging is frequently inventive, with young directors – often from film or theatre – given free rein. Surtitles make life easier for monolingual opera buffs. Tickets ($35-$128) can be obtained from the Opera House box office or via a ticket agency (*see chapter* **Theatre & Dance**).

Brandenburg Orchestra

The Brandenburg (9363 2899/fax 9327 2593) is Australia's only early instrument group. Its concerts are fashionable events, rich mixes of visual and musical experience. A series was held in the Art Gallery of NSW, for example, and their occasional concerts with Australian counter-tenor Graham Pushee (with whom the orchestra has recorded Handel's operatic arias) are always eagerly anticipated.

Musica Viva

Musica Viva (9698 1711/fax 9698 3878) is the world's largest chamber music organisation, touring a dozen international and Australian groups around the country each year as well as providing a schools programme of enormous geographical spread. The organisation, which celebrated its

Home-grown talent

From the lush environmentalism of veteran **Peter Sculthorpe** to on-the-edge musical experimentation by Michael Smetanin, Australian composition is alive and flourishing. The **Sydney Symphony Orchestra**, smaller ensembles such as **Elision** and soloists interested in contemporary music (for example, **Lisa Moore**, the expatriate Australian pianist who plays with the Bang on a Can Allstars in New York) make a point of playing local music and commission regularly.

The ABC records Australian music, played by Australian orchestras and soloists, on the ABC Classics label which is available at record shops and ABC shops around the city and suburbs (phone 9950 3999 for your nearest stockist). The best shops for classical CDs are Michael's Music Room in the Town Hall Arcade, the HMV Shop in the Mid City Centre, and Blockbuster in the Pitt Street Mall (*see chapter* **Shopping & Services**).

Sydney Festival's Opera in the Park.

In January, the popular open-air Symphony Under the Stars is held in The Domain, and December sees two performances of Handel's 'Messiah'. The symphony season runs from March to November, offering a constantly changing round of local and overseas soloists. Tickets may be obtained from the Opera House box office, or from the SSO (9334 4600/general enquiries 9334 4644/fax 9334 4660); prices range from $17 to $75.

Other Musical Ensembles

Other musical outfits to watch out for include the **Philharmonia Choirs** (9251 2024), which have been going strong for 70 years, and stun audiences with a lusty Carmina Burana or a luscious Missa Solemnis several times a year; the **Song Company** (9364 9457), based at Sydney University, which performs early operas and oratorios in concert or partial costume; and the highly regarded local chamber groups, the **Macquarie Trio** and **Australia Quartet**.

Soloists from the Sydney Symphony Orchestra also band together in various permutations to perform chamber music. When cutting-edge ensemble **Elision** – which plays in Europe a couple of times a year and is now based at the University of Queensland – and the respected Adelaide-based **Australia Ensemble** play in town, they are definitely worth seeing.

fiftieth anniversary in 1995, has broadened its brief in recent years, touring famous choirs such as St John's College Choir, but it remains conservative in its programming. Still, a roll-call of the world's best outfits, including the Emerson Quartet and the Beaux Arts Trio, are regulars on its impressive calendar. Concerts are normally held in the Concert Hall of the Opera House.

Sydney Symphony Orchestra

Under the artistic directorship of Dutch conductor Edo de Waart, the Sydney Symphony Orchestra (SSO) is being developed into the flagship of a network of Australian state capital city orchestras. Established in 1932 as a radio-broadcasting orchestra, the SSO has grown into the biggest and the best in the country, attracting the finest musicians and offering a varied programme of more than 150 concerts a year.

In 1995, the gnashing of musical teeth could be heard around the country when the federal government announced the partial separation of the SSO from the national network and gave it a handsome increase in funding. More than 200,000 people attend their concerts in Sydney each year – most of them at the Concert Hall of the Opera House. More irregularly, the Eugene Goossens Hall provides a venue for contemporary and experimental music (a cut-down version of the SSO plays there under the name the Twentieth Century Orchestra). Recitals are also held occasionally at Sydney and Paddington Town Halls, and at St James' Church (*see chapter* **Sightseeing**).

Guided Tours

Opera Centre

480 Elizabeth Street, Surry Hills (enquiries 9319 6333/24-hour booking 9319 1088). CityRail Central. **Tours** *basic* 10am, 2pm, *lunch-time* 11am, Mon-Fri. **Rates** $8 incl tea; $18 incl lunch.
Visitors can go behind the scenes at the Australian Opera's vast headquarters in Surry Hills, where singers rehearse, sets are built and costumes are made. The tour takes in the costume, millinery and wig-making departments; the props manufacturing and storage department; set design and building; and rehearsal spaces for singers and musicians.
Tours of the **Opera House** (*see p191*) are run daily between 9am and 4pm, and take about an hour. Tickets cost $6-$9.

On Air

Sydney is relatively well served with classical music radio stations: ABC Classic FM (29.9 FM), tends towards slick presentation, conservative content and a populist agenda, while 2MBS (102.5 FM) is funded by subscription and offers meatier fare, often quirkily presented by amateur broadcasters. On Radio National, the countrywide AM network, the Saturday morning 'Music Show' provides an overview of the week in classical music, covering both live performances and new recording releases, with interesting interviews, many with Australian musicians and composers.

Music: Rock, Folk & Jazz

Sydney is a rock town. It does size. It does power. It also does contemporary jazz, funk, latin, blues, and more tribute bands than you can shake a plectrum at.

Thanks to the weather, the distance and a whole load of other factors, including the lack of something decent to watch on television at the weekends, Sydney is a 'Let's go out' city all year round.

Rock & Folk

In any given week, there are hundreds of bands to see – more even than in New York or London. For the visitor, the number of unrecognisable band names can be quite mind-boggling. Of course, many of these bands will be about as enjoyable as a trip to the dentist, but heck, the beer is usually cheap.

There is a historical reason for this multiplicity of choice. Until the 1960s, pubs in Australia had a strict 6pm closing time. This meant that people had to squeeze as much drinking as possible in the sliver of time left after work. To make it easier for beer lovers to lift their elbow, pubs were built much larger than their UK counterparts, with longer bars. Subsequently, when the laws that created the Six O'Clock Swill were lifted, pub owners found themselves in competition to attract punters, who could now be more choosy about their time and place of alcohol consumption. Someone came up with the idea of hiring bands to attract customers, and in no time at all, a national circuit sprang into being.

The heyday of Australian pub rock was in the late 1970s and early 1980s, when road warriors like AC/DC, Cold Chisel, Midnight Oil and The Angels slogged up and down the East Coast (it's

*Packing them in at the **Annandale Hotel**. See page 198.*

"AACUDOON ABROON"

ROUGH TRANSLATION:
Landlord, I require a bottle of your superlative ale forthwith.

Readily available on tap, and in good liquor outlets throughout NSW.

a ten hour drive from Sydney to Melbourne alone), playing in small towns and big cities. The late 1980s saw something of a musical recession, with a swathe of venues closing their doors because of the enforcement of fire restrictions, but the scene has warmed up again this decade. Sydney is more guitar-oriented, more rockist and more visceral than Melbourne, which leans towards arty, cerebral and exploratory music. The smaller population size means tickets often don't sell out as quickly in Sydney as they do in London and elsewhere, so it's possible to pick up seats for an international act you'd have to queue for days to see at home. The biggest shows will attract scalpers, but they aren't as frequent, or as expensive, as elsewhere. You will often be able to buy a ticket at, or near, to the real price.

A word of warning: Sydney is a rock town. It does size. It does power. It doesn't really do subtlety. If it's complexity, texture or maturity you're looking for in music, hire a guide.

Major Venues

Enmore Theatre

130 Enmore Road, Newtown (9550 3666). CityRail Newtown. **Open** *box office* 9am-6pm Mon-Fir; 10am-2pm Sat. **Tickets** $20-$50. **Credit** AmEx, BC, DC, MC, V.
An old, wooden-floored cinema-style theatre, with a balcony and foyer bar. It holds about 1,700 people, and is a haunt for low level international acts and popular local bands. European stars also feature – you'll often drive by and spot a poster advertising 'The Greek Madonna' or 'The Turkish Julio'. Ever so slightly down-at-heel, but that just adds to the charm.

Hordern Pavilion

Sydney Showground, Moore Park, Driver Avenue, Paddington (9331 9263). Bus 373, 377, X77.
Open *box office* 9am-5pm Mon-Fri, plus day of event.
Tickets $22-$50. **Credit** AmEx, BC, DC, MC, V.
The building is under threat from Rupert Murdoch's Fox studio project, which is set to eat up the Royal Agricultural Showground area, of which this is a part. The Hordern squeezes in around 5,000 people, and can be as hot as Hades on a humid summer night. When Nirvana played here at the start of 1992, they had to use the fire hoses to spray the audience because people were passing out from heat exhaustion. That aside, the Hordern has been the scene of many of the best ever Sydney gigs. With bleacher seating around an open floor, it can be a terrific place to see a band, even if Moore Park is not the easiest place to get to (parking prices vary, but it usually costs about $5). The line-up consists of alternative international acts and the biggest of the local groups.
Disabled: access; toilets.

The Metro

624 George Street, Sydney (9264 2666). CityRail Town Hall. **Open** *walk-in bookings* 9am-9pm Mon-Fri; noon-9pm Sat, Sun; *telephone bookings* 9am-5pm Mon-Fri; noon-5pm Sat, Sun. **Tickets** $8-$30. **Credit** AmEx, BC, MC, $TC, V.
The best, purpose-built venue in Sydney. The Metro holds about 1,200 (seated and unseated), arranged in a series of tiers, which allows for good sound and sight lines all the way to the back wall. It's intimate, well air-conditioned, easy to get to, and increasingly popular with the local bands and indie internationals who play here.
Disabled: access; toilets.

Opera House

Bennelong Point, Circular Quay (box office 9250 7777/information 9250 7111/fax 9251 3943). CityRail or ferry Circular Quay/438 bus. **Open** *box office* 9am-8.30pm Mon-Sat; two hours before show Sun. **Credit** AmEx, BC, DC, MC, V.
Great in theory but not so often in practice, this venue is occasionally trotted out for a rock performance (most recently for kd lang), but tends to lack the atmosphere of the State Theatre. The building (capacity 2,000) is beautiful, but the acoustics of the hall are configured for an entirely different kind of sound, and rock shows tend to be a little boomy. *See also chapter* **Sightseeing**.
Car park. Disabled: access; toilets; hearing loop; information (9250 7185); TTY for hearing impaired (9250 7347). Shuttle bus from The Domain car park.

Selinas

Coogee Bay Hotel, Corner of Arden Street and Coogee Bay Road, Coogee (9665 0000). Bus 314, 315, 372, 373, 374. **Open** 9am-3am Mon-Fri; 9am-5am Sat; 9am-midnight Sun. **Performances** Wed-Sun evenings. **Tickets** $25. **No credit cards**.
Probably the biggest beer barn left in Sydney, and home to many of the loudest rock acts. A balcony allows great views of the mosh pit. It's attached to the Coogee Bay Hotel, out on one of Sydney's prime eastern beaches. There's occasionally a bit of aggro around on a Friday or Saturday, but it's easily avoidable. The venue itself, which holds about 2,000 people, gets extraordinarily hot when there's a full house -- go in shorts and T-shirt in summer.
Disabled: access; toilets.

State Theatre

49 Market Street, Sydney (9373 6655/advance bookings Firstcall 9320 9000). CityRail Town Hall. **Open** *box office* 9am-5.30pm Mon-Sat, until 8pm on performance nights. **Tickets** $50-$60. **Credit** AmEx, BC, DC, MC, V.
First choice venue for artistes looking to inject some style. The opulent entertainment palace, built in 1929, boasts massive chandeliers, abundant statuary, an imported marble staircase and more gilt than is good for the eyes. It's a rococo-cum-deco treat, never short of atmosphere. And it's right in the middle of the CBD. Dancing is restricted to the side aisles only though. It holds more than 2,000 people. *See also chapter* **Sightseeing**.
Disabled: access; toilets.

Sydney Entertainment Centre

Harbour Street, Haymarket (9320 4200/information 1800 957 333/Ticketek bookings 9266 4800). CityRail Central or Town Hall/monorail Haymarket. **Open** *box office* 9am-5pm Mon-Fri. **Tickets** $50-$60. **Credit** AmEx, BC, DC, MC, V.
Still living off winning *Performance Magazine*'s Best Venue in The World gong a couple of years ago (don't be fooled – that just means roadies love it), the 'Ent Cent' is Sydney's biggest indoor venue. Situated at the intersection of Darling Harbour and Chinatown, it holds around 12,000 people – an auditorium planned for the 2000 Olympic Games will seat half as many again. The Ent Cent is a great place to see the Sydney Kings basketball team go through their paces, but it turns into just another concrete, soulless barn when a band is playing. It takes an exceptional act to create any feeling of warmth or intimacy. Sound, security and seating are reliable but don't expect to be able to dance in the aisles or rush to the front. Major international acts perform here.
Disabled: access; toilets.

Pubs

Where to start? They come and go with extraordinary frequency. There are more than 100 pubs and clubs – Returned Services Leagues (RSL) clubs and Worker's clubs) – in Sydney, offering regular bands of all types. Here are some of the best of them.

Annandale Hotel

Corner of Nelson Street and Parramatta Road, Annandale (9550 1078). Bus 413, 436, 437, 438, 439, 440, 461, 480, 481, 482, 483. **Open** 10am-midnight Mon-Sat; 3-10pm Sun. **Performances** from 10pm. **Tickets** free-$10. **No credit cards.**
A long-time hangout of indie bands and up-and-comers, on busy Parramatta Road in the inner west. Smoky, humid and often jam-packed with punters, it offers the quintessential pub rock experience.

The Basement

29 Reiby Place, Sydney (9251 2797). CityRail/ferry Circular Quay. **Open** noon-2am Mon-Thur; noon-4am Fri; 7pm-4am Sat; 7pm-2am Sun. **Tickets** $7-$25. **Credit** AmEx, BC, DC, MC, TC, V.
This popular jazz venue makes room for other kinds of music every now and then. Booking is essential – the views from the tables are great, but if you're stuck at the bar, it's not worth it. *See also p201.*

Beach Palace

169 Dolphin Street, Coogee (9664 2900). Bus 314, 315, 372, 373, 374, X74. **Open** 11am-midnight Mon-Wed, Sun; 11am-3am Thur-Sat. **Tickets** $7-$10. **No credit cards.**
A new venue at Coogee, right on the beach. Mainstream fare, cover bands and recognisable oldies are what's on offer at this domed building.
Disabled: access; toilets.

Birkenhead Tavern

11 Roseby Street, Drummoyne (9181 4238). Bus 501, 502, 503, 504, 505, 506/ferry Drummoyne Wolseley Street. **Open** 10am-midnight Mon-Sat; noon-10pm Sun. **Tickets** free-$30. **Credit** AmEx, BC, DC, JCB, MC, TC, V.
A centre for local and touring folk acts. It's not the easiest place to get to without a car, but if you can beg or borrow one, there's plenty of parking, the drink prices are reasonable and a surprising number of internationally known names pass across the small stage.
Disabled: access; toilets.

Bridge Hotel

135 Victoria Road, Rozelle (9810 1260). Bus 500, 501. **Open** 24 hours Mon-Sat; 5am-midnight Sun. **Tickets** free-$25. **Credit** AmEx, BC, DC, MC, TC, V.
Blues-oriented acts and local rockers play the large room here (capacity 700). A disco swings into action most nights at about 11pm.

General RW Bourke Hotel

74 Church Street, Parramatta (9635 8811). CityRail/Rivercat Parramatta. **Open** 9.30am-1am Mon-Thur; 9.30am-5am Fri, Sat; 11.30am-midnight Sun. **Tickets** free Mon, Tue, Thur, Sun; $5-$12 Wed, Fri, Sat. **Credit** AmEx, BC, DC, MC, V.
Go west! Parramatta's numero uno rock space hosts a heap of bands, known and unknown, from 8pm nightly.

Hopetoun Hotel

416 Bourke Street, Surry Hills (9361 5257). Bus 301, 302, 303. **Open** 10am-midnight Mon-Sat; noon-10am Sun. **Tickets** free-$8. **No credit cards.**
A traditional inner city rock venue. You'll have to queeze into this tiny corner pub, where many rock acts that went on to minor notoriety played their first gig. It was closed for a year, but is now open once more.

Kinsela's

383 Bourke Street, Darlinghurst (9331 3299). Bus 378, 380, 382, L82. **Open** 8pm-3am Tue-Sat; 7pm-midnight Sun. **Admission** ground level free; upper levels $5-$10. **No credit cards.**
Chic and self-conscious types stand around pool tables in singlets, trying to hold their cigarettes fashionably. In the heart of Darlinghurst, just off Oxford Street, this perennial club often has great acts playing on its various levels. Don't clap too loudly though – it's uncool. *See also chapter* **Nightlife.**

Revesby Workers Club

Brett Street, Revesby (9772 2100). CityRail Revesby. **Open** 10am-midnight Mon-Wed, Sun; 10am-1am Thur; 10am-3.30am Fri, Sat. **Tickets** $5-$25. **Credit** BC, MC, V.
Along with the Rooty Hill RSL and Panthers Leagues Club, this is the place to go for the full-tilt suburban experience. Middlebrow music, entertainment and fashion rule.
Disabled: access; toilets.

Sandringham Hotel

387 King Street, Newtown (9557 1254). CityRail Newtown/422, 423 bus. **Open** noon-midnight Mon-Sat; 3-10pm Sun. **Tickets** free-$5. **No credit cards.**
This pub has been plying its musical trade at the south end of Newtown for what seems like an eternity. Never exactly swish, it deals in beer-guzzling indie acts from around the country, and is exactly the wrong shape to be a good venue. But somehow it works. Sunday evening shows are a highlight.

Jazz

In the late 1980s there was talk of an Australian jazz renaissance, but if you visited certain clubs in the CBD you might have been forgiven for concluding that the whole thing was a chimera.

But had you chanced on the right night in the right place, you would have found the music happening and the venue packed, with young listeners far outnumbering the old guard. The younger fans included a generous mix of latter-day hippies and skate-boarders (there's a funky jazz skateboard band that plays at competitions). Creative levels were high – startlingly so – given Australia's sparse population.

It all looked like yet another revival movement, pretty much in parallel with London. Young turn boppers in three-button suits followed Wynton Marsalis' guidelines to academic correctness, and some of them reached very high levels: tenor saxophonist Dale Barlow even made it into one of the last editions of the Jazz Messengers. James Morrison presented a more eclectic mix of trad, swing and modernism, which was sometimes overshadowed by a panoply of stunts, plus jokes so tired you almost had to laugh. Vince Jones, the Melbourne singer and trumpeter, visited Sydney many times with a moodier show that appealed to those bemused by James Morrison's early Australian performances. Morrison was connected

---

Tuesdays and Wednesdays are jazz nights at the **Strawberry Hills Hotel**. *See page 202.*

to the vaudeville aspect of jazz, Jones to the *film noir* images of the young Miles and Chet. Between the two of them they raised the profile of jazz, which had gone into a steep decline since the last creative period in the 1970s.

But behind the scenes, young experimentalists were working independently, or in company with such older players as Bernie McGann, Mike Nock, John Pochee and Mark Simmonds, whose work was either still in motion, or somehow retained an edgy intensity which put it outside the finished academic schools. From this has emerged a bewildering array of contemporary bands, including Clarion Fracture Zone, Wanderlust, The Catholics, The Necks, the Bernie McGann Trio, Ten Part Invention, Alisons Wonderland, Australian Creole, First Light, the Scott Tinkler Trio, Twentieth Century Dog, Engine Room, AustraLysis and

Big days out

Australian music fans have long bemoaned the lack of a festival culture. Though there were irregular festivals in the 1970s and 1980s, it wasn't until the 1990s that anything even approaching the annual Glastonbury or Reading bashes was tried. **The Big Day Out**, a venture of long-time promoters Ken West and Vivien Lees, held on or about Australia Day (26 January), was a huge success for four years, but breathed its last in January 1997. Held on three or four stages at the Showgrounds, it attracted about 30 acts, with a handful of major international bands sharing the stage with the locals. There was more than just music to the event, too: art exhibitions, skateboarding demonstrations, rides, sideshows and all kinds of international food stalls made up the event.

Other promoters have been trying to get festivals up, with mixed success (**Summersault** was great, **Alternative Nation** not so), but have yet to attain The Big Day Out's regularity and bankability. It's a safe bet that now Lees and West have announced their intention to take a breather, others will jump into the vacuum left by their departure, so keep your eyes and ears open for January and February events. Meanwhile, if your imagination is fired by something groovier than long-haired boys with guitars, **Vibes on a Summer's Day** is also held around Australia Day, and has succeeded in creating a more laidback atmosphere. Vibes attracts DJs and dance acts from around the world for a daytime, outdoor frolic at Bondi.

Artisans Workshop. A comparable list of bands could be drawn up for Melbourne.

Some of the above groups have been very enthusiastically received at international festivals. Clarion Fracture Zone's CD *Zones on Parade* scored a five star review in *Downbeat* magazine – almost unprecedented for a non-American band. The Engine Room was the first western band to tour Russia after Glasnost, and was applauded ecstatically by re-emerging members of the Russian avant-garde. Indeed, the influence of the avant-garde lives in many of the current Australian bands, adding bite and a degree of wildness to the prevalent 'world music' influence. Many contemporary jazzers earn their living in rock, funk, Latin and blues bands and have allowed these influences to colour their jazz playing, while avoiding any hint of 'fuzak'.

That this movement has been able to emerge from underground, and that some of the bands have been able to tour extensively, is largely due to the efforts of the Sydney Improvised Music Association (SIMA), who have maintained a venue (in the **Strawberry Hills Hotel**, *see page 202*) on Tuesday and Wednesday nights for more than six years. (The same venue, at the weekend, is one of the last bastions of traditional pub jazz.) There's also a major contemporary label, Rufus, which is run by Tim Dunn, a minister in the Uniting Church. Meanwhile, the young and old boppers and traditionalists can still be heard playing marvellously, though not always regularly. The devil's music still haunts Sydney.

Venues

For the **Harbourside Brassserie**, which hosts jazz and cabaret evenings, *see chapter* **Nightlife**.

The Basement
See page 198 for listings.
One of the best-appointed clubs in the world, and now a mixed popular music venue. It still serves as the ideal forum for visiting jazz artists, and periodically, for local jazz talent.

Bowlers Club of New South Wales
95 York Street, Sydney (9290 1155). CityRail Town Hall.
Open 10am-11pm Mon-Sat. **Performances** jazz one Tue a month, phone for details. **Tickets** $7 members, $12 non-members. **No credit cards.**
A Sydney licensed club (a phenomenon all visitors should experience) complete with poker machines, the Bowlers is also a monthly venue for concerts of traditional, mainstream and modern jazz, usually presented by Sydney's Jazz Action Society or the Musician's Club. The acoustics are very odd, varying from quite good to deplorable in different parts of the room. Concerts are often worth catching, however.

Cafe De Lane
15 Brisbane Street, Surry Hills (9314 3797). CityRail Museum. **Open** times vary. **Tickets** $5. **No credit cards.**
Nothing to do with Franklin D, this occasional venue is down a tiny lane. Pretty small itself, it more closely resembles Sydney's once-famous El Rocco club than any other place around. Young players and still-adventurous veterans are the usual bill of fare.

Randwick Labor Club

135 Alison Road, Randwick (9399 3342). Bus 372, 373, 374, 375, 377, X74, X77. **Open** 11am-11.15pm Mon-Fri; 10am-1.30am Sat; 11am-11.30pm Sun. **Tickets** free. **No credit cards.**
Promoter Sil Ventura has found a pleasant Friday night venue for traditional and mainstream as well as modern jazz, within the hallowed Randwick Labor Club.
Disabled: access; toilets.

Round Midnight

2 Roslyn Street, Kings Cross (9356 4045/mobile 015 412 222). CityRail Kings Cross. **Open** 6pm-3am Tue-Thur, Sun; 6pm-6am Fri, Sat. **Performances** from 11pm. **Tickets** $5-$8 Mon-Fri; $10 Sat, Sun. **Credit** AmEx, BC, JCB, MC, V.
Head for Roslyn Street in Kings Cross, for some late-night jazz and blues.

Soup Plus

383 George Street, Sydney (9299 7728). CityRail Town Hall or Wynyard. **Open** noon-midnight Mon-Sat. **Performances** from 8pm. **Admission** $5 cover Mon-Thur; $20 incl two-course meal Fri, Sat. **No credit cards.**
A long-standing traditional jazz forum, the Soup now presents mostly mainstream and bop stylists, as well as jam sessions. Its central-city location on George Street and restaurant layout mean that the music has always competed with diners, office parties and weekend revellers. But the last set is for listening.
Advance booking essential.

Strawberry Hills Hotel

453 Elizabeth Street, Surry Hills (9698 2997). CityRail Central. **Performances** 8.30pm-12.30am Tue, Wed, Sat; 8-11pm Sun. **Tickets** $6-$10. **No credit cards.**
There's music every night of the week, but jazz nights are Tuesdays and Wednesdays, when contemporary bands present largely original programmes, and weekends, when traditionalists such as Tom Baker and Jeff Bull play for an older audience – many of whom actually dance. The atmosphere is dismal when the audience is sparse, euphoric when the fans turn out in force.

Unity Hall Hotel

292 Darling Street, Balmain (9810 1331). Bus 441, 442. **Open** times vary. **Admission** $5. **No credit cards.**
A surviving trad pub of renown in what was a working-class suburb, built in Sydney sandstone. The Café Society Orchestra (an 11-piece swing band) plays on Tuesdays; soulful ex-Brit trombonist Roger Janes leads a spirited band on Fridays and Sundays.

Woollahra Hotel

116 Queen Street, Woollahra (9363 2782). Bus 389. **Open** *back bar* (pool room, pinball, card tables) 10am-midnight Mon-Sat; noon-9pm Sun; *front bar* (jazz) noon-midnight Mon-Sat; noon-9pm Sun. **Performances** 6-10pm Sun. **Admission** free. **No credit cards.**
Having found an audience through SIMA's efforts at **Strawberry Hills** (*see above*) some contemporary musicians have also found surprising acceptance here on Sunday afternoons. The pub is pleasant but echo-ey, and set in a leafy suburb (think Hampstead in London).

Rock's undead

In Sydney, if you plan your week well enough, you can see pretty much every great band in the history of rock. There's just one hitch. They're all fake.

The dead walk here. It's not something that anyone is particularly proud of, but Sydney is the undisputed worldwide home of the Tribute Band. It's Impostor Central, a home for *doppelgänger* acts who live on their ability to pretend that they're something and someone else. Some, such as Bjorn Again (ABBA) are exercises in campness and cabaret, knowing parodies of their chosen act. Others are deadly serious, trainspotters determined to get every nuance exact. Kiss (Dynissty), U2 (Sunday Bloody Sunday), Led Zeppelin (Gold Zeppelin), Madonna (Physical Attraction), Elton John (Elton Jack), AC/DC (Dirty Deeds), Pearl Jam (Pearl Jammed), The Beatles (The Beatnix), The Cure (Love Cats) and many, many others have inspired impersonators – more than 150 tribute bands have hit the circuit this decade. In the case of the defunct/dead acts, it gives punters the chance to glimpse what might have been. In the case of the acts that are still kicking, the imitators are both accessible and affordable – the Rolling Stones (Rolling Clones) don't play your local every Friday night. And

rock gigs are for getting drunk at – who's going to notice after a dozen songs? If you must stay sober, the whole idea can be so surreal that it's worth seeing anyway.

Sport & Fitness

Cricket dominates the sporting life and rugby league is big business, but gambling's the winner in the nation which spends more than any other on games of chance.

If Australians in general are religious about sport, Sydney represents the libertarian, non-dogmatic wing of the religion. In Melbourne, everyone is fanatical about sport because the weather leaves them with little else to do (in Sydney, people are still going to the beach in winter). In Brisbane and Perth, they're fanatical about their teams because they love to beat Sydney or Melbourne. In Sydney, there are so many options to choose from that sport is like a fashion accessory. You support your team if they're winning, but if they're losing, you take up rollerblading instead.

Sport in Sydney is a seasonal, fickle thing. When the local Australian Rules football (Swans), basketball (Kings), rugby union, league and cricket (all called Blues) teams are doing well, you'll find it hard to get into one of their matches. If they're doing badly, you'll struggle to find out where and when they're playing. Great clumps of tumbleweed will roll through the stadium carparks. The media will gleefully dissect the downturn of interest.

When Sydney-based teams lose, this is traditionally blamed on there being too many other things to do. Instead of training, kids want to surf or skateboard, go sailing or play golf and tennis. It's not that Sydney people aren't committed to their sports. It's that they're gluttons who can't get enough. And they're not choosy, as long as it all tastes good.

VENUES

As well as being major venues, Sydney Cricket Ground and Sydney Football Stadium both handle more than one sport (cricket and Australian football at the SCG; rugby league, rugby union and soccer internationals at the SFS). For other venues see the relevant sport listed below.

Sydney Cricket Ground & Sydney Football Stadium

Driver Avenue, Moore Park (ground & trust office 9360 6601/match information SCG 0055 63 132; SFS 0055 63133/booking via Ticketek only). Bus 372, 373. **Open** 9am-5pm Mon-Fri and match days. **No credit cards.** *Disabled: access; toilets.*

TICKETS

For many sporting events tickets can only be booked in advance through a ticket agency. Phone **Ticketek** (9266 4800) and expect to pay a booking fee of $3.20. For the big matches and tournaments you may be able to buy tickets at the ground or course on the day, if seats are still available, but remember that they tend to accept cash only.

Athletics

Athletics has never been a big spectator sport in Australia – only six per cent of the population went to see an event in 1995. But with the Olympics approaching, big track and field events are marked down for the Sydney International Athletics Centre, which will be the warm-up facility for the 2000 games. **Athletics New South Wales** (9552 1244) provides information on forthcoming events.

Australian Football

Sydney has a fickle relationship with this sport, symbolised in the fortunes of its local team. **The Swans** used to be the South Melbourne team but were transplanted to Sydney in the early 1980s when the Victorian Football League got starry-

Six-pack and out?

eyed about a national competition. Sydney has no real participatory base in the sport so the Swans have needed outside financial support and player-draft to stay afloat. 1996, however, was the Swans' most successful year to date, culminating in the team making the Grand Final. Sydney had a love affair with the team and by the end of the season, their fortnightly matches were regularly selling out the 40,000 seat SCG (*see page 203*). Match tickets cost $13 for adults, $3-$6.50 for concessions.

Baseball

Sydney has one baseball team in the national league, **The Blues**. Their home ground was the Sydney Showground, but with that site being turned over to Rupert Murdoch's Fox Studios, the Blues had to find another home, in the west. Affiliated to the Toronto Blue Jays, the Blues have been reasonably successful over the years, winning their most recent national title in the summer of 1995-96. Meanwhile, suburban baseball teams are on the increase, boosted by US and Canadian expats. For information about games phone the **Australian Baseball Federation** (9437 4466).

The Blues
Parramatta Stadium, O'Connell Street, Parramatta (9331 3655). CityRail Parramatta. **Open** 9am-3pm Mon-Fri. **Tickets** $12 adults; $5 5-16s; free under-5s. **Credit** AmEx, BC, DC, MC, TC, V.
Disabled: access; toilets.

Basketball

To the consternation of older generations, Michael Jordan is the most recognised sportsman among Australian adolescents. Young people's participation in basketball has not yet filtered through to the senior ranks but the **Kings** (men's) and the **Flames** (women's) teams in the national leagues regularly draw crowds of more than 15,000 at the Sydney Entertainment Centre. Both teams are owned by the same company and often play on the same bill. For wider participation information phone the **NSW Basketball Association** (9746 2969).

Sydney Kings & Sydney Flames
Sydney Entertainment Centre, Harbour Street, Haymarket (9319 7777). CityRail Central/monorail Haymarket. **Open** 9am-6pm Mon-Fri. **Tickets** *for 2 games (Kings & Flames)* $16 adults; $11 5-15s; free under-5s. **Credit** AmEx, BC, DC, MC, V.
Disabled: access; toilets.

Bowls

Lawn bowls, the 'young people's sport that old people play', is surprisingly well attended in Australia. It has its own TV show and nearly every suburb has a bowling club. The **Royal NSW Bowling Association** (9283 4555) is always happy to furnish information.

Get bowled over by the views at Kirribilli Bowling Club.

The sporting year

There is only one day of the year that escapes Australians' obsession with sport, though for many 25 December is just an annoying disruption to the cricket season. But because it's the only day when nothing's on, Christmas Day is where the year starts and ends.

Cricket is Australia's favourite spectator sport. One in two Australians watch it on television, while one in five go to see a match. In Sydney, the highlight of the cricketing year is the five-day Test at the Sydney Cricket Ground (SCG), usually in the first week of January. The Australian cricket team also plays five or six one-day internationals (known as 'pyjama cricket', for the players' colourful kit), which are played under floodlights at the SCG between December and February. Up to 40,000 people watch these matches. One-day cricket is the preferred option for visitors and the softer fringes of cricket-watchers who fear getting bored by a sport Robin Williams once referred to as 'baseball on valium'.

At state level, the New South Wales cricket team, the NSW Blues, plays about eight matches at the SCG between October and March in the interstate Sheffield Shield competition (plus some one-day matches). The final, if NSW makes it, often takes place in Sydney in early March.

During the summer, cricket competes for spectators with **tennis and golf**. But it is Melbourne, rather than Sydney, that hosts the biggest tennis and golf events. The White City courts, in the eastern suburbs, stage the NSW (or some sponsor's name) Open tennis tournament in late December or early January, as a warm-up for the Australian Open in Melbourne. In golf, Sydney gets one or two big tournaments a year, usually scheduled either side of Christmas.

Ironman is a peculiarly Australian sport, and is fun to watch if you get off on seeing big beefy men and women nearly killing themselves in big surf. The professional circuit travels around Australia during the summer, with events in

Sydney – usually at Manly and Bondi – held in January or February. Surf lifesaving carnivals, which are the nurseries for ironman and also a great club ritual, are amateur events staged at Sydney beaches on several weekends until March.

Soccer, never a big spectator sport in Australia, has recently switched to summer in an attempt to pull more crowds. Sydney has several teams in the national A-League, some identified with particular ethnic communities: Croatian, Italian, and Serbian, for example. A-League finals are in March-April; if the final is played in Sydney it's held at Parramatta Stadium.

Easter heralds the **horse racing** carnivals, with Sydney's richest race, the Golden Slipper Stakes, at Rosehill Gardens on the weekends leading up to the Easter Carnival at Randwick. The year's other big racing carnival in Sydney is held on the public holiday weekend at the beginning of October.

Of the winter sports, **rugby league** is the biggest, with Sydney represented in 1996 by 11 of the 20 teams in the national competition. The game is in turmoil, with Rupert Murdoch's Super League looking likely to succeed in wresting control from the traditional Australian rugby league bosses. If the next couple of years see anything like normal service, the highlights of the season will be the State of Origin series in May and June, with NSW and Queensland fighting it out in what have seemed like routinely legendary matches, and the Premiership final series, in September.

Rugby union is less popular at club level, but the NSW team is strongly supported in the Super 12 competition, which runs through April and May. Rugby union's biggest matches are the internationals in June, July and August between Australia and touring teams. Thanks to a recent deal, Sydney will host one match a year between Australia and either New Zealand or South Africa, the other two big powers in the world of rugby union.

Sydney has a team in the national **Australian Football League** competition, though that sport is based in Victoria, South Australia and Western Australia. The Sydney Swans survive on the largesse of the Melbourne-based AFL, but when they're winning it seems all of Sydney wants to be their friend. They play at the SCG from March to September.

Sydney puts up teams in **basketball** (the Kings, the Flames) and **baseball** (the Blues), while the city is represented by several sides in the national **netball** competition. The netball finals are in June, basketball in October. And by then it's time to start thinking about cricket again…

Odds on favourites

Depending on your point of view, gambling is a sickness, a sport, a business or a fantasy. Whichever, Australians are in it up to their necks. The only people in the world who gamble more than Sydneysiders are Tasmanians. In Sydney, people spend an average of $400 a year each on gambling – which doesn't sound that much until you realise that babies and children are included in this calculation. By comparison, people in Hong Kong spend $370 a year, Americans $170.

In the state of New South Wales, 13 per cent of the government's revenue comes from taxes on gambling. Racing provides $12 billion, lotteries nearly $4 billion, and gambling machines $2 billion. With 74,000 poker machines, NSW has more of them per head than Nevada. Walk into almost any pub in Sydney – not to mention the new Sydney Harbour Casino – and you can lose your money to blackjack-playing card machines as quick as you can say Las Vegas.

Among the gambling sports, there's a definite food chain. At the top is horse racing, then harness racing, and at the bottom are the dogs. The phrase 'gone to the dogs', says it all for greyhound racing.

Even within each sport, there is a hierarchy. Sydney has four horse racing venues. Randwick (just south of the city) and Warwick Farm (in the far west) are run by the traditional body, the Australian Jockey Club (AJC). 'Royal Randwick' hosts the big traditional races: Epsom Handicap and The Metropolitan in the spring; Doncaster Handicap, AJC Derby and Sydney Cup in the autumn. Warwick Farm is the AJC's second-ranking course, and usually has midweek meetings on Wednesdays.

The upstart body in racing is the Sydney Turf Club (STC), based at Rosehill Gardens in western Sydney and Canterbury in the south-west. The STC has tried to overtake the AJC with a big-money, glamour carnival in the autumn.

From the punter's point of view, the clubs look pretty much the same. A meeting has eight races, spaced about 35 minutes apart, starting around noon. You can bet either with a bookmaker or on the electronic totalisator (tote). The bookies are much more fun. Harness racing and greyhound meetings happen at night, which is more suited to the nocturnal types you meet there.

If you come across any characters known as an 'eastern suburbs racing identity', steer clear. This is a euphemism for a criminal, arising from the fact that some dodgy characters, when caught with unexplained amounts of money, claim to have won it at the races. This merely serves to incriminate them further because the only way you can win at the races is by obtaining insider knowledge from trainers and jockeys.

It is often said that Australians will bet on two flies crawling up a wall. This is true. But if an Australian offers you odds on one fly or the other, beware – it has probably been drugged, injured or told to go slow.

Cricket

The growth – some would say overgrowth – of international cricket in Australia has broken down regional identities, so that major events on the Sydney cricketing calendar are not state but national games (*see page 205* **The Sporting Year**). Meanwhile, on Saturday afternoons in summer, hundreds of fields around Sydney host cricket matches of all levels and standards. Contact the **NSW Cricket Association** (9261 5155) for more information. Tickets cost from $20 for a one-day match to $100 for a five-day Test. For **Sydney Cricket Ground** (SCT) details, *see page 203*.

Dog Racing

Greyhounds race at night every week at Wentworth and Harold Parks. The **NSW Greyhound Breeders, Owners & Trainers Association** (9649 7166) is the canine sport's administrative body. If you get your jollies from watching muzzled dogs chase a stuffed bunny in a circle and then attack each other when it disappears down a chute, this one's for you. The human life – most of it also stuffed – is interesting too.

Harold Park Paceway
Wigram Road, Glebe (9692 0546/9660 3688). Bus 432, 433, 434.

Wentworth Park Greyhound Track
Wentworth Park Road, Glebe (9660 4308). Bus 468.

Golf

Golf in Sydney is cheap and plentiful. Most suburbs have a public course where, depending on the standard of facilities, the price of a round is $10-$25. Golf clubs can be hired for less than $20 at most places. The very best courses, unfortunately, are private and you need a member's invitation to play. Phone the **NSW Golf Association** (9264 8433) for more information.

Spectatorwise, Sydney usually hosts one or two big tournaments in summer, at the **Lakes Golf Club** (9669 1311) in Mascot, the **Australian Golf Club** (9663 2273) in Rosebery, **Royal Sydney Golf Club** (9371 4333) in Rose Bay or the **Terrey Hills Golf & Country Club** (9450 0155). Tournament ticket prices vary from about $15 to $25 per day's play.

Gyms

The gymnasium boom has not left Australia untouched, and gyms are now as plentiful as post offices in Sydney. Weight and circuit training, and high- or low-impact aerobic classes are available, though the variation in standard and value for money between gyms is considerable so it's worth shopping around. One-off visits cost about $10, while monthly and short-term memberships are also relatively cheap. There is no centralised association for gyms, but if you're staying anywhere near the CBD and feel like a laugh, try the City Gym Health & Fitness Centre for 24-hour showtime.

City Gym Health & Fitness Centre
107 Crown Street, East Sydney (9360 6247). Bus 200, 323, 324, 325, 327. **Open** 24 hours Mon-Fri; midnight-9pm Sat; 8am-8pm Sun. **Admission** $8 per day. **Credit** AmEx, BC, DC, MC, V.

Harness Racing

'The trots', as they are misnamed – it's parallel-gait pacing, not square-gait trotting – are held at Harold Park Paceway (*see above* **Dog Racing**) on most Friday nights. The sport's image was tarnished in 1996 when a leading driver was banned for cheating, but harness racing retains a hard core of punters and owners.

Horse Racing

On Saturdays and Wednesdays, all year round, there is a race meeting in Sydney. The **Australian Jockey Club** (9663 8400) runs meets at Royal Randwick and Warwick Farm, while the **Sydney Turf Club** (9930 4000) organises programmes at Rosehill Gardens and Canterbury. The big carnivals are in the spring and autumn (*see page 205* **The Sporting Year**). Newspapers provide form guides. Admission to meets is usually $5 or $6 with under-18s allowed in free.

Canterbury Park Racecourse
King Street, Canterbury (9930 4000/9930 4050). CityRail Canterbury then shuttle bus. Disabled: access; toilets.

Rosehill Gardens Racecourse
Grand Avenue, Rosehill (9930 4070/9930 4080). CityRail Rosehill/Rivercat Parramatta then shuttle bus. Disabled: access; toilets.

Royal Randwick Racecourse
Alison Road, Randwick (9663 8400). Bus 372, 373, 374. Disabled: access; toilets.

Warwick Farm Racecourse
Hume Highway, Warwick Farm (9602 6199). CityRail Warwick Farm then shuttle bus. Disabled: access; toilets.

Netball

Another huge participation sport, netball has burgeoned in recent times. The **NSW Netball Association** (9552 6077) administers competitions at all levels, while the national competition is televised each week during the season, which runs from summer until midwinter.

Rugby League

Sydney is the only city in the world where rugby league is the biggest of the football codes. The **Australian Rugby League** (9232 7566) has been based in, and controlled from, Sydney, a fact that has led to serious upheavals in recent years. In October 1996, after a previous ruling against him was overturned, Rupert Murdoch won his court battle (subject to High Court appeal) to start a breakaway Super League competition. The victory (intended to boost the audience for his Foxtel cable TV channel) has thrown the game into confusion.

Rugby league has always drawn its players from a lower socio-economic base. The game's heartland has shifted, with that sector of the population, from the inner city to the western suburbs. The season has usually run from March to September, with the Premiership finals held at the Sydney Football Stadium. The big representative matches have, since 1980, been the State of Origin series, with NSW taking on Queensland. The future of International Rugby League, pretty much shelved in 1996 while Australia battled Murdoch's global ownership of the game, may be brighter now.

To see the State of Origin series, expect to cough up $50 a match for premium seating. Ticket prices for the Premiership matches have ranged from $12 to $50 a match. Sydney had 11 teams in 1996. There's no guarantee they will survive the current war, but we've listed a contact number for each.

Canterbury-Bankstown Bulldogs *(9789 2922)*.
Cronulla-Sutherland Sharks *(9523 0222)*. **Manly-Warringah Sea Eagles** *(9938 3677)*. **North Sydney Bears** *(9923 1633)*. **Parramatta Eels** *(9683 6311)*.
Penrith Panthers *(4720 5666)*. **South Sydney Rabbitohs** *(9319 4156)*. **St George's Dragons** *(9587 1022)*. **Sydney City Roosters** *(9386 3248)*. **Sydney Tigers** *(9555 1650)*. **Western Suburb Magpies** *(4628 4200)*.

Rugby Union

The difference between the two rugby codes is that union seems messier: the ball is hidden under piles of players for much of the time, there is more kicking, and union supporters wear tweed jackets with elbow patches. Until 1996, union was supposedly amateur. Now it is fully professional at the top level.

The Australian Wallabies play about six home internationals a year. Matches against Northern Hemisphere teams, used as warm-ups for clashes with the big boys (South Africa and New Zealand), are also well attended at the SFS. The **NSW Blues** play against regional teams from Australia, South Africa and New Zealand, also at the SFS, in the Super 12 competition.

Since the strengthening of international and state rugby, the Sydney club competition has been weakened, with poor turnouts at matches. The finals are in September. **Australian Rugby**

Union (9955 3466) has information on matches and teams. Ticket prices for the big matches range from $10 to $30.

Soccer

A lot of Australian kids play soccer, but only nine per cent of the population go to see any pro games. In fact, most fans follow overseas soccer more closely than the local action through TV coverage from Europe. The national A-League now plays its matches in summer and Sydney has three teams. Tickets cost from $6-$10.

Marconi-Fairfield *Club Marconi, Social Recreation & Sporting Centre Limited, Marconi Road, Bossley Park (9823 2222). CityRail Fairfield then 826 bus.*

Sydney Olympic *64 Tennent Parade, Hurlstone Park (9558 5355). CityRail Hurlstone Park.*

Sydney United *223 Edensor Road, Edensor Park (9610 6111). CityRail Cabramatta.*

Squash

Squash has had a solid core of participants since the 1960s, evinced by the number of suburban squash centres in Sydney. Courts cost around $15 an hour to hire – if you can last that long – and all courts allow you to hire racquets and balls. **NSW Squash** (9660 0311) can provide more information.

Swimming

As with athletics, swimming's popularity is set to rise in the lead-up to the Olympics. The Sydney International Aquatic Centre, an Olympic venue, is due to hold one world championships before 2000. There are 50-metre swimming pools in many suburbs across Sydney. For information call the **NSW Swimming Association** (9552 2966).

Sydney International Aquatic Centre
Sydney Olympic Park, Homebush (9752 3666). CityRail Strathfield then 401, 402, 403, 404 bus.

Tennis

Like golf, tennis is a sport in which Sydney is generously blessed with facilities. At almost any time of the day or night you can hire a court near wherever you are. Local councils administer them and charge around $12-$15 an hour. Courts are also owned by local associations, and the best way to find one nearby is to check the Yellow Pages, ask the local council who runs it, and book your slot.

From the spectator's point of view, tennis in Sydney has fallen on hard times with only one Association of Tennis Professionals (ATP) event, the NSW Open at **White City Tennis Club** (30 Alma Street, Paddington; 9360 4113), remaining.

Theatre & Dance

Love it or hate it, you'll never be indifferent to the larrikinism of Sydney theatre.

If there is one word that sums up the feeling of Sydney theatre, the word is 'larrikin'. A larrikin in Oz lingo is a bit of a stirrer – rough, tough and definitely cheeky: an iconoclast who loves to take the mickey out of everyone and everything, but especially anything that represents authority. Which translates into theatre that often has a political edge, carrying social criticism but painted in bold colours and performed with lots of lip and humour.

Sydney today is one of the most cosmopolitan and multicultural cities in the world, and this is reflected in its theatre scene. What is most striking, however, is the way it is divided up quite distinctly into two categories. The division is ideological. There is mainstream, traditional, language-based theatre; and there is contemporary, image-based theatre. Sydney audiences (apart from the extremists in both camps) patronise both.

The listings below are split along these lines. Dance venues and companies are listed separately at the end of this chapter, but they too display the same ideological divisions.

TICKETS

Generally, tickets obtained directly from theatre box offices are the cheapest and can be booked in advance. Alternatively, you can use a telephone booking agency such as **Ticketek** (9266 4800) or **FirstCall** (9320 9000), but they do charge a booking fee ranging from $1.20 to about $3 per ticket. If you're prepared to take a gamble, head down to Martin Place after midday to the **Halftix** booth (0055 26655), where you can obtain unsold tickets released by various theatre companies for half price on the day of the performance (24 hours in advance for matinées). Not all theatre companies use this service, but most of them do.

Mainstream

Whatever might be playing at either venue, a visit to the **State Theatre** or the **Capitol Theatre** (*see below*) is a must for anyone interested in experiencing the excesses of Sydney dressed in its florid, rococo style. While the experience is more architectural than theatrical, it offers an insight

*The splendidly rococo **State Theatre**: more gold than is good for the eye.*

The city's flagship, the **Sydney Theatre Company**, operates out of a wharf on Walsh Bay.

into the city. The Capitol is likely to be running the latest imported Broadway musical, but with Australian cast and production team; the State, ditto, but it often hosts upmarket pop concerts or the occasional solo show.

Bell Shakespeare Company

Information (9241 2722).

Being a touring company, the Bell Shakespeare Company has no fixed performing abode. But if they happen to be in town when you are, try to see them. They perform at the Playhouse in the Sydney Opera House (*see p213*) twice a year. The company was formed by John Bell, one of the country's leading actors, with the specific aim of building up an Australian company trained to the task of performing Shakespeare. The hope was that an indigenous Shakespearean theatre might develop. The company's approach is frequently iconoclastic, often fumbling and sometimes messy, but always interesting and occasionally inspiring. Romeo with an Aussie accent? 'Onya, Juliet!'

Belvoir Street Theatre

25 Belvoir Street, Surry Hills (9699 3444). CityRail Central. **Open** *box office* 9am-5pm Mon; 9am-7.30pm Tue-Sat; 3-7pm Sun. **Tickets** $32 adults; $20-$23 concessions. **Credit** AmEx, BC, MC, V.

Some say this is Australia's, not just Sydney's, leading theatre space. Actors scramble over each other to work at the Belvoir – even Mel Gibson has elbowed his way on to the stage here. More specifically, they want to work with its artistic director, Neil Armfield, who delivers beautiful, translucent readings of the classics or Oz's latest in highly idiosyncratic style, producing tough, politically committed but very Australian theatre. The Belvoir's programming leans toward the adventurous and the risky while delivering a mix that might include a new indigenous play alongside an old European one. Its production style is minimalist, leaning heavily on the actors. There are two stages: the large **Upstairs** theatre which stages the main programme, and the intimate **Downstairs** space, which is usually rented out to itinerant groups and co-ops. The standard Downstairs is

unpredictable, but always interesting. Here you might sample *Waiting for Godot* set in the Simpson Desert or a lesbian fantasy set in a seashell. The Belvoir after-show foyer carries the best buzz in town.

Capitol Theatre

13 Campbell Street, Haymarket (9320 5000). CityRail Central. **Open** *box office* 9am-8.30pm Mon-Sat. **Tickets** $26-$75 adults; $20 concessions. **Credit** AmEx, BC, DC, JCB, MC, V.

See introduction p209.

Disabled: access; toilets.

Ensemble Theatre

78 McDougall Street, Milsons Point (9929 0644). CityRail Milsons Point. **Open** *box office* 10am-5pm Mon; 10am-7.30pm Tue-Sat. **Tickets** $23-$35 adults. **Credit** AmEx, BC, MC, V.

Founded in 1960, the Ensemble is Sydney's oldest professional theatre company. It began life above a fruit shop in North Sydney, and went on to create its own theatre in a converted boatshed by the harbour, where it still resides. The Ensemble is famous for introducing Sydney to its first acting school, theatre-in-the-round and the delights and palls of the Method – using all, nevertheless, to produce some of the best acting and most rigorous theatre in the country during its heyday in the 1960s and early 1970s. Today, the Ensemble is no longer in the round, and it offers safe, middle-class fare to a mainly middle-aged, middle-class audience. It's still worth a visit, though, either to enjoy the harbour view or simply to pay homage to an Australian theatrical sacred site.

Disabled: access; toilets.

Harold Park Hotel

115 Wigram Road, Glebe (9552 2999). Bus 433. **Open** *hotel* 11am-midnight daily; *theatre* 8-11pm Mon, Wed-Sat. **Tickets** $5-$15 adults. **Credit** AmEx, BC, MC, V.

This is a Sydney institution. In the front part of the hotel are the punters; in the back are the loonies. Or perhaps it's the other way round. That is, Harold Park is a racing pub, adjacent to one of Sydney's better-known race tracks. But it is also home to stand-up comedians, impromptu acts, and all the would-be-if-they-could-bes, both on and off the tracks. Sometimes even a writer or poet drifts through, looking for a willing audience. And if you get tired of the jokers in the back room, you can always join the ones in the front bar. Harold Park is part of Sydney racing, theatrical and literary lore – over the years, it has been the venue for play readings, book readings, brawls and arrests. There's usually a show on Thursday, Friday and Saturday nights, but check the newspapers for details, dates and times, since everything changes here with alarming frequency and mysterious rationale. *See also chapter* **Nightlife**.

Lookout Theatre Club
Woollahra Hotel, 116A Queen Street, Woollahra (9362 4349). Bus 389. **Open** *box office* times vary. **Tickets** $25 adults; $16 concessions. **No credit cards**.
A unique theatre space in Sydney, the Lookout is a room on the first floor of a pub, the Woollahra Hotel, and seats only about 30 people. But less is more. Depending on the quality of the production, which varies as dramatically as the material it offers to its sardine-packed audience, the Lookout's tiny space means confronting theatre, whatever your position. Programmes range from the highly avant-garde

theatrical collage to the traditional play, the classic to the experimental. The standard is usually well above average. If you like theatre in-your-face, this is it.

New Theatre
542 King Street, Newtown (9519 3403). CityRail Newtown. **Open** *box office* times vary. **Tickets** $20 adults; $15 concessions. **No credit cards**.
Although an amateur group, the New Theatre is the oldest continuously running theatre company in the country, and occupies a proud place in Australian theatre history. Formed as part of a workers' theatre movement in the 1930s, it survives today in the same format: a theatre dedicated to producing works that take a critical stance on today's social issues. Many an Australian actor has felt the warmth of their first follow-spot here.
Disabled: access; toilets.

Stables Theatre
10 Nimrod Street, Kings Cross (9361 3817). CityRail Kings Cross. **Open** *box office* 9am-5pm Mon-Fri (and an hour before show). **Tickets** $15-$28 adults. **Credit** BC, MC, V.

Dance encounters

Aboriginal Islander Dance Theatre
PO Box 15, Millers Point, NSW 2000 (9252 0199).
At the time of writing, AIDT was housed temporarily on Windmill Street in The Rocks, preparatory to moving to new premises reputed to be a vault under the Sydney Harbour Bridge. For further information on AIDT's address and programme, phone the National Aboriginal Islander Skills Association (NAISA) on the number listed above. AIDT is the national Aboriginal and Torres Strait Islander dance company, formed in the 1970s from students attending the NAISA school. It regularly tours nationally and internationally, presenting a choreographed fusion of modern and traditional dance.

The Australian Ballet
Its headquarters are in Melbourne, but the Australian Ballet performs a summer and winter season each year at the **Sydney Opera House** (*see above*). Formed in 1962, the national ballet company has grown from a derivative, third-rate mix into a first-rate, internationally acclaimed

touring ensemble, with its own athletic stamp and style (pictured here on tour, performing *Onegin* (left) and *Of Blessed Memory*). The repertoire is mainly traditional, but recently the company has been adding more home-grown ballets to its permanent repertoire, drawn from a growing pool of talented choreographers nurtured within its ranks.

Bangarra Dance Theatre
Information (9569 4555).
Like AIDT (*see above*), Bangarra was on the move at the time of writing. New premises are likely to be in the Aboriginal Cultural Centre, Pier 4/5, Hickson Road, Walsh Bay. Although it has toured Europe and the Pacific, Bangarra is most famous for having been chosen to perform the flag-exchange ceremony for the 1996 Olympics, when Atlanta handed over the Olympic banner to Sydney. Bangarra is an offshoot of AIDT and while their aims are similar, under former Sydney Dance Company member Stephen Page, the company has become more oriented towards contemporary dance that incorporates the traditional, rather than the other way around.

Dance Exchange
With no fixed abode or itinerary, you have to watch out for this ensemble (get details from **The Performance Space** *above*). Dance Exchange is one of the most interesting groups performing in the contemporary dance scene, using the body to explore the language of dance itself. Artistic director Russell Dumas always choreographs the dancers to their limits, sometimes to a work's detriment, but at other times to its most exciting fulfilment.

Sydney Dance Company
Performs at the **Sydney Opera House** (*see above*) two seasons a year, using its box office facilities (and the Sydney Theatre Company's Wharf Two space for rehearsals and workshops). An ensemble of 15 dancers, under the long and enduring artistic directorship of dancer Graeme Murphy, the Sydney Dance Company is the city's leading contemporary dance group. Like that of the Australian Ballet (Murphy's previous home), the SDC's style is highly muscular and energetic, but with a camp patina.

Originally founded as an actors' co-op in 1978, the Griffin Theatre Company has dedicated itself to producing only Australian work, especially new pieces by young, untried writers. It offers the chance of readings and full productions to scores of budding playwrights. This is theatre in the raw staged in an auditorium with tiers to the ceiling, often filled exclusively with fellow writers, out-of-work actors and a sprinkling of strays. The building itself is the famous Stables Theatre (a nineteenth-century horse stable converted into a minute stage with seating for about 120, if everyone budges up), once home of the famous Nimrod Company that helped bring about the renaissance of Australian theatre in the 1970s. Seats are not allocated, so when the bell rings for the start of a performance, it's first elbow in, first served.

State Theatre

49 Market Street, Sydney (9373 6655/advance bookings Firstcall 9320 9000). CityRail Town Hall. **Open** *box office* 9am-5.30pm Mon-Sat, until 8pm on performance nights. **Tickets** $50-$60. **Credit** AmEx, BC, DC, MC, V.
See introduction p209 and chapter **Sightseeing**.

Sydney Opera House

Bennelong Point, Circular Quay (box office 9250 7777/information 9250 7111/fax 9251 3943). CityRail or ferry Circular Quay/438 bus. **Open** *box office* 9am-8.30pm Mon-Sat; 2 hours before show Sun. **Tickets** $31-$128 adults; $8-$20 concessions. **Credit** AmEx, BC, DC, MC, V.

The city's top mainstream venue. In addition to the **Opera Theatre** and **Concert Hall** (*see chapter* **Music: Classical & Opera**), the famous building has two drama theatres. The inventively named **Drama Theatre** is the Sydney Theatre Company's main stage (*see p214*), while the equally imaginatively named **Playhouse** is a venue for touring commercial productions, usually international or interstate, although some local theatricals plays too. Consequently the standard and type of show in the Playhouse varies quite a bit, from a Sydney-produced Noel Coward play to a confronting piece of Western Australian Aboriginal theatre to a variable West End or Broadway import. *See also chapter* **Sightseeing**.
Carpark. Disabled: access; toilets; hearing loop; information (9250 7185); TTY for hearing-impaired (9250 7347). Shuttle bus from The Domain carpark.

Sydney Theatre Company

Pier 4, Hickson Road, Walsh Bay (9250 1777).
CityRail/ferry Circular Quay then 15-minute walk. **Open**
box office 10am-8.30pm Mon-Sat. **Tickets** $41-$46
adults; $32-$36 concessions (Mon-Thur only). **Credit**
AmEx, BC, MC, V.

The STC is Sydney's flagship company and reflects the city
well. Here you will find the latest David Williamson
(Australia's most popular playwright) and the latest British
and US mainstream fare, but all delivered in the vernacular.
Like its home city, the company is eclectic, even daring, in
outlook, but brazenly pragmatic in deed. Style is everything.
Intellectual content is minimal and where possible avoided,
or – if all goes well with the choice of director – even annihilated. Sometimes, however, to the embarrassment of all, an
occasional knockout slips through. The STC makes use of
three stages: the **Drama Theatre** at the Sydney Opera
House (*see p213*) is where the company stages what it
regards as heavyweights (Williamson, Sondheim, even
Brecht gets a look-in here); **Wharf One** is for the
middleweights (David Hare, Edward Albee, Nick Enright);
Wharf Two hosts the 'experimental' work (works in
progress or the occasional classic done with some abandon
and flair). It's the latter which is more likely to be the knockout, but Wharf One has also been known to throw the occasional stunner. As there is no direct public transport to the
Walsh Bay wharfs, it's a good idea to take a cab at night. *See
also* **The Wharf** *in chapter* **Restaurants**.

*Disabled: access; toilets. Matinée shuttle service (Wed,
Sat) from Queen Victoria Building.*

Contemporary Performance

Elsewhere, the groups listed here might go under
the heading 'alternative' or 'underground', but in
Sydney they are a very active and significant part
of the theatre scene. What's more, the performance
groups you are likely to catch here are those that
usually end up on the international touring circuits
under the banner of 'Australian theatre'.

The Performance Space

199 Cleveland Street, Redfern (9319 5091). Bus 372.
Open *box office* times vary. **Tickets** $10-$20 adults; $10
concessions. **Credit** BC, MC, V.

This is contemporary performance's headquarters, and
nearly every contemporary performance company in the
city operates from here. On the first floor are galleries and
a small studio space for intimate installation and devel-
opmental work; downstairs at the back is the huge open
performing space, where you can see everything from *The
Pornography of Performance* to *The Aboriginal Protesters
Confront the Proclamation of the Australian Republic on
January 1, 2001* or a production of *The Commitment* by
Heine Muller. The kind of work you get here is usually
multimedia based and corporeal, with image taking prece-
dence over language. Film, video, dance and theatre merge.
The Performance Space hosts a major conference on contemporary performance annually for two weeks, (usually
in late July or early August) which is a must for head-
bangers. Performers to watch out for include Legs on the
Wall, Entr'acte, Open City, Post Arrivalists, Tess de
Quincey, Nigel Kellaway, Splinters and Gravity Feed. *See
also chapter* **Museums & Galleries**.

Sidetrack Performance Group

9/142 Addison Road, Marrickville (9560 1255). Bus 428.
Open 9am-5pm, 7.30-8pm, Mon-Fri. **Tickets** $15-$20
adults; $10 concessions. **No credit cards**.

If you reach up, you might just be able to touch the jumbo
jet coming into land over your head. It's all part of Sidetrack,
which has been producing some of the best contemporary
performance work in the country for 20 years in a small community hall in the wilds of inner-city Marrickville, right
under the flight path. But Sidetrack takes comfort in Cage,
who says an artwork unable to survive the noises of the modern world ain't modern. This group most certainly is –
multilingual, multicultural, multi-skilled and multi-critical.

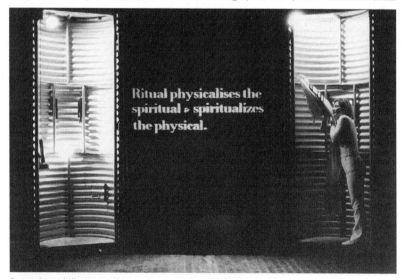

Ritual physicalises the
spiritual & spiritualizes
the physical.

Image-based theatre at the very contemporary **Performance Space**.

In Focus

Business

As Sydney takes her place as one of the business capitals of the Pacific, her financial services have met the challenge head on.

Making a fast buck at the **Australian Stock Exchange**.

Think of Sydney, and images of busy executives wielding mobile phones and thrashing out multi-million-dollar deals don't exactly spring to mind. But you'd better get used to the idea, because this is a city on the move. Having traded for so many years on the attractions of its stunning setting, Sydney has begun to take on a much more serious role as one of the major capitals of the Asia-Pacific region and a business city of international standing.

It may be many hours' flying-time from the corporate capitals of the world, but modern communications have thrown Sydney into the thick of international affairs, and it is meeting the challenge head on. The city's central business district (the CBD), once a low-rise collection of nondescript buildings, now boasts a towering skyline to rival any in Europe, the United States or Asia. From the golden crown of Centrepoint to the sleek lines of Chifley Square, Sydney both looks and feels like a city ready to do business. To fit this new-found status, services have improved beyond recognition.

Doing business in Sydney is easy. The CBD is contained within a small, mostly walkable area, serviced by taxis, trains, ferries and buses. From Circular Quay to Central Station, the city operates largely on a grid system, with the major streets of Clarence, York, George, Pitt, Castlereagh, Elizabeth, Phillip and Macquarie running in a north-south direction. This area houses most of the major banks, corporations, law firms and up-market businesses and is also the city's main commercial and tourist centre. You can shop, eat, drink and take in the major sights in between your business appointments.

If you're in town for a conference, your business day will focus on Darling Harbour and the **Sydney Convention & Exhibition Centre**. If you need to do business in North Sydney, the city-within-a-city, it's an easy cab ride across the Harbour Bridge. Nowhere is very far in Sydney, which means that business can be conducted on the run, leaving time to enjoy the more relaxing aspects of the place. After all, who wants business to be all work and no play?

DOING BUSINESS IN SYDNEY

Despite its fun-loving image, Sydney prides itself on being the corporate and commercial hub of Australia and is surprisingly formal when it comes to business. A dress code of business suit for both men and women is pretty strictly adhered to, though it is generally swapped for skimpy jogging gear at lunchtime.

The business day starts early – usually by 8am – and ends late, to take account of the time difference with the major international markets. Most Forex and money markets operate 24 hours a day, however, so you're never really out of touch. The long lunch went out with the 1980s, so you can expect people to be back in their offices by 2.30pm. The general business atmosphere combines a mix of British formality, American drive and Australia's preference for understatement and lack of pretension. In short, it'll pay to be on your toes.

Conventions

Sydney Convention & Exhibition Centre
Darling Harbour (9282 5000/5050). Monorail Convention/ferry Darling Harbour.
The Sydney Convention Centre lies in the heart of Darling Harbour, a dazzling complex of shops, restaurants, cafés, bars and tourist attractions, perched on Cockle Bay. With magnificent views of the city skyline, the centre plays host to dozens of conferences and special events each year. There are five halls of 5,000 sq metres, each with its own offices, hospitality lounges and catering facilities. It lies next to the Harbourside Festival Marketplace, and the National Maritime Museum, and is a short stroll from the Powerhouse Museum, Sydney Entertainment Centre, Chinese Garden, Tumbalong Park, and the CBD. Even if you're not doing business, it's well worth a visit (*see chapter* **Sightseeing**).

Banks

For information on currency exchange, branches of the major high-street banks and emergency numbers for lost or stolen credit cards, *see chapter* **Essential Information**.

ANZ
20 Martin Place, Sydney (9227 1911). CityRail Martin Place.

Bank of America
Level 18, 135 King Street, Sydney (9931 4200). CityRail Martin Place.

Bank of China
65 York Street, Sydney (9267 5188). CityRail Wynyard.

Bank of New Zealand
333 George Street, Sydney (9290 6666). CityRail Wynyard.

Bank of Tokyo
1 Macquarie Place, Sydney (9255 1111). CityRail/ferry Circular Quay.

Banque Nationale de Paris
12 Castlereagh Street, Sydney (9232 8733). CityRail Martin Place or Wynyard.

Hong Kong Bank
Level 9, 1 O'Connell Street, Sydney (9255 2888). CityRail Martin Place or Wynyard.

Lloyds Bank
Level 40, Governor Phillip Tower, 1 Farrer Place, Sydney (9375 5555). CityRail/ferry Circular Quay.

Bank Information Lines

National Australia Bank
(13 2265).

Westpac
(13 2032).

Commonwealth Bank of Australia
(13 2221).

Citibank
(13 2484).

Useful Addresses

Australian Stock Exchange
20 Bond Street, Sydney (general enquiries 9227 0000). CityRail Wynyard. **Open** 8.30am-5.30pm Mon-Fri.

Bureau of Statistics
Level 5, St Andrew's House, Sydney Square, Sydney (9268 4111). CityRail Town Hall. **Open** 8.30am-4.30pm Mon-Fri.

Chamber of Commerce
83 Clarence Street, Sydney (9350 8100. CityRail Wynyard. **Open** 9am-5pm Mon-Fri.

Chamber of Manufacturers
157 Liverpool Street, Sydney (9372 0444). CityRail Museum. **Open** 8.30am-5.30pm Mon-Fri.

Customs Service
477 Pitt Street, Sydney (9213 2000). CityRail Wynyard. **Open** 10am-5pm Mon-Fri.

Document Exchange
153 Phillip Street, Sydney (9221 2677). CityRail Martin Place. **Open** 8am-5.30pm Mon-Fri.

Industrial Property Organisation (Patents)
45 Clarence Street, Sydney (9262 6304/9262 6305). CityRail Wynyard. **Open** 10am-4pm Mon-Fri.

Legal Aid Commission of NSW
323 Castlereagh Street, Sydney (9219 5000). CityRail Central. **Open** 8.30am-5.30pm Mon-Fri.

Tax Office
Podium Level, 100 Market Street, Centrepoint, Sydney (13 2861). CityRail St James. **Open** 8.30am-4.45pm Mon-Fri.

Trade Commission

AIDC Tower, 201 Kent Street, Sydney (9390 2000).
Open 8.45am-6pm Mon-Fri.

Courier Services

Want to send an important document across town within the hour? No worries. Sydney's courier services are now an industry in their own right, and a highly competitive one at that. Courier companies fill no less than seven pages of the Yellow Pages, each vying for a slice of the corporate action. Pick up the telephone, and a kamikaze of the cycling world will set off at breakneck speed to dispatch your document. Australia Post can deliver overnight to most city locations across the continent. Check the Yellow Pages for details of more services. For more on the postal system, *see chapter* **Essential Information**.

DHL Worldwide Express

24-hour hotline (9317 8333).
A leader in express delivery – operating door-to-door, around the world.

Allied Express

24-hour hotline (13 1373).
Australia's largest independent courier company with 400 vehicles servicing Sydney.

Ansett Courier

24-hour hotline (9748 4111).
A subsidiary of the domestic airline, which promises 90-minute, door-to-door service anywhere in Sydney.

Australia Post

General enquiries (13 1317). **Open** 8am-6pm Mon-Fri; 8am-noon Sat.

Hotels

Sydney's top-drawer hotels are all within easy walking distance of the CBD. Among those that offer full business facilities are **The Park Hyatt**, which provides personal fax machines and voice-mail; **The Regent**, which has a dedicated business centre with secretaries, boardroom, computers, fax machines and photocopiers; and **The Inter-Continental**, which also incorporates a business centre complete with fax, photocopying and secretarial services, as well as a telecommunications room. Alternatively, you can choose a cheaper hotel and work out of one of the city's business centres (*see below* **Office Services**). For details of the hotels above, together with other accommodation options, *see chapter* **Accommodation**.

Libraries

State Library of NSW

Macquarie Street, Sydney (9230 1414). CityRail Martin Place. **Open** 9am-9pm Mon-Fri; 11am-5pm Sat, Sun.
It's a case of quality rather than quantity when it comes to Sydney's public libraries. The State is the biggest and best,

promising 'information from anywhere in the world to anywhere in the State' which is no mean boast. The library, in Macquarie Street next to the State Parliament building, is a superb research centre with well-trained staff on hand to offer assistance. *See also chapter* **Sightseeing**.

Office Services

Comb the Yellow or White Pages under B for Business, and you'll find scores of companies providing office services, from equipment to computers, printing, photographic services, typing, word processing, faxing, and photocopying – everything the travelling executive could want. The centre below offers several of these services under one roof.

The Business Centre

12th Floor, Colonial Mutual Building, 14 Martin Place, Sydney (9232 6139). CityRail Martin Place. **Open** 8.30am to 5.30pm Mon-Fri. **No credit cards.**
No job is too big or too small for this outfit – the only problem may be the queue. One of Sydney's leading office centres, it offers typing, as well as word processor and desktop publishing services. Staff can also fax documents, although there are no modem or Internet facilities. The centre is always busy, so you may have to be patient, although urgent requests are usually met.

Translators

Given Sydney's multi-cultural mix, it's not surprising that you can find a translator for just about every language. All promise fast, accurate and low-cost services covering documents of any nature and content. Check the Yellow Pages for a complete list.

Ethnic Affairs Commission

164 Liverpool Road, Ashfield (9716 2248). CityRail Ashfield. **Open** 9am-5pm Mon-Fri. **Credit** BC, MC, V.
A NSW Government service offering all-language translations and interpreting of legal, commercial, medical, technical and other documents.

Commercial Translation Centre

Level 20, 99 Walker Street, North Sydney (9954 4376). CityRail North Sydney. **Open** 9am-5.30pm Mon-Fri. **Credit** BC, MC, V.
Express translations and typesetting, business and conference interpreting, in Japanese, Korean, Chinese, Russian and all European languages. All documents considered.

Newspapers & Magazines

There are four major dailies, the *Sydney Morning Herald*, the *Australian*, the *Australian Financial Review*, and the *Daily Telegraph*. The *Sun Herald* and *Sunday Telegraph* are Sunday tabloids. All have business sections. *See chapter* **Media** for more details.

Business magazines include the *Business Review Weekly*, printed by Kerry Packer's Australian Consolidated Press; the international edition of *Business Week*; and the London edition of *The Economist*, all of which are available from leading newsagents.

Babies & Children

Practical details on travelling with tots Down Under, plus all the activities you need to know about to keep the sprogs amused.

Sydney is a laidback city with a climate that makes family life pretty easy. Crammed full of beaches, parks, waterways, and other outdoor activities, it's not a hard place to keep children amused, and there are plenty of shops and museums to take refuge in when it rains.

Before you arrive, bear in mind that hats and sunblock are essential protection from the super-strong Oz sun, especially during the summer, so it'll help if your children are used to the idea of wearing both before you arrive. Swimming practice is also a good idea, if you want to reap the full advantage of the dozens of beaches.

*Sleeping over at the **Hyde Park Barracks**.*

The Journey

If you have small children and are travelling the lengthy journey from the UK, prepare for a gruelling flight. Reserve bassinette seats for babies (suitable for infants weighing up to 16kg), since flying for more than two hours with a baby in your arms is impossible.

Breastfeeding mothers should remember that both mother and baby will need extra fluid due to the dehydrating effects of the flight. Bottle-fed babies require a bit more planning and baggage. Cabin staff are usually willing and able to heat chilled bottles for you. They will also wash and sterilise bottles on request.

If you have the time, the benefits of even one night's stopover are worth the hassle of getting in and out of planes and airports. The best location for this is undoubtedly Singapore; check out stopover packages with your travel agent.

Where to Stay

Serviced apartments are a good self-catering option and usually work out more economical for families than hotels; they also offer more privacy and freedom. Renting a house is another good option for families; holiday lets are often advertised in the *Sydney Morning Herald* and are worth investigating if you're staying any length of time. Prices rise sharply for the summer/Christmas period, and

it's always a good idea to book well ahead. *See chapter* **Accommodation** for more information.

Sightseeing

For more information on the following places, *see* chapters **Sightseeing** *and* **The Great Outdoors**.

If the sun's out (as it frequently is), a ferry cruise on the harbour, or boat trip to **Taronga Zoo** is a great introduction to the city. Alternatively, take a trip on the **Bounty**, a replica of the famous ship, which offers special pirate cruises during the school holidays. In the city centre, take in the view from **Sydney Tower** (choose a clear day), or climb up inside the **Harbour Bridge** for an equally stunning vantage point.

Then there are the beaches. **Bondi** is lively and child friendly, with a good playground next to the Pavilion and plenty of space for rollerblading and skateboarding, as well as the usual beach activities. Neighbouring, sheltered **Bronte** is a favourite with families, and has a park complete with barbecue facilities and play areas. Also worth checking out for families are peaceful **Nielsen Park** and **Parsley Bay**, **Watsons Bay** with its harbourside and cliff-top walks and fish and chip restaurants, and the double bay of **Balmoral Beach**, which is great for picnics. And if your kids are fans of *Home and Away*, then a trip to the **Northern Beaches** where the series is filmed is essential. Whichever beach you decide to use, respect the surf and stay within the marker flags when swimming.

If you've seen enough water, try an expedition to **Centennial Park**, an enormous open space buzzing with activity. Rollerblades, bikes and pedal cars can all be hired from Centennial Park Cycles, at the Musgrave entrance (*see chapter* **Shopping & Services**). The café in the park (*see chapter* **Cafés & Bars**) is right next to a toddlers' playground.

Rainy Days

Kidsports

65 Ebley Street, Bondi Junction (9386 9966). CityRail Bondi Junction. **Open** 10am-6pm Mon-Wed; 9am-6pm Thur-Sun. **Admission** $6.50 per child. **Credit** AmEx, BC, MC, V.

If tiring out the kids is essential, then try out this indoor recreation centre for children aged between 6 months and 12 years. The entry fee enables them to run, crawl and climb off excess energy for as long as it takes. There are toddler safe areas too.

Sega World

Scheduled to open some time in 1997, this will be an interactive family theme park based at Darling Harbour. Attractions include large-scale rides featuring the latest in computer graphics and Virtual Reality, and live entertainment. Family tickets will be available and opening hours are likely to be from 10am-10pm daily. Telephone the Darling Harbour Visitors Centre (9286 0110) for more information.

Museums

Activities for children are run every Sunday afternoon at 2.30pm at the **Art Gallery of New South Wales**. They range from Aboriginal storytelling to Asian dance and drama. The **Australian Museum** has plenty of dinosaur exhibits and much more besides, while the **Powerhouse**, near Darling Harbour, is packed with hands-on technological gadgetry. At the **Hyde Park Barracks**, you can investigate Sydney's past. There are convict hammocks to try out, a room 'haunted' with the moans and groans of transportees, and computers on which you can trace your family name. *See chapter* **Museums & Galleries** for more information on all of these.

Aquariums

Sydney has two excellent aquariums, at Darling Harbour and at Manly. Both afford close encounters with sharks and stingrays, as well as hands on experiences with starfish and sea urchins.

Oceanworld Manly

West Esplanade, Manly (9949 2644). Ferry Manly. **Open** 10am-5.30pm daily. **Tickets** $13.50 adults; $10 concessions; $7 children; free under 4s. **Credit** BC, MC, V.
Sharks are hand-fed by divers twice a day and there are four seal shows daily. Children over 12 can also dive with the sharks – beginners' dive courses cost $99. Phone Sydney Ferries (13 1500) for details of the Oceanworld Pass, which

includes entry to the aquarium and the Manly Art Gallery and Museum, as well as the return ferry ride to Circular Quay.

Sydney Aquarium

Aquarium Pier, Darling Harbour (9262 2300). CityRail Town Hall/monorail Darling Park/ferry Aquarium. **Open** 9.30am-9pm daily; *seal sanctuary* 9.30am-sunset daily. **Tickets** $14.90 adults; $7-$11 concessions; $34.90 family ticket. **Credit** AmEx, BC, DC, JCB, MC, TC, V.
See also chapter **Sightseeing**.

Visit the Tropics

Sydney International Aquatic Centre

Olympic Park, Homebush Bay (9752 3666). CityRail Strathfield, then shuttle bus. **Open** 5am-9.45pm Mon-Fri; 6am-6.45pm Sat, Sun. **Admission** $4 adults; $3 4-15s; free under 4s; $12 family ticket. **Credit** BC, MC, V.
Has a 'tropical wonderland' as well as state-of-the-art swimming pools.

Theatre & Music

The **Marian Street Theatre** runs plays and performances for children all year round. At the **Sydney Opera House**, the Bennelong Programme involves children from as young as two, giving them hands-on experience of an orchestra, as well as presenting a series of workshops (*see chapter* **Music: Classical & Opera**).

Marian Street Theatre

2 Marian Street, Killara (9498 3166). CityRail Killara. **Open** 10am-7pm Tue-Sun. **Admission** $8.50 adults; $6.50 children; $24 family ticket. **Credit** AmEx, BC, MC, V.

Trips Out of Town

For more excursions in New South Wales, *see chapter* **Trips Out of Town**.

Australia's Wonderland

Wallgrove Road, Eastern Creek (9830 9100). CityRail Rooty Hill, then shuttle bus. **Open** 10am-5pm daily. **Admission** $31.95 adults; $21.95 children; free under 4s. **Credit** AmEx, BC, DC, MC, JCB, TC, V.
A theme park, wildlife park and beach all rolled into one. Wonderland is the largest theme park in the southern hemisphere, offering more than 80 wild rides and shows staged across seven different fantasy theme lands. *See also page 94.*

Blue Mountains

Two hours' drive from Sydney, the Blue Mountains are just a small part of the Great Dividing Range that stretches for thousands of kilometres across the continent. Formed by rivers eroding a vast plateau, these unique gum tree-covered mountains offer breathtaking views. Special points of interest for children include the pinnacles that make up the Three Sisters, the ultra-steep scenic railway and cable car that runs from Katoomba, and the Jenolan Caves. *See page 249* for more information.

Mowbray Park Farm Holidays

Barkers Lodge Road, Picton (4680 9243). CityRail Picton, then 5-minute taxi ride. **Open** 9.15am-5pm daily. **Admission** *day ticket* $40 adults; $28 5-14s; $10 1-4s; *overnight ticket* $100 adults; $55 5-14s; $25 1-4s. **Credit** BC, MC, V.
Just over an hour's drive from Sydney, this offers the chance to see a working Australian farms, with hayrides, milking,

*Feeding time for all manner of strange underwater creatures at **Oceanworld Manly**.*

sheep-sheering and more. A day ticket buys you a tractor ride, all sorts of farm activities including horseriding, and lunch, although the farm is primarily geared towards overnight stays. Also in Picton is the family-friendly King George pub, one of NSW's oldest, which has its own garden.

Services

There are plenty of useful services in child-friendly Sydney. Smooth out the wrinkles in your holiday by availing yourself of some or all of the following.

Dial an Angel
(9362 4225/0412 289 789). **Open** *office* 8.30am-8.30pm daily. **Rates** from $48 first 3 hours, Mon-Fri. **Credit** BC, MC, V.
Offers an excellent nannying/babysitting service, 24 hours a day. All carers are carefully screened.

Nipper Nosh
(9310 7787). **Open** 9am-5pm Mon-Fri. **No credit cards.**
Nipper Nosh will deliver wholesome, freshly cooked, preservative- and salt-free food for babies and toddlers. The usual range of prepared baby foods and formula is available in supermarkets and chemists, including Only Organic, a selection of additive-free meals.

Sydney Nappy Wash
(9418 1884). **Open** 9am-5pm Mon-Fri. **Credit** BC, MC, V.
For the environmentally conscious holidaying parent, Nappy Wash will deliver and pick up terry nappies, at a cost of $20-$25 per week for 50-70 nappies.

Shopping

Toys

The toy sections of Sydney's two main department stores, **David Jones** and **Grace Bros** (are

you being served?) are well stocked, with toys to try, as well as buy *(see chapter* **Shopping & Services***)*. There are also five branches of **Toys R Us** across the city, the most central of which is listed below. If it's a quaint toy shop you're after, try **Kidstuff**, which specialises in high quality, low tech toys aimed at 'interesting and challenging' children up to the age of 12. For children's books go to **Lesley McKay's Children's Bookshop**.

Kidstuff
126A Queen Street, Woollahra (9363 2838). Bus 389. **Open** 9.30am-4.30pm Mon-Sat. **Credit** AmEx, BC, MC, TC, V.
Branch: 780 Military Road, Mosman (9960 5298).

Lesley McKay's Children's Bookshop
401 New South Head Road, Double Bay (9363 0374). CityRail Edgecliff/323, 324, 325 bus. **Open** 10am-6pm Mon-Fri; 10am-5pm Sat; 11am-5pm Sun. **Credit** AmEx, BC, DC, MC, TC, V.

Toys R Us
Shop 1C, The Retail Supa Centa, South Dowling Street, Moore Park (9313 8355). Bus 301, 302, 303. **Open** 9am-5pm Mon, Tue, Fri; 9am-9pm Thur; 9am-5pm Sat, Sun. **Credit** AmEx, BC, MC, TC, V.

Clothes

There are an increasing number of enticing Australian kids' labels. Look for them at David Jones and Grace Bros, or try The Kids Room.

The Kids Room
83 Paddington Street, Paddington (9328 6864). Bus 378, 380, 382. **Open** 10.30am-5.30pm Mon-Fri; 10am-4.30pm Sat. **Credit** AmEx, BC, MC, $TC, V.

Queer Sydney

Boys and girls come out to play for Mardi Gras and the Sleaze Ball, but it's mostly a man's world in the hot spots and flesh pots of Sodom-by-the-sea.

Without a doubt, Sydney is the queer capital of Australia, and probably south-east Asia. It has the largest gay and lesbian population in the country, the largest commercial 'scene' and the biggest dance parties in the world. The pooftars, dykes, trannies and bis of the Harbour City also enjoy an unrivalled social presence, cultural influence and political impact. They're everywhere, and highly visible. Chasing the 'pink dollar' is a city-wide occupation.

Queers in NSW are legally protected against discrimination and vilification, as are people living with HIV/AIDS. Same-sex sex is completely legal (the age of consent is currently 16 for females but 18 for males, though they're working on that) and, at least in the inner city, you can walk around holding your lover's hand without raising a glance (except of the admiring kind).

Sydney's queer communities for the most part are clustered in two central suburbs. The biggest is Darlinghurst (aka Darlo), around Oxford Street ('the Golden Mile'). Initially, Sydney's gay male community was centred around Kings Cross, but the influx of hetero sleaze in the 1970s pushed the gay bars south to Darlo, where they have remained, prospered and multiplied ever since.

Darlinghurst is a suburb where residential buildings, supermarkets and restaurants rub shoulders with pubs, clubs and bonking palaces. It still has traces of late-Victorian charm beneath the renovations and demolitions. If you're wondering why everything's painted in shades of cream, green and brown, it's because they're officially sanctioned 'Heritage Colours', though rainbow flags predominate. The area is fast-paced, vibrant and hedonistic: a great place to eat, drink, go people-watching or person-catching.

Newtown is a slightly more easygoing suburb. Its focus is King Street, a cosmopolitan but traffic-choked main drag. The large queer community lives side-by-side with students, ferals, twentysomething straight nesters and the area's earlier migrant communities. Newtown also boasts Sydney's greatest concentration of good, inexpensive restaurants and some of the most entertaining street fauna.

Of course, gays and lesbians live right across Sydney – there's a legendary colony of lesbians in Leichhardt (known as 'Dykeheart'), for instance. San Francisco may be the queer capital of the world, but Sydney lacks the right-wing loonies, has a nicer harbour and a much sillier bridge.

SAFETY

While Sydney is one of the most tolerant places on earth for gays and lesbians, bashers and homophobes do still exist. At night, be sensible. Stick to busy, well lit streets. Walk quickly and with a sense of purpose. If you're intoxicated or just nervous, play safe and catch a cab.

LUSCIOUS LATEX

Safe sex is a way of life – 'if it's not on, then it's definitely not on', as the local slogan goes. Sydney is the epicentre of Australia's experience of the HIV/AIDS pandemic, and while a decade of safe sex campaigns has hugely reduced the incidence of new infections, the evil lurgie is still out there. Below are listed some useful sources of information, medical help and safer-sex supplies. For 24-hour helplines, *see chapter* **Survival**. The necessary equipment is readily available – finding someone to use it on is up to you.

AIDS Council of NSW

9-25 Commonwealth Street, Surry Hills (1800 063 060/ fax 9206 2069). CityRail Central. **Open** 10am-6pm Mon-Fri.
HIV/AIDS information, counselling and medical referrals.

King Street Chemist

293 King Street, Newtown (9557 3575). CityRail Newtown. **Open** 9am-6.30pm Mon-Wed, Fri; 9am-9pm Thur; 9am-6pm Sat; 10am-6pm Sun.
If you want an intimate Oz experience, check out Wetstuff, a highly recommended Australian-made lube.

Sharpes Pharmacy

12-14 Flinders Street, Surry Hills (9360 4446). Bus 377, 378, 380, 382, 390. **Open** 9am-midnight daily.

Sydney Sexual Health Clinic

Sydney Hospital, Macquarie Street, Sydney (9283 7440). CityRail Martin Place. **Open** 8.30am-7pm Mon, Tue, Thur, Fri; 2.30-7pm Wed.
Anonymous testing and advice, plus free condoms and lube.

Further Enlightenment

In any world city with a sizeable queer scene, things change faster than a drag queen between shows. Clubs open and close in a matter of minutes, pubs go gay and then go straight again at the drop of a hairpin, and the cultural geography is in a state of permanent, hysterical flux. Sydney is no exception.

For the latest on the street, the best forthcoming dance parties and even directions on 'which way to the Albury', the friendly and often spunky staff at **The Book Shops** (*see chapter* **Shopping & Services**) can't be bettered. Drop by the one in Darlo or Newtown and ask them anything that's on your mind. Then check out their stock of Oz and overseas gay and lesbian literature and non-fiction.

Also wander into the PRIDE Centre, Sydney's queer community centre, which has a plethora of information resources and pamphlets. Another source of info is the queer media. Sydney has three publications (all available from The Book Shops, PRIDE and most venues). Dykes will find the monthly news mag, *Lesbians on the Loose*, required reading. The city's two free weekly queer newspapers, *Sydney Star Observer* and *Capital Q*, also have full and up-to-the-minute 'what's on' and venue guides. For a non queer-specific events guide, pick up the *Sydney Morning Herald*'s Metro supplement, published every Friday.

PRIDE Centre
26 Hutchinson Street, Surry Hills (9331 1333/fax 9331 1199/email pride@geko.net.au). Bus 377, 390, 398, 399. **Open** 10am-6pm Mon-Fri.

Darlinghurst

For women, there isn't a huge choice in Darlo. The only regular women's venue is **On the Other Side**, on the top floor of Kinsela's (*see chapter* **Nightlife**) on Sunday nights. It starts at 8pm but doesn't hot up until around 10pm, and only goes on till midnight, so you have to be quick. It plays some very cool music and attracts a youngish, glam-dyke crowd. The occasional boy is permitted to attend on a leash. But for men, it's your suburb so you can cry if you want to… or at least crawl to another bar for that last Long Island.

Bars & Pubs

There are plenty of pubs in Darlo, catering to a wide variety of tastes. Most of the venues listed below are pretty queer from Monday to Thursday and on Sunday, but they become much more mixed (and crowded) on Friday and Saturday. Many locals avoid the Darlo strip on these nights, saving their energies for Thursday and Sunday, but there are still queers aplenty every night of the week. All pubs welcome dykes as well as gay men.

The Albury
6 Oxford Street, Paddington (9361 6555). Bus 378, 380, 382. **Open** 2pm-2am Mon-Fri; 1pm-2am Sat; 2pm-1am Sun. **No credit cards.**

If drag is the drug, at the Albury (nicknamed 'The Ordinary') they're mainlining. In the front bar it puts on drag shows seven nights a week from around 11pm, and they're widely regarded as having Sydney's highest drag production values. The much more relaxed **Piano Bar** also has entertainment nightly, usually of the homo-cabaret variety. The crowd as a whole is young and pretty, with quite a few of those straight girls who like hanging around with gay men. The music is as girlie as the clientele – expect Kylie about once every half-hour (still).

The Beauchamp
267 Oxford Street, Darlinghurst (9331 2575). Bus 378, 380, 382. **Open** noon-midnight Mon, Tue, Sun; noon-1am Wed; noon-2am Thur-Sat. **Credit** AmEx, BC, DC, MC, TC, V.
On its street level, the Beauchamp is just another 'local pub' with a friendly and unpretentious atmosphere. It gets a big after-work crowd from the local queer businesses, and is an essential place to visit on a Sunday arvo when the beer swilling gets serious. Downstairs is **Base**, the latest in queer Sydney's ongoing infatuation with unfinished wall surfaces. Basically a stone box hollowed out of the foundations, it's small, dark, minimalist and cooler than thou. The toilets (the best lit in Sydney) are shared with the ground-floor bar, so there's some cross-trade. People dance here at their own risk.

The Beresford
354 Bourke Street, Darlinghurst (9331 1045). Bus 378, 380, 382. **Open** 6am-midnight Mon; 11.30am-1am Tue-Thur; 11.30am-2am Fri, Sat; 11am-midnight Sun. **Credit** AmEx, BC, DC, MC, TC, V.
The Beresford is a local boozer, with a laid-back feel – until around 10pm on a Friday or Saturday, when it fills to the gills with (often straight) young ravers. Its big claim to fame is the range of beer on tap: try a schooner (375ml) of Coopers or a middy (250ml) of Cascade. Other attractions include an annex with pool tables and a couple of pinball machines, plus the infamous three-metre finger pointing up to the heavens on the balcony at the front.

The Exchange
34 Oxford Street, Darlinghurst (9331 1936). Bus 378, 380, 382. **Open** *Street bar* 9pm-3am Mon-Wed; 5pm-3am Thur, Fri; 5pm-6.30am Sat; 9am-2am Sun. *Lizard Lounge* 5pm-midnight Mon-Wed; 5pm-2am Thur; 5pm-3am Fri-Sun. *Phoenix* 10pm-4am Tue-Thur; 10pm-3am Fri; 10pm-noon Sat-Sun; 10pm-2am Sun. **No credit cards.**
The Exchange comes in three parts. The street-level bar, which has drag shows between 1am and 3am, occasionally applies a cover charge at the weekend, but is free on mid-week nights. It's a big bar, with some stools and a dance-floor playing popular dance tracks. Upstairs is the **Lizard Lounge**, a cocktail bar popular with dykes. Check out the balcony with a calming G&T in hand for a cool view of the

*Drag seven nights a week at **The Albury**.*

Darlo strip. Downstairs is **Phoenix**, a small and sweaty box of a dance club (also with a cover charge). There are special nights for Sydney's Asian queers, but any time it's mostly men and mostly shirtless. The fun goes on till very late and the toilets are extremely interesting, if you like that type of thing.

Flinders
63-65 Flinders Street, Surry Hills (9360 4929). Bus 377, 390, 398, 399. **Open** phone for details.
For those staying up late, the Flinders offers dancing, drinking and collapsing into corners until the small hours. Early (around 9pm), the place is often completely empty. The dancefloor is tiny but the punters don't care, gyrating away in a square centimetre of personal space. The place tends to be a migration point when other venues close, for those who don't want to pay a nightclub cover charge. As a result, the crowd is uncategorisable, ranging across ages, genders and sexualities. Worth a visit for the adventurous night owl.

The Lava Bar
Burdekin Hotel, 2 Oxford Street, Darlinghurst (9331 3066/Lava Bar 9331 8065). Bus 378, 380, 382. **Open** *street bar* 11am-12.30am Mon-Thur; 11am-3.30am Fri, Sat; *Lava Bar* 5pm-12.30am Wed, Thur; 5pm-3.30am Fri, Sat; 7pm-1am Sun.
Don't let the street-level pub downstairs (full of straight suits and hen parties) fool you... sneak a peek through a door on the side, climb a few flights of stairs, and suddenly you're in lounge lizard heaven. A young, highly hip and pierced crowd sprawls across big lounges while post-apocalyptic cocktail trash mellows out the room. It's got lots of interesting nooks and crannies and a very calming vibe. Great for a pitstop between busier scenes.

The Oxford
134 Oxford Street, Darlinghurst (9331 3467). Bus 378, 380, 382. **Open** *Street bar* 5pm-2am Mon-Thur; 5pm-3am Fri, Sat; 5pm-midnight Sun. *Gilligan's* 5pm-late daily. **Credit** AmEx, BC, DC, MC, V.
The Oxford is legendary, though for what no one's really sure. At street level is a big bar, almost universally male. It's quite sociable early in the evening, but gets cruisier and cruisier as the evening wears on. The crowd ranges across the ages and, if you're lucky, you might spot one of Sydney's few remaining clones. Upstairs is **Gilligan's**, a cocktail bar and lounge room. It gets horribly crowded (and rather straight) late in the evenings, but is actually best around sunset. If you can get a seat by the window, sip your very large drink and watch Darlo fade into the dusk.

Stronghold
227 Goulburn Street, Surry Hills (9332 2676). Bus 301, 302, 303. **Open** phone for details.
The hangout of choice for Sydney's leather community. Here you get men and women draped in acres of dead cow skins, drinking beer, talking bikes and politics and new knot techniques and generally hanging out. It's got a good feel, if a tad monocultural (though if you don't have leather, denim will do), and there's a very pleasant courtyard for the warmer months. Best in the early evening and late at night.

Mixed Bars

Grand Pacific Blue Room
See page 111 for listings.
It offers cool food until around 11pm, then becomes a laid-back but very classy jazz-soaked cocktail hangout.

Green Park Hotel
See page 129 for listings.
Stylish and buzzy local bar on Victoria Street with a huge cross-section of clientele. If you're staying at the Cross, this makes a nice first port of call before heading up the road to Oxford Street.

Essential for dancing queens: **Midnight Shift**.

Judgement Bar
Courthouse Hotel, 189 Oxford Street, Darlinghurst (9360 4831). Bus 378, 380, 382. **Open** 11am-3am Mon-Thur; 24 hours Fri, Sat; 11am-midnight Sun.
Though not strictly a queer venue, this is the place where various Darlo tribes meet to mingle – poofs, dykes, ferals, punks, sex-radicals, backpackers and straights from the suburbs. It can get nasty, but there's very efficient security.

Clubs

DCM
31-33 Oxford Street, Darlinghurst (9267 7380). Bus 378, 380, 382. **Open** 11pm-5am Thur; 11pm-6am Fri; 11pm-9am Sat; 10pm-8am Sun. **No credit cards**.
Sydney's biggest dance club, with more Hi-NRG than is decent, a very large dancefloor and excellent lighting. There's also a large and buzzy bar, plus a few lounges to collapse on to. Gets rather straight on Fridays and Saturdays – the discerning queer should try Thursday or Sunday after midnight. Very popular with gym bunnies and usually a shirt-free zone on the dancefloor.

The Midnight Shift
85 Oxford Street, Darlinghurst (9360 4319). Bus 378, 380, 382. **Open** noon-3am Mon-Wed; noon-4am Thur; noon-5am Fri, Sat; noon-midnight Sun. **No credit cards**.
Another Sydney legend. At street level is a dark but friendly bar, with no cover charge and a wide range of punters. Upstairs is the dance club (men-only at the weekend and mostly men the rest of the time). It's not quite as big as DCM (*see above*) and squeezes the boys into a sweaty ruck of flesh, which is exactly how they like it. The dancefloor gets like a furnace, but fortunately the bar area has windows overlooking Oxford Street. Utterly essential for dancing queens.

Festive occasions

Queer Sydney's big night out is the **Gay & Lesbian Mardi Gras Parade**, held annually on the first Saturday of March. As many as half a million people line the inner-city streets to watch the spectacular procession, with hundreds of floats and thousands of exotically frocked or semi-naked participants. It takes three hours to pass by and is the largest street event in Australia.

The parade began in June 1978 as a Stonewall riot commemoration, then moved to late summer in 1980 to allow the activists to bare more flesh in warmer weather. Since then, some people complain it has lost any political edge, yet its core message of 'reclaiming the streets' remains as potent

as ever. And, of course, it's fabulous fun, a huge tourist drawcard and a defiantly sexual spectacle.

After the parade is the Mardi Gras Party, when upwards of 22,000 scantily clad queers and friends gyrate furiously in five halls until 8am, interrupted only by spectacular shows, drunken drags and fascinating trips to darkened lavatories.

The parade and party are preceded by a month-long cultural festival in February, presenting the best in local and overseas gay and lesbian arts (performance, visual and cinematic) and culture (from a huge outdoor fair to leather cruises and sporting events). Full programmes are available in the months before each year's festival. To find accommodation at this time, you have to book well in advance.

October sees the **Sleaze Ball**, a huge party similar to the Mardi Gras bash, but with a darker and more erotic slant. Both are open only to Mardi Gras members. Tourists can get individual membership allowing them to buy one ticket each. Tickets have to be bought in advance: Mardi Gras and Sleaze tend to sell out a month beforehand, so get your travel agent to make arrangements or contact the Mardi Gras office (9557 4332/fax 9516 4446) in advance. Don't turn up a week before expecting a ticket because you won't get one, no matter how much you beg or plead. If you do miss out, there are plenty of smaller alternative parties on the night. Throughout the year, there's also a biggish dance party every month or so (keep an eye out in the queer press for details).

Sydney Gay & Lesbian
MARDI GRAS

This year and every year – travel with us to the largest gay party on earth

Travelling over the Mardi Gras period? Then don't forget that we have guaranteed accommodation in Sydney just off Oxford Street, and anyone travelling with us to the Mardi Gras can pre-purchase their Party Ticket! Call for our Mardi Gras brochure.

ATOL 3231
CIVIL AVIATION AUTHORITY

Accredited Agents for
Sydney Gay & Lesbian Mardi Gras '97

0181 902 7177

MAN
AROUND

Holidays of a Lifestyle

Taxi Club

See page 130 for listings.

When everything's closed, when desperation strikes, never fear – there's always the Taxi. This is the venue for the adventurous, the serious drinker or, more usually, both. You have to be a member to get in, but you can get temporary membership easily. There's a bar on the first level with millions of slot machines, while upstairs on Friday and Saturday nights is Sydney's most tragic dancefloor. Favoured by drag queens after work, the Taxi's major attraction (apart from the strange and messy clientele) is that it provides the cheapest drinks in queer Sydney. It's often quite dull before 3am.

Cafés & Restaurants

Eating well in Darlo is easy – it's such a hyper-competitive market that dud eateries simply fall by the wayside within a few weeks of opening. The strip of Oxford Street between Bourke and South Dowling Streets has a plethora of fine but inexpensive restaurants covering a broad range of cuisines from Vietnamese to Balkan. All have their menus displayed on the door, so comparative gastronomy is dead simple. There aren't really queer-specific restaurants in Sydney, though cafés are a different matter. Almost anywhere on Oxford Street is fine, though the best foccacia on the strip comes from the **New Spanish Deli** (88 Oxford Street; 9331 5883), while **Cafe 191** has excellent coffee, a more pretentious atmosphere and is a great place for people-watching (191 Oxford Street; 9360 4295). Have a double macchiato and watch Darlo slip by.

Shopping

Shopping is a matter of walking. The Pop Shop has Sydney's best queer gifts with a selection of deeply camp merchandise. Both sides of Oxford Street offer quality clothing retailers – for a younger, ravey feel try Crown Street. At Gowings (*see chapter* **Shopping & Services**) you can buy that ultimate, unisex, Oz-made queer accessory, the Blundstone boot – cheaper than Docs and longer lasting.

The Pop Shop

143 Oxford Street, Darlinghurst (9331 7849). Bus 378, 380, 382. **Open** 9am-6pm Mon-Wed, Fri, Sat; 9am-7.30pm Thur; 11am-5.30pm Sun. **Credit** AmEx, BC, DC, MC, TC, V.

Newtown has a smaller commercial queer scene than Darlo, so all venues are generally both gay and lesbian apart from the Bank Hotel and Sirens for women, and the Imperial and Newtown Hotels for men.

Pubs & Bars

Bank Hotel

324 King Street, Newtown (9557 1280). Bus 422, 423. **Open** phone for details.

The Bank and its excellent cocktail bar, Sleepers, are usually a crossover space, but on Wednesdays it's dykes getting serious over a legendary pool competition. After the comp's over, they usually move out back for a few drinks with endless Etheridge and Lang on the jukebox.

Imperial Hotel

35 Erskineville Road, Erskineville (9519 9899). CityRail Erskineville or Newtown. **Open** noon-10.30pm Mon; noon-2am Tue; noon-3am Wed; noon-4am Thur; noon-8am Fri-Sun. **No credit cards**.

The pub from which the bus in 'Priscilla' departed (going the wrong way down a one-way street actually). It has three bars, all open late. The front bar is mixed, local and rather quiet. It's the best art deco bar in queer Sydney and is fun on a summer afternoon. Downstairs is mostly boys, kind of cruisey and very dark. The back bar has the drag shows, the dancing and the crush. Very mixed: since that film alerted suburban Australia to drag queens, the place has been packed out – but it's still definitely worth a trip. Open till later than you think.

Newtown Hotel

174 King Street, Newtown (9557 1329). Bus 422, 423. **Open** 11am-midnight Mon-Fri; 10am-midnight Sat; 10am-10pm Sun. **No credit cards**.

Start at the Newtown, a classic local gay pub. The comfy piano bar upstairs aims for that smoky cocktail feel, while downstairs the neighbourhood boys and girls are on the make, on for a chat or out on the tiles. There's a fiercely contested pool table, drag shows on Thursdays and Saturdays, and dancing the rest of the time. After closing, the crowd departs *en masse* down the road to the Imperial (*see above*).

Sirens

12-14 Enmore Road, Newtown (9519 5877). CityRail Newtown. **Open** 8pm-3am Fri, Sat. **Credit** BC, MC, V.

Sydney's top dyke dance spot (reputedly once a Greek wedding venue). Climb two flights of stairs to reach pulsating lesbian paradise, with varied punters – young and old, glam and butch, girlie and… well, not so girlie. A bar, a side area with tables and a biggish dancefloor are the facilities; the music veers towards popular techno, but it depends who's playing; and the atmosphere is welcoming. Friday is girls only; on Saturday, boys are allowed in if accompanied by two dykes.

Restaurants & Shops

Like Darlo, Newtown has a huge variety of restaurants, and almost any Newtown café can cut the mustard – take your pick from a seemingly endless string of them up and down King Street. Menus are usually on the door, and if a place is crowded, it's usually good. Newtown's queer shopping section is in the same block as the Newtown Hotel (*see above*). **The Greed Sisters Emporium** (178 King Street; 9516 1448) is similar to The Pop Shop (*see above*) and there are a couple of overpriced 'modern collectibles' retailers here as well, should you be lusting after an art nouveau smoker's stand.

The Gym Thing

If you're planning on doing the tiny-little-party-costume trip – or just want to get semi-naked with complete confidence – the following Sydney sweat joints will cater to your every desire for self-punishment. Legendary is **City Gym Health & Fitness Centre** (*see chapter Sport & Fitness*), offering everything and open round the clock. Bayswater Fitness is a more modern mirrors-and-carpet number that boasts 45 different aerobics classes as well as the usual fitness facilities. Both have a large gay and lesbian clientele, and offer short-term membership for those last-minute flesh-sculpting preparations.

Bayswater Fitness

33 Bayswater Road, Kings Cross (9356 2555). CityRail Kings Cross. **Open** 6am-1am Mon-Thur; 6am-10pm Fri; 8am-9pm Sat, Sun. **Credit** AmEx, BC, DC, MC, V.

Getting Your Rocks Off

Should you feel the need to get down and dirty (and this is boy's territory here), Sydney has a wide range of sex-on-premises venues. They come in two flavours: 'wet' and 'dry'. Pick up any essential accessories at your nearest Tool Shed.

Tool Shed

The Basement, Taylor Square, under 191 Oxford Street, Darlinghurst (9360 1100). Bus 378, 380, 382. **Open** 10am-1am Mon-Thur, Sun; 10am-3am Fri, Sat. **Credit** AmEx, BC, DC, MC, TC, V.
Should you feel the need for an extra sexual accessory during your stay, the places to go are the Tool Sheds, which stock a vast range of appliances, protuberances and fetish wear. **Branches:** 81 Oxford Street, Darlinghurst (9332 2792); 196-198 King Street, Newtown (9565 1599).

Wet: Saunas

Bodyline

58A Flinders Street, Surry Hills (9360 1006). Bus 378, 380, 382. **Open** noon-7am Mon-Thur; noon-7am Fri-Mon. **Credit** AmEx, BC, DC, MC, V.
According to reputation, Bodyline attracts the young gym-pumped spunks, while Kingsteam (*below*) caters to the more mature man, but it's very much a case of the trade on the night.

Ken's @ Kensington

83 Anzac Parade, Kensington (9662 1359). Bus 390, 391. **Open** noon-6am Mon-Thur; noon-7am Fri-Mon. **No credit cards.**
Ken's @ Kensington, or KKK (Ken's Karate Klub, Ken's Knitting Kircle… who knows?), is Sydney's oldest sauna. It's also the biggest and possesses the usual steam room, cubicle maze and coffee facilities.

Kingsteam

First Floor, 38-42 Oxford Street (9360 3431). Bus 378, 380, 382. **Open** 10am-6am Mon-Thur; 10am-6am Fri-Mon. **No credit cards.**

Dry: Clubs

The Den

First Floor, 97 Oxford Street, Darlinghurst (9332 3402). Bus 378, 380, 382. **Open** 8pm-5am Mon-Thur; 8pm-5am Fri-Mon. **No credit cards.**
The biggest (and best). Beyond a pool table and café lie corridors, cubicles, private rooms and other delights. It gets very busy at the weekend and one can usually find a like-minded soul or three.

Headquarters on Crown

273 Crown Street, Darlinghurst (9331 6217). Bus 301, 302, 303. **Open** 4pm-3am Mon-Thur, Sun; 4pm-8am Fri, Sat. **No credit cards.**
Specialises in 'fantasy play areas' (for example, a fake toilet block, plastic trees), though only the 'Ute Room' is quintessentially Australian.

Signal

Corner of Riley Street and Arnold Place, Darlinghurst (9331 8830). Bus 378, 380, 382. **Open** 11am-3am Mon-Thur, Sun; 11am-6am Fri, Sat. **No credit cards.**

Places to Rest Your Haircut

It can safely be said that any 'international' (glass front, big lobby, expensive cocktails) hotel in Sydney will be queer-friendly. A large chunk of staff at any of these places will be 'family', so you should have no hassles (rumour has it there was once a straight porter at the Hilton, but he was never found). If you want the full ghetto-accommodation experience, the place to enquire pre-embarkation is the **Australian Gay and Lesbian Travel Association** (AGLTA). It has a website at http://aglta.asn.au, which will refer you to accommodation-providers.

Travel Operators

If you're planning to travel to Sydney for the Gay & Lesbian Mardi Gras, booking ahead is essential – allow at least six months, though even that is optimistic. The following gay and lesbian travel operators (all three are AGLTA members) can take care of all your touring needs, from recommending local guesthouses to details of *bijou*, queer-owned country estates.

Breakout Tours

10 Roseby Street, Marrickville, NSW 2204 (9558 8229/ fax 9558 7149/email brkout@world.net).
Breakout can also send you a copy of AGLTA's Tourism Services Directory, which lists all Australian AGLTA members with descriptions.

Beyond the Blue

Suite 205, 275 Alfred Street, North Sydney, NSW 2060 (9955 6755/fax 9922 6036/email btb@msn.com).

Jornada

6 Manning Road, Double Bay, NSW 2028 (9362 0900/fax 9362 0788). Bus 323, 324, 325.
Specialises in the luxury gay market with an emphasis on swanning around island resorts.

Students & Backpackers

Where to study, where to stay, and where to hang out in between.

Academics may be able to explain the many complexities of our world, but ask them to organise the simplest of events – like student enrolment day – and it sends the most experienced administrators into a spin. But despite the crisis that is enrolment, the rest of the academic year is plain sailing; all Sydney universities offer a relaxed environment and plenty of study choice.

The experience students have of tertiary education in Sydney is still largely dependent on where they study. Universities differ largely in what they offer – not only in the subject matter taught and the specialities, but in the all-important campus vibe.

The Universities

Semesters run from the beginning of March to the end of June, and from August to late November. Below is a brief rundown on where to study.

University of NSW

Postal address *University of NSW, Sydney 2052 (0385 1000).*
Kensington Campus *Anzac Parade, Kensington (9385 1000). Bus 393, 394, 395, 399.*
St George Campus *Corner of Hurstville Road and Oatley Avenue, Oatley (9385 9999). CityRail Oatley.*
College of Fine Arts *Corner of Selwyn and Albion Streets, Paddington (9385 0888). Bus 378, 380, 382.*
Australian Defence Force Academy (Canberra) *Northcott Drive, Campbell, ACT 2601 (6268 8111).*
There are about as many student clubs at the UNSW as there are courses, covering all possible areas of interest – from sporting to religious, intellectual to political. UNSW started life in 1949 with only 46 students; now there are more than 28,000 students, 5,000 staff and three separate campuses. The Fine Arts faculty is particularly strong (and correspondingly popular), offering courses in photomedia, ceramics and clay, film, video art, installation and performance art.

University of Sydney

Postal address *University of Sydney, NSW 2006 (9351 2222).*

*The **University of Sydney** combines a strong academic tradition with a laidback vibe.*

Main campus *Parramatta Road, Camperdown (9692 2222). Bus 413, 436, 461, 480.*
Cumberland College *East Street, Lidcombe (9646 6356). CityRail Lidcombe.*
Orange Agricultural College *Leeds Parade, Orange (6363 5555). CityRail Orange.*
Sydney College of Arts:
Postal address *24 Mansfield Street, Balmain, NSW 2041 (9692 0266).*
Administration *58 Allen Street, Glebe (9351 1000).*
Art schools *6 Mansfirld Street, Rozelle (9351 1000). Bus 500, 501/44 Smith Street, Balmain (9351 1000). Bus 441, 442.*
Sydney Conservatorium of Music
Macquarie Street, Sydney (9230 1222). CityRail Martin Place.

Economics students, preparing themselves for the affluence they hope for on finishing their degree, can be seen leaving lectures early in their (parent's) BMWs. Most of them flock to nearby cafés in Glebe or Leichhardt or the university pub. Despite the relaxed atmosphere on campus, the University of Sydney has a strong academic and research tradition, attracting some of the State's top students. It has almost 5,000 staff and some 30,000 students. It offers both specialised courses, as well as a good choice of general degrees for students after a broader education.

Macquarie University
Herring Road, North Ryde (9850 7111). Bus 288, 292.
A multitude of road signs along the three-lane freeway north of Sydney leads you to this university, set in 130 hectares/321 acres of bushland. It offers a rural alternative to the shoulder-to-shoulder education of the city centre campuses. As a comparatively young university (it was established 30 years ago), it has maintained a tradition of innovation. It was responsible for developing the Macquarie dictionary of Australian English, and was the first university to send students to Egypt on archaeological digs. There is also a healthy music scene on campus, and bands play regularly in the university's courtyard. Tucked away in a corner of Macquarie stands the small, but by no means insignificant, Australian Radio, Film and Television School (ARFTS). This offers short courses in multimedia, film production, radio training and writing.

University of Technology Sydney
Main campus *Broadway, Sydney (9514 2000). CityRail Central.*
Ku-Ring-Gai *Eton Road, Lindfield (9514 1900). CityRail Roseville then 15-minute walk.*
St Leonards *Pacific Highway, Gore Hill (9514 1900). Bus 288, 292.*

UTS prides itself on preparing students to be professionals, and has strong links to industry. Most of the courses are vocationally based, many of the classes being scheduled at night. Because many students choose to study part-time there is less chance for socialising, though the uni bar is always full. There are no expansive grounds here – the main city campus is a collection of buildings next door to Central Station. Beyond the austere concrete of the Broadway Tower, lies the technical prowess of the engineering faculty, where both electrical and chemical engineers live. At the basement of the Tower is the cafeteria, home of the 50¢ bowl of rice. Unusually, UTS offers its students free internet access.

University of Western Sydney
Postal address PO Box 10, Kingswood 2747 (4736 0222).
Nepean/Westmead Campus *Hawkesbury Road, Westmead (9685 9273). CityRail Richmond.*
Kingswood/Werrington Campus *Second Avenue, Kingswood (4736 02222). CityRail Kingswood.*
Macarthur/Bankstown Campus *Bullecourt Avenue, Milperra (9772 9200).*
Campbelltown Campus *Goldsmith Avenue, Campbelltown (4620 3136). CityRail Macarthur.*

Hawkesbury/Richmond Campus *Bourke Street, Richmond (4571 0333). CityRail Richmond.*
Nirimba Campus *Eastern Road, Quakers Hill (9678 4002). CityRail Quakers Hill.*
The six campuses which makes up UWS offer a great alternative to the city-based universities, and the university offers strong faculties in a range of areas. Because of the its location in the west, UWS has a diverse student population. It also manages to churn out more graduates each year than any other university. Prospective students can be assured of finding nearly every conceivable discipline of study at one of the campuses here, which clock up an impressive choice of 728 undergraduate and post-graduate courses between them. In recent years, the Arts faculty has produced an increasingly reputable Communications course, and there are also excellent modules in history, psychology and computing. The university is particularly supportive to women, and has one of the country's highest number of female academic staff.

Australian Catholic University
Castle Hill Campus *521 Old Northern Road, Castle Hill (9739 2800). CityRail Parramatta, then 600 bus.*
MacKillop Campus *40 Edward Street, North Sydney (9739 2368). CityRail North Sydney/288, 292 bus.*
Mount Saint Mary Campus *179 Albert Road, Strathfield (9739 2100). CityRail Strathfield, then 414, 483 bus.*
Although associated with the Catholic Church, this university does not make a religious background part of its selection criteria. But be warned, there are statues of the Virgin Mary. ACU may not have the academic background of some of Sydney's older universities, but it does offer good quality education, with a less competitive entrance level. Smaller classes, and a tendency for students to have the same tutor for the duration of their degree, means it provides one of the more personal experiences of tertiary education.

University of Wollongong
Northfields Avenue, North Wollongong (4221 3555). CityRail Wollongong.
The University of Wollongong, south of Sydney, attracts a mixture of students from the surrounding area as well as those who choose to relocate from Sydney for the duration of their studies. Wollongong itself is about a 90 minute drive from Sydney and offers affordable accommodation and student housing in a beachside setting. It's not a university dominated by school-leavers, with 41% of undergraduates on campus being over 21. Student/staff ratios are good and the library is well-stocked. The university's isolation from the city creates a close-knit student community. Entry levels to the courses are slightly lower than at the city-based universities, with the emphasis placed on work experience and previous studies.

Eating & Drinking

All unis have their own cafeterias, but while eating on campus may be cheaper than in nearby cafés (it's subsidised by the student unions), it's not exactly haute cuisine. For students willing to venture from their ivory towers, there is an abundance of affordable cafés and restaurants in **Glebe**, **Darlinghurst**, **Newtown** and **Bondi**, all of which serve caffe lattes, nachos and focaccia as their low-cost staples.

Glebe Point Road offers a multitude of student hangouts, all within strolling distance of the University of Technology and the University of Sydney. On neighbouring St John's Road, the **Nag's Head Hotel** operates by day as a place where old-timers gather for an afternoon sherry, but come Saturday night, the place buzzes with twentysomethings, milking it for its cheap alcohol and early kick-off.

Bill and Tony's, located on East Sydney's Stanley Street has been serving up $5 pasta for over a decade now. Along the stretch of King Street, Newtown, cafés have sprung up at every second shop, changing hands with alarming frequency. The cosmopolitan **Green Iguana** is popular as an employer of students, as well as a hangout between lectures.

Moving into Darlinghurst, the **Brighton Hotel** – itself the most unassuming of all watering holes – is tucked among some of the hippest clubs and shops on Oxford Street. With its plush-pile carpet and late-night strobe lighting, it's an unlikely venue for some serious techno.

In the summer, the place to head is the **Bondi Hotel**. Its prime location on Campbell Parade overlooks the beach and there are plenty of pool tables, an accommodating dance floor and a friendly atmosphere. Not surprisingly, the pub pulls in the crowds. For more beach-front hangouts, groovy bars, as well as more gourmet eateries, *see chapters* **Restaurants** *and* **Cafés & Bars**.

Brighton Hotel
77 Oxford Street, Darlinghurst (9331 5153). Bus 378, 380, 382. **Open** 8am-midnight Mon-Sat; noon-midnight Sun. **Credit** BC, MC, TC, V.

Bill and Tony's
74 Stanley Street, East Sydney (9360 4702). CityRail Town Hall. **Open** noon-2.30pm, 6-10.15pm, daily. **No credit cards.**

Green Iguana
6 King Street, Newtown (9516 3118). Bus 422, 423. **Open** 7am-midnight daily. **No credit cards.**

Hotel Bondi
178 Campbell Parade, Bondi Beach (9130 3271). Bus 380, 382. **Open** 11am-midnight Mon-Sat; noon-midnight Sun. **Credit** AmEx, BC, DC, MC, $TC, V. *See also chapter* **Accommodation**.

Nag's Head Hotel
162 St John's Road, Glebe (9660 1591). Bus 431, 434. **Open** 11am-midnight Mon-Sat; noon-midnight Sun. **Credit** AmEx, BC, DC, MC, V.

Concessions & ID

All full-time students qualify for a student concession card. This allows heavily discounted rail, bus and ferry travel, as well as cheaper cinema and theatre tickets and entry to some museums. The cards are issued annually and are only updated if students continue in full-time study. Overseas students are eligible for an International Student Concession Card which entitles them to similar discounts.

Be prepared to show photo identification for entry into any licensed venue, including clubs, hotels and restaurant bars. The legal drinking age in NSW is 18 years.

Accommodation

Universities provide limited accommodation and usually have on-campus student housing officers who can help students find a place to live. This on-campus accommodation is limited and in high demand, so early application, before the start of each year is essential.

Universities also keep a register of accommodation available to rent in nearby areas. Inner city suburbs tend to be the most popular and convenient locations for students from UTS and the University of Sydney. **Chippendale**, **Ultimo** and **Glebe** are good areas to investigate. A number of high-rise apartments have recently been built in these areas to cater for the increasing number of overseas students who want to rent or buy in the inner city. UNWS's students head for the eastern suburbs, such as Kensington, Randwick and even Bondi.

Rent in Sydney is the most expensive in Australia, and so a room in a shared house or apartment is often the most affordable option: check local café and university noticeboards for rooms advertised for rent, or contact the university student housing officer.

For short-term options, such as backpacker and youth hostels, *see chapter* **Accommodation**.

Bookshops & Libraries

Besides the major departmental bookshops found in the city and suburbs and the various university libraries, there are a few less obvious institutions that are worth seeking out. **Gleebooks** is a gem for contemporary Australian fiction, non-fiction and poetry, as well as specialist publications both obscure and mainstream. For the spiritually-minded, the **Aquarian Bookshop**, behind the Queen Victoria Building, covers all things emotional and spiritual and is crammed with self-help, astrological and religious books. There's also a resident astrologer on hand, and the shop sells a myriad of candles and aromatherapy oils.

On a more serious note, the **NSW State Library** is one of the country's finest. The computer catalogues list a vast range of literary resources, including all the major newspapers and magazines. The staff are experts in research, and if you have time to wait for the stack service, they will scour the hundreds of bookshelves at the library for your request. On the same site is the **Mitchell Library**, where you can access hundreds of archives, plans and other primary sources. Security is understandably tight in this library. For Gleebooks, and many more bookshops, *see chapter* **Shopping & Services**. For the NSW State Library, *see chapter* **Sightseeing**.

Aquarian Bookshop
129 York Street, Sydney (9267 5969). CityRail Town Hall. **Open** 9am-6pm Mon-Wed, Fri; 9am-8pm Thur; 9am-5pm Sat; 11am-4pm Sun. **Credit** AmEx, BC, MC, $TC, V.

Backpacking

Backpackers inject a massive $820 million into the Australian tourist economy annually, much of it channelled into cafés, pubs, and supermarkets. Sixty per cent of these backpackers start their journey through Australia in Sydney.

The **Youth Hostel Association** (YHA) does much to support backpackers in their travels across Australia (422 Kent Street, Sydney, NSW 2001; 9261 1111/fax 9261 1969). The association provides a range of useful information on where to stay and how to find work, and will also put you in contact with other backpackers staying in Sydney and organise local tours. Initial membership costs $42 for the first year and $26 for renewal. This is valid worldwide to backpackers of all ages.

Travellers can expect to pay anywhere between $7 and $19 per night per person, for dormitory-style accommodation in hostels across the city. The beachside suburbs of **Bondi** and **Coogee**, 20 minutes from the city, are a mecca for backpackers, particularly in the summer months, and the impromptu party held on Bondi Beach on Christmas Day, has become notorious.

Kings Cross, Sydney's all-night suburb, is another popular place to park your pack, and is full of cheap cafés, pubs and hostels. It is also site of the **Kings Cross Car Market** (*see above and chapter* **Getting Around**), the centre for buying and selling second-hand cars, and a useful place to get advice before you set off on your travels.

If you're heading out of town, to the national parks and pristine, deserted beaches of the South Coast (*see chapter* **Trips Out of Town**), there are hostels at Bundanoon in the Southern Highlands, at Nowra, Bateman Bay, Bega, Gerringong and Merimbula.

For more information on where to stay, *see chapter* **Accommodation**; for information on working visas, and finding employment, *see chapter* **Survival**.

Women's Sydney

Q: How many Australian men does it take to change a lightbulb? A: None – it's a woman's job.

Australian chauvinism may still be alive and struggling for breath even in relatively urbane Sydney but Australian women – characteristically confident, practical and capable – more than hold their own. In fact, many are leaving their men far behind; girls consistently perform better at school than boys, and female university students now outnumber the males. And while older (45 and over) Australian professional males are being regularly retrenched with re-employment only a remote possibility, women in the same age bracket, seen as experienced flexible workers, are often snapped up by employers.

The roots of Australian male chauvinism probably go back to early settlement days, when women were regarded as convict descendants useful only for sexual gratification. But, ironically, it was precisely this that determined the world-leading, groundbreaking character of the Australian feminist movement. The nation now has one of the best records for sexual equality on the planet.

Australia was the second country to give women the vote (1894 in South Australia, 1902 federally). By 1974 equal pay for equal work had been attained, and many other pressing issues had been addressed. The sex discrimination act was subsequently passed in 1984, but there are still many goals to achieve. In real terms, Australian women still do not earn the same as their male counterparts, and in New South Wales only around 15 per cent of local government members are women. Only 10.2 per cent of the federal House of Representatives are women, compared with nearly 13 per cent in the US. At home, even when an Australian couple are both fully employed – surprise surprise – the female still does twice her share of the housework.

Q: Why do Australian women prefer chocolate to sex? A: With chocolate there's no need to fake it. Forget the clichéd Australian male's idea of foreplay: 'Brace yourself, Sheila.' In reality, a 1996 global sex survey of 10,000 people across 15 countries revealed that when it comes to sex, Australians score. The survey, conducted by condom manufacturer Durex, rated Australians up there with the French as some of the world's best lovers. Australians were equal second (alongside the British and the Americans) in the sexual

The Women's Library. *See page 236.*

prowess stakes after comparisons on a range of factors. Not only do they have sex more frequently than most nations (an average of 116 times a year, against Italy's paltry 96), but they are relatively considerate lovers, with 42 per cent concerned about 'partner satisfaction', beating hands down the Americans, the South Africans and the Germans, among others (girls, a tip: make Canada your next stop). For such a laid-back nation, Australians are also surprisingly keen on 'safe sex', the majority using a condom with a casual partner.

Q: How many Australian men does it take to change a lightbulb? A: 16. One to change the bulb and 15 to stand around saying 'Goodonya mate'. If you find yourself sweet on an Aussie, bite your tongue if you don't like his buddies. Aussie male bonding is no myth. One theory behind it, is that male comradeship was fostered by the tough life of the early white settlement days when females were scarce. In fact, the truth is that the only people prepared to listen to endless footie talk are other men.

Health & Safety

Sydney is well served by health centres, advisory services and information lines. For specific contacts check the White Pages under 'Women' and the Yellow Pages under 'Community Health Centres'.

As far as safety is concerned, it's wise not to get too relaxed about Sydney's easygoing attitude. Buses are safer than trains at night. On the train, always sit in the carriage next to the guard, indicated on the platform by the 'nightsafe' markings. Or take a cab. Hitch-hiking is no longer considered safe; the gruesome 1992 'backpacker murders' of travellers hitching just outside Sydney highlighted the dangers. Public transport is cheap and a lot safer. If you unlucky enough to be assaulted, contact the Sydney Rape Crisis Centre first; they will direct you to the nearest sexual assault centre. A worker will counsel you and ensure that you are seen by a sympathetic, trained police officer. *See chapter* **Survival** for more information on health services available in Sydney.

Leichhardt Women's Community Health Centre

55 Thornley Street, Leichhardt (9560 3011). Bus 436, 437, 438, 461, 480. **Open** 9.30am-1pm, 2-5.30pm Mon, Fri; 9.30am-1pm, 2-7.30pm Tue, Thur (by appointment).
Medical help for all women, including free consultations.

NSW Women's Information & Referral Service

(1800 817 227). **Open** 9am-5pm Mon-Fri.
Helpful organisation with information on rape, violence, sex discrimination, legal referrals, education, work, accommodation, government services, support groups and health centres offering medical help. Interpreters are available.

Pregnancy Advisory Services

195 Macquarie Street, Sydney (9221 7338). CityRail Martin Place. **Open** 8.30am-4pm Mon-Wed, Fri.
Offers pregnancy testing, contraception, the morning-after pill, counselling and ultrasound scanning.

Rape Crisis Centre

(1800 424 017). **Open** 24 hours daily.

Travelwatch

(1800 673 305).
A free phone-in security service. Details of your travel plans and expected time of arrival are taken, then handed to the police if you don't report in. You can also have a mailbox number (costing $5 per month) and a free voicebox number on which your contacts can leave recorded messages.

Women's Legal Resources Centre

PO Box H154, Harris Park, NSW 2150 (9637 4597). **Open** *free legal helpline* 9.30am-12.30pm, 1.30-4pm Mon, Tue, Thur, Fri; 9.30am-12.30pm Wed.

Accommodation

If you're travelling alone and looking for somewhere extra secure to stay, there are some women-only hostels in Sydney. The **Elevera Private Hotel** (9929 7441) in the affluent north shore suburb of Neutral Bay and **Vita's Place** (9810 5487) in Birchgrove cater exclusively for women.

Alternatively, try one of the following (*see chapter* **Accommodation** for more information on them). If you're looking for a home-from home, try one of the bed & breakfast/guesthouses such as the **Periwinkle Guest House** (9977 4668/fax 9977 6308) in Manly, or **Tricketts Luxury B&B** (9552 1141/fax 9692 9462) in Glebe.

Pub hotels are often cheap (though not recommended for the shrinking violet). Good ones to go for are the **Lord Nelson Brewery Hotel** (9251 4044/fax 9251 1532), the **Palisade Hotel** (9247 2272/fax 9247 2040) or the **Mercantile Hotel** (9247 4306/ 9247 3570/fax 9247 7047), all in The Rocks area.

Backpacker-style hostels are good for meeting other like-minded women travelling solo. Some dorms sleep both sexes, so check first if it's important to you. **Alishan International Guesthouse** (9566 4048/fax 9525 4686) in Glebe and Newtown's **Billabong Gardens** (9550 3236/fax 9550 4352) are popular and offer comprehensive facilities. Affordable and right in the heart of the CBD is the **Y on the Park Hotel** (9264 2451/fax 9285 6288).

Mid-range security-conscious options include the **Wynyard Vista Hotel** (9290 1840/1800 652 090/fax 9290 1870) and **The Russell** (9241 3543/fax 9252 1652). If money is no object, get a room with extra security on floors two or three at the **Observatory Hotel** (9256 2222/fax 9256 2233), or indulge in an all-frills Corporate Woman Room at the **Ritz-Carlton Sydney** (9252 4600/ fax 9252 4286).

Books

See also page 266 **Further Reading**.

Feminist Bookshop

Shop 9, Orange Grove Plaza, Balmain Road, Lilyfield (9810 2666). Bus 440. **Open** 10.30am-6pm Mon-Fri; 10.30am-4pm Sat. **Credit** BC, MC, $TC, V.
Good stock of books, journals and mags by and about women.

The Women's Library

73 Garden Street, Alexandria (9319 0529). CityRail Redfern. **Open** 11am-8pm Tue-Fri; 11am-5pm Sat, Sun.
Friendly voluntary library carrying books by and about women. Browsing is encouraged and there's a children's room. A small joining fee is charged to borrowers.

Film

Australian women film-makers who have made their cinematic mark include **Gillian Armstrong**, whose string of fine credits incorporates *The Last Days of Chez Nous*, *My Brilliant Career* (based on the Miles Franklin novel and starring Australian actress Judy Davis) and, more recently, the Winona Ryder vehicle *Little Women*. **Jocelyn Moorhouse's** *Proof* – a highly charged, steamy thriller in which a young housekeeper manipulates her blind employer – won seven AFI awards. Producers like **Jan Chapman** (*The Piano*, *Love Serenade*) have also make an impact over the years. And there is a new generation of female cineastes, like producer **Glenys Rowe**, and directors **Shirley Barrett** and **Emma-Kate Crogan**. *See also* **Women on Women** *in chapter* **Film**.

Women with attitude

Jennie George
A former head of the NSW Teachers' Federation and the first woman president of the the Australian Council of Trade Unions (ACTU), Jennie George has long championed the rights of working women. Part of her mission is to modernise working conditions so that they better meet the needs of families.

Germaine Greer
For many, Germaine Greer epitomises the female liberation of the 1960s and 1970s. Her  bestseller, *The Female Eunuch* (1970), portrayed marriage as a form of legalised slavery for women. Now an advocate of radical celibacy in middle age and a passionate opponent of hormone replacement therapy, she is a lecturer at Cambridge University in England.

Janet Holmes à Court
Australia's richest woman. Describing herself as a humanitarian socialist, she is on the board of the Reserve Bank of Australia and is chairman of the Australian Children's Television Foundation, which produces and lobbies for quality children's programming.

Dame Leonie Kramer
Politically astute former ABC TV chairwoman and one of the nation's most prominent businesswomen. She became the first female professor at Sydney University in 1968 and, subsequently, Chancellor in 1991.

Jana Wendt
One of the nation's most successful television interviewers. On *A Current Affair* she walked out in protest at a story on topless hardware shop assistants. Thereafter she was permitted to vet all *ACA* stories before screening. Turning down lucrative US offers, she currently hosts Seven's popular current affairs programme *Witness*.

Theatre

Theatres that regularly stage plays written and direct by women include **The Performance Space** (9319 5091) in Redfern. This contemporary movement and dance-based performance theatre also houses an art gallery that features unorthodox artwork by female artists. The **Stables Theatre** (9361 3817) in Kings Cross puts on work by new female playwrights and the **Belvoir Street Theatre** often uses women writers and directors. For full listings *see chapter* **Theatre & Dance**.

Fitness & Relaxation

See also **Health & Beauty** *in chapter* **Shopping & Services** *and chapter* **Sport & Fitness**.

Unlimited Fitness
55 Christie Street, St Leonards (9906 5997). CityRail St Leonards. **Open** 6am-9pm Mon-Fri; 8am-7pm Sat, Sun. **Admission** $10 ($4 pool only). **Credit** AmEx, BC, MC, V. This north shore centre has a 25m swimming pool, gym, circuit and aerobic classes, and childminding facilities.

World of Club Fitness
167 Castlereagh Street, Sydney (9267 6644). CityRail Town Hall. **Open** 6.30am-8.30pm Mon-Fri; 9am-12.30pm Sat. **Admission** $8-$10. **Credit** AmEx, BC, MC, $TC, V. A large city fitness centre with computerised gym equipment, circuit and aerobics classes, massage, physio, beauty therapists, sauna and solarium.

Zanadu Health
248 Pitt Street, Sydney (9283 5888). CityRail Town Hall. **Open** noon-2am daily. **Admission** $22 ($56 incl 45-minute massage). **Credit** AmEx, BC, DC, MC, $TC, V. Located above Brashs record shop, Zanadu's ladies section has a hot spa, cold plunge pool, sauna and steam room. It also offers shiatsu, body scrubs and a beauty salon. fresh Fruit juices, sandwiches and robes come free.

Media

The quarterly *Refractory Girl Established* ($6.95) is a popular Australian feminist journal, while quirky computer mag *Geek Girl Respected* ($6), also quarterly, caters to cyberwise lasses.

Radio programmes particularly aimed at women include *Women on the Line* (current affairs, Monday 9am); *Sheherezade* (women's issues, Wednesday 8.30pm); and *Crystal Set* (feminism for the 1990s, Wednesday 9pm), which can all be heard on 2SER (107.3 FM). *See also chapter* **Media**.

Events & Activities

Every year, to celebrate **International Women's Day** in March, there is a month-long series of events and well attended street marches.

If you're feeling hearty, contact **BreakOut** (9558 8229/fax 9558 7140) who run adventure tours for women – including mountain-biking and abseiling – to the Hunter Valley and Blue Mountains.

"AACUDOON ABROON"

ROUGH TRANSLATION:
Landlord, I require a bottle of your superlative ale forthwith.

Readily available on tap, and in good liquor outlets throughout NSW.

Trips Out of Town

Trips Out of Town

Bushwalks and beaches, winetasting, time-wasting in cafés, or pottering around on the river – New South Wales is just one big outdoor playground.

Sydneysiders are lucky. The city they live in may be part of Australia's biggest and most populous urban concentration but, within little over a three-hour radius, they can access huge pockets of remote rainforest and wilderness, some of the country's cleanest, bluest bays and expanses of empty, white sandy beach.

In fact, much of the area surrounding Sydney itself is one big playground for the city's inhabitants, be it aquatic (diving, surfing or sailing on the coast, fishing on the Hawkesbury river) or land-based (bushwalking in the national parks or rock climbing in the Blue Mountains). There's also plenty nearby for those with more sedate pleasures in mind – the vineyards of the Hunter Valley lie inland to the north, while the gentle landscape and period villages of the Southern Highlands are within an hour-and-a-half's drive of the city.

There's Aboriginal heritage everywhere, some of it dating back over 40,000 years, colonial history from the earliest days of settlement, and even a species of tree prevalent 150 million years ago, discovered in 1994 only 150 kilometres (93 miles) from the city centre. Much younger and just over three hours' drive away, is the federal capital, Canberra, with its national buildings, galleries and monuments.

Most areas are easier to get to by car (particularly those off the beaten track), but where possible we have included details of local train or bus routes. We've also included suggestions for where to eat or stay – local tourist offices will have details of further options, as well as information on campsites. Unless otherwise stated, room rates quoted below are for a double room; restaurant averages are for a three-course meal without drink. Journey times are estimated from central Sydney.

For more general information on the areas surrounding Sydney contact the Countrylink NSW Travel Centre (*see below*). For details of car rental companies *see chapter* **Getting Around**.

Central Station
CityRail Central. (Countrylink Central Reservations 13 2232/Public Transport Infoline 13 1500).

Countrylink NSW Travel Centre
11-31 York Street, corner of Margaret Street, Sydney (9224 2742/13 2077). CityRail Wynyard. **Open** 9am-5pm Mon-Fri; 9am-1pm Sat.
Branches: phone 13 2232 for the location of your nearest.

Heading North

Hawkesbury River

The Hawkesbury River, which for much of its length skirts the outer edges of Australia's biggest city, is a great greeny-brown giant, licking over 1,000 kilometres of foreshore as it curls first north-east and then, from Wisemans Ferry, south-east towards the sea, emptying into an estuary at Broken Bay. In parts, despite its proximity to Sydney, it is so sparsely populated (road access to much of its wooded slopes is limited) that sightings of a Loch Ness-type monster have been reported along it. But the river's course is also rich both in Aboriginal heritage (there are rock engravings and cave paintings that date back 14,000 years around the river they called Deerubbun and settlement history (upstream are towns like Windsor and Richmond, which are nearly as old as Sydney itself).

Although the uncontrolled growth of Sydney has polluted the Hawkesbury – there was an outbreak of toxic algae in the early 1990s – its fjord-like saltwater creeks and inlets are still ideal for exploring by boat. Houseboating holidays are increasingly popular: pottering around on the river brings with it a palpable sense of peace and a miraculous feeling of isolation, given that Sydney is just around the corner. Late autumn and early winter (May-July), with their crisp blue skies, morning mists and lack of crowds, are good times to go.

Like the nearby Blue Mountains, the Hawkesbury has long been a source of inspiration to painters and writers. Nineteenth-century artists

Telephone number changes
From 18 August 1997, as the final phase of a vast re-numbering scheme, the area code for the whole of NSW and the ACT will change to 02. If you are phoning a non-Sydney number listed in this guide from within Australia before August 1997, you'll need to add a 0. *See also chapter* **Essential Information**.

Watch the world float by from the **Berowra Waters Boatshed**. *See page 242.*

Charles Conder, Julian Ashton and Arthur Streeton all worked here; Streeton painted *The Purple Noon's Transparent Might* at Freeman's Reach, overlooking the river near Richmond.

RICHMOND & WINDSOR

European settlers explored upstream as early as 1789 when Governor Phillip reached what is now Richmond Hill and recognised the area's agricultural potential. It wasn't long before the land was being tilled with basic tools and supplying much-needed food to Sydney, which in its early years was near starvation. So sprang up the towns of Windsor and Richmond (recalling the names of villages on the banks of the Thames back in England), which, along with nearby Pitt Town, Wilberforce and Castlereagh, later became known as the Macquarie Towns, after the 'Father of Australia', Lachlan Macquarie.

The town of **Windsor** retains many of its original buildings, including Australia's oldest inn (the Macquarie Arms, built in 1815), its oldest Courthouse (1822) and St Matthew's Anglican Church, built by convict labour from a design by convict architect Francis Greenway (also in 1822). Australian soap addicts may recognise some of Windsor's other buildings from *A Country Practice*, which was originally filmed here; also of note (literally) is John Tebbutt's house and observatory (with its outsized telescope) which are depicted on the $100 bill. With its riverside setting, restored period cottages and pedestrianised mall

complete with small shops and a water-wheel, Windsor is a place of some charm.

It's worth taking a cruise down river from Windsor aboard the Deerubbun (Windsor River Cruises; 9831 6630). Alternatively, join one of the Hawkesbury Heritage Discovery Tours (4577 6882), and you'll get an enthusiastic low-down on the area's history from a local guide. Within easy reach of Windsor, there's more colonial architecture at **Richmond**, a tree-lined garden town where the railway station dates back to 1822, and **Ebenezer**, which claims to have Australia's oldest church (Ebenezer Uniting Church on Coromandel Road, built 1809). It's also home to the more modern Tizzana winery (Tizzana Road, Ebenezer; 4579 1150), with good reds and a zesty port, catering to an age-old thirst.

Continuing on the colonial heritage trail, the fourth Macquarie Town of **Wilberforce** (established 1810) has a collection of original nineteenth-century buildings grouped together in the Australian Pioneer Village (Buttsworth Lane, Wilberforce; 4575 1457). These include a police station (1891) in which there's barely enough room to swing a cat burglar and Rose Cottage (home of Australia's first free settler family), the country's oldest timber building (built 1811, mind your head). The village also has demonstrations of traditional skills such as billy tea-brewing, damper-making, boomerang-throwing (mind your hand) and sheep-shearing blindfold (mind everything). You can view much of the lush upper Hawkesbury valley from the rolling foothills of the Blue Mountains at **Kurrajong Village** (all craft shops and cafés) and you can sometimes see as far as Sydney Harbour Bridge from **Kurrajong Heights**.

WISEMANS FERRY & ST ALBANS

The Hawkesbury's change of course in its midreaches is marked by an S-bend at **Wisemans Ferry**, another of the river's historic villages. Named after Solomon Wiseman who, after being sent to Australia for stealing, was granted land in the area as an emancipist, it has the country's oldest ferry service (which Wiseman established in the 1820s). The ferry still runs 24 hours a day (one of the few remaining free rides in New South Wales; 4566 4337) and the wealthy merchant's former home, Cobham Hall (built 1826), now houses the Wisemans Ferry Inn. Up the road in the Macdonald River Valley, at the secluded hamlet of **St Albans**, is another colonial inn – the Settlers Arms – and in the Old Cemetery lies the grave of William Douglas, a First Fleeter who died in 1838. Strong rumours also suggest that St Albans was Windsor magistrates' preferred venue for illicit nooky over the years.

BEROWRA

The lower reaches of the Hawkesbury are its most spectacular, with forested steep-sided banks and a number of sizeable creeks branching off its wide sweep. Near the end of one of them, **Berowra Creek** (west of the Pacific Highway), at the foot of two deep bush-covered hills, is beautiful **Berowra Waters**. There's not much more here than a small car ferry, a cluster of bobbing boats and a few restaurants offering fine cuisine (including Hawkesbury oysters). Much of the remainder of the river, as it makes its way to the sea, is equally tranquil – notably the slender fingers of water that make up **Cowan Creek** (east of the Pacific Highway). It's here, in the **Ku-Ring-Gai Chase National Park**, that many people choose to cruise or to moor for a sedentary spot of fishing (*see chapter* **The Great Outdoors**). If you haven't yet gone for houseboating, Australia's last riverboat postman may be the answer. The four-hour cruise from **Brooklyn** allows you to participate in the delivery of mail to such local personalities as the Pink Elephant, while taking in the scenery (runs from Brooklyn Wharf at 9.30am weekdays; 9985 7566).

Getting There

By Car

Richmond & Windsor Via Hornsby: Pacific Highway (Route 83) to Hornsby; Galston Road; then Pitt Town Road. Via Pennant Hills: Epping Road (Route 2) to Pennant Hills; then Route 40. Via Parramatta: Western Motorway (Route 4) to Parramatta; then Route 40. Sydney to Windsor 59km (37 miles); journey time 1-1½ hours.
Wisemans Ferry & St Albans Pacific Highway (Route 83) to Hornsby; Galston Road; then Old Northern Road.

Berowra Waters Pacific Highway (Route 83); 12km (7½ miles) north of Hornsby, Berowra turn-off signposted. **Brooklyn** turn-off 12km (7½ miles) further north.

By Train

Regular train service to **Windsor** and the upper Hawkesbury River area on the Richmond line (via Blacktown) from Central Station. Journey time 1 hour 20 mins.
Wisemans Ferry & St Albans are inaccessible by train. Main Sydney-Newcastle line from Central Station to **Berowra Waters** (via Berowra Station) and **Brooklyn** (via Hawkesbury River Station). Journey time approx 1 hour (not all trains stop at both stations). For details contact Public Transport Infoline on 13 1500.

By Bus

For details of coach services to the Hawkesbury region contact the Hawkesbury Visitor Centre or the Countrylink NSW Travel Centre (*see page 240*).

Tourist Information

Hawkesbury Visitor Centre

Ham Common, Bicentenary Park, Richmond Road, Clarendon (4588 5895/fax 4588 5896).
There is also tourist information (including houseboating details) at 1/5 Bridge Street, Brooklyn (9985 7947).

Where to Stay & Eat

Able Houseboats

River Road, Wisemans Ferry (4566 4308). **Rates** from $290 two days, one night. **Credit** AmEx, BC, MC, V.

Berowra Waters Boatshed Restaurant

Berowra Waters Road, Berowra (9456 1025).
Open lunch Wed-Sun; dinner Fri, Sat. **Average** $35. **Credit** AmEx, BC, DC, MC, V.
Great setting and an à la carte menu. BYO. Opening hours vary, according to demand.

Court House Guest House

19 Upper Macdonald Road, St Albans (4568 2042). **Rates** from $95. **Credit** BC, MC, V.

Hawkesbury Lodge

61 Richmond Road, Windsor (4577 4222/fax 4577 6939). **Rates** from $142. **Credit** AmEx, BC, DC, MC, V. Moderate to expensive with good facilities.

Luxury Afloat Houseboats

Kangaroo Point Marina, Brooklyn (9985 7344/fax 9985 7407). **Rates** from $495 (three days). **Credit** AmEx, BC, MC, V.

Peats Bite

(water access only) Berowra Creek (9985 9040). **Open** times vary. **Average** $65. **Credit** AmEx, BC, MC, V. Views and oysters; open on demand.

Ripples Houseboat Hire

87 Brooklyn Road, Brooklyn (9985 7333). **Rates** from $360 (two days, one night). **Credit** AmEx, BC, MC, V.

Settlers Arms Inn

Wollombi Road, St Albans (4568 2111). **Rates** from $100. **Credit** AmEx, BC, MC, V.
Food and accommodation available.

Wisemans Ferry Country Retreat

Old Northern Road, Wisemans Ferry (4566 4422/fax 4566 4613). **Rates** from $90. **Credit** AmEx, BC, MC, V.

Wisemans Ferry Inn
Old Northern Road, Wisemans Ferry (4566 4201).
Average $20. **Credit** MC, V.

Hunter Valley

Wine. These days the Lower Hunter Valley is synonymous with the word. No matter how people try to reinvent the region as something else, it's the wine label that sticks (even though the Hunter does not necessarily produce Australia's best wines). In some ways that's a tribute to local wine-industry marketing, which has put Hunter wines on tables around the world, not to mention in bottle shops the length and breadth of Australia. In others it's a triumph for a well organised (and relatively recent) tourism campaign, coaxing visitors to the area with the promise of fine wine, good food and upmarket guest houses.

The slight hills of the Hunter Valley around **Pokolbin** are certainly well equipped to deliver on this promise. The region boasts more than 50 wineries (from the smallest boutique to the big boys like Lindemans), which offer tastings and cellar-door sales of wine ranging from semillons and shiraz to sweet spätlese or buttery chardonnays. Mingled among the vineyards are award-winning restaurants (such as Roberts and Chez Pok) and luxury accommodation ranging from the quirky Casuarina (its eight themed suites include the 'French Bordello') and the surprisingly cosy Peppers Guest House.

While such wine-based indulgence has put the Hunter firmly on the tourist map, the area's personality is schizophrenically bound up with the vastly different industry of coal mining. Plump grapes and deep coal seams may seem an unlikely combination, but historically they've both been part of the Hunter equation. The very waterway from which the region gets its name was originally known as the Coal River (it was renamed in 1797 after the then NSW Governor, John Hunter), and the founder of the Hunter's wine-growing industry, Scottish civil engineer James Busby, arrived in Australia in 1824 partly to oversee coal-mining activities in nearby Newcastle. But while the Hunter Valley once boasted the largest shaft mine in the Southern Hemisphere which held the world record for coal production in an eight-hour shift (Richmond Main Colliery, now a museum and open irregularly; 4936 1124), all but two of its mines have now shut down. Only a few, sometimes painful, signs of the once-prime industry remain (the Bellbird Mine Disaster Memorial in **North Rothbury** marks the death of 21 men in an underground fire in 1923).

The wine industry, which sprouted from a few hundred European vine cuttings introduced to the Hunter Valley by Busby in the 1830s, has fared rather better. Seeing out the tough nineteenth

Grapemobile. *See page 244.*

century, then the Depression of the 1930s, and fighting off competition from other antipodean wine-growing regions such as South Australia, the Hunter made it to the 1970s wine-rush and flourished. In 1994, the retail value of wine produced in the Hunter was $240 million, with exports accounting for 25 per cent of that figure. Meanwhile, the amount of land under vine has increased by over 20 per cent since 1989.

Despite its small area (the main vineyard district north of the town of **Cessnock** is only a few kilometres square), the sheer number of wineries in the Lower Hunter can present the wine tourist (as opposed to the expert) with a problem. Namely, where to start? Inevitably, familiarity leads many to the bigger, more established wineries first and this is a good way of gaining an insight into the Hunter's wine-growing traditions. Large family companies such as Tyrrells (founded 1858, Broke Road, Pokolbin; 4998 7509), Draytons (Oakey Creek Road, Pokolbin; 4998 7513) and Tullochs (Glen Elgin Estate, Debeyers Road, Pokolbin; 4998 7580) have been producing wine in the area for over 100 years, while at Lindemans (McDonalds Road, Pokolbin; 4998 7684) there's a museum exhibiting old winemaking equipment. Other big wineries such as McGuigan Brothers (McDonalds Road, Pokolbin; 4998 7402) offer full on-site facilities including accommodation (*see page 245* Vineyard Resort), a gallery, a restaurant and crumbly handmade cheeses from the Hunter Valley Cheese Company.

But it would be a shame to miss out on the smaller wineries. Places like Oakvale (set against the Brokenback Range, Broke Road, Pokolbin; 4998 7520) offer the time and space for a more individual experience of tasting. Many of these boutique wineries are set in picturesque surroundings. The grounds of Pepper Tree Wines (Halls Road, Pokolbin; 4998 7539) incorporate a former Brigidine convent, now the area's swishest guest house, moved lock, stock and barrel to the Hunter for the purpose, as well as an 1870s cottage and fragrant gardens. Further afield, in **Rothbury**, the 100-acre

Wandin Valley Estate offers villas to stay in and has its own cricket ground.

Since the Hunter is reasonably flat and compact, and the wineries are never far apart, it's a good place to ditch four-wheel transport. Bicycles are available from some guest houses; they're free at Peppers and Splinters. Grapemobile (tel/fax 4991 2339) runs enjoyable day and overnight cycling and walking tours of the wineries from Cessnock. Finally, if you're not high enough already, see the regimented rows of vines from above with a sunrise balloon flight (Balloon Aloft; 4938 1955/1800 028 568).

Although locals may point to the area's galleries – Butterflies, with its small café, is a pleasant spot (Broke Road, Pokolbin; 4998 7724) – and such historic towns as **Morpeth** to the east of the region (one of the country's busiest seaports in the 1820s) and **Wollonbi** to the south (an early nineteenth-century village) it's only after you've visited a few wineries, sampled a couple of the region's restaurants and pampered yourself in one of its guest houses that you'll feel you've explored the Hunter.

BARRINGTON TOPS

Although it's less than an hour north of the Hunter Valley, the Barrington Tops (with the exception of the thinly wooded foothills around **Dungog** and the cute village of **Paterson**) is as different from the wine-growing district as it's possible to be. A national park with a World Heritage listing, its upper slopes are thick with sub-tropical rainforest containing thousand year-old trees, clean mountain streams and abundant wildlife. With its swimming holes, camping and bushwalking possibilities, the Barrington Tops is a domain for out-there enthusiasts but can also be explored with mechanical help (try Hunter Valley 4WD Tours; 4938 5031).

Further south, it's the land of green hillocks and even greener valleys, the sort of landscape that insists you jump out of bed straight on to the back of a horse or a mountain bike. Catering to exactly that desire, are country retreats like Barringtons and Eaglereach Wilderness Resort, where eco-tourism meets the comfort zone.

Getting There

By Car
Lower Hunter Valley Sydney-Newcastle Freeway (Route 1) to Freemans Interchange; then turn-off to Cessnock (Route 82). Alternatively, leave Route 1 much earlier at Calga; head through Central Mangrove (via Peats Ridge and Bucketty) towards Wollonbi; then turn-off to Cessnock (Route 132). Journey time 2-2½ hours. The main wine-growing district around Pokolbin and Rothbury is a dozen kilometres north-west of Cessnock.
Barrington Tops (just north of **Dungog**). Direct route: Sydney-Newcastle Freeway to Maitland turn-off on New England Highway (Route 15); Paterson Road; then turn right for Dungog approx 5km (3 miles) beyond Paterson. Via Hunter Valley: follow signs from Cessnock to Maitland (via Kurri Kurri) then as above. Journey time 3 hours.

The sub-tropical **Barrington Tops**.

By Train
Hunter Valley coaches connect with the regular Sydney-Newcastle commuter service. For details call Rover Motors (4990 1699) or the Public Transport Infoline (13 1500). Journey time from Newcastle to Dungog roughly 1 hour 20 minutes.
Dungog, just south of **Barrington Tops**, is served by a few daily trains from Newcastle (journey time approx 1 hour 20 minutes). Some guest houses will pick up from Dungog.

By Bus
Keans Travel (4990 5000) runs regular daily coach services to the **Hunter Valley** from Sydney. Rover Coaches offers day and weekend tours of the region (4990 1699/1800 801 012). For details of other tours contact the tourist offices (*see below*).

Tourist Information

Cessnock Tourist Information Centre
Turner Park, Aberdare Road, Cessnock (4990 4477/fax 4991 4518).
The main Hunter Valley tourist information source.

Gloucester Tourist Information Centre
34 King Street, Gloucester (6558 1408).
For information on the Barrington Tops try here or at the Cessnock Tourist Information Centre (*above*).

Maitland Visitors Bureau
King Edward Park, Banks Street, East Maitland (4933 2611).

Where to Stay & Eat

Most guest houses in the Hunter region will not take bookings for less than two nights, especially over weekends. There are more, cheaper hotels and motels in Cessnock.

Barrington Guest House
Salisbury via Dungog (4995 3212/fax 4995 3248).
Rates from $79 (full board). **Credit** AmEx, BC, MC, V.
Basic accommodation right on the edge of the rainforest.

The Barringtons Country Retreat
Chichester Dam, Dungog (4995 9269/fax 4995 9279).
Rates from $110. **Credit** BC, MC, V.
Cabins overlooking the valley, spa baths and imaginative country cooking at moderate rates.

Casuarina Restaurant and Country Inn
Hermitage Road, Pokolbin (4998 7888/fax 4998 7692).
Rates from $170. **Credit** AmEx, BC, MC, V.
Pricey, but accommodation here is the stuff of fantasy. Owner Peter Meier is also a gastronomic legend in these parts (average spend $45).

The Convent Guest House
In the grounds of Pepper Tree Wines, Halls Road, Pokolbin (winery 4998 7539/convent 4998 7764).
Rates from $255. **Credit** AmEx, BC, DC, MC, V.
The Hunter's ultimate indulgence.

Eaglereach Wilderness Resort
Summer Hill Road, Vacy via Paterson (4938 8233/fax 4938 8234). **Rates** from $150. **Credit** AmEx, BC, DC, MC, V.
Great views from the top of Mount George.

Montagne View Estate Guest House
Hermitage Road, Pokolbin (4998 7822/fax 6574 7276).
Rates from $140. **Credit** AmEx, BC, DC, MC, V.
Luxury (and a vineyard on the doorstep).

Peppers Guest House
Ekerts Road, Pokolbin (4998 7596/fax 4998 7739).
Rates from $228. **Credit** AmEx, BC, DC, MC, V.
Expensive but a real star in the Hunter, providing accommodation and an excellent restaurant in the shape of **Chez Pok** (average $40).

Roberts
Pepper Tree Estate, Halls Road, Pokolbin (4998 7330).
Average $50. **Credit** AmEx, BC, DC, MC, V.

Splinters Guest House
24 Hermitage Road, Pokolbin (tel/fax 6574 7118).
Rates from $75. **No credit cards.**
Ask about the excellent lodges.

Thistle Hill Guest House
Hermitage Road, Pokolbin (6574 7217). **Rates** from $70.
No credit cards.
This pleasant B&B with a duck and a pet kangaroo, is one of the few places that cater for one-nighters.

Vineyard Resort
Next to McGuigan Brothers winery, McDonalds Road, Pokolbin (4998 7600). **Rates** from $95. **Credit** AmEx, BC, DC, JCB, MC, V.

Wandin Valley Estate
Wilderness Road, Rothbury (4930 7317). **Rates** from $40. **Credit** AmEx, BC, DC, MC, V.

Central Coast & Port Stephens

This coastal strip, stretching from the Hawkesbury River in the south to glorious Port Stephens in the north, is one big aquatic playground. It encompasses superb surf beaches and calm seaside lagoons before industrial Newcastle, and impossibly blue waters further north around Nelson Bay. Most weekends, what seems like half the population of Sydney floods north in search of an unforgettable wave or a teeming underwater cave, the Big Fish or the perfect sheltered family beach. They are accommodated in anything from caravan parks and run-of-the-mill motels to luxurious houseboats, from nudist resorts to spoil-yourself-rotten hotels like the Holiday Inn Crowne Plaza in Terrigal and the exquisite Anchorage in **Corlette**.

The Central Coast, just an hour's drive from Sydney, has grown particularly popular, with a doubling of visitor numbers in just five years (1991-96), while more and more people opt to live in the area and commute to the city. The region has thus sprouted a mini-urban sprawl around **Gosford** (replete with misguided architecture) to add to that in Newcastle. Yet, originally, this was an area that the settlers were slow to populate, partly because it took a while to 'persuade' the indigenous Kooris to give up their rich fishing grounds.

The early days of Sydney are recreated by actors at Old Sydney Town (Pacific Highway, Somersby; 4340 1104), off the Sydney-Newcastle Freeway, near Gosford. Nearby there's the Australian Reptile Park (4340 1022/recorded information 4340 1146) which has a slithery-scuttling selection of crocs, spiders and other beasties, including a snake capable of killing 200,000 mice with one burst of venom. Outside Gosford, there are two galleries worth visiting: Gallery 460 (460 Avoca Drive, Green Point; 4369 2111), with its large sculpture park, is one of the coast's more surprising offerings; while the Ken Duncan Australia Wide Gallery (Oak Road, Matcham; 4367 6777) lets you travel around the continent in a series of lustrous (if a little too perfect), panoramic studies taken by the great exponent of wide-angle landscape photography.

It would be a shame, though, not to get out in the great outdoors. There are many opportunities, the simplest of which is to take a cruise around **Brisbane Water** aboard the MV Lady Kendall (departs Gosford Wharf; 4323 2974), Australia's oldest working vessel. A little further afield, the inspiring Central Coast Kayak Tours, based at **Patonga** (at the mouth of the Hawkesbury River; tel/fax 4381 0342), promises to help you 'fall off the planet' as well as guide (and glide) you through unspoilt estuaries and creeks to secluded beaches. From Patonga, a sleepy fishing village, there's also a fine walk over the headland to the pretty hamlet of **Pearl Beach**.

A mecca for divers, bottlenose dolphins and other aquatic types: **Port Stephens Bay.**

The Central Coast's most fashionable resort is **Terrigal** – the 196-room Holiday Inn is often booked out at weekends – 12 kilometres (7.5 miles) east of Gosford. The restaurant and café atmosphere of the place is reminiscent of Coogee or Manly. Apart from the decent beaches on the doorstep (Wanberal, Terrigal and Avoca), the town also has good access to a wealth of watersports including boating (on the Tuggerah Lakes), sailboarding, water-skiing and parasailing (contact Central Coast Tourism for details). Around Terrigal, and a short drive north at **Norah Head** (beyond The Entrance), the diving possibilities (in usually good visibility) include reefs, caves, dropoffs and shipwrecks. Several dive shops in the area run trips and rent equipment (try Pro Dive at 15 Mitchell Street, Norah Head; 4396 3652).

At the top end of the Central Coast lies Australia's major port and its sixth largest city, **Newcastle**. Although it's hardly a tourist destination, it does have a few notable Victorian and Edwardian public buildings (survivors of the 1989 earthquake) and a well-known family beach – Nobby's. Seen at night, the lights and smoke of the city's steelworks and other heavy industry have a certain grim appeal.

Around four-and-a-half times the size of Sydney Harbour, **Port Stephens Bay** is another mecca for divers (at weekends top spots like Halifax Reserve and Fly Point near Nelson Bay are prone to underwater congestion), with a reliable resident bottlenose dolphin population. For details of Dolphin Watch trips contact Port Stephens Visitor Centre (*see page 247*). The **Tomaree Peninsula** on the southern shore is the focus of holiday activity with its series of blue bays (Salamander, Shoal, Fingal and Anna), glinting marinas (Nelson Bay and Corlette Point), outstanding coastal beaches (Wreck, Samurai and Stockton Bight) and all manner of accommodation choices.

One exhilarating, wind-rushing-through-your-hair way to get your bearings in the area is to see it from the back of a Harley Davidson with Freedom Thunder Tours (4984 6262). Get them to take you to the **Gan Gan Lookout** from where there are 360-degree views over the coast. A little less comfortable but no less inspiring is a camel ride (Walkabout Camel Adventures; 4964 8996) along Stockton Beach, whose mountainous dunes are also made for four-wheel driving (Horizon Safaris; tel/fax 4982 6328). If that doesn't thrill you enough, try not using the brakes on the local toboggan run (Toboggan Hill Park, Salamander Way, Nelson Bay; 4984 1022).

The peninsula is also home to two groundbreaking (as opposed to neck-breaking) ventures. Bardots Nude Village Resort ('happiness is no tan lines'), set amid a cluster of trees behind legally nude Samurai Beach, is a sanctuary for the open-minded. The Dolphin Within Society, which uses as a base the Anchorage Marina on Corlette Point, is currently researching the potential benefits to humans of contact with dolphins. As part of their work, founders Dr Olivia de Bergerac and William McDougall take small groups out for weekends (twice a month) aboard their yacht, Sirius, to swim with the dolphins, closely monitoring the effects of interaction on an EEG machine. For more details contact them on (9665 0712/fax 9664 2014).

This region offers a number of other ways to experience nature at first hand. In winter, up to 3,000 humpback and southern right whales pass Port Stephens, *en route* to their breeding grounds at Hervey Bay, while all year round the **Tilligerry Peninsula**, on the southern shore of the inner harbour of Port Stephens, is a tranquil haven for wildlife. It offers some of the best odds in New South Wales for finding koalas in their natural habitat. Another common sight is that of low-flying pelicans skidding in to land on the water near **Lemon Tree Passage**.

Getting There

By Air
The northern part of this region is served by Newcastle Airport, situated at Williamtown, 25 minutes' drive from Nelson Bay and 20 minutes from Newcastle. Eastern Australian Airlines runs up to eight flights a day from Sydney (for reservations phone 13 1313). Commuter airlines link the Central Coast with Sydney.

By Car
Central Coast (Patonga, Gosford, Terrigal, The Entrance): Sydney-Newcastle Freeway (Route 1) connects with all of this stretch of coast. For **Patonga** take Gosford exit then turn off towards Woy Woy. For **Terrigal** continue through Gosford; then turn-off to Terrigal.
For **The Entrance** take Tuggerah exit then turn-off to The Entrance via Tumbi Umbi or drive north from Terrigal via Wanberal and Forresters Beach. Journey time approx 1½ hours.
Lower North Coast Sydney-Newcastle Freeway (Route 1) and/or Pacific Highway (Route 83). For **Anna Bay**, **Nelson Bay** and **Port Stephens** take Route 122 off the Pacific Highway (just north of Hexham) or go via Newcastle taking the road out of Mayfield (past the steelworks) signposted Williamtown (Route 121). Journey time approx 2½ hours.

By Train
CityRail runs regular services from Sydney's Central Station to Newcastle (journey time approx 2 hours 40 minutes), stopping at Woy Woy (for **Patonga**, journey time 1 hour), and **Gosford** (for **Terrigal**, journey time 1 hour 20 minutes). A bus service (up to eight times a day on weekdays, less at weekends) links **Nelson Bay** to Newcastle Station. For details phone the Public Transport Infoline (13 1500).

By Bus
Several major coach companies link Sydney with the **Central Coast** and **Newcastle**. For the **Lower North Coast**, Port Stephens Buses runs a daily service to **Nelson Bay** (with an additional bus during the summer) from Bay 14, Eddy Avenue, Sydney (for details phone 4981 1207).

Tourist Information

Central Coast Tourism
Rotary Park, Terrigal Drive, Terrigal (4385 4431).
Branches: Marine Parade, The Entrance (4332 9282); 200 Mann Street, Gosford (4385 4430/fax 4385 4435).

Newcastle Tourism Information
92 Scott Street, Newcastle (4929 9299/recorded information 1800 654 558).

Port Stephens Visitor Centre
Victoria Parade (PO Box 435), Nelson Bay (4981 1579/ 1800 808 900/fax 4984 1855).

Where to Stay & Eat

The Anchorage
Corlette Point Road, Corlette (4984 2555/fax 4984 0300). **Rates** from $160. **Credit** AmEx, BC, DC, JCB, MC, V.
Unusually designed luxury accommodation next to marina; also has houseboats.

Bardots Nude Village Resort
288 Gan Gan Road, Anna Bay (4982 2000). **Rates** from $110. **Credit** BC, MC, V.

The Beach House
The Haven, Terrigal (4385 3222). **Average** $30. **Credit** AmEx, BC, DC, MC, V.
Formerly called the Galley Restaurant, this eaterie overlooks the beach, has a good atmosphere and serves fine food.

Clan Lakeside Resort
1 Ocean View Drive, Terrigal (4384 1566). **Rates** from $80. **Credit** AmEx, BC, DC, MC, V.
Average spend at the restaurant is $20 a head.

Croft Haven B&B
202 Salamander Way, Nelson Bay (4984 1799). **Rates** from $85. **No credit cards.**

Holiday Inn Crowne Plaza
Pine Tree Lane, Terrigal (4384 9111). **Rates** from $160. **Credit** AmEx, BC, DC, MC, V.
It also has three restaurants (average spend from $35 a head).

Nelson Towers Motel
71 Victoria Parade, Nelson Bay (4984 1000/fax 4984 1020). **Rates** from $88. **Credit** AmEx, BC, DC, MC, V.
Ask for a room with a view.

Red Bellies Restaurant
Nelson Lodge Motel, 1 Government Road, Nelson Bay (4981 1705/fax 4981 4785). **Average** $30. **Credit** AmEx, BC, DC, MC, V.
Delicious Australian cuisine (using native ingredients) including famous Port Stephens oysters, kangaroo, crocodile and emu. Rooms at the motel cost from $77.

Salamander Shores
147 Soldiers Point Road, Soldiers Point (4982 7210/ fax 4982 7890). **Rates** from $69. **Credit** BC, DC, MC, V.
Luxury and ocean views at an affordable price). There is a restaurant too (average $40 a head).

Shoal Bay Country Club
Shoal Bay Road, Shoal Bay (4981 1555/1800 040 937/fax 4984 1315). **Rates** backpacker from $35; hotel from $70. **Credit** AmEx, BC, DC, MC, V.
Unbeatable location and great seafood at the on-site restaurant, Gelignite Jacks (average $40).

Heading West

For a note on changes to NSW phone numbers see page 240.

Blue Mountains

The Blue Mountains, top of the must-see list of destinations within striking distance of Sydney, can seem like something of a paradox. On the one hand it's an area of spectacular wilderness, so resistant to the city's relentless westward sprawl that it can hide in its midst a species of tree (the Wollemi pine) thought to have been extinct for 150 million years. On the other, with its dainty villages where portraits of Queen Elizabeth crown mantelpieces and neat English gardens vie with native plants and bushes, the area embodies the struggle by European settlers to tame the Australian landscape and recreate a little piece of home in cooler mountain climes.

It's also a place of many moods. In summer, with the eucalyptus oil rising off the leaves of the trees and refracting the sun's rays, it really is blue. In winter, embalmed in mist and, occasionally, snow, it's an atmospheric, upside-down venue for Christmas celebrations, complete with turkey and tree.

Whatever the time of year, the region offers a vast, clean-aired refuge from the hectic pace of Sydney – the Blue Mountains National Park alone covers nearly 250,000 hectares (617,750 acres) of wilderness. The best way to experience the area is to try one of the many signed bushwalks (ranging from a few minutes to several days trekking), or by trying out a more challenging pursuit such as abseiling or mountaineering. Failing that, there are plenty of day tours run by larger companies from Sydney, which provide a cursory look around, and there's a shuttle bus which operates daily from Katoomba railway station. Best of all if your time is limited, are the smaller, more sensitive Blue Mountains-based operations such as Cox's River Escapes (4784 1621), which have a more intimate feel for the area.

Of the 26 townships in the Blue Mountains, **Katoomba** is the most popular starting point, thanks to its proximity to some of the major attractions. These include the mountains' most photographed feature, the Three Sisters, near Echo Point, a rock formation as shrouded in Aboriginal legend as it often is in mist; the world's steepest rail incline, the Scenic Railway; and the equally giddy Scenic Skyway (both open 9am-5pm daily; 4782 2699). If you've got time, descend the precipitous 841-step Giant Staircase, next to the Sisters and then do the two-and-a-half-hour walk through the **Jamison Valley** to the foot of the railway. If time's short or the weather's bad, the film, *The Edge*, on show at the spanking-new Maxvision cinema (47828 928) back in Katoomba, is a startlingly photographed insight into the mountains'

more hidden beauties, despite the PC commentary. Katoomba itself is the region's most feral town and its attractions don't go much beyond its art deco façades, the historic Carrington Hotel (built in the 1880s) and the marvellously dowdy Paragon café. But it's here and in the nearby town of **Blackheath** that you'll find cheaper accommodation options such as the Cecil Traditional Guest House – the grand exception being the lovely, top-of-the-range Lilianfels Blue Mountains Hotel, which overlooks the Jamison Valley.

Linked to Katoomba by a panoramic cliff drive – and altogether more yuppie – is **Leura** with its slightly snooty but comfortable guest houses, kempt gardens (an annual Gardens Festival is held here in early October; 4784 1258) and chichi shops and galleries. Leura's also home to some of the area's better quality restaurants such as The Ferns. Just down the road are the **Wentworth Falls**, another much loved Blue Mountains attraction, which have been known to flow upwards when strong winds blow up the valley. There's an excellent, if occasionally arduous, undercliff-overcliff walk nearby. Other places of interest on the Sydney side of Katoomba, lower down the Blue Mountains, include Norman Lindsay's Home & Gallery in **Faulconbridge** (*see* **The Far Side** *in chapter* **Sightseeing**) and the town of **Springwood**.

Further into the mountains beyond Katoomba, the Hydro Majestic Hotel in **Medlow Bath** – once frequented by Sydney's chattering classes and still rather precious – is popular for coffee with a view. More down-to-earth is the World Heritage-listed village of **Mount Victoria**, where John F Kennedy is reputed to have stayed in a Repatriation Hospital (at the site of the present Victoria & Albert Guest House – ask to see his carved autograph) after World War II. It's also the starting point for many fine walks.

On the northern side of the mountains, off the Bells Line of Road above the Grose Valley, is the quintessentially English hamlet of **Mount Wilson** – a riot of russet in autumn – where Nobel Prize-winning author Patrick White once lived. His family's old summer house, Withycombe (built 1878), is now a classy guest house featuring one of the many serene gardens in the area. For flora that's more native, continue on to the hushed **Cathedral of Ferns** at the end of the lane. But if it's European order you're after, head for the landscaped Botanic Gardens at **Mount Tomah** (Bells Line of Road; 4567 2154). Whatever your taste, the views from Mount Tomah are wonderful.

You'll need to travel to the south-western edge of the Blue Mountains to reach the other of the area's main attractions, the **Jenolan Caves** (open daily; 6359 3311): a series of extraordinary underground limestone caverns within a peaceful 2,400-hectare (5,930-acre) nature reserve. Some caverns are large and easily accessible; some, such as the

River Cave, feature stalagmites and stalactites; and others, such as the Adventure Cave, can be explored in more depth in overalls and helmets.

Getting There

By Car

Via Penrith: for **Springwood**, **Faulconbridge**, **Wentworth Falls**, **Leura**, **Katoomba**, **Mount Victoria** take Western Motorway (Route 4) and/or Great Western Highway (Route 32). Sydney to Katoomba is 109km (68 miles); journey time approx 2 hours. Alternatively, go via Richmond: for **Kurrajong** and **Mount Tomah** take Great Western Highway (Route 32) or Western Motorway (Route 4); turn off to Richmond via Blacktown; then Bells Line of Road (Route 40). **Mount Wilson** is 6km (3¾ miles) off Bells Line of Road. For **Jenolan Caves** take Great Western Highway (Route 32) via Katoomba and Mount Victoria; then turn off south at Hartley.

By Train

Hourly departures from Central Station. Journey time to **Katoomba** approx 2 hours (for details phone Public Transport Infoline, 13 1500). Aussie Tours (4782 1866) runs buses regularly from Katoomba Station.

By Bus

A number of coach companies offer day trips to the Blue Mountains, departing from Sydney. These include Australian Pacific Tours (13 1304) and the more backpacker-oriented Wonderbus (9247 5151).

Tourist Information

Blue Mountains Information Centres

Echo Point, Katoomba (4739 6266); Great Western Highway, Glenbrook (4739 6266).

Where to Stay & Eat

See also **Vulcan's** and **Cleopatra** in chapter Restaurants.

Avalon Restaurant

98 Main Street, Katoomba (4782 5532). **Average** $30. **Credit** BC, MC, V.

Cecil Traditional Guest House

108 Katoomba Street, Katoomba (4782 1411/fax 4782 5364). **Rates** from $45. **Credit** AmEx, BC, DC, MC, V.

Echoes

3 Lilianfels Avenue, Katoomba (4782 1966/fax 4782 3707). **Rates** from $310 (half board). **Credit** AmEx, BC, MC, V.
Upmarket guest house with wonderful views.

The Ferns Restaurant

130 Megalong Street, Leura (4784 3256). **Average** $35. **Credit** AmEx, BC, DC, MC, V.

Hotel Imperial

Great Western Highway, Mount Victoria (4787 1233/fax 4787 1461). **Rates** from $98. **Credit** AmEx, BC, MC, V.
Historic building; good counter meals.

Hydro Majestic Hotel

Great Western Highway, Medlow Bath (4788 1002). **Rates** from $194 (half board). **Credit** BC, DC, MC, V.

Jenolan Caves House

Jenolan Caves (6359 3304/fax 6359 3227). **Rates** from $120. **Credit** AmEx, BC, DC, MC, V.

Leura House Guest House

7 Britain Street, Leura (4784 2035/fax 4784 3329). **Rates** from $65. **Credit** BC, MC, V.
'Yuletide' celebrations a speciality (in June).

Lilianfels Blue Mountains

Lilianfels Avenue, Echo Point, Katoomba (4780 1200/1800 024 452/fax 4780 1300). **Rates** from $335 (half board). **Credit** AmEx, BC, DC, MC, V.
Look out for the self-playing piano in the lobby. It also has two good restaurants: Lilians and the award-winning Darleys.

Little Company Retreat

2 Eastview Avenue, Leura (4782 4023/fax 4782 5361). **Rates** from $170. **Credit** BC, MC, V.

Victoria & Albert Guest House

19 Station Street, Mount Victoria (4787 1241/fax 4787 1588). **Rates** from $45. **Credit** AmEx, BC, MC, V.

Whispering Pines

178-186 Falls Road, Wentworth Falls (4757 1449/fax 4757 1219). **Rates** from $130. **Credit** BC, MC, V.
Set in a secluded spot with access to great walks.

Withycombe

Corner of The Avenue and Church Lane, Mt Wilson (4756 2106/fax 475 62177). **Rates** from $425 (full board for two). **Credit** AmEx, MC.

Blue Mountains Adventures

Australian School of Mountaineering

182 Katoomba Street, Katoomba (4782 2014/fax 4782 5787).

Blue Mountains Adventure Company

190 Katoomba Street, Katoomba (4782 1271/fax 4782 1277).

Cox's River Escapes

PO Box 81, Leura (4784 1621/fax 4784 2540/mobile 015 400 121).
Sensitively geared walking tours and four-wheel drive trips.

Werriberri Trail Rides

Megalong Road, Megalong Valley (4787 9171).

Wild Escapes

PO Box 116, Asquith (9482 2881/fax 9477 3114).

Around Bathurst

Stretching from the western slopes of the Great Dividing Range, beyond the Blue Mountains, is a land of endless skies over seemingly infinite plains, ridges and valleys. The sort of country where 'just down the road on the right' means a four-hour drive; where the summers are baking hot and the winters are crisp and occasionally cold enough for snow. At its centre lies the major regional city of **Bathurst**, Australia's first inland settlement (pre-dating most of the coastal capitals) and the focus of an area rich in agricultural assets. It is also one of the towns (along with **Sofala**, **Hill End** and **Trunkey Creek**) that swelled with successive waves of hopeful diggers in the mid-nineteenth century gold-rush frenzy.

Once home to Australia's raunchiest painter and sculptor, Norman Lindsay. See page 249.

Before European settlers arrived, the semi-nomadic Aborigine Wiradjuri tribe, the largest in New South Wales, had lived happily undisturbed in the area for more than 40,000 years. Although the tribe mistakenly believed the pale interlopers to be the blanched souls of dead Aborigines, settlement brought them the usual combination of displacement, fatal disease and slaughter, almost eliminating them completely. The area was opened up to Europeans through the building, by convicts, of the first cross-Blue Mountains road in 1816, following in the footsteps of explorers Blaxland, Lawson and Wentworth.

The way to Bathurst from Sydney is still through the Blue Mountains, along the Great Western Highway or via the Bells Line of Road. Both routes eventually descend to the former steel and coal-mining town of **Lithgow**, but on the way down the Great Western Highway takes in the historic village of **Hartley** with its sandstone Court House. With the mountains for its backdrop and some period buildings, Lithgow is not unattractive and all manner of oddities (mainly to do with coal and steel) are on display at Eskbank House (corner of Bennett and Inch Streets; 6351 3557). Lithgow is also a reasonable base from which to explore Wollemi National Park to the north.

Bathurst is around 60 kilometres (37½ miles) further west and has played a central role in the development of the region almost from the day it was declared a settlement by Governor Macquarie in 1815. For much of that time it has prospered through agriculture and, of course, gold (though the latter brought with it *nouveau-riche* excess and criminal activity in the form of bushrangers like Ben Hall). Wide avenues, parks and civic structures help the city retain an air of affluence today, mixing the

modern and the historic with some success. A few simple colonial buildings are worth seeing, for example, Government Cottage (built 1820, behind 1 George Street; 6332 4755). There are also some Victorian edifices of which Miss Traill's House is an early example (321 Russell Street; 6332 4232).

Although Bathurst missed out on becoming the federal capital in the 1890s, its most famous son, Ben Chifley, was to have great influence in shaping twentieth-century Australia as prime minister from 1945 to 1949. The small cottage he shared in Bathurst with his wife Elizabeth is open to the public for a couple of hours daily (10 Busby Street; 6332 1444).

On the edge of the city, Mount Panorama is the venue for the annual rubber-burning ritual of the Bathurst 1,000 touring car race, which each year attracts 40,000 fans. As the track is also a public road, you too can pretend you're Damon Hill, albeit at maximum speeds of 60 kilometres (37½ miles) per hour and with traffic coming from the opposite direction.

Enjoying the view (and quality of light) is something that artists have done a lot of in the area over the years, from Conrad Martens in the 1840s to modern Australian guru Brett Whiteley, who went to school in Bathurst and returned many times until his death in 1992. The Regional Art Gallery (Keppel Street; 6331 6066) displays a collection of Australian works, including significant pieces by Lloyd Rees.

The artists' favourite places, such as the former gold-mining towns of Sofala and Hill End, the Abercrombie Caves (15 kilometres/nine miles south of Trunkey Creek) and the village of **Carcoar** (National Trust classified) are still worth a look. Overrun in the 1850s and 1860s by hungry gold-diggers (including some 10,000 Chinese), Sofala is quieter now. The village's main street is still intact, complete with original post office, pub

i-D=instinctive+
debonaire+eclec
tic+nonconformis
t+textural+ideos
yncratic+transmut
ant+you-identity

SUBSCRIBE
TO THE WORLD'S FINEST FASHION MAGAZINE

12 MONTHS OF GOOD i-DEAS FOR £27!
AND GET A FREE i-DENTITY T-SHIRT WORTH £16

---

subscription rates for 12 i-Ds per year plus free i-Dentity T-shirt

uk	europe	world [airmail]
☐ (£27.00)	☐ (£36.00)	☐ (£58.00)

Value of order £ _____

Access/Visa number:

☐☐☐☐☐☐☐☐☐☐☐☐☐☐☐☐

Signature: _____

Expiry date: _____

Yes please, this offer is (i·D)eal!

Name: _____

Address: _____

_____

_____

Tel: _____ **Date:** _____

and fire station. The frantic activity around the nearby Turon River, where gold was discovered, has also died down – though apparently there is still the odd nugget floating around.

Getting There

By Car
Bathurst Take Great Western Highway (Route 32) via Katoomba and Lithgow or via Bells Line of Road (Richmond to Lithgow). Journey time 2½-3 hours. **Sofala** is 45km north of Bathurst; **Hill End** is another 40km; **Carcoar** is south-west of Bathurst on the Mid Western Highway.

By Train
Bathurst and **Lithgow** are served by both Countrylink XPT (express) and local trains from Central Station. Journey time to Bathurst is a minimum of 3 hours. For details call Countrylink (13 2232) or the Public Transport Infoline on (13 1500).

By Bus
Local companies include Rendell's Coaches (6884 4199). There are also rail/coach connections. Contact one of the tourist information centres listed below for more details.

Tourist Information

Bathurst Visitors Centre
28 William Street, Bathurst (6332 1444).

Hill End Visitors Centre
High Street, Hill End (6337 8206).

Lithgow Visitors Centre
1 Cooerwull Road, Lithgow (6353 1859).

Where to Stay & Eat

There is camping at Carcoar Dam and by the Turon River in Sofala, among other good spots in this region. Contact the tourist information centres listed above for details.

Blandford Bed & Breakfast
214 Lambert Street, Bathurst (6331 9995). **Rates** from $90. **Credit** AmEx, BC, MC, V.

Dalebrook
Naylor Street, Carcoar (6367 3149). **Rates** from $95. **No credit cards**. Meals also served ($35 set menu).

Governor Macquarie Motor Inn
19 Charlotte Street, Bathurst (6331 2211). **Rates** from $79. **Credit** AmEx, BC, DC, MC, V.

Royal Hotel
Denison Street, Sofala (6337 7008). **Rates** from $15 per person. **No credit cards**.

Strathmore Victorian Manor
202 Russell Street, Bathurst (6332 3252). **Rates** from $100. **Credit** AmEx, BC, DC, MC, V.

Winter Rose Cottage
79 Morrissett Street, Bathurst (6332 2661). **Rates** from $70. **Credit** AmEx.

Woolstone House & Stables Restaurant
24 Gilmour Street, Kelso (6332 3900). **Rates** from $90. **Credit** AmEx, BC, DC, MC, V. The average price in the Stables is $30 a head.

Heading South

For a note on changes to NSW and ACT phone numbers see page 240.

Canberra

Canberra was conceived as the compromise choice of federal capital to end the squabbling between arch-rivals Sydney and Melbourne. But since its creation in 1911, Canberra has been dogged by bad press. It's the city that people from other Australian cities love to hate, the New Zealand of intra-Australian jokes ('a waste of a good sheep paddock'), regarded by detractors as a sterile, low-level metropolis full of also-(Canber)rans, a mundane mecca for politicians and bureaucrats. For those Australians that have visited the city, Canberra can also evoke less than favourable memories: of being escorted (by the ears) around endless exhibitions and galleries as a school kid, or being driven mad by getting lost in the car among the city's eccentric circles.

Those clichés wouldn't exist if there wasn't some truth in them. Yet Canberra is also loved with a passion by many of its residents, who point to its space, tranquillity, clean air and proximity to unspoilt bushland. In fact, with bushland making up 70 per cent of the national capital, Canberra

Canberra's sobering war memorial. See p254.

is, as has been remarked, 'much more a city scattered through a park than a city through which parks are scattered'.

Whether you side with Canberra's detractors or its defenders is partly a matter of taste (the city's design is either your dream or your nightmare) and partly a matter of perception. On a clear day, viewed from **Mount Ainslie**, the **Telstra Tower** (Black Mountain Drive, Acton; 1800 806 718) or the basket of a hot air balloon (Balloon Aloft, 15 Fitzgerald Street, Yarralumla; 6285 1540), Canberra can appear stately, elegant and positively Washingtonesque. Back on the ground, the city may seem less disorienting from the saddle of a bicycle (bikes for hire from Mr Spokes, Lake Burley Griffin, Barrine Drive, Acton Park; 6257 1188). In fact, compared with the murderous streets of Sydney, Canberra is a cyclist's heaven, with relatively flat terrain, plenty of cycle paths, negligible traffic (riding is permitted on pavements anyway) and most of the sights within easy pedalling distance.

Doing a circuit of the central man-made **Lake Burley Griffin** (a two-hour ride) might even win you over to the vision of 'the city beautiful' that Canberra's architect, Walter Burley Griffin, originally had in mind. The **National Capital Exhibition**, on a knoll overlooking the lake – near the submerged whale pretending to be a fountain (Regatta Point, Commonwealth Park; 6257 1068) – gives further insights into Griffin's plans for Canberra (eloquently drawn by his wife Marion Mahoney), which won the competition for the design of the capital. There is also a model of the city (with blinking lights indicating attractions) which makes it a good starting point for a tour.

Whatever Canberra's faults, as federal capital it can claim to have many of Australia's most important national monuments, buildings and galleries, the most significant (and visited) being Parliament House, the Australian War Memorial and the National Gallery of Australia.

It might look like an over-sized wigwam from afar – thanks to an 81-metre (222-foot) stainless-steel flagpole – but **Parliament House** (opened 1988, Capital Hill; 6277 5399) is as imposing as it is humble, as human as it is functional. From its position on Capital Hill it dominates Canberra's landscape, yet its turfed roof allows the people to stand above their elected representatives. Inside, the foyer (complete with marble columns and staircases), the Great Hall (an Arthur Boyd tapestry – one of the world's biggest – hangs here) and both chambers (Senate and House of Representatives) are airy and refreshingly bathed in natural light. Throughout the building there are displays of Australian art and photographs, including portraits of the country's ex-prime ministers in the Members' Hall. There are interesting free guided tours every 30 minutes from 9am (try and get on one before the coaches arrive).

Beneath this comparative baby of a building, but far from eclipsed by it, stands **Old Parliament House** (also home to the National Museum of Australia, the National Portrait Gallery and the Australian Archives, King George Terrace, Parkes; 6273 5130), which was the country's seat of democracy from 1927 to 1988. With leather sofas and *film noir*-ish frosted windows embossed in gold lettering, this place reeks of the machinations of Australia's political past. Just down the road and reputedly once linked to Old Parliament House by a white line so that worse-for-wear politicians could find their way there at night, is the **Hotel Kurrajong**. Once the Canberra home of prime ministers (among them Robert Menzies) and other eminences, it's now a lovely boutique hotel whose bar is often abuzz with bright young locals chewing the present-day political fat.

Also nearby is Australia's foremost art institution, the **National Gallery** (Parkes Place, Parkes; 6240 6411), which houses good collections of international, Australian, Aboriginal and Torres Strait Islander art, as well as hosting major exhibitions from overseas that often bypass Sydney. It also has a sculpture garden. Next door to the National Gallery is the innovative **Questacon National Science and Technology Centre** (King Edward Terrace, Parkes; 6270 2800) with a number of hands-on exhibits, including a frighteningly realistic recreation of an earthquake.

On the other side of the lake is another of Canberra's major sights, the **Australian War Memorial** (Anzac Parade, Campbell; 6243 4211). Commemorating the country's 102,000 war dead from 11 international military involvements since 1860, this is obviously a poignant place – especially the Hall of Memory (the mosaic contains six million enamelled glass tiles) and the Tomb of the Unknown Soldier. Also housed here is an extensive exhibition detailing the Australian experience of war, vividly retold using a combination of personal testimony, film, photography, art work and other original material.

If you've ever wondered how Australia, with its relatively small population, is able to produce so many top-class athletes, a visit to the **Australian Institute of Sport** on the city's outskirts (Leverrier Crescent, Bruce; 6252 111) and its new Ansett Visitor Centre will shed some light. It's a sort of university for the country's élite sportspersons (there are 160 on scholarships here, including a couple of ten year-old gymnasts), and a tour of this coco pop-free zone (led by one of its resident athletes) will leave you fingering your fat content guiltily.

The high life: for the best views of Canberra, take to the skies.

Or it may drive you to drink. In which case, head south to Canberra's wine-growing region around **Murrumbateman**, with its 16 boutique wineries. Premium cooler-climate wines are produced here by such magnetic *vignerons* as Ken Helm (Helms, Butts Road, off Yass River Road, Murrumbateman; 6227 5536) and Rob and Kay Howell (Jeir Creek, Gooda Creek Road, Murrumbateman; 6227 5999). At weekends, National Capital Wine Tours (tel/fax 6231 3330) runs trips to the vineyards, taking in three wineries.

The name Canberra is an Aboriginal word for 'meeting place' and in the past, local tribes gathered here to feast on bogong moths. While the range of Canberra's cuisine has grown since then – try the legendary Malaysian Sammy's Kitchen or the modern Italian La Scala – it can still seem something of a ghost town after Sydney. However, in the suburb of **Manuka**, not far from the Parliamentary triangle, you'll find the city's café culture alongside a cluster of clubs and restaurants, while in **Lyneham**, Tilly's licensed café attracts an alternative crowd for its eclectic mix of music, poetry and comedy. Back in the city centre, the arty set hang out at the Phoenix, an Irish pub with a pulse which serves a decent pint of Guinness.

Canberra rarely gets overcrowded, except during its annual ten-day Festival in March (for details phone 6207 6477), a colourful celebration including hot air ballooning, exhibitions, theatre, music and dance, marking the founding of the city in 1913. But the city does have one of the highest room-occupancy rates in Australia. So it pays to book ahead for accommodation, particularly at weekends.

GOULBURN

If you're driving or taking the train to Canberra (Countrylink offers packages to the capital which include accommodation; 13 2829), you may want to stop in Goulburn, Australia's first inland city. Once the centre for tracking down the infamous bushrangers in the 1830s, it has a couple of old cathedrals and a number of historic houses. It also boasts the Big Merino (a giant ram symbolising the importance of the wool industry to the city) into which – if you're so inclined – you can climb for a sheep's-eye view of Goulburn.

Getting There

By Air

Canberra has a small domestic airport about 15 minutes' drive from the city centre. Both national airlines fly to the capital several times a day. For details contact Qantas Airways (13 1313) or Ansett Australia (13 1344). Flying time from Sydney is roughly 30-40 minutes.

By Car

Canberra is 288km (179 miles) south of Sydney. Take Hume Highway (Route 31); turn off to Canberra on Federal Highway beyond Goulburn. Journey time 3 hours in a Ferrari, but allow up to 4.

By Train

Countrylink's Xplorer service runs from Sydney to Canberra three times a day. Journey time just over 4 hours.

By Bus

Most major coach companies operate services to Canberra. Try one of the following: Firefly Express (9211 1644/1800 631 164); Greyhound Pioneer (13 2030); McCaffertys (1800 076 211).

Tourist Information

Canberra Visitor Information Centre

Northbourne Avenue, Canberra City (6205 0044/1800 026 166).

Where to Stay & Eat

Brassey Hotel

Belmore Gardens, Barton (6273 3766/fax 6273 2791). **Rates** from $105. **Credit** AmEx, BC, DC, MC, V. Historic boutique hotel offering accommodation plus champagne and ballooning packages.

Chelsea Lodge B&B

(reception at Miranda Lodge, 534 Northbourne Avenue) 526 Northbourne Avenue, Downer (6248 0655). **Rates** from $60. **Credit** AmEx, BC, DC, MC, V. The longest established B&B in ACT.

Hotel Kurrajong

National Circuit, Barton (6234 4444/fax 6234 4466). **Rates** from $150. **Credit** AmEx, BC, DC, MC, V.

Kythera Motel

98-100 Northbourne Avenue, Braddon (6248 7611/ fax 6248 0419). **Rates** from $77. **Credit** AmEx, BC, DC, MC, V.

Olims Canberra Hotel

corner of Ainslie and Limestone Avenues, Braddon (6248 5511/1800 020 016/fax 6247 0864). **Rates** from $95. **Credit** AmEx, BC, DC, JCB, MC, V.

The Phoenix Pub

21 East Row, Canberra City (6247 1606).

Rydges Canberra

London Circuit, Canberra City (1800 026 169/fax 6257 3071). **Rates** from $135. **Credit** AmEx, BC, DC, JCB, MC. *The* address to stay at, by Lake Burley Griffin.

Sammy's Kitchen

Bunda Street, Canberra City (6247 1464). **Average** $10. **Credit** AmEx, BC, MC, V. Chinese and Malaysian dishes at reasonable prices.

La Scala Restaurant

Bunda Street, Canberra City (6248 8338). **Average** $35. **Credit** AmEx, BC, DC, MC, V.

Tilly's Cafe

96 Wattle Street, Lyneham (6249 1543). **No credit cards**. Music, poetry and comedy.

Wig & Pen Pub

Corner West Row and Alinger Street (6248 0171). **No credit cards**.

South Coast

According to the people who live there, particularly those living in the Shoalhaven region (stretching 160 kilometres/98 miles south of the town of Berry), this is the area of New South Wales that has it all: wilderness galore (including large tracts of national park and state forest); beaches so long and white they make Bondi look like a house party at an ex-sewage dump; some of the cleanest, clearest water in Australia (offering incomparable diving, fishing, swimming and surfing); a bay they say is 8½ times the size of Sydney Harbour, complete with pods of crowd-pleasing dolphins; easy access to magnificent mountain vistas; heritage and antiques; 'surfing' kangaroos; and, hey, it's even got the best fish and chips in the world.

Sound idyllic? Well, a lot of the South Coast is. And luckily, up until recently locals have been understandably slow to give their area the hard sell. It's the old tourism quandary: let too many people in on the secret and the area's unspoilt essence becomes threatened. But there's also some confusion on which direction to go in terms of tourism – whether to continue with the traditional family-oriented camping and caravan-park approach, or to target a more affluent eco-tourist, activity-based 'escape the city' market. For the moment, the former prevails (in terms of accommodation and activities), but things may change.

Travelling south from Sydney along the Princes Highway (Route 60), beyond the Royal National Park (*see chapter* **The Great Outdoors**), the first region you encounter is **Illawarra**, the administrative centre of which is the city of **Wollongong**. It's perhaps unfair to view Wollongong as one of the two ugly sisters on either side of Sydney (the other being Newcastle), but, as you approach its smoking industrial surroundings, it's hard not to. Nevertheless, Wollongong does have a couple of decent city beaches, coastal views and a resident collection of Aboriginal and other Australian art at the City Gallery (corner of Kembla and Burelli Streets; 4227 7461).

It's not long before the road begins to slide prettily between the coast on one side and the beginnings of the Southern Highlands on the other (Illawarra comes from an Aboriginal word meaning 'between the high place and the sea'). You soon come upon the first of the seaside towns worthy of a stop, **Kiama**. The town's main attraction is the Blow Hole (set that freeze-frame camera option), which spurts spray up to 60 metres (197 feet) into the air from a slatey, crenellated outcrop next to a comparatively tranquil harbour (weather permitting). Also by the harbour is a fresh fish market, while on the way into town there's a block of quarrymen's cottages dating from 1885, which have been done up and turned into restaurants and craft shops. Nothing in Kiama, however, prepares you

for the sign: 'Stan Crap – Funeral Director' (Life's crap and then you die?) on the way out of town.

Kiama is a good base for exploring the subtropical **Minammurra rainforest**, the **Carrington Falls** and nearby **Seven Mile Beach**. This undeniably impressive caramel arc, backed by a hinterland of fir trees, is best viewed from **Kingsford Smith Lookout**, just beyond Gerrigong.

An alternative base in these parts is the tree-lined inland town of **Berry**, a little further south. It's an entertaining hybrid of hick-town and quaint yuppie heaven, where earthy locals mix with weekending Sydneysiders in search of antiques and fine dining. The former are catered for by a couple of daggy pubs (look out for the priceless Bob Hawke wine flagon at the Great Southern Hotel), while the latter eat at the Baker & Bunyip Restaurant and like to bed down at the Bunyip Inn Guest House (in a National Trust-classified former bank).

Given the beauty of the surrounding coast, nobody could pretend that **Nowra**, commercial centre of the Shoalhaven region, is an attractive town. But it does have an Animal Park, with native animals and birds on the banks of the **Shoalhaven River** (4421 3949), and the Naval Aviation Museum (Albatross Road, Nowra Hill; 4421 1920).

JERVIS BAY

Undoubtedly the Shoalhaven region's greatest attraction, and the one that drives normally restrained commentators (and, it seems, the shopkeepers of **Huskisson**, the bay's main village) to reach for their superlatives, is Jervis Bay. Pronounced 'jur-', after British naval Commander Jervis, and not 'jar-' (this was determined by a special sitting of Parliament in 1972), this huge bay with 56 kilometres (35 miles) of shoreline has a history of close shaves. First, in 1770, Captain Cook sailed straight past it on the way to Botany Bay, recording it as 'low-lying wetlands' rather than noting its deep, wide natural harbour (which made it an ideal alternative to Sydney as fulcrum for the new colony). Later, this ecologically sensitive beauty spot was mooted as a possible port for Canberra and the ACT. And in 1975 **Murrays Beach**, at the tip of the Jervis Bay National Park, was chosen as a site for a nuclear reactor (a project thankfully defeated by public protest).

These narrow escapes and a fortuitous lack of population growth around Jervis Bay mean that this coastal area remains one of the most undisturbed and beautiful in Australia. Divers (and commercial directors who use the bay for underwater shots) testify to the clarity of its waters; swimmers are sometimes literally dazzled by the whiteness of its sands (**Hyams Beach** is said to be the whitest in the world); the National Park is booked out by campers months in advance; and regularly visiting sea and bird life includes fur seals, giant rays, whales (southern right, pilot and killer), sharks, sea eagles, penguins and many, many more.

A good way to get a feel for Jervis Bay as a whole and meet its resident dolphins is to go on a Dolphin Watch Cruise (74 Owen Street, Huskisson; 4441 6311/fax 4441 5885). Huskisson, the launching point for the cruise, is one of six villages on the shores of the bay and has a couple of accommodation options, two dive shops (Pro Dive and Seasports), wonderful fish and chips, and a pub (the Husky) with a bistro. Just south of Jervis Bay there is excellent sailing, snorkelling and swimming on the trapped body of water at **St George's Basin** and great fishing at **Sussex Inlet**.

ULLADULLA

Despite all the stunning scenery around Jervis Bay, it can be worth venturing further south to the sleepy fishing town of **Ulladulla** for a place to stay. The homely Ulladulla Guest House is about the best value for money in the area. Ulladulla's protected harbour may not quite recall Sicily, but the town has a sizeable Italian fishing community (guaranteeing decent local pizzas and pasta) and the Blessing of the Fleet is an annual event here on Easter Sunday. From Ulladulla it's also easy to access wilderness areas to the west and further south (**Budawang** and **Murramarang National Parks**) plus yet more expansive beaches such as Pebbly (which is actually sandy) with its resident kangaroos.

Getting There

By Car
Princes Highway (Route 60). Journey time to **Pebbly Beach** approx 3 hours (on a good day). Allow at least 2¼ hours to **Jervis Bay**, and 2½ hours to **Ulladulla**.

By Train
For **Wollongong**, **Kiama**, **Gerrigong**, **Berry** and Bomaderry for **Nowra** there are regular trains from Sydney's Central Station via the South Coast line. Journey time to end of line (Bomaderry) approx 2½ hours. From Bomaderry an infrequent coach service continues on through Nowra as far as **Ulladulla**. For details call the Public Transport Infoline (13 1500).

By Bus
Interstate coaches travelling the Princes Highway (Route 60) between Sydney and Melbourne stop at many of the towns mentioned above. There are also other local bus and coach services along the coast. Contact the local tourist offices for more details.

Tourist Information

Jervis Bay National Park Visitors Centre
Village Road, Jervis Bay (4443 0977).

Kiama Visitors Centre
Blowhole Point, Kiama (4232 3322).

Shoalhaven Tourist Centres
Princes Highway, Bomaderry (4421 0778); Princes Highway, Ulladulla (4455 1269/1800 024 261).

Wollongong Visitors Centre
93 Crown Street, Wollongong (4228 0300).

Where to Stay & Eat
For camping and caravan sites, contact the nearest tourist office (*see above*).

Baker & Bunyip Restaurant
23 Prince Alfred Street, Berry (4464 1454). **Average** $38. **Credit** AmEx, BC, MC, V.
Cooking classes also available.

Bunyip Inn Guest House
122 Queen Street, Berry (4464 2064/fax 4464 2364). **Rates** from $100. **Credit** AmEx, BC, DC, MC, V.

Cookaburra's Restaurant
Shop 2, 10 Watson Street, Ulladulla (4454 1443). **Average** $35. **Credit** AmEx, BC, DC, MC, V.
Modern Australian cooking.

Huskisson Beach Motel
9-11 Hawke Street, Huskisson (4441 6387). **Rates** from $60. **Credit** AmEx, BC, DC, MC, V.

Jervis Bay Motel
Owen Street, Huskisson (4441 5781/fax 4441 7072). **Rates** from $55. **Credit** AmEx, BC, DC, MC, V.

Pleasant Way Motor Inn
Pleasant Way, Nowra (4421 5544). **Rates** from $72. **Credit** AmEx, BC, DC, JCB, MC, V.

Ulladulla Guest House
39 Burrill Street, Ulladulla (tel/fax 4455 1796). **Rates** from $45. **Credit** AmEx, BC, DC, MC, V.
Luxury (including spas, a saltwater pool, sauna and small gym) at an affordable price.

Villa Dalmeny
72 Shoalhaven Street, Kiama (4233 1911). **Rates** from $95. **No credit cards**.

Woodbyne Gallery & Guesthouse
4 O'Keefe Lane, Jaspers Brush (4448 6200). **Rates** from $195. **Credit** BC, MC, V.
On the road out of Berry, this charming and spotless establishment has an interesting gallery and provides food (average $40 a head) as well as lodging.

Southern Highlands

Known by nineteenth-century wealthy Sydney-siders as the 'Sanitarium of the South', for its cooler climes and fresh air, and favoured by honeymooners in the 1930s and 1940s, the Southern Highlands has recently been experiencing something of a renaissance as a tourist destination.

It's easy to see why. Just a short drive or train ride from Sydney, the area is dotted with well preserved historic villages such as **Berrima** (founded 1831) and fading stately homes like Ranelagh House in **Robertson** (a thriving country club in the 1930s and now a guest house). All in a gently undulating landscape so easy on the eye that it

evokes a different country (even before the area was first settled – and European trees introduced – Governor Macquarie said it reminded him of England). This is the sort of the place where you feel you're bound to bump into some maiden aunt (perhaps long since dead) taking Devonshire tea in a drowsy tea shop, or failing that, find one of her old knick-knacks for sale in one of the area's countless antique shops.

But even if there's some truth to the local saying that the Southern Highlands are for 'the newly weds and the nearly deads', there is something here for most tastes. Apart from the area's interesting settlement period, Aboriginal history in the area (through the Wadi Wadi tribe) goes back 40,000 years. Nor are the Southern Highlands merely an imitation of the green pastures of Europe, encompassing areas of tropical and subtropical rainforest, the second largest falls in New South Wales (Fitzroy) and the northern edge of Morton National Park, where you can really take a walk on the wild side.

Of the many pleasant approaches by car, two leading from the main coastal road (Princes Highway) stand out. The first is to take the Illawarra Highway (from Albion Park) through **Macquarie Pass National Park**, and the second is to take the tourist drive from just beyond Berry. The route from Berry – rising, bending and finally dropping towards the popular **Kangaroo Valley** – is often atmospherically thick with mist, but on even a partly clear day it affords luscious views of the countryside. Kangaroo Valley village, despite its iron roofs and sandstone-pillared Hampden Bridge (built

in 1897, but pure Disney) is a little disappointing. However, the walking and camping nearby are excellent, as are the canoeing and kayaking on the Kangaroo River (contact Kangaroo Valley Tourist Park near the bridge; 4465 1310).

Leaving Kangaroo Valley, the road rises and twists once more before leading you to the **Fitzroy Falls**. A short saunter (note the construction of the boardwalk in harmony with the rainforest) from the impressive Fitzroy Falls Visitor Centre and you are amid scenery that's as Australian as Paul Hogan. There are actually five falls in the vicinity, but Fitzroy is the nearest and biggest, plummeting 81 metres (266 feet) into **Yarunga Valley**. Take any of the walks around the falls (the steep Valley Walk leads to the base of Fitzroy) and you'll encounter are up to 48 species of gum tree, lyre birds and possibly the odd wombat.

Another way of exploring the top end of underrated **Morton National Park** is to use the town of **Bundanoon** as a base for bushwalking and/or cycling. Bundanoon, which means 'a place of deep gullies', is as Scottish in flavour as its name sounds. Each year (the week after Easter) the town transforms itself into *Brigadoon* to host an authentic Highland gathering, featuring traditional games, Scottish dancing and street parades. Bundanoon was also once the honeymoon centre of the Southern Highlands – in its heyday it had 51 guest houses – but these days the bedsprings are rarely rattled. A fun accommodation option still available here is the creaky old Bundanoon Country Hotel, which boasts a billiard table to die for, Nea Hayes' famous pies and the occasional poetry reading (on a Sunday).

Slightly north of the forgettable town of Moss Vale is **Berrima**, considered Australia's finest example of an 1830s village. Berrima is the town the railways forgot. They bypassed the then thriving regional centre in the 1860s, so many of its early buildings remain in pristine condition. The highlight is a visit to the neo-classical courthouse (built in 1838, Wiltshire Street; 4877 1505) with its sandstone portico and curved wooden doorways. Don't miss the reconstruction of the 1843 trial of the adulterous Lucretia Dunkley and her lover, particularly the judge's sentencing of the pair for the murder of her dull husband. Berrima's other historic buildings include Harper's Mansion and Australia's oldest continually licensed hotel, The Surveyor General Inn (both built 1834). Otherwise there are enough antique, craft and coffee shops to keep even the most dedicated tourist happy.

An unexpected delight on the road to **Bowral** is Berkelouw's Book Barn (4877 1370), a treasure trove of yellowing knowledge (check out the students' notes in the margins), which houses over 200,000 old books. Bowral itself is attractive enough, especially during the spring Tulip Festival, but its biggest claim to fame is as the town that gave Australian cricket Donald Bradman. The great man is honoured in the Bradman Museum (4862 1247) on the edge of the lush Bradman Oval, opposite the old Bradman home. There's even a Bradman Walk around the town (pads and cricket box optional). If cricket doesn't captivate you, take a trip up to **Mount Gibraltar**, overlooking the town and much of the surrounding countryside, and the view surely will.

There's not much more to the town of **Mittagong** than meets the eye, although Lake Alexandra reserve (where the Mount Alexandra Walking Trail begins) is a pleasant spot for a picnic. About 60 kilometres (37½ miles) west of Mittagong are the **Wombeyan Caves** (via part-sealed and part-dirt road). These limestone caverns are thousands of years old, featuring a number of unique encrustations and deposits. You can take a guided tour of several caves and there's on-site accommodation and camping available. Contact the visitor centre (4843 5976) for details.

Destined to become the Southern Highlands' most famous village, and all because of a talking pig, is the one-spud (look out for it on the roadside) town of **Robertson**, where the film *Babe* was largely shot. Actually the biggest potato-growing (rather than sheep-rearing) area in the region, Robertson is a sleepy hollow that has evaded much change since the film's release. However, if you have a drink at the County Inn, Robertson's prime watering hole, you'll probably find them still talking about their satellite link-up with the 1996 Oscar ceremony. Unfortunately, *Babe* failed to bring home the bacon (winning just one Academy Award) and you can find almost the entire cast on the breakfast menu at rambling Ranelagh House.

Getting There

By Car

Inland route: Hume Highway (Route 31); distance approx 120km (75 miles); journey time just under 2 hours. Coastal route: Princes Highway (Route 60) then turn inland on Illawarra Highway (Route 48) by Albion Park; distance 130km (81 miles); journey time just over 2 hours).

By Train

Trains to the Southern Highlands depart from Sydney's Central Station regularly every day. Most stop at **Mittagong**, **Bowral**, **Moss Vale** and **Bundanoon**. Journey time 1¾-2½ hours. For details call the Public Transport Infoline (13 1500).

By Bus

Several companies serve the area including Greyhound Pioneer (13 2030); Firefly Express (9211 1644/1800 631 164); McCaffertys (1800 076 211); and Priors Scenic Express (1800 816 234).

Tourist Information

Fitzroy Falls Visitor Centre

Fitzroy Falls (4887 7270).

Shell Centre

Sutton Forest (4878 9369).

Southern Highlands Visitor Information Centre

Winifred Park West, Old Hume Highway, Mittagong (4871 2888/1800 656 176).

Where to Stay & Eat

Briars Country Lodge Motel

Moss Vale Road, Bowral (4868 3566/fax 4868 3223). **Rates** from $140. **Credit** AmEx, BC, DC, MC, V. Strong on comfort and food.

Bundanoon Country Hotel

Erith Street, Bundanoon (4883 6005). **Rates** from $46 per person. **Credit** BC, MC, V.

Gibraltar Park B&B

Corner of Mittagong and Old Bowral Roads, Bowral, (tel/fax 4861 4422). **Rates** from $130. **Credit** BC, MC, V. Expensive for a B&B, but it in sumptuously beautiful surroundings.

Ranelagh House Guesthouse

Illawarra Highway, Robertson (4885 1111/ fax 48851 051). **Rates** from $85 per person (half board). **Credit** AmEx, BC, DC, MC, V. The place for devonshire teas. Also does a country-style lunch and dinner menu.

The Surveyor General Inn

Old Hume Highway, Berrima (4877 1226). **Rates** from $70. **No credit cards**. A good spot for chips with your heritage.

White Horse Inn

Market Place, Berrima (4877 1204). **Rates** from $65. **Credit** AmEx, BC, DC, MC, V. Motel-style accommodation.

Survival

Survival

How to keep healthy, become wealthy and get wise – from helplines and medical advice to temping and tax tips.

1800 numbers can be dialled free of charge from within Australia.

Agencies & Helplines

See also page 264 Health Advice.

Alcoholics Anonymous
(9799 1199). **Open** 24 hours daily.
Manned by volunteers who are recovering alcoholics.

Alcohol & Drug Information Service
(9331 2111/1800 422 599). **Open** 24 hours daily.
Crisis counselling, information, assessment and referrals.

Australian Maritime Rescue
(Co-ordination centre 06 253 4400). **Open** 24 hours daily.
Call the centre in an emergency.

Child Protection & Family Crisis Service
(1800 066 777). **Open** 24 hours daily.
Investigates allegations of child abuse and offers help to families whose children may be at risk.

Crime Stoppers
(9384 6467/1800 333 000). **Open** 7am-11pm Mon-Fri; 8am-5pm Sat, Sun.
The organisation receives information on any crime anonymously, issues press releases and appeals to the public for information.

Department of Fair Trading
(9286 0006). **Open** 9am-5pm Mon-Fri.
For all consumer-related problems, enquiries and complaints.

Domestic Violence Line
(1800 656 463). **Open** 24 hours daily.
Call the police on 000 if you are in immediate danger; otherwise, this service offers 24-hour counselling and advice for those suffering domestic abuse.

Eastern & Central Sexual Assault Services
(9am-5pm 9515 7566/6pm-8am 9515 6111).
A crisis service for victims of sexual assault, offering medical and legal support as well as counselling.

Gamblers Counselling Service
(13 1114). **Open** 24 hours daily.
Run by Lifeline, this is a telephone counselling and referral service run by trained volunteers.

Gay & Lesbian Counselling Line
(1800 805 379). **Open** 4pm-midnight daily.
See also chapter Queer Sydney.

Government Information Service
(9743 7200). **Open** 9am-5pm Mon-Fri.
Provides information on NSW legislation and government publications. Be prepared to wait in a phone queue.

Grief Support Inc
(9489 6644). **Open** 24 hours daily.
A listening service for those suffering grief and loss, run by experienced volunteers.

HIV/AIDS Information Line
(9332 4000/after hours 9382 2222). **Open** 9am-8pm Mon-Fri; 10am-6pm Sat.
This is a statewide information service. *See also chapter* **Queer Sydney**.

Law Society of New South Wales
(9926 0333). **Open** 9am-5pm Mon-Fri.
For legal information or referral to a solicitor over the phone.

Lifeline Counselling Service
(13 1114). **Open** 24 hours daily.

Poisons Information Centre
(13 1126). **Open** 24 hours daily.
Offers advice in an emergency to those who have been exposed to any form of poison, as well as supplying more general information on the use of drugs and chemicals.

Police Switchboard
(9281 0000). **Open** 24 hours daily.
Phone for the location of your nearest police station.

Rape Crisis Centre
(1800 424 017). **Open** 24 hours daily.
The centre offers rape counselling over the telephone.

Salvation Army
Salvo Care Line (9331 6000)/Salvo Crisis Line (9331 2000). **Open** 24 hours daily.
These lines, run by the Salvation Army, offer 24-hour counselling and help for those in crisis or contemplating suicide.

Emergencies

The following are all 24-hour emergency numbers that serve the Sydney metropolitan area. For fire brigade, police or ambulance, **dial 000**.

Electricity
Energy Australia Emergency Line (13 1388).

Gas
Emergencies (13 1909); supply difficulties, service and information (13 1606).

Water
Water Board Service Breakdown & Emergency Northern Region (9952 0600); Great Western Region (9828 8600); Southern Region (9551 4600).

Airlines

The following airlines operate regular flights into Kingsford Smith Airport at Mascot.

Ansett Australia (13 1300)
Air New Zealand (13 2476)
British Airways (9258 3300)
Canadian Airlines (9299 7843/1800 251 321)
Cathay Pacific (13 1747)
Continental Airlines (9321 9242)
Northwest Airlines (1800 505 747)
Qantas (13 1313)
Singapore Airlines (13 1011)
Virgin Atlantic Airways (1800 646 747)
United Airlines (9237 8888)

Communication

For information about telephones, poste restante, buying stamps and the address of the General Post Office *see chapter* **Essential Information**.

Telephone Directories

The Yellow Pages and residential White Pages contain a mine of useful information at the front, from entertainment and transport details to local resources. Copies can be found in the larger hotels, at post offices and the Telstra Payphone Centre in Pitt Street (*see chapter* **Essential Information**).

Consulates & Legations

Canada

Level 5, 111 Harrington Street, Sydney (9364 3000/ visa information 9364 3050). CityRail Circular Quay. **Open** 9.30am-12.30pm Mon-Fri; *phone enquiries only* 1.30-3pm Mon-Fri.

Republic of Ireland

20 Arcana Street, Yarralumla, Canberra (6273 3022). **Open** 9.30am-12.45pm, 2-5pm, Mon-Fri.

New Zealand

1 Alfred Street, Sydney (9247 1999/passport office 9247 1999). CityRail Circular Quay. **Open** 10am-4pm Mon-Fri.

United Kingdom

Level 16, Gateway Building, 1 Macquarie Place, Sydney (9247 7521/24-hour passport & visa information 9247 9731). CityRail Circular Quay. **Open** 10am-4.30pm Mon-Fri.

USA

39 Castlereagh Street, Sydney (9373 9200/24-hour visa information 1902 262 682). CityRail Martin Place. **Open** 8.30am-noon Mon-Fri.

Driving in Sydney

See chapter **Getting Around** for details of car rental companies, NSW road regulations and the National Road & Motorists Association (NRMA).

Accident Information

Motor Accidents Authority of NSW

(9252 4677). **Open** 9am-5pm Mon-Fri.
Phone the state authority for information and advice regarding personal injury in motor accidents.

Breakdown Services

NRMA

(13 1111). **Open** 24 hours daily.
Round-the-clock emergency breakdown service.

Car Parks

Consult the Yellow Pages under 'Parking Stations' for more locations. Those listed below are in the centre of Sydney. Many have 'Early Bird' special rates if you park before 9am and leave before 5.30pm.

Apple Car Park

169 Thomas Street, Haymarket (9281 2066). **Open** 6.30am-1am daily. **Rates** $4 one hour; $8 two hours; $13 9am-6pm. **No credit cards**.

Cinema Centre Carpark

521 Kent Street, Sydney (9264 5867). **Open** 6.30am-1am Mon-Thur; 6.30am-2am Fri; 7.30am-2am Sat; 8.30am-1am Sun. **Rates** $3 30 mins; $19 day rate. **Credit** AmEx, BC, DC, MC, V.

KC Park Safe

109 Pitt Street, Sydney (9232 7868). **Open** 7am-7pm Mon-Wed; 7am-11pm Thur; 7am-1am Fri; 8am-6pm Sat. **Rates** $4 30 mins. **No credit cards**.

Kings Cross Car Park

Corner of Ward Avenue and Elizabeth Bay Road, Kings Cross (9358 5000). **Open** 24 hours daily. **Rates** $4 one hour; $12 day rate. **No credit cards**.

Kings Parking

55 Elizabeth Street, Sydney (9232 7485). **Open** 7.30am-6.30pm Mon-Fri. **Rates** vary according to site. **No credit cards**.

Branches: 300 Elizabeth Street, Sydney (9212 7418); 345 George Street, Sydney (9299 7496); 363 George Street, Sydney (9283 5444); 71 York Street, Sydney (9299 2609).

Secure Parking

155 George Street, Sydney (9241 2973). **Open** 7am-10.30pm Mon-Wed; 7am-11pm Thur; 7am-1am Sat; 9am-10pm Sun. **Rates** $7 one hour; $13 two hours; $19 three hours; $25 four hours; $32 maximum. **Credit** AmEx, BC, DC, MC, V.

Sydney Opera House Carpark

2A Macquarie Street, Sydney (9247 7599). **Open** 6.30am-1am daily. **Rates** $4 one hour; $12 maximum to 7pm; $16 evening flat rate; $20 maximum day rate. **Credit** AmEx, BC, DC, MC, V.

Health Advice

See also page 262 **Agencies & Helplines**. For information on health insurance and Medicare's overseas reciprocal agreement *see chapter* **Essential Information**.

Health Information Service

State Library of NSW, Macquarie Street, Sydney (9230 1414/fax 9223 3369/email grl@ilanet.slnsw.gov.au). *CityRail Martin Place.* **Open** 9am-9pm Mon-Fri.
The service will help you find up-to-date and reliable information on health issues.

Working in Sydney

If you want to find work in Australia to finance your travels, you'll need to have entered the country on a working holiday visa. This is valid for 13 months from the date of issue (so don't apply for it until a month before you leave) and allows you to stay in Australia for a maximum of 12 months. During that 12-month period you are allowed to work for any employer for up to three months. You can apply for an extension of this visa, but you must do this at least two months before the visa expires. The visas are principally granted to those between the ages of 18 and 25, but those between 26 and 30 are sometimes given the visas (the requirements are more rigorous). Those eligible must hold a valid UK, Dutch, Irish, Canadian or Japanese passport and have no children. Contact the Australian Embassy (*see chapter* **Essential Information**) for more information on the requirements and cost of a working holiday visa. If you enter Australia on a tourist visa, you cannot work. *See also chapters* **Students & Backpackers** *and* **Business**.

Job-hunting

The backpacker-oriented TNT *Australia & New Zealand Travel Planner* contains useful tips on looking for temporary work in Australia. It's available from the Australian High Commission in London and selected travel agents. You can also get a copy from TNT for Backpackers at: 5th Floor, 55 Clarence Street, Sydney. It's worth looking at the job ads in local newspapers, and in the *Sydney Morning Herald* on Mondays, Wednesdays and Saturdays. Otherwise, try the federal-run Commonwealth Employment Service (CES) or one of the temp agencies listed below, all of which offer temporary secretarial, accounting and clerical work (you'll find more listed under 'Employment Agencies' in the Yellow Pages).

Bligh Appointments
9th Floor, 428 George Street (9235 3699). CityRail Town Hall. **Open** 8am-6pm Mon-Fri.

Commonwealth Employment Service
345 George Street, Sydney (9320 2600). CityRail Martin Place or Wynyard. **Open** 8.45am-5pm Mon-Fri.

Drake International
Level 12, 60 Margaret Street, Sydney (9241 4488). CityRail Wynyard. **Open** 8am-6pm Mon-Fri. **Branches**: Level 1, 13 Spring Street, Chatswood (9419 7799); Level 9, 77 Pacific Highway, North Sydney (9957 5888); Level 3, 69 Phillip Street, Parramatta (9891 1022).

Manpower
34 Hunter Street, Sydney (9231 4844). CityRail Wynyard. **Open** 9am-5pm Mon-Fri.

Tax

Non-residents are taxed at source at a rate of 29%, which rises to 50% if you don't have a tax file number. These are issued by the Australian Taxation Office and take around six weeks to be processed: pick up a form at your local post or tax office.

Contraception/Abortion

Bessie Smyth Foundation
Powell Street Clinic, 80 Park Road, Homebush (9764 4133). CityRail Homebush. **Open** 9am-5pm Mon-Fri; 8am-2pm Sat.
Offers counselling and pregnancy termination, advice on contraception, plus other gynaecological health services. The clinic will provide you with a month's free supply of the Pill. Medicare covers 35% of other costs.

Family Planning NSW
Phone the head office on 9716 6099 for details of your nearest clinic.
Offers advice about, and practical assistance with, contraception, pregnancy testing, gynaecological healthcare and infection checks, plus sexual counselling. All services are free.

Dentists

Dental treatment is not covered by Medicare, so the only option available to overseas visitors is to find a local dentist and pay for their services. The Australian Dental Association (ADA) provides an after-hours referral service for emergency treatment.

After Hours Dental Emergency Service
75 Hall Street, Bondi Beach (9130 4221). Bus 380, 382. **Open** 24 hours daily.
The consultation fee is $20.

Dental Emergency Information Service
Australian Dental Association (9369 7050). **Open** 24 hours daily.

United Dental Hospital of Sydney
2 Chalmers Street, Surry Hills (9282 0200). CityRail Central. **Open** 8.30am-4.30pm Mon-Fri.

Hospitals

All of the following hospitals have casualty departments which are open 24 hours a day.

New Children's Hospital
Hawkesbury Road, Westmead (9845 0000). CityRail Westmead then shuttle bus.

Prince Henry Hospital
Anzac Parade, Little Bay (9661 0111). Bus L94, 394.

Prince of Wales Hospital/Sydney Children's Hospital
High Street, Randwick (9382 2222/9382 1111). Bus 400.

Royal Prince Alfred Hospital
Missenden Road, Camperdown (9515 6111). Bus 412.

St Vincent's Public Hospital
Corner of Burton and Victoria Streets, Darlinghurst (9339 1111). CityRail Kings Cross.

Sydney Hospital and Sydney Eye Hospital
8 Macquarie Street, Sydney (9382 7111). CityRail Martin Place.

Medical Treatment

If you need medical treatment while in Sydney, check the Yellow Pages for your nearest medical centre or phone the hotel service listed below. In an emergency, call 000 for an ambulance or go to the casualty department of one of the hospitals listed above.

Hotel Doctor
(9962 6000). **Open** 24 hours daily.
A quick-response, four-doctor practice serving any hotel or apartment in the centre of Sydney. The service has an agreement to deal directly with several travel insurance companies and will make a claim on your behalf; otherwise the doctor will advise you on how to make a claim on your insurance yourself or arrange a Medicare rebate. Consultations cost $100 during office hours, and $150 after hours.

Pharmacies (late-opening)

Chemist Emergency Prescription Referral Service
(9235 0333). **Open** 24 hours daily.
Phone this number for the location of your nearest after-hours chemist.

Left Luggage

There are left luggage lockers at Kingsford Smith Airport and Central Station. At the airport, storage for extra-large baggage costs $6 for 24 hours, lockers in the international terminal cost $4 for 24 hours. At Central Station, lockers cost $1.20 for 24 hours. The Travellers Contact Point (9221 8744) will also arrange to store baggage for you.

Lost Property

For belongings lost on State Transit buses and ferries, CityRail trains or in taxis, *see chapter* **Getting Around.** For property lost in the street, contact the police. For items lost at the airport, phone 9667 9583 or contact the relevant airline.

Money

For currency details, bureaux de change and lost or stolen travellers' cheques/credit card emergency numbers *see chapter* **Essential Information.**

Public Lavatories

There are plenty of public lavatories to be found dotted around town, in department stores, shopping centres and at train stations, as well as at beaches and in parks.

Religion

Every suburb has its parish church, and all religions are represented in multicultural Sydney. Consult the Yellow Pages under 'Churches & Synagogues' for full details of places of worship.

Further Reading

Travel & Reference

David Dale *The 100 Things Everyone Needs to Know About Australia*
Essential background reading covers everything from Lamingtons and Vegemite to Malcolm Fraser's trousers.
Terry Durack & Jill Dupleix (eds): *The Sydney Morning Herald Good Food Guide*
Recommendations for eating well in and around Sydney, published annually.
Susan Hawthorne and Renate Klein (ed): *Australia for Women, Travel & Culture*
The title says it all.
Jan Morris: *Sydney*
Personal and highly readable account of the city 'left on the shores of history by Empire's receding tide'.
Barbara Sweeney (ed): *Cheap Eats*
Another annual food guide – covers where you can eat two courses for under $25.

History & Politics

Manning Clark: *A History of Australia*
Six-volume history of the white settlement with sympathy for the underdog.
Robert Hughes: *The Fatal Shore*
Epic tale of brutal early convict life, written by New York based art critic.
John Pilger: *A Secret Country*
Passionately critical account of Australia written by the ex-patriate journalist.

Autobiography & Biography

Albert A Facey: *Fortunate Life*
Enormously successful autobiography tracing Facey's life from outback orphanage to Gallipoli, the Depression and beyond.
Sara Henderson: *From Strength to Strength*
Tough times on an outback cattle farm.
Sally Morgan: *My Place*
Best-selling autobiography of a Western Australian Aboriginal woman.

Fiction

Peter Carey: *Bliss, Illywhacker, Oscar and Lucinda* and others
Booker Prize-winning novelist who started life as an ad agent.
Bryce Courtenay: *The Power of One; The Potato Factory*
Australia's best-selling writer, though he tends not to stick to Oz-related subject matter.
Miles Franklin: *My Brilliant Career*
Novel written in 1901 about a rural woman who refuses to conform.
Helen Garner: *Monkey Grip*
Sex, drugs and rock 'n' roll in 1970s Melbourne.
ibid *Postcards from Surfers*
Short stories.
May Gibbs: *Snugglepot and Cuddlepie*

The most famous of Gibbs' successful children's books about the gumnut babies.
Thomas Keneally: *Bring Larks and Heroes, The Chant of Jimmy Blacksmith*
Two novels about oppression – of convicts in the former, Aborigines in the latter. His *Schindler's Ark* was made into the Oscar-winning film *Schindler's List*.
Henry Lawson: *Joe Wilson and his Mates*
Collection of short stories about mateship and larrikinism by the first Australian writer to be given a state funeral (1922).
Norman Lindsay: *The Magic Pudding*
Splendidly roguish children's tale – as Australian as a book can get.
David Malouf: *Johnno*
First novel by one of Australia's most popular contemporary writers, about a Brisbane boyhood.
Ruth Park: *The Harp in the South, Poor Man's Orange*
Tales of inner-city struggle, written in the 1940s. Ruth Park wrote the wonderful children's book, *The Muddle-Headed Wombat*.
Dale Spender (ed): *The Penguin Anthology of Australian Women Writers*
Celebrating the work of female writers, past and present.
Patrick White: *Voss, The Eye of the Storm*
Heavy-going fiction about a mad desert explorer and an individual's triumph over adversity, by the winner of the Nobel Prize for Literature (1973) who died in 1990.
Tim Winton: *Cloudstreet, That Eye, The Sky*

Glossary

For further enlightenment, consult the standard Australian English dictionary – called the Macquarie Dictionary – compiled by Macquarie University in Sydney.

ANZAC Technically, a member of the First World War Australian and New Zealand Army Corps, but often used in phrases like 'Anzac spirit', referring to the pluck of the Australian soldiers sent to die at Gallipoli by the English (who haven't been forgiven). Sadly, there are only a handful of ANZACs left.

arvo the bit of the day between lunchtime and evening.

barbie the plastic princess. Also, hotplate or grill used for the ritual ruination of perfectly fine pieces of meat.

bloody all-purpose Aussie adjective.

bottle shop off-licence or liquor store.

bludger lazy person, often used in connection with social security frauds, as in 'dole bludger'.

bush like shrubbery, only bigger.

bushrangers highwaymen, mainly prominent in the nineteenth century. Most now have office jobs in the city.

chook chicken. Also, to be out of control, as in 'run around like a headless chook'.

cossie the thing that stops you from being arrested for indecency when you're at the beach. In Melbourne: bathers.

crim see *crook*.

crook see *crim*. Also, to be sick, as in 'Geez I'm crook Beryl'.

daggy originally referring to the particles of faecal matter which collect in the wool around a sheep's rear end, now mostly means someone or something considered unfashionable.

damper bread made in the ashes of a fire.

dob in to snitch, generally considered un-Australian, unless there's a dollar in it.

doona duvet or continental quilt.

dinky di Small British princess. Verification that something is genuine. Also true blue, dinkum.

dunny toilet. Also, thunderbox, shithouse, lav, loo, little boy's room.

esky sacred cooling device for beer and picnic materials on hot day.

feral wild. Also refers to the dreadlocked types who lie in front of bulldozers in old growth forests.

fossick search about for something.

galah attractive pinkish bird. Also, an out and out fool, as in 'You stupid galah'.

grog alcohol. Also piss, turps.

hoon noun and adj. Foul-mouthed, petrolhead male (usu.), his behaviour.

Koorie Aborigine.

Lamingtons sponge cake dipped in chocolate and rolled in coconut. Considered a delicacy by small children and nostalgic adults.

larrikin tearaway.

mate friend. Someone you would get in a fight for, but not lend 50¢.

middy beer glass measure; not as big as a *schooner*.

nick off please go away.

no worries expression of reassurance that everything is OK. Also she'll be right, she'll be apples, no wuckin' furries, and no wuckers.

ocker Alf Garnett, Australian style.

pokies electronic poker machines, still called one-armed bandits, though they don't have arms to pull anymore. In pubs and clubs all over Sydney.

Pom, Pommie unfortunate person of English extraction (comes from 'Prisoner of the Motherland').

rack off! excuse me, I thought I asked you to leave!

ripper expression of approval. As in 'You beauty! You little ripper!'.

RSL Returned Services League. Also their clubs, as in 'I'm just shooting off down to the RSL, dear'.

schooner beer glass measure, not as small as a *middy*.

shonky A spiv, like Arthur Daley. Also shady, dodge.

shout noun and verb. Buy a round of drinks, as in 'It's my shout'.

sickie day off work, not necessarily due to illness.

silvertail rich person

slab 24-can box of beer – a party pre-requisite in many suburbs.

smoko a work break (you'll probably take a smoko in the arvo, if you're not already taking a sickie).

spewin' vociferously angry. As in 'I'm just spewin'. about what those silvertail bastards are doing.

squatter early colonial sheep farmer. Also, squattocracy, meaning long-established wealthy landowners.

stubby short, fat, brown bottle of beer. Tends to be local brew. The opposite of modern, sleek, clear bottles of beer, which tend to be imported and expensive.

tall poppy the much debated Tall Poppy Syndrome has it that Australians will always criticise the successful, because they don't believe one person should have much more success than another.

thongs flip-flops.

tinnie can of beer.

Vegemite non-toxic vegetable extract (like Marmite), and a national icon. An excellent hangover cure.

waxhead surfie. Also sharkfucker or sharkbait.

westies denizens of the western suburbs, stereotypically thong-wearing, beer-gut carrying, idiot, rednecks.

yabbie freshwater crustacean. To die for.

yakka work, as in 'I put in some hard yakka today'.

Index

Sydney Guide
Advertisers' Index

Please refer to the relevant sections for addresses/telephone numbers

Maps

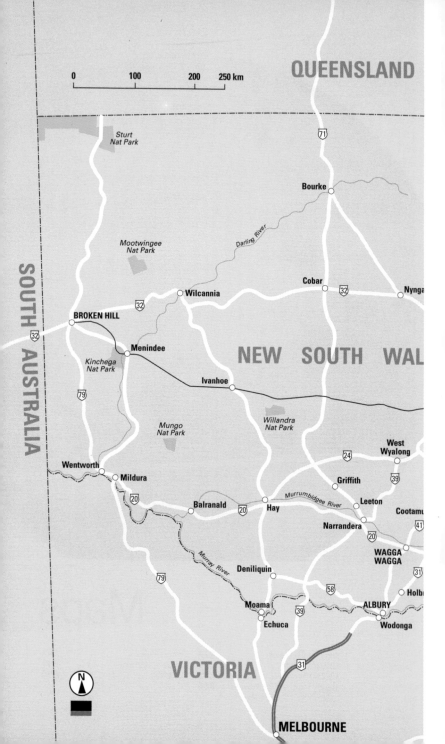

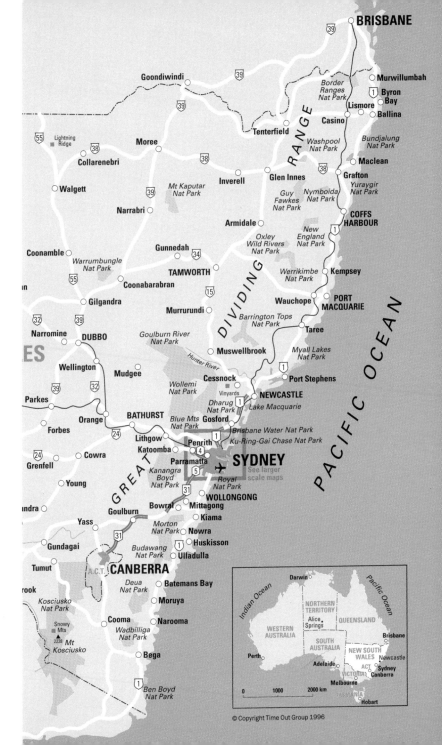

© Copyright Time Out Group 1996

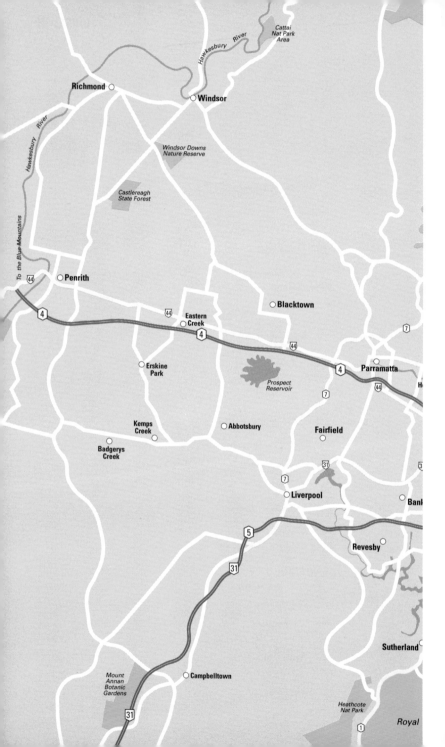

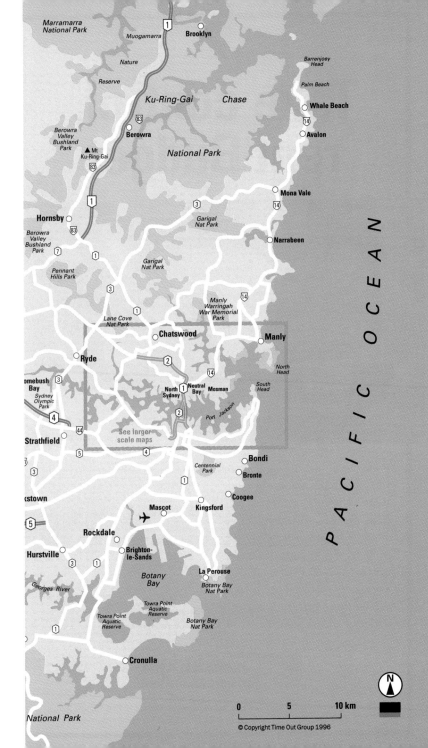

Take control, rent Budget

Experience the freedom to do what you want, when you want. Rent your own set of wheels from Budget. Whether you're after the versatility of a 4WD, the comfort of a campervan or the convenience of a sedan, Budget has exactly what you need. All at competitive prices, with the option of one way rentals.

For bookings call your travel agent or Budget on:

Australia	13 28 48
New Zealand	0800 652 227
United States	1800 527 0700
Canada	1800 268 8900
United Kingdom	0800 181 181
France	0510 0001
Italy	6 229 356 20
Germany	89 66 695 128
Switzerland	1 813 5797
Netherlands	23 567 1222

Budget.
All The Difference In The World.

ResponseAbility BUD/0804

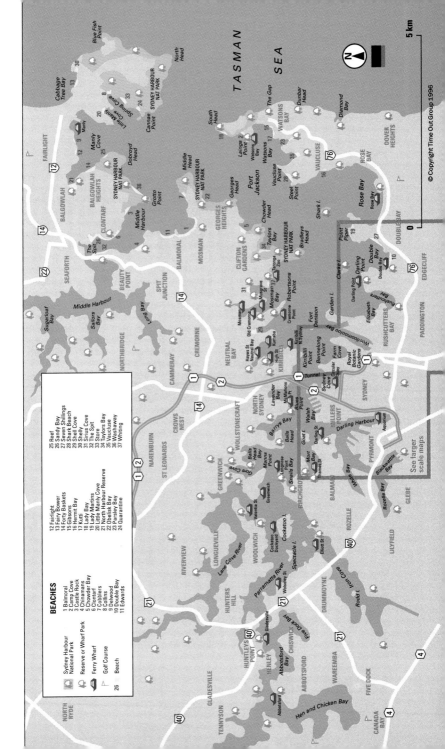

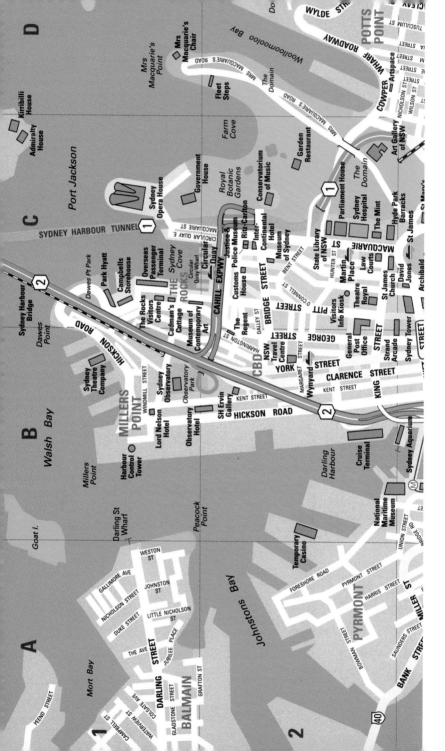

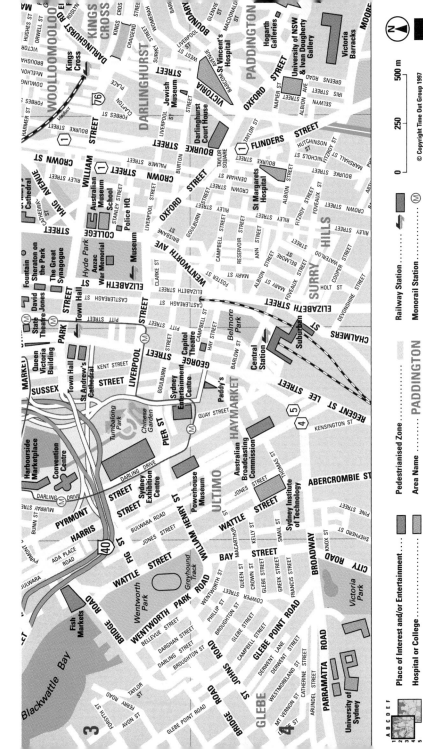

© Copyright Time Out Group 1997

0   250   500 m

A B C D E F
1
2
3
4
5

Place of Interest and/or Entertainment . . . .

Hospital or College

Pedestrianised Zone . . . .

Area Name . . . . PADDINGTON

Railway Station . . . .

Monorail Station . . . . Ⓜ

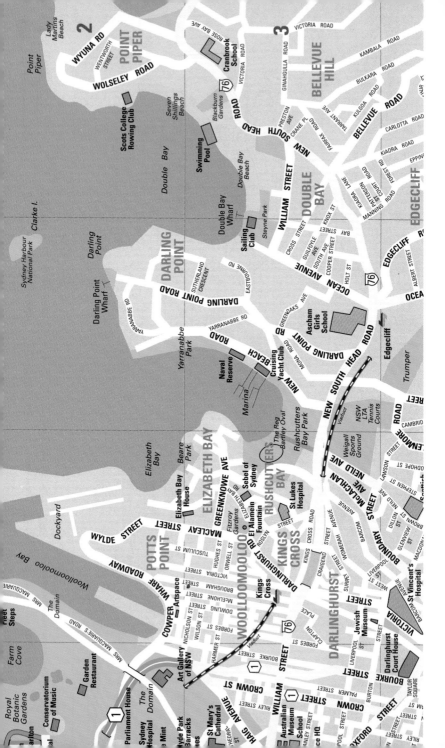

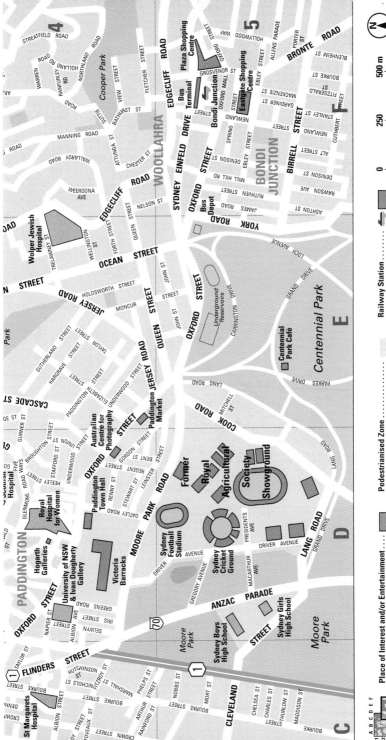

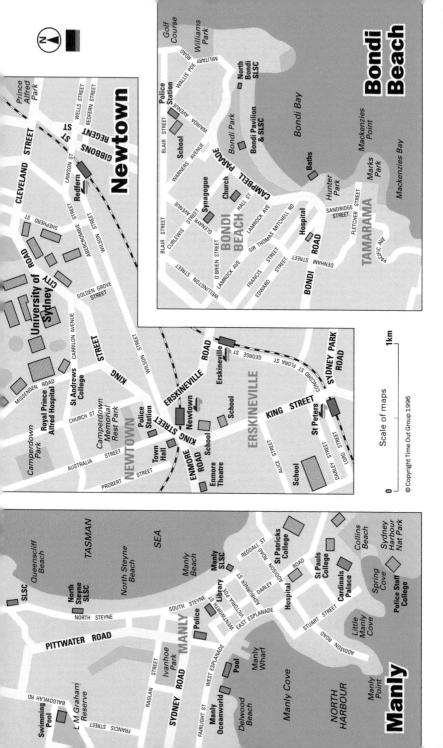

Manly

SLSC
Queenscliff Beach
TASMAN
North Steyne SLSC
North Steyne Beach
SEA
Manly Beach
Manly SLSC
Library
Police
SOUTH STEYNE
MANLY
PITTWATER ROAD
NORTH STEYNE
Swimming Pool
BALGOWLAH RD
FRANCIS STREET
L M Graham Reserve
STREET
Ivanhoe Park
RAGLAN
FAIRLIGHT ST
SYDNEY ROAD
WEST ESPLANADE
Manly Oceanworld
Pool
Delwood Beach
Manly Cove
WENTWORTH ST
EAST ESPLANADE
VICTORIA PDE
Manly Wharf
ASHBURNER ST
DARLEY ROAD
ADDISON ROAD
REDDALL ST
St Patricks College
St Pauls College
Hospital
Cardinals Palace
Police Staff College
STUART STREET
ADDISON ROAD
NORTH HARBOUR
Manly Point
Little Manly Cove
Spring Cove
Collins Beach
Sydney Harbour Nat Park

Newtown

Prince Alfred Park
WELLS STREET
REDFERN STREET
CLEVELAND STREET
SHEPHERD ST
GIBBONS ST
REGENT ST
Redfern
LAWSON ST
University of Sydney
CITY ROAD
University of Sydney
MISSENDEN ROAD
Royal Prince Alfred Hospital
ST
ABERCROMBIE STREET
WILSON STREET
GOLDEN GROVE STREET
CARRILON AVENUE
KING STREET
St Andrews College
Camperdown Park
St Patricks College
CHURCH ST
Camperdown Memorial Rest Park
WILSON STREET
NEWTOWN
Police Station
Town Hall
KING STREET
School
Newtown
ENMORE ROAD
School
Enmore Theatre
AUSTRALIA STREET
PROBERT STREET
ERSKINEVILLE ROAD
Erskineville
GEORGE ST
CONCORD ST
FLORA ST
ERSKINEVILLE
School
KING STREET
St Peters
ALICE STREET
DARLEY STREET
LORD STREET
SYDNEY PARK ROAD

Scale of maps

0 ——————— 1km

© Copyright Time Out Group 1996

Bondi Beach

Golf Course
Williams Park
MILITARY RD
WALLIS ROAD
North Bondi SLSC
Police Station
School
BLAIR STREET
WARNERS AVENUE
WAROA AVENUE
Bondi Park
CAMPBELL PARADE
Bondi Pavilion & SLSC
Bondi Bay
Synagogue
Church
HALL ST
BONDI BEACH
CURLEWIS STREET
GLENAYR AVENUE
Baths
Hunter Park
Mackenzies Point
BLAIR STREET
O'BRIEN STREET
LAMROCK AVE
SIR THOMAS MITCHELL RD
Hospital
BONDI ROAD
Marks Park
WELLINGTON STREET
LAMROCK AVE
FRANCIS STREET
EDWARD STREET
DENHAM STREET
SANDRIDGE STREET
FLETCHER STREET
TAMARAMA
PACIFIC AVE
Mackenzies Bay

Bondi Beach

Street Index

Take control, rent Budget

Experience the freedom to do what you want, when you want. Rent your own set of wheels from Budget. Whether you're after the versatility of a 4WD, the comfort of a campervan or the convenience of a sedan, Budget has exactly what you need. All at competitive prices, with the option of one way rentals.

For bookings call your travel agent or Budget on:

Australia	13 28 48
New Zealand	0800 652 227
United States	1800 527 0700
Canada	1800 268 8900
United Kingdom	0800 181 181
France	0510 0001
Italy	6 229 356 20
Germany	89 66 695 128
Switzerland	1 813 5797
Netherlands	23 567 1222

Budget.
All The Difference In The World.

ResponseAbility BUD/08/04

CityRail Suburban Network

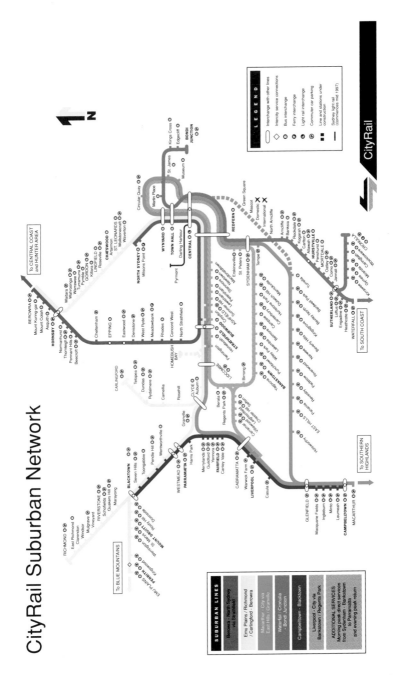

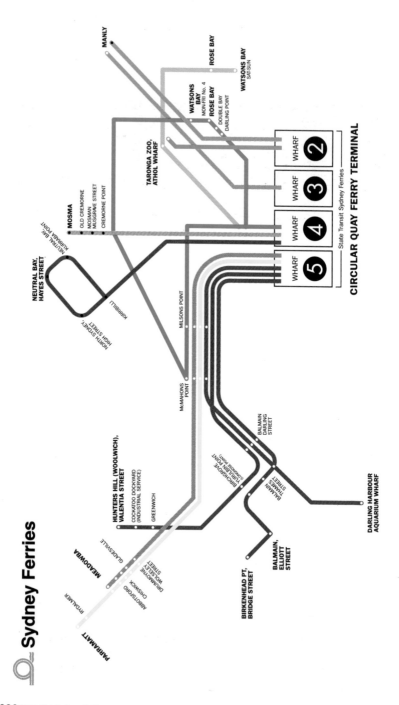

Sydney Ferries

CIRCULAR QUAY FERRY TERMINAL

State Transit Sydney Ferries

MANLY

ROSE BAY

WATSONS BAY
SAT-SUN

WATSONS
BAY
MON-FRI No. 4
ROSE BAY
DOUBLE BAY
DARLING POINT

TARONGA ZOO,
ATHOL WHARF

MOSMA
OLD CREMORNE
MOSMAN
MUSGRAVE STREET
CREMORNE POINT

NEUTRAL BAY,
KURRABA POINT

WHARF 2

WHARF 3

WHARF 4

WHARF 5

NEUTRAL BAY,
HAYES STREET

KIRRIBILLI

NORTH SYDNEY,
HIGH STREET

MILSONS POINT

McMAHONS
POINT

HUNTERS HILL (WOOLWICH),
VALENTIA STREET

COCKATOO DOCKYARD
(INDUSTRIAL SERVICE)

GREENWICH

BALMAIN
DARLING
STREET

BIRCHGROVE
(LONGNOSE POINT)
BALMAIN POINT

BALMAIN
THAMES
STREET

MEADOWBA

GLADESVILLE

RYDALMER

PARRAMATT

ABBOTSFORD

CHISWICK

DRUMMOYNE
WOLSELEY
STREET

BIRKENHEAD PT,
BRIDGE STREET

BALMAIN,
ELLIOTT
STREET

DARLING HARBOUR
AQUARIUM WHARF

Time Out Sydney Guide Reader's Report

Name:
Address:

Telephone:

Age: up to 19 ☐ 20-24 ☐ 25-29 ☐ 30-34 ☐ 35-44 ☐ 45+ ☐

Nationality:

Occupation:

Did you travel to Sydney:

Alone? ☐ With partner? ☐
As part of a group? ☐ With children? ☐

How long is your trip to Sydney?

Less than three days ☐ three days-one week ☐
One week-two weeks ☐ Over two weeks (please specify) ☐

Are you a *Time Out* magazine reader? Yes ☐ No ☐

Have you bought other *Time Out* guides? If so, which ones?

Amsterdam Guide ☐	Barcelona Guide ☐
Berlin Guide ☐	Brussels Guide ☐
Budapest Guide ☐	London Guide ☐
Los Angeles Guide ☐	Madrid Guide ☐
New York Guide ☐	Paris Guide ☐

Prague Guide ☐ Rome Guide ☐
San Francisco Guide ☐ Eating & Drinking in London Guide ☐
London Visitors' Guide ☐ Shopping & Services Guide ☐

Would you like to receive information about new titles? Yes ☐ No ☐

How useful did you find the following sections?

	Very	Useful	Fairly	Not very
Accommodation	☐	☐	☐	☐
Sightseeing	☐	☐	☐	☐
History	☐	☐	☐	☐
Sydney by Area	☐	☐	☐	☐
Eating & Drinking	☐	☐	☐	☐
Shopping & Services	☐	☐	☐	☐
Museums & Galleries	☐	☐	☐	☐
Arts & Entertainment	☐	☐	☐	☐
In Focus	☐	☐	☐	☐
Trips Out of Town	☐	☐	☐	☐
Survival	☐	☐	☐	☐

Is there anything you'd like us to cover in greater depth?

AFFIX
STAMP
HERE

Time Out Magazine
Universal House
251 Tottenham Court Road
London
United Kingdom
W1P 0AB